LITERATURE, RELIGION, AND POSTSECULAR STUDIES
LORI BRANCH, SERIES EDITOR

IMAGINED SPIRITUAL COMMUNITIES IN BRITAIN'S AGE OF PRINT

JOSHUA KING

THE OHIO STATE UNIVERSITY PRESS
COLUMBUS

Copyright © 2015 by The Ohio State University.
All rights reserved.

Library of Congress Cataloging-in-Publication Data
King, Joshua, 1979– author.
 Imagined spiritual communities in Britain's age of print / Joshua King.
   pages cm — (Literature, religion, and postsecular studies)
 Includes bibliographical references and index.
 ISBN 978-0-8142-1293-6 (cloth : alk. paper)
  1. Religion and literature—England—19th century—History. 2. Religion and the press—England—19th century—History. 3. Christianity and literature—England—History—19th century. 4. Spiritual formation. I. Title. II. Series: Literature, religion, and postsecular studies.
 PR145.K56 2015
 820.9'382—dc23
                    2015020921

Cover design by TG Designs
Text design by Juliet Williams
Type set in Adobe Garamond Pro
Printed by Thomson-Shore, Inc.

♾ The paper used in this publication meets the minimum requirements of the American National Standard for Information Sciences—Permanence of Paper for Printed Library Materials. ANSI Z39.48–1992.

9 8 7 6 5 4 3 2 1

*For Naomi, my wife,
and Elise, my daughter,
who surprise me with joy*

CONTENTS

ACKNOWLEDGMENTS • IX

INTRODUCTION
Religion, Reading, and Imagining Nineteenth-Century Britain • 1

PART 1
APOLOGISTS FOR PRINT-MEDIATED SPIRITUAL COMMUNITIES

CHAPTER 1
Coleridge's *Aids to Reflection*: The Clerisy and a National Spiritual Republic of Letters • 21

CHAPTER 2
F. D. Maurice's Universal Society: National Spiritual Community in a Sectarian Print Culture • 57

CHAPTER 3
Arnold's Poetic National Church: Anarchy and the Charming Force of Poetry • 96

PART 2
VIRTUAL CONGREGATIONS AND PRINTED POETIC CYCLES

CHAPTER 4
John Keble's *Christian Year*:
Private Reading and Imagined
National Religious Community • 129

CHAPTER 5
Tennyson's "New Christian Year":
In Memoriam and the Minimum of Faith • 159

CHAPTER 6
In Memoriam's Open Secret:
The Public Forms of Private Faith • 189

CHAPTER 7
Christina Rossetti's *Verses*:
A Multi-Fashioned Community of Strangers • 232

CONCLUSION
The End of Print-Mediated Christian Britain and
the Rise of Digital Spiritual Communities • 289

Bibliography • 303

Index • 323

ACKNOWLEDGMENTS

I have benefitted immensely from responses to portions of this book by audiences at the University of Toronto, Wheaton College, Baylor University, the Coleridge Summer Conference, and several conferences held by the North American Society for the Study of Romanticism and the North American Victorian Studies Association. Baylor University generously supported my research with summer sabbaticals in 2010 and 2012 and a research leave in fall 2012. The staff at Ohio State University Press has been exceptional. I am especially indebted to (then) Senior Editor Sandy Crooms, who first inquired into my work on this project in 2011 and remained invested even when my own will was close to faltering. Lindsay Martin, who became Acquisitions Editor for Literary Studies when Sandy went to the University of Pittsburgh, is everything I could wish for in an editor—highly skilled, patient, and ready to cheer when at last the finish line is crossed. Suggestions from the two outside reviewers for OSUP have made this book much better than it would have been otherwise. I would never have reached this point without the talented staff at the Armstrong Browning Library at Baylor University, especially Rita Patteson, Cyndie Burgess, Melvin Schuetz, Jennifer Borderud, Christi Klempnauer, Glenda Ross, and Melinda Creech (who is also one of my graduate students). Mary Shrader heroically sifted through hundreds of periodicals in support of my work. My cooperation with the Library has entered a new stage with my appointment as the Margarett Root Brown Chair in Robert Browning and Victorian Studies in 2014. I am thrilled to be working with such an outstanding group of people.

Few English departments have been blessed with a chair as wise and devoted to the success of her faculty as Dianna Vitanza. Colleagues in Baylor's Nineteenth-Century Research Seminar (19CRS), for several years now an indispensable intellectual community for me, have joined many others across campus in challenging my thinking and preserving my belief in the value of the academy. I cannot name all who should be recognized, but several deserve special mention: James Barcus, David Clinton, Michael DePalma, Luke Ferretter, Tom Hanks, David Jeffrey, Hope Johnston, David and Maura Jortner, Kristen Pond, Richard Russell, Lisa Shaver, Joe Stubenrauch, Dan Walden, and Ralph Wood. Kara Poe Alexander, Sarah Rude, and Danielle Williams joined several of those already mentioned in pointing me to the digital spiritual communities discussed in my conclusion. Michael Milburn, my research assistant at the time of writing this book and one of my graduate students, belongs in all these categories. He is also one of the most intellectually gifted yet unpretentious people I know. Many colleagues outside of Baylor have been instrumental to the formation and completion of this book, among them Kirstie Blair, Lori Branch (the editor for this series), Daniel Cook, Graham Davidson, Karen Dieleman, Anne Frey, Dayton Haskin, Diane Hoeveler, Regina Hewitt, Colin Jager, Mark Knight, Charles LaPorte, Meredith Martin, Emma Mason, William McKelvy, John Powell, Marjorie Stone, and Susan Wolfson. Adam Potkay graciously sent me penetrating and encouraging feedback on my manuscript in the nick of time.

Johnny Jones has helped me weather more crises of confidence than I care to count in the past few years, and in the process taught me the discipline of true friendship. During leaves from Baylor for writing, my parents, Robert Stephen King and Mae Belle King, offered the harbor of their home and, as always, their unconditional love. My brother, Caleb Barrett King, among the most brilliant people I know, has fanned my intellectual curiosity back into flame when it felt closest to extinguishment. Naomi, my wife, and Elise, my daughter, continually rescue me from myself by their love and the sheer delight of their company. This book, to which they have contributed more than I could hope to acknowledge, is for them.

Less than a page of the introduction appeared in "A Post-Secular Victorian Study: Religion, Reading, and Imagining Britain" in *Nineteenth-Century Prose* 39.1/2 (Spring/Fall 2012), used by permission of the editor, Barry Tharaud. An earlier and shorter version of chapter 1 appeared as

"Coleridge's *Aids to Reflection,* Print Culture and Mediated Spiritual Community" in *European Romantic Review* 23.1 (2012) (journal website: www.tandfonline.com / http://www.tandfonline.com/doi/full/10.1080/10509585.2012.639183), used by permission of Taylor & Francis Ltd./Routledge. A different version of the last two sections of chapter 1 appeared as "Coleridge's Clerisy and Print Culture" in *The Coleridge Bulletin* 40 (2012), used by permission of the Friends of Coleridge. A small and altered portion of chapter 3 will be included in "The Inward Turn: The Role of Matthew Arnold" in *The Routledge Companion to Literature and Religion,* ed. Mark Knight (Routledge 2015), used by permission of Taylor & Francis Ltd./Routledge. An earlier version of chapter 4 appeared as "John Keble's *The Christian Year:* Private Reading and Imagined National Religious Community" in *Victorian Literature and Culture* 40.2 (2012), used by permission of Cambridge University Press. A few paragraphs in chapters 5 and 6 appeared, in different form, in "Christianity: Introduction" in *Reading the Abrahamic Faiths: Rethinking Religion and Literature,* ed. Emma Mason (Bloomsbury 2014), used by permission of Bloomsbury Academic.

INTRODUCTION

RELIGION, READING, AND IMAGINING NINETEENTH-CENTURY BRITAIN

We are in the silent school of Reflection, in the secret confessional of Thought.
—Samuel Taylor Coleridge, *Aids to Reflection in the Formation of a Manly Character* (1825)

If you looked down upon [London] from the top of St. Paul's, . . . you would not have such a panoramic view of the streets and houses as you have in a large sheet of advertisements. *There* you see the outsides of the houses and some indistinguishable figures walking about in the streets; *here* you have a glimpse into the insides of them, some little hint of what these people are walking about for, of some of the thoughts that are going on in their hearts. [Such anonymous] notices . . . tell us of *some* fellow citizen, *some* fellow-creature of ours . . . [T]hese advertisements [tell us] that there must be something else than [buying and selling] to bind us together, and make us live together and work together, as men are meant to do.
—Frederick Denison Maurice, "On the Use and Abuse of Newspapers" (1852)

We [have] felt that through [*The Christian Year*'s] pages of hallowed thoughts we could hold communion with thousands of pious hearts, whose prejudices and convictions otherwise separate us most widely.
—Braden William, *The British Quarterly Review* (July 1867)[1]

---

1. *Aids to Reflection:* 84; *The Friendship of Books:* 73–74; William, "The Works of George Herbert": 123.

Lifted from untold myriads of printed texts dispersed through nineteenth-century Britain with a reach, speed, and diversity unmatched in any previous age, the three remarks above illustrate the subject of this book: the many efforts during that century to turn the circulating printed page into a medium for imagining and participating in competing versions of a British Christian community. In the first quotation, Coleridge interrupts his meditations on Christian reflection in his book *Aids to Reflection* (1825) to make one of his many intimate addresses to his imagined audience of young, educated men who are preparing to serve as Britain's future clergy, educators, and professional intellectuals. As discussed in chapter 1, Coleridge's rhetoric represents *Aids to Reflection* as the site of community among strangers who are in fact isolated in space and time. The "secret[s]" discovered in this "confessional of Thought" are open secrets, "silent[ly]" shared in a "school" with the group invoked by "we"—the inquiring reader, a classroom of fellow young seekers, and Coleridge their tutor. Coleridge constructs this virtual classroom as a training ground for the "clerisy" that he will announce four years later in *On the Constitution of the Church and State* (1829). This body of Anglican educators and ministers, Coleridge hoped, would establish literal classrooms in a national education system that would extend to all Britons the reflective awareness of moral and spiritual truths cultivated in *Aids to Reflection*. With this training, journalists would transform the rapidly expanding mass media into a widely diffused medium through which British citizens could imagine themselves in a spiritually and ethically united community with strangers from across their nation.

The second quotation comes from an early and enthusiastic graduate of Coleridge's virtual school in *Aids*, the Anglican clergyman, journalist, educator, and reformer Frederick Denison Maurice, whom I discuss in chapter 2. Here Maurice adds to his thirty-year effort to extend and fulfill Coleridge's vision of a British print network transformed into a medium for imagining national Christian community. Even newspaper advertisement pages, Maurice insists in this 1852 lecture to a London audience, could enable British readers to imagine their lives linked to a vast host of unseen fellow citizens in a Christian society capable of overcoming the sectarianism, class conflict, and valuation of products over persons stimulated by industrialism and print capitalism. In my third quotation, Braden William, a Congregationalist minister, reflects on the significance of *The Christian Year* (1827), the immensely popular collection of devotional lyrics by the Anglican priest John Keble, which forms the focus of chapter 4 and sets the context for those following. A year after Keble's death, William portrays the poet's "pages of hallowed thoughts" as a virtual interdenominational meeting place between "pious hearts" across the nation who are otherwise separated by the sectarian conflicts still fueling a wide array of Victorian newspapers, journals, pamphlets, and books. Here William joins many Victorian commentators in representing Keble's *Christian Year* as a medium for imagining private poetry reading as a way of participating in a British Christian, and basically Protestant, community that transcends denominational and party boundaries.

Taken from the beginning, middle, and later decades of the nineteenth century, and taking in a wide range of genres—a work of religious philosophy, a lecture on reading, newspaper advertisements, a blockbuster volume of poetry, and a periodical review—these quotations indicate the scope of this book. I believe such a wide lens is necessary for understanding both the reasons and the diverse ways in which nineteenth-century British imaginative authors, journalists, educators, and clergy represented the printed page as a medium for envisioning and partaking in a national Christian community. While I concentrate on literature, I do so in an interdisciplinary fashion with an interdisciplinary audience in mind. My argument will be of primary interest to literary scholars, but it also intervenes in discussions among political scientists, historians of religion and nationalism, sociologists, scholars debating the nature and effects of secularization, and those involved in media studies.

My title, *Imagined Spiritual Communities in Britain's Age of Print*, alludes to Benedict Anderson's well-known *Imagined Communities* (1983, rev. 1991). I wish to extend and revise Anderson's account of the ways modern national imagination was enabled by the spread of mass print media. While Anderson's claim that print capitalism provided the *basis* of popular national consciousness has been questioned (Van Young 41, 59; Thompson 63), his primary assumptions about national identity and media retain explanatory power: (1) a nation is not a concrete entity, but a discursively constructed community imagined as limited to a finite territory and composed of members who see themselves progressing simultaneously through history; (2) national communities should be studied in terms of the media through which they are imagined (Anderson 5–7, 22–46). Scholars continue to rely on these two principles when studying phenomena ranging from national and regional identity to cyberspace "nationhood" (Kriegel 232–33; Dicks and Van Loon 209; Pearse 112; Sherman 32–54). In *Imagined Spiritual Communities*, I retain Anderson's concentration on the mediated nature of national consciousness, treating it as a constructed image of communion dependent on specific media and ways of using them. I do so, however, by studying nineteenth-century Britain and its increasing immersion in printed media, rather than outlining a genealogy of nationalism; and I resist Anderson's implication that imagining national communities is an essentially secular activity coordinated with the decay of religious forms of imagined community (Anderson 11–12, 22–36).

Furthermore, while Anderson almost exclusively emphasizes the unifying dimension of print-mediated national communities, I stress the competing and often contradictory efforts of nineteenth-century commentators and authors from the middle and upper-middle classes to imagine a Christian British reading nation. As a result, I agree with recent critics of Anderson's theory in stressing the degree to which nearly every image of communion depends, ironically, on the displacement of others through the very act of representing them (Dicks and Van Loon 210, 213). When envisioning Britain as a nation of Christian readers, I argue, nineteenth-century authors participated in the tendency to imagine community by stereotyping enemies or outsiders, but they also consciously resisted it. In chapter 2, for example, I discuss Frederick Denison Maurice's effort, in nearly half a century of publications and public addresses, to encourage others to read in such a way that they would cultivate a mental image of a united and generally Protestant nation under the Anglican Church, an image that could provide the mental and emotional background for their daily individual and collective life. This vision of Christian Britain required Maurice to forget or sideline the Catholics, Jews, Hindus, Muslims, spiritualists, agnostics, atheists, and other non-Protestants also living within Britain and its empire. Yet he promoted such a print-mediated national Protestant community precisely because of his sensitivity to the process of inclusion by exclusion: his early experience as a journalist convinced him that newspapers and periodicals projected a shared identity for their readers only by reinforcing prejudices about other social classes, political groups, and religious confessions.

This book takes up a question in a nineteenth-century British context still debated in the public square and at academic conferences: how do modern religious and national ways of imagining community relate? The public force of religion remains a controversial and unsettling subject in Western democracies. In France, for example, arguments about how boundaries between religion and the public sphere should be policed erupted when its *parlement* banned the Islamic *burqa* (or *niqab*) from public spaces (effective April 11, 2011). Such anxiety over the public presence of religion seems to derive at least in part from the belief that the nonsectarian democratic nation has become the center of imaginative and political allegiance for modern societies, and that this requires the privatization of religious forms of community. As Jo Carruthers has argued, the strong prejudice against Muslims recently discernible in British politics, news, and opinion polls is triggered by a popular image of "Islam . . . as an *unavoidably* public religious identity: . . . a set of practices that cannot be relegated to a private space" (98).

This idea—that religious belief and community tends to retreat from the public spheres of modern nations—has been powerfully challenged in academic circles by sociologist of religion José Casanova in his *Public Religions in the Modern World* (1994). Once controversial, Casanova's argument for the public vitality of religion in nations around the world, especially in the United States and countries outside the West, has been confirmed by recent global history, and respect for his claims has grown among sociologists. The sociologist Steve Bruce now feels the need to defend, against many detractors, the inevitable decline of religion's "social presence" in modern industrial liberal democracies (76).

Bruce's view still finds occasional support among influential scholars of nationalism, several of whom remain willing to characterize national consciousness as the secularizing successor of religion. In the introduction to *Nations and Nationalism: A Global Historical Overview* (2008), a massive anthology aimed at scholars, teachers, and students, the authors proclaim that in the nineteenth century "the nation filled the gap" left by "traditional religions" (Herb and Badescu, I:xix). The conviction that national consciousness is inherently secular drives Liah Greenfeld's analysis of English identity in *Nationalism: Five Roads to Modernity* (1992). After the English Civil War, Greenfeld argues, the "nation as the primary object of loyalty was established," and it was only "natural" that "religion" thereafter "ceased to be the source of social values"—inevitably, it would "be pushed aside" as a foundation of national identity (77). Greenfeld's historical argument has been refuted by Krishan Kumar (96–103), but the influence her book has enjoyed among scholars of nationalism indicates the durability of her belief in national consciousness as an agent of inevitable secularization. In the 2008 anthology I mention above, for instance, Greenfeld, now joined by Jonathan Eastwood, repeats her basic claim that "the national image of the world is a secular one" (I:5).

By contrast, religious historians such as Stewart Brown in *Providence and Empire* (2008), and literary historians such as William R. McKelvy in *The English Cult of Literature* (2007), have demonstrated that narratives of religious decline can no longer account for the history of nineteenth-century Britain, the era in which most scholars believe national consciousness became particularly strong in Britain and Europe.² Recently, Hilary M. Carey, in her history of the role of religion in nineteenth-century Britain and its colonies, has fully rejected Anderson's notion that nationalism develops at the expense of religion, agreeing with scholar of nationalism Adrian Hastings that "religion, like language, [is] a component of all nationalisms" (10). In affirming and seeking to contribute to this growing body of scholarship, I am particularly indebted to McKelvy's *English Cult of Literature*.

McKelvy and I agree on many points: we both reject traditional secularization narratives as inadequate for describing the vital role played by religion in nineteenth-century culture; highlight the intersection of nineteenth-century reading, religion, and conceptions of the nation; and include in our studies a wide range of texts, from poems to newspapers. McKelvy also stresses that the emergence "of a reading nation" over the century "was widely perceived as a religious event" (255). Furthermore, our arguments rest upon the shared assumption that two of the most important historical changes over the course of the nineteenth century were the transformation of reading into a socially normative activity and the removal of nearly all penalties for nonconformity with the Church of England. While building on McKelvy's study, this book stands apart by analyzing a phenomenon still largely overlooked by scholars of literature, history, political science, and religion: how a range of nineteenth-century creative authors, clergy, educators, and journalists made commentary on reading, reflective attention to the act of reading, and attempts to model reading practices central to imagining membership in conflicting versions of a Christian British community, even as the state severed its exclusive connections to the Anglican Church.

Aiming to expand the dialogue on reading, religion, and national imagination in nineteenth-century Britain, in this book I also join a wider endeavor to rethink simplistic notions of "the religious" and "the secular." A growing number of anthropologists, sociologists, philosophers, scholars of religion, and (somewhat less often) literary scholars are asserting that the "secular," rather than some obvious category left behind by the retreat of religion, is in fact a uniquely Western construction (Taylor, "Western Secularity" 33–34), and that the "secular" and "religious" are mutually con-

---

2. McKelvy reaffirms this point in his essay on "Post-Secular Victorian Studies and Victorian Secularization Theory," which is part of a recent forum of articles on "The Sacralization of Literature in the Nineteenth Century" in *Nineteenth-Century Prose*. In my own contribution to that forum, "Religion, Reading, and Imagining Britain," I make a case for the kind of study pursued in this book.

stituted categories whose significance depends on when and where they are used (Asad, *Formations* 17, 25). For this reason, rather than hunting for an "essential" religious quality shared by the imagined communities surveyed in this book, I emphasize the strategies and aspirations authors and readers pursue in *constructing* the significance of "religion." This is evident in my analysis, in chapter 3, of Matthew Arnold's ambition to define the role and meaning of "religion" in public discourse. Yet it also characterizes my sustained focus on the diverse ways nineteenth-century authors continued, and sometimes resisted, the long process by which "religion" had by their time been reconfigured into "a primarily epistemological concern, a matter of minds rather than of bodies" (Jager, *Unquiet Things* 243).[3]

I use "spiritual" rather than "religious communities" in my title not to highlight nineteenth-century spiritualism, but because, although I concentrate on Christian imagined communities, the kinds of communion under consideration elude any single religious institution's boundaries, whether by design or by religiously diverse receptions and redeployments in print culture. Furthermore, whereas several authors I discuss, such as John Keble and Christina Rossetti, emphasize the creedal and ecclesiastical dimensions of the communities they invoke, very often others, such as Alfred Tennyson, contribute to the nineteenth-century tendency to identify faith with inwardness by presenting intuitions about God as if they were somehow innate to the soul and beyond or below the reach of any specific creed.

My explication of these imagined spiritual communities frequently relies on political philosopher Charles Taylor's now-familiar concept of the "immanent frame." Discussed at greater length in chapters 3 and 5, the "immanent frame" describes the possibility, uniquely shaped by Western history and fully in place by the nineteenth century, of experiencing the world as an immanent or "secular" order that operates according to secular time and impersonal cause-and-effect without necessary reference to God or a transcendent realm (Taylor, *A Secular Age* 541–44). Complementary to this sense of the world, Taylor argues, is the inward view of religion and spiritual experience I have described above. Following Taylor, I do not believe the immanent frame is inevitably closed to something beyond, though it *may* be experienced that way (543–44). Rather, it gives rise to

---

3. I do so intermittently in chapter 1 but at length in chapters 3, 5, and 6. The latter three chapters provide a fuller discussion of this inward understanding of "religion" and its relationship to nineteenth-century print-mediated imagined communities. For a concise summary of the modern construction of "religion" and scholarship touching upon it, see Jager's *Unquiet Things* (5–6, 248–49 n.15–17).

"multiple modernities," various ways of relating a secular immanent frame to spiritual experience, belief in God, and religious practice (Casanova, "The Secular" 61).

Hence, national imagination, as Benedict Anderson rightly notes, is characterized by a sense of moving simultaneously with hosts of other citizens through secular time in a shared finite destiny (35–36). While in this way national imagination is a major component of the modern immanent frame, it is not of necessity closed to religious communal imagination or providential conceptions of history. Without these phenomena national imagination is in fact incomprehensible in nineteenth-century Britain. Rather than portraying as neutral the divergent strategies by which authors negotiate senses of the secular and religious, I attend to their political consequences. The tendency to distinguish inward "religious" or "spiritual" experience from a secular immanent frame, for example, can facilitate not only greater tolerance of diverse religious expressions but also, as chapters 3 and 6 demonstrate, a willingness to sanction the liberal state's control over the secularized body, as well as state suppression of religious expression that transgresses the tolerated inward boundary.

Yet why, in the first place, should the nineteenth century be the moment when so much energy in Britain was devoted to imagining spiritual community through print? Several developments had converged to accustom a broad range of middle- and upper-class Britons to imagining their religious belonging in terms of solidarity created with strangers through texts circulating in a competitive religious market. Historians such as Linda Colley (1992), Hugh McLeod (1999), and Krishan Kumar (2003) have shown that Christianity, particularly Protestantism, became fundamental to British identity over the eighteenth century. Divisions between Protestants outside and within the Church of England, and the completion in the nineteenth century of a longer process of demolishing exclusive ties between this Church and the British state, meant that British identity could not be securely linked to a dominant religious institution. In 1689, the Act of Toleration, in permitting unrestricted worship of Trinitarian Protestant Dissenters, began a process of decoupling public, political, and social life from submission to the teaching and practice of the Church of England. Glimpsed in the 1689 Act were the legal separation between citizens' personal beliefs and matters of public security and peace (McKeon 39), and the principle of voluntary religious association, which were to be more fully witnessed in the official admission of Catholics and Dissenters to Parliament in 1828 and 1829, and the abolition of most Anglican restrictions on civil life, political participation, and education between 1850 and 1871.[4] By the 1830s, John Keble, the Anglican priest mentioned above, was witnessing tangible evidence of the swift process he prophesied in his well-known 1833 "National Apostasy" sermon: the Anglican Church was "henceforth to stand, in the eye of the State, as one sect among many" (*Sermons* 127). By the 1851 census, the shift from a confessional to a voluntary religious settlement revealed its effects. On the day of the census, only "about 20 per cent of adults" in England and Wales "attended an Anglican service," with an almost equal number showing up at Nonconformist chapels (McLeod *Religion and Society* 20, 11–12).

The principle of voluntary religious affiliation was speedily restructuring nineteenth-century British life. At the same time, the activity of reading, and the immense proliferation of reading materials, was taking off as never before in the middle and upper classes and reaching downward, aided by reforms to copyright laws in the late eighteenth century (St. Clair 111–21); improving printing technology since the early nineteenth century (Altick 262); enhancement of postal, distribution, and communication services (assisted by mid-century by the railway and telegraph); an expanding network of lending libraries and coffeehouses and reading rooms; and (especially by mid-century) the lowering prices of reprinted literature, newspapers, and periodicals (Altick 322–64). Put together, the rise of a voluntary establishment and the spread of reading created an environment in which competition for religious allegiance through the print market was essential (Hempton 90). Led especially by evangelicals, this broadcasting effort meant that from "1796 to 1914, Britain was immersed in the greatest exercise in Christian proselytism" the "country has ever seen" (C. Brown 39). In the resulting print-mediated battle for influence, full identification of a "truly national Christian culture" with either the institutions and membership of the Church establishment or its well-publicized religious competitors became impossible (Hempton 93).

---

4. The confirmation, in 1886, of Charles Bradlaugh as the first openly atheistic MP (after he won a series of elections for the position since 1880), was in many ways the end of a process beginning with the repeal of the Test Acts (1828) and the passing of the Catholic Relief Act (1829): Parliament, which had allowed Jewish members in 1858, was now fully secularized, in the sense of non-sectarian. Between 1850 and 1871, the Church of England lost most of its official control over British social and intellectual life: Nonconformists were admitted to Oxford and Cambridge in 1854; divorce was removed from ecclesiastical control in 1857; blasphemy was relatively free from prosecution after 1860; compulsory church rates were abolished in 1868; subscription and oath requirements were fully removed at Oxford, Cambridge, and Durham in 1871; national primary education was comprehensively established by the state in England, and non-confessional school boards were founded in districts underserved by religious schools, in 1870; such education was made compulsory through age ten in 1880; and Anglican control over burial services in the English countryside was removed in 1880.

The enormous efforts of the religious press, and the implication of religion in nearly every public or political conflict, ensured that Christianity did not lose, but increased, its public profile in nineteenth-century Britain. In 1877, Matthew Arnold could still claim in his "Preface" to *Last Essays on Church and Religion* that it was impossible to avoid his title subject "in all serious literary work" about issues of politics or national culture (*Complete Prose* VIII:148). Yet consumption of religion through the printed page, and competition for audiences in an increasingly crowded religious market, might have ironically weakened regular participation in religious institutions by the next century. By the twentieth century, the long-term consequences of this "struggle for" religious "influence" were beginning to show in a British populace that shared a "vague unaffiliated popular piety," but that had comparatively slackened its active commitment to religious institutions (Cox 213).

The period on which this book concentrates, the 1820s through the early 1890s, witnessed the relatively rapid creation of a situation with which all the commentators and authors I discuss felt compelled to grapple. Britain remained, in the imagination of the great majority of its citizens, a Christian nation. Yet Christianity retained its *public* and *national* force as an increasingly voluntary, competitive, and print-mediated phenomenon, rather than one *primarily* identified with any single group's site or institution.[5] Actual institutional participation became less essential to a sense of religious belonging than it would have been before 1780 (Hempton 84). Even though nineteenth-century Britain was "a deeply Christian country of unprecedented churchgoing levels" (C. Brown 9), worship spaces ceased to be the uncontested dominant means for imagining religious unity on a national scale, envisioning the place of one's own religious group within the nation, or seeking influence over potential believers. These acts were increasingly conceived as dependent on appeals to unity with a community of strangers through texts circulating within a competitive print market. Political and social conflicts between the 1820s and 1870s drove home this fact for authors, educators, and clergy seeking to reinforce the nation's

---

5. I include these italics to clarify that I do *not* believe church services and membership declined or became unimportant to religious life in nineteenth-century Britain. In fact, several of my chapters (especially 3 and 6) concentrate on the powerful public resonance of church buildings and forms of worship in nineteenth-century print culture. Instead, I am claiming that in attempts to *imagine* and *publicize* British Christian identity, no *single* religious institution, membership apparatus, or form of public worship could claim universal assent, or even the allegiance of a decisive majority. This meant that imagining oneself in spiritual community with other Britons through reading, rather than through shared physical sites and acts, became increasingly important.

sense of spiritual unity, even as they recognized that the rapidly expanding activity of reading, which eluded any institution's total control, was powerfully determining how Britons imagined themselves in community.

While devoting substantial attention to many non-Anglican authors, this book highlights authors from across the nineteenth century who aligned themselves with the Church of England and attempted to turn the printed page into a means of imagining a Christian community for a nation in which their church was losing its hegemonic status. Strengthened by several centuries of privileged legal, political, and social standing, the Church of England's position as a cultural center of gravity was difficult to displace (Knight and Mason 7). By 1851 the Church of England was drawing less than half of the nation's Sunday worshippers to its churches, but it remained the nation's largest Christian church: for every 1,000 live births in 1900, 609 baptisms were still performed in the Church of England (C. Brown 6). Anglicanism therefore retained a prominent hold on nineteenth-century poetics, church architecture, and definitions of national identity (Blair, *Form and Faith* 122). Nearly all nineteenth-century British efforts to imagine print-mediated national spiritual communities, even by figures outside the Established Church, were staged with awareness of Anglican authors and aesthetics, and often examined the problematic relationship of the Church of England to the state and the nation's other Christian groups. Moreover, precisely because their church was experiencing a steady decline in social and political strength, Anglican authors were sensitive to the ways in which competing sources of allegiance were exerting widespread influence through printed media. If, for this reason, Anglican writers examined in this book often displayed conservative, reactionary alarm in the face of Britain's expanding print culture, they also engaged in detailed and self-conscious reflection upon the ways in which imagining oneself in religious and national community was becoming inseparable from immersion in a media-saturated world.

In the first half of the book, *Apologists for Print-Mediated Spiritual Communities*, I discuss a series of middle-class authors, clergy, and educators who allied themselves with the Anglican Church: Samuel Taylor Coleridge, Frederick Denison Maurice, and Matthew Arnold. I analyze their differing attempts to promote reading strategies and educational programs to help Britons transform the millions of texts daily circulating through their nation into mediums for imagining themselves in a united spiritual, and generally Protestant, community. In chapters 1 and 2, I examine efforts by Coleridge and Maurice, the nineteenth-century theologian who most creatively adapted Coleridge's ideas, to envision and promote a reformed public sphere for a British national Christian community. Flourishing between the early and late decades of the eighteenth century, the ideal of a public sphere, or "republic of letters," was conceived—especially by middle-class writers—as a virtual space sustained in print in which citizens of all classes could rationally discuss and read about issues of national and common concern. This ideal seemed to flounder in the 1790s, with the proliferation of politically divided reading audiences, and of what Michael Warner would call radical and artisanal "counterpublics" that defied the discursive norms of the bourgeois and upper-class reading public (*Publics and Counterpublics* 118). Yet most middle-class authors continued to appeal to what Warner has called the imagined "unity of the public sphere," sustaining in their rhetoric the "fiction of 'public opinion' as the ideal background of all possible" reading "publics" (*Publics and Counterpublics* 56). To this "virtual social object" (*Publics and Counterpublics* 55), an imagined national community of readers, Coleridge and Maurice continued to appeal, but on new grounds. They did not think readers and writers recognized transparent standards for the "public use of their reason" of the kind that Habermas has associated with the ideal of the public sphere (Habermas 27). Coleridge and Maurice instead located the source of consensus in the inner witness of God within the conscience, which each Briton could learn to access through methods of reflective reading. They differently sought to promote a spiritual republic of letters, a reformed public sphere, in which the nation's vast network of print would become a medium for imagining and participating in a united Christian national community under a tolerant Anglican Church.

Coleridge and Maurice tempered their high hopes for the Church of England as an agent of national unity by acknowledging that the religious and social reach of their church was limited, and that the activity of reading, which was becoming the determining force in how Britons imagined themselves in community, resisted any institution's comprehensive control. Coleridge, in his later prose of the 1820s, and Maurice, in a wide range of publications between the 1830s and 1860s, reluctantly acknowledged that British citizens would not finally awaken to their spiritual unity through the institutions of the Church of England (or those of any single religious group), but through the ways they imagined themselves in community while reading and because of reading. This concession tacitly fuels Coleridge's and Maurice's most creative and idealistic attempts to guide British readers' interpretations of their increasingly mass-mediated world— whether dreaming of a clerisy that would train up journalists and professionals capable of converting the press into a form of daily national scripture, or modeling strategies of sympathetic reading that could turn even advertisements into aids to reflection upon a united British community under Christ.

In chapter 3, I turn to Matthew Arnold, often portrayed by scholars as a promoter of literature and culture, rather than institutional Christianity, as the source of modern British unity. By contrast, I claim that Arnold joins Coleridge and Maurice as a more heterodox, but no less earnest, apologist for the transformation of Britain's print network into a medium through which readers of all classes could imagine themselves in a Christian, and largely Protestant, national community. This way of comparing the careers of Coleridge, Maurice, and Arnold better illustrates their common concerns than the "Broad Church" label still often used by religious historians and literary scholars to group them together. Coleridge and Maurice share many theological concerns, but they share few with Arnold. What Coleridge, Maurice, and Arnold undeniably have in common is anxiety over the rapid expansion of print culture and of non-elite reading audiences—and the support seemingly lent by these developments to sectarianism, class tensions, and the decline of the Anglican Church's political power and social influence. In response to these trends, they all variously envisioned establishing, through reading, an imagined national Christian community in the minds of Britons, and sustaining this unifying act of imagination through Britain's print and mass communications network.

In the period following Maurice's death, the early 1870s to the later 1880s, Arnold clarified how he hoped a reformed Anglican Church and national education system would cooperate in shaping the consciousness of the reading nation. Guided by critics of culture administering their influence through the public sphere, Britons of all classes would, with the aid of state-funded literary education, learn to interpret the Bible and the rites of the Anglican Church as a national, public poetry—in effect, a poetic National Church. The shared ethical "poetic" language of liturgy and Scripture would enable British readers to rise above their sectarian and class-based identities into supposedly higher, more tolerant selves capable of achieving a harmonious national community. Rather than relying on the decline or replacement of institutional religion, then, the Arnoldian program of culture depends on defining the meaning of "religion" so as to set the terms on which it could bind together the British reading public. Arnoldian culture requires not the rejection of institutional Christianity but a sustained attempt to articulate and defend its moral and poetic force in a national public sphere, and a less obvious recovery of its theological authority for the regulation—sometimes forceful—of that reading public by critics and the state.

The hard-dying habit of characterizing Arnold as a "replacement" theorist, dedicated to substituting secular culture and literature *for* institutional Christianity, has obscured the aims of his later career. This misunderstanding has often been accompanied by relative scholarly neglect of nineteenth-century attempts very different than Arnold's to promote a national Christian community through poetry. To one such effort the second half of my book, *Virtual Congregations and Printed Poetic Cycles,* is devoted. In this section, I turn to the role of long poetic cycles in fostering extra-institutional communities of Christian readers. In chapter 4, which opens this part of the book, I concentrate on *The Christian Year* (1827), published by John Keble to bring Britons' reading back under the imaginative and moral discipline of the Anglican Church, an institution he regarded not as Protestant but as the most authentic branch of the true Catholic Church. Keble's well-selling volume soon ironically became a means for many inside and outside the Church of England to imagine a national Christian, and generally Protestant, community that was sustained by private reading. Poets and critics, therefore, could represent private poetry reading as participation in a national Christian community by alluding to *The Christian Year,* and by adapting its model of a cycle of poems that coordinated private reflection with membership in a worshipping community. *The Christian Year* informs and helps illuminate the structure and reception of best-selling poetic cycles as diverse as Tennyson's *In Memoriam* (1850) and Christina Rossetti's *Verses* (1893).

In chapter 5, I survey a wide field of Victorian responses to Tennyson's *In Memoriam* (1850), explaining why the poem struck so many Victorians as a strong public testimony to a "minimum of faith," an intuitive belief in God and immortality lodged in the bedrock of the soul. Perhaps unintentionally, Tennyson presented his minimal confession of faith in a poetic cycle that Victorian readers compared to Keble's *The Christian Year.* To these Victorians, Tennyson's poem appeared to rework the alignment of private reading with participation in an imagined British Christian community that Keble had unwittingly put into circulation across a large number of Christian denominations in Britain. Tennyson's apology for a minimal, internal faith appealed to a broad spectrum of middle- and upper-class readers used to imagining their religious belonging in terms of the intuitions of the heart and solidarity created with strangers through a competitive religious market. Within some sectors of Victorian print culture, Tennyson's "New Christian Year" rivaled and even replaced Keble's as the poetic cycle best suited for helping British readers imagine themselves in a Christian community that transcended denominations. *In Memoriam* thereby offered an important medium for mid-century British readers of the middle and upper classes to imagine their spiritual relationship to strangers across their society in ways that eluded denominational boundaries—even if this meant conceiving of themselves as part of an orthodox subculture destined to resist the spiritual apathy of a reading public enchanted with the watered-down faith of the Queen's laureate.

Tennyson's appeal to interior, non-dogmatic faith in *In Memoriam* seems to confirm the story that was once widely circulated among twentieth-century scholars: in modernizing nations, religion is inevitably banished from the public sphere to the realm of private opinion. In chapter 6, I contest this deceptive impression by analyzing *In Memoriam*'s open secret, its convincing location of faith within the private soul through its appeal to public forms, religious and otherwise. If faith in *In Memoriam* explicitly inhabits the region of internal mood and suggestion, its communicability depends on a wide range of public allusions and shared forms—the Christian calendar; hymns and church bells; the Prayer Book and Bible; Christian typology represented as subjective insight; and a regular stanza and meter entangled in a thick net of public religious associations. The creation of an individual experience silently—but noticeably—textured by communal structures makes Tennyson's journey to faith seem "our" journey for many Victorian readers. By relying on internalized public forms to validate intuitions of the private soul, I argue, *In Memoriam* ironically facilitated a vague British piety that could sanction imperial expansion, repression of political protest, and sacrifice of one's body for war and economic production as signs of faith in a sacred British community. In pointing to spiritual intuitions that supposedly eluded sectarian warfare, Tennyson's "New Christian Year" could for some inspire a nationalistic and aggressive form of British sanctity.

In Memoriam's reception points to changes in the way the Christian unity of Britain is imagined after the mid-century. Moving away from a fundamentally Protestant (and often anti-Catholic) conception, British spiritual unity increasingly becomes attached to a broad sense of shared Protestant Christian values and civilization, a vision of unity easily tied to a Christian imperial mission for a superior British nation to spread enlightenment to the world. Yet for many Britons this sense of community did not become the dominant point of allegiance; rather, it was often viewed in competition with more specific religious and irreligious imagined communities. A vaguely Christian Britain could serve as the openly or silently acknowledged counterpoint against which to define a more deeply Christian and international form of imagined community.

As I discuss in chapter 7, Christina Rossetti (1830–94), in her late spin on the paradigm established by *The Christian Year* in *Verses* (1893; her last and best-selling volume), firmly resisted the national and imperial forms of imagined community enabled by Tennyson's *In Memoriam*. *Verses* invited readers to imagine themselves in an ecumenical and international community of saints whose hope for citizenship in a resurrected nation under Christ would spur its members to acts of love and justice now, even as it estranged them from total identification with any national society, branch of the Church, or reading audience. Rossetti sought to bring this vision of community to a wide readership by anticipating the reception of *Verses* in a competitive and diversified late-century market in which a thickening wall had arisen between "general" and "devotional" literature. Rossetti therefore created an updated *Christian Year* whose multidimensional language and structure were true to her own Anglo-Catholic convictions even as they appealed to audiences sensitive to distinct modes of understanding poetry and Christianity. Yet the very success of Rossetti's bid for a diversified reception eventually contributed to the editorial dismemberment and market demise of *Verses,* and the reinterpretation of the communally focused poetry within it as the increasingly irrelevant outpourings of a sweet, cloistered spirit. The construction and fate of *Verses* reflect the multiplicity of attempts to carve out readerships at the century's close, as well as the deepening estrangement between explicitly Christian and other spiritual and national visions of community formed by reading. Passing from the varying efforts to envision a spiritually united reading public by Coleridge, Maurice, and Arnold, and surveying adaptations of the poetic paradigm that Keble's *The Christian Year* popularized, a broad but uneven trend emerges. The labor to imagine and build a truly *national* Christian community through reading is replaced by demarcations of competing religious and irreligious audiences within a still broadly "Christian" national reading public that itself remains unidentified with any single religious institution or group.

My conclusion links the design and demise of Rossetti's *Verses* to the substantial weakening of print-mediated Christian Britain by the 1920s. For reasons elaborated in that closing chapter, in the 1890s the bond between active Christian allegiance and British national imagination was already buckling under pressure exerted by three developments: the diversification of Britain's religious and print market; the emergent international, rather than primarily national, focus of many British churches and missionary societies; and the dramatic rise in the number of Britons willing to imagine and passively symbolize their Christian identity rather than actively practice their faith in church or chapel. The last trend was, ironically, encouraged by this book's subject, the tremendous nineteenth-century efforts to circulate Christian identity and community through the printed page. By the early decades of the twentieth century, the growing international and ecumenical focus of churches and missions, spurred in part by outrage over military and economic atrocities committed in the British Empire, combined with the telecommunications revolution to signal the end of *print-mediated* Christian Britain. Even after print ceased to be the dominant medium of national imagination and virtual religious community in the next decades of the century, Christian Britain survived on a public scale as a widely broadcast and multi-mediated, but thinning, discourse reinforced by domestic ideology. When that ideology fell apart in the late 1950s and 1960s, so did Christian Britain.

Many of the questions with which the authors in my study were faced by their peculiar historical situation, and which their responses to that context suggest, remain relevant, even urgent. How does daily immersion in a mass-mediated world inform the ways people imagine themselves in communities, socioeconomic classes, religious groups, and nations? Wide diffusion of mass media in a competitive market can paradoxically increase social isolation, sectarianism, ideological fragmentation, and the power of commercial interests over politics and public opinion. How could these same media be reclaimed in (and between) national societies as means for motivating sympathetic imagination, shared values, cooperation for common causes, and reform of inequalities? What contribution could and should religious belief and practice make to this effort? How could national education contribute, and what is the place of religion in education? Do all attempts to imagine and solicit a public audience in some way involve distorted representations of those not included? How have exclusive, conservative efforts to link religious community to widely diffused media fortuitously fueled interdenominational and inclusive ones? On the other hand, how has liberal tolerance of religious diversity in the marketplace of ideas unexpectedly combined with approval of state coercion and violence?

Not all of the authors examined in this book asked these questions directly. They would have trouble comprehending them posed in these words. Yet such issues are constantly raised by their intricate, evolving, and often contradictory attempts to turn the circulating printed page into a medium for imagining and forming religious and national community. Translated from their printed age into our digital age, the questions confronted and indicated by these nineteenth-century British authors are largely still our own, and at several points along the way I consider their contemporary relevance explicitly, most fully in the conclusion. On the whole, this book indicates the wisdom of respecting the commanding roles media and mass communications have played and continue to play in attempts to imagine religious and national community. What periodicals and printed books were to nineteenth-century figures such as John Keble and Matthew Arnold, social media are for many today when it comes to imagining and debating their positions in national and international space and time. Media are not simply the *means* by which we imagine community; they partially *constitute* the communities we envision.

Imagined Spiritual Communities indicates another way in which scholarship on the nineteenth century might speak to the twenty-first. Taking seriously the roles that religion and theology played in the multifarious constructions of British identity in nineteenth-century print culture could change more than the ways scholars imagine the past. It might also help us better engage the present world, in which a variety of religious faiths and their detractors aim for public influence on a national and global scale.

PART 1

APOLOGISTS FOR PRINT-MEDIATED SPIRITUAL COMMUNITIES

CHAPTER 1

COLERIDGE'S *AIDS TO REFLECTION*

The Clerisy and a National Spiritual Republic of Letters

Writing for the *Athenaeum* in 1828, the young John Sterling lamented that "nine-tenths of the minds of this country" were passively measuring life not by seasons and church bells, but by the "monthly, weekly, tridiurnal, and daily" consumption of periodicals and newspapers (695).[1] "Saturated and overwhelmed with details, and opinions, and thoughts, . . . and feelings" circulating through print, "we live," he complained, "amid a succession of moments[,] . . . a repetition of ephemeral impulses: and England has become a mighty stock-broker, to whom ages past and future are nothing, and whose sole purpose . . . is to watch the news" (695). Sterling's portrayal of a nation of text druggies might recycle statements made by the sage at Highgate, whom he had met the year before (Nye, *DNB*), and whose words he had been reporting to friends (C. Sanders 136): Coleridge's notes for an 1811 lecture declare that "9/10ths of the Reading of 9/10ths of the reading Public" is supplied by a mind-numbing diet of "Reviews, Magazines, . . . Newspapers & *Novels*" (*Lects 1808–1819 [CC]* I:186).[2] Coleridge and Sterling are unremarkable for their time in protesting mindless overconsumption

---

1. The article is signed "Theodore Elbert, a young Swede," a pseudonym that Sterling used when contributing to the *Athenaeum* (Marchand 12).
2. Unless noted otherwise, all citations of Coleridge's works are from *The Collected Works of Samuel Taylor Coleridge* (Princeton UP and Routledge) and follow the abbreviations for Coleridge's works adopted in this series.

of printed works. Sterling indicates Coleridge's distinctive influence, however, when he calls for periodical authors to redeem the oversaturated print network by diffusing timeless "principles" and "*idea[s]* which the nation . . . should seek to realize," ideas that are not "drawn from . . . outward phenomena," and that shine a "light" on the unity of humanity in "God" while exposing the shallowness of "the philosophy of sensation and 'utility'" (695).

This vision—of a spiritual republic of letters, a print network sustaining a national community irradiated by divine light—Coleridge increasingly promoted in his later prose. As I discuss later in this chapter, in *On the Constitution of the Church and State* (1829) Coleridge imagined a learned order that could bring about this spiritual print republic: the clerisy, a National Church committed to cultivating the inward life and unity of the nation through publications, public lectures, instruction at universities and local schools, and Christian worship services. Yet before *Constitution of the Church and State*, Coleridge's vision of a spiritual republic of letters informed his most frequently republished work of prose in the nineteenth century (*Critical Heritage [1995]* II:8): *Aids to Reflection in the Formation of a Manly Character* (1825). Shortly after its publication, Sterling remarked, "I have read the *Aids to Reflection* again and again, with ever new advantage" (C. Sanders 136); nearly two decades after his first exposure to the volume, Frederick Denison Maurice, Sterling's friend and an early champion of Coleridge among the Cambridge "Apostles," could still declare that "The 'Aids to Reflection' is a book . . . to which I feel myself under much more deep and solemn obligations" than Coleridge's other writings (*Kingdom of Christ* I:6).

The enthusiasm of these and other Cambridge "Apostles" for *Aids*[3] supports narratives with which scholars have long been familiar: the Coleridgean origins of the so-called "Broad Church Movement" (C. Sanders) and of various nineteenth-century dreams of a cultural clerisy (Knights). It can also indicate, however, that these young intellectuals found in *Aids* not only a guide in religious inquiry but also a way of adapting to the matrix of print into which they felt the minds of the nation were being rapidly absorbed. *Aids* seemed to promise them a method of participation, through the medium of print, in a divinely illumined community.

The provision of such a method is a structuring motive of *Aids*. The reinforcement of utilitarian empiricism by reading habits formed among middle- and upper-class readers, Coleridge asserts throughout the volume,

---

3. Hereafter I abbreviate *Aids to Reflection* as *Aids*.

is undermining belief in intuitive knowledge—that is, those speculative and moral certainties provided, in Coleridge's view, by the reflection of God's light (the Logos) at a level of the self that normally remains subconscious. Coleridge therefore addresses those who can shape the print culture of the future: young men of the middle and upper classes "at the close of their education or on their first entrance into the duties of manhood," particularly those intending to enter "the Ministry" or serve as "Instructors of Youth" (6). He offers to lead them in developing "the art of REFLECTION" (9) through a series of meditations pursued in dialogue with passages drawn mainly from seventeenth-century English divines, especially Archbishop Robert Leighton (1611–84).

Coleridge's effort to encourage ways of achieving spiritual community within print culture helps explain his intimate form of address to readers in *Aids,* and his representation of the text as a virtual form of classroom instruction—"we are in the silent school of Reflection, in the secret confessional of Thought" (84). In this classroom of mediated intimacy, the reader of *Aids* is invited to reflect on his or her own mind to experience intuitions of the divine light, and to regard this reflective activity as shared within a community sustained by the virtual space and time of Coleridge's printed text. In the next sections, I analyze how Coleridge's invitation of readers of *Aids* into his virtual school of reflection follows from his vision of a spiritual republic of letters. I then examine his explicit formulation of the clerisy in *On the Constitution of the Church and State.* This independent body of ethical and humanistic educators and parish priests would, Coleridge hoped, restrain the rapidly expanding influence of a commercialized and sectarian mass media upon the ways British citizens imagined their membership and responsibility in the national community. Yet the clerisy would also reform the same mass media into a medium through which Britons would become aware of themselves as a community united by the intuitive moral and spiritual truths articulated in *Aids.*

As even this short summary indicates, participation in Coleridge's spiritual republic of letters is limited by class and gender. His clerisy would, if realized, exclude his own daughter Sara from positions of institutional leadership within its ranks, even though she was his most gifted nineteenth-century interpreter and editor. Her gender would also bar her from the projected audience of *Aids,* which, like *The Statesman's Manual* (1816), courts a readership of well-educated, reflective, implicitly Anglican young men from the professions and higher classes, and screens out the supposedly unpredictable and easily manipulated mass public (Canuel 99–100). These writings thereby invite the criticism first memorably made by William Hazlitt, who, in one of several antagonistic reviews of *The Statesman's Manual,* posed as an artisan outraged at having been "throw[n]" aside, along with other intelligent members of the mass public, by Coleridge, who had abandoned the cause of liberty to cater exclusively to the higher orders (Hazlitt 1817: 29).

Yet it is misleading to follow Hazlitt's once-common strategy of splitting Coleridge's life into a radical phase before 1798 and a reactionary one thereafter. Coleridge "did move from being a radical dissenter to being a proponent of the established Church and State, from being a democrat and republican to being a monarchist and a defender of a restricted franchise, from being a severe critic of the rights of property to being one of its stoutest defenders" (Kitson 157). Surprisingly consistent convictions, however, guided Coleridge's shifting political positions. If, for example, Coleridge switched from attacking personal property to defending it, both stances were rooted in his championship of personal and public liberty, with the change resulting from his later view that property prevented tyranny and affirmed the moral agency of the individual (Leadbetter 5). As fundamental to Coleridge's thought in 1825 as in 1795 was his "social idealism" (4), a belief that all lasting social reform depended on awakening "human consciousness" to feel and apply principles of moral responsibility (7). Coleridge, as he put it in 1818, urged a "more permanent revolution in the moral world" (*SWF [CC]* 1:685), by which active self-reflection would empower individuals to change—rather than simply react to—their environments. Belief in the primacy of mental revolution marked Coleridge's radical and conservative phases, and in both he called for the leadership of "an intellectual vanguard," ultimately leading to his late championship of "the clerisy" (Kitson 162). This explains Coleridge's dedication, as early as 1795, to cultivating critical reflection "by way of the print media" (Leadbetter 2) among those able to influence public opinion, rather than to reaching the mass reading public (12).

Prioritizing intellectual and moral revolution did not harden Coleridge to the oppression of the working classes in early nineteenth-century Britain. During his conservative period, he drew up petitions to Parliament, gave speeches, wrote pamphlets, and argued in his critical prose for affordable food, better labor standards, and education for the poor (Leadbetter 12). From his 1795 radical Bristol lectures to his 1829 *On the Constitution of the Church and State,* Coleridge asserted the government's active responsibility for the well-being of its people (Kitson 157), which he outlined, among other places, in his 1817 *Lay Sermon:* "1. To make the means of subsistence more easy to each individual. 2. To secure to each of its members the hope of bettering his own condition or that of his children. 3. The development of those faculties which are essential to his Humanity, i.e., to his rational and moral Being" (*LS [CC]* 216–17). Coleridge's later political philosophy, then, "always showed concern for the social (if not the political) welfare of the labouring classes" (Kitson 165). It was rooted in the assumption "that a person can never become a thing, nor be treated as such without wrong" (*Friend [CC]* I:190), and was therefore bitterly opposed to the status quo, in which "the machinery of the wealth of the nation" was "made up of the wretchedness, disease and depravity of those who should constitute the strength of the nation!" (*C&S [CC]* 63).

For all this, Coleridge's social idealism, before and after 1798, enabled his comfort with elitist rhetoric and with the exclusion from the intellectual vanguard of those currently denied positions of public and intellectual influence. At the root of Coleridge's clerisy is his elitist faith that in every age a philosophic few remain attuned to the light amidst general darkness: all history shows, he claimed in the 1809 *Friend,* "noble structures raised by the Wisdom of the Few, and gradually undermined by the Ignorance and Profligacy of the Many" (II:52). In this sense, the Neo-Platonic view of reflective reason on which Coleridge founds the clerisy, discussed below, is a paternalistic construction that constantly locates the best hope of the masses in their guidance by a (male) intellectual aristocracy, even though in principle members of any class might join this contemplative elite (Leadbetter 10). Yet Coleridge's paternalistic complacency is arguably less a sign of reactionary or hypocritical conservatism than of blind spots entailed in his early and foundational assumption that social reform depends more on an enlightened few gradually changing minds through print culture than on reforms to government or electoral politics.

Already tendentious in his time, Coleridge's vision of national spiritual community now seems even more of a pipe dream, as do the related projects of early graduates from Coleridge's virtual school of reflection in *Aids*. In my conclusion, I turn briefly to one of these graduates, Frederick Denison Maurice, who became the leading Victorian champion of Coleridge's efforts to reform print culture, and who is the central figure in my next chapter. While I recognize the elitism and ideological exclusivity of Coleridge's, and later Maurice's, ambitions for a spiritual republic of letters in Britain, I conclude by suggesting that the clerical calling they affirm for the humanities remains a challenging point of vocational reference for scholars and educators in a mass-mediated world where spaces for cultivating and practicing critical thinking are rapidly disappearing.

I. REFLECTIONS OF THE LOGOS IN *AIDS TO REFLECTION*

Coleridge's assumptions about reflection guide his criticism of print culture and empiricism in *Aids*, and are central to his promotion of a divinely illuminated republic of letters. In the "Preface" to *Aids*, Coleridge apostrophizes his imagined university or seminary student: "Reader! . . . you are born in a Christian land" with a storehouse of "Revelation," but the only "key to this casket" is "Self-knowledge," obtained by reflecting "on your own thoughts, actions, circumstances" (9–10). There is in each person, Coleridge asserts, a "truest *self, the* man *in* the man," a "house gloriously furnished" with "truths and realities" that each might glimpse through the "*enlightening* eye" of "Reflection" (*AR [CC]* 15). "Reflection," then, means active intuition of those "truths and realities" abiding at a level of the self deeper than biographical identity or daily consciousness. Considered in isolation, the biographical self is a shallow "complexus of visual images, cycles or customs of sensation" (*CM [CC]* III:720); it is the "*you*—you—you yourself on to the end of the Chapter" that Coleridge felt popular Methodist teaching and preaching emphasized (*CM [CC]* III:528). Yet Coleridge does not think the "truest self" is some insulated ideal form. The core of our selfhood, our "soul" (*AR [CC]* 15) or self-determining "finite will" (42), is defined by membership in what Coleridge calls "the System of intelligent and self-conscious Beings, . . . the great Community of *Persons*" (77). Such a view of the true self as simultaneously individual and transpersonal, a distinct realization of a universal humanity shared with others, informs Coleridge's comment on the way Shakespeare "shaped his characters out of the Nature within": "It was S[hakespeare]'s prerogative to have the *universal* which is potentially in each *particular,* opened out to him—the *homme generale* not as an abstraction of observation from a variety of men; but as a Substance capable of endless modifications of which his own personal Existence was but one—& to use *this one* [his personal existence] as the eye that beheld the other [the universal humanity], and as the tongue that could convey the discovery" (*Lects 1808–1819 [CC]* II:148).

Yet if a reflecting person ever lights upon "truths and realities" by contemplating his "truest *self,*" it is because his act of contemplation "is *but* a reflection" of a greater "light" (*AR [CC]* 16). This greater, originating "light" Coleridge identifies as "the Messiah, . . . the Logos, or co-eternal Filial Word" (219). Here Coleridge depends on an idea developed in the 1820s in his notebooks and in his draft for the *Opus Maximum,* according to which the Second Person of the Trinity is the eternal "Principle or Idea of the divine Humanity" (Perkins 231). The Logos is the universal pattern of human nature and human knowledge reflected in each person's truest self *and* the power by which this true self is realized in community with God and others (262–64). The reflection of the Logos in the true self and the possibility of becoming this self in human community exist because the Logos has taken "flesh" to "assume our humanity personally" in Jesus (*AR [CC]* 323). The life, death, and resurrection of the historical Jesus have provided the basis and universal pattern for each person's communion with the eternal Logos, the divine humanity reflected in his or her truest self, as well as the potential for any truly united and healthy national community.

Coleridge in this way creatively adapts the view of reflection held by seventeenth-century Cambridge Platonists, such as John Smith (1618–52) and Benjamin Whichcote (1609–83). As Douglas Hedley describes it, "the doctrine of reflection which Coleridge shares with the Cambridge Platonists is that the reflection of the soul upon itself reveals the immutable verities which are simultaneously the principles of human action and knowledge and the ideas of God [or Logos]" (226–27). The "nature and ultimate object of reflection," Coleridge explains to the student reader of *Aids,* is "to discover the living fountain and spring-head of the evidence of the Christian faith in the believer himself"; it is to recognize within one's intuitions of moral and spiritual truths the illuminating presence of the Second Person of the Trinity, that "which we find within ourselves, which is more than ourselves, and yet the ground of whatever is good and permanent therein, . . . the source and substance of all other knowledge" (*AR [CC]* 30n).

This method of reflection depends on Coleridge's distinction between Reason and Understanding. Coleridge adapts the Christian Neo Platonic tradition to equate "Reason" with the Divine "Logos," and to identify the sense-abstracting power that John Locke called "reason" with the lower faculty of "Understanding," "the Faculty by which we reflect and generalize" from "impression[s] on the Sense" (*AR [CC]* 224–25). Hence Coleridge can apply the prologue of St. John's Gospel[4] to "Reason" in distinction from "Understanding": "There neither is nor can be but one Reason, one and the same: even the Light that lighteth every man's individual Understanding" (218).

In *Aids,* Coleridge claims that "the main chance of ["my youthful Readers"] *reflecting* on religious subjects *aright,* and of their attaining to the *contemplation* of spiritual truths *at all,* rests on their insight into the *nature*

---

4. "In the beginning was the Word, and the Word was with God, and the Word was God . . . [The Word is] the true Light, which lighteth every man that cometh into the world" (John 1:1, 9 AV).

of this disparity" between Reason and Understanding (224). By my Understanding, for example, I might see that it is prudent, before building a new store, to evaluate my available capital, expected revenues, and the solidity of the ground. By the light of Reason illuminating my sense of moral law, what Coleridge calls "Conscience" (AR [CC] 286), I might intuit—rather than analyze abstractly—the "sacred distinction between Things and Persons" (140), and connect this unconditional moral law with what it implies: my daily experience of having a "Will" (140) not fully determined by the cause and effect of my environment, and therefore capable of responsible moral action. I might decide to abandon building the store, even if the ground is good and the capital available, because it would mean expelling families from the apartment complex currently on the lot.

Yet I could experience this intuitive moral recognition and still selfishly resolve on destroying the apartment building. My violation of conscience could lead to indifference; but it could also, Coleridge contends, open me to another truth, spiritual in nature: the reality of "Sin," some mysterious "By-law in the Will contrary to the universal Law of right Reason in the Conscience" (AR [CC] 286), a self-corrupting tendency affirmed by "every Religion, and . . . every Philosophy, in which the reality of a responsible Will and the *essential* difference between Good and Evil have been recognized" (289). Reading the letters of St. Paul, I might find in their pages testimony to the same light of Reason by which I have intuited sin, and, further, the revelation of an answer to my dilemma in the "doctrine of Redemption from Sin" through Christ, which could then supply me with "motives and reasons for" affirming "the divinity of the Redeemer . . . in the economy of [my] own Soul"—that is, in my own moral struggle and need for a supra-human answer (188). In these writings, too, I might find fuller disclosure of what Seneca (146) partly discovered when striving after his intuitive sense of the moral law: that there is "One present to all and in all" within "the great Community of *Persons*" (77), an empowering Holy Spirit "acting *in* the Will[s]" (77) of cooperating individuals to enable them to conform to the "Will of Reason," the universal moral law (217).

With this view of reflection in mind, Coleridge makes his well-known declaration: "Make a man feel the *want* of" Christianity; "rouse him, if you can, to the self-knowledge of his *need* of it; and you can safely trust it to its own Evidence" (AR [CC] 405–6). Rather than reducing religion to ethics or existential struggle, Coleridge encourages readers to turn inward to participate—contemplatively and practically—in the divine life disclosed in Reason, the goal of the process ultimately being "the entrance of the Soul into Glory, *i.e.* its union with Christ," who is Reason (160). For Coleridge, the light of Reason is "present to all and in all" (77), source of the "sustaining Law of visible natures" (323) in the universe, and of the speculative, but especially moral, truths by which any nation can enter into a just cooperative life.

Crucial to right reflection is the realization that "*empirical* data," to which the Understanding is confined, can be the "indispensible condition, of our reflecting on" absolute "Truths" of Reason already present at an unconscious level; but "our conviction" of these truths is never "derived . . . from outward Experience" (*AR [CC]* 291). The apple hits Newton on the head and he *becomes aware* of the invisible power of gravity; one learns of slaves treated as property in the Empire and, however imperfectly, *recognizes* the violation of "the sacred distinction between Things and Persons"; Coleridge peruses the "Books of the Old and New Testament" and discovers "words for" his "inmost Thoughts," so that its revelation of redemption, for example, "*finds*" him at the deepest level of his moral struggle (*SW & F [CC]* II:1121).

II. PRINT CULTURE IN THE AGE OF UNDERSTANDING

Coleridge's view of reflection required him to believe that a divine and vital communication network, the Logos that indwells humanity and renders reality intelligible, provided the ultimate conditions—recognized or not— for middle-class, early nineteenth-century England, a world in which tons of paper circulated between steam-powered presses, bookstores, circulating libraries, post offices, and homes in a vast print matrix. Yet in the last decades of his life, Coleridge repeatedly criticized "the present much-reading, but not very hard-reading age" (*C&S [CC]* 134), and suggested that its excesses contributed to the disregard of Reason. In the flyleaf of a copy of the 1818 *Friend,* he wrote "the Present is the Epoch of the Understanding and the Senses" (*Friend [CC]* I:203n.). Narrowly empiricist and utilitarian attitudes, Coleridge thought, were spreading among "the higher and middle Ranks" (*AR [CC]* 405), and were encouraged by "the enormous multiplication of Authors & Books" (*Lects 1808–1819 [CC]* I:186).

Coleridge saw the real danger coming from books by the learned pious, especially those by the Anglican professor and clergyman Dr. William Paley. Drawing heavily on Locke, Paley authored works on moral philosophy (*The Principles of Moral and Political Philosophy,* 1785), Christian apologetics (*View of the Evidences of Christianity,* 1794), and natural theology (*Natural

Theology, 1802). These had already gone through numerous editions, and were standard textbooks at Cambridge, by the time Coleridge was writing *Aids*. Paley assumed an empiricist epistemology: he defined (like Hume) the human mind as "a bundle of habits" formed by experience (Hedley 174), and he ultimately treated God as an empirical hypothesis to be proven according to Jesus' recorded miracles. Paley's evidentiary approach is exemplified in a passage from *Principles* that Coleridge disapprovingly quotes in the conclusion of *Aids*:

> Had Jesus Christ delivered no other declaration than the following—"The hour is coming, in which [the dead] shall come forth: they that have done good, unto the resurrection of life; and they that have done evil, unto the resurrection of damnation"—he had pronounced a message of inestimable importance, and well worthy of that splendid apparatus of prophecy and miracles by which his mission . . . was attested . . . [N]o man can prove [the reality of the future state], but the teacher who testifies by miracles that his doctrine comes from God. (qtd. in *AR [CC]* 411)

For Paley, Jesus' message, demonstrated by miracles, is of value not only because it "prove[s]" the reality of the afterlife but also because it provides incentive for a good (and submissive) life now, lest one awake to eternal damnation later. For this reason, in an aphorism entitled "PALEY NOT A MORALIST," Coleridge equates Paley's ethics with "Schemes of conduct, grounded on calculations of Self-Interest; or on the average Consequences of Actions" (*AR [CC]* 293)—Paley himself declared "Whatever is expedient, is right" (qtd. in Crimmins, *DNB*). Substantiated by Jesus' miracles, Paley's God threatens hell and promises heaven to encourage compliance in a society of utility, one in which the members are ultimately conceived, Coleridge felt, as "*things* [that] *find their level*" within a laissez-faire economy (*LS [CC]* 205).

Coleridge believes that the passage he quotes from Paley's *Principles* will sound "plausible and popular . . . to the great majority of Readers" (*AR [CC]* 410). In the conclusion of *Aids*, Coleridge imagines one such reader from the middle and upper ranks, a "*rational* Christian," looking up from Paley's page to say, "with a sighing, self-soothing sound between an Ay and an Ah!—*I* am content to think, with the *Great* Dr. Paley . . ." (410). Popular books such as Paley's promote an inadequate form of reason (confined to the Understanding) as the standard of truth for self-satisfied readers of "the higher and middle Ranks," among whom, as a result, "there is an inward withdrawing from the Life and Personal Being of God, a turning of the Thoughts exclusively to [His] so called physical Attributes," such as "Ubiquity" (405). Early into *Aids,* Coleridge imagines an anonymous "Review" of the volume he has composed. Coleridge describes the reviewer piecing together adverse quotations from Hanoverian literary and religious authorities ("Swift, . . . Warburton"), interspersed with "allusions" to Coleridge's own "supposed . . . Infirmities": "'It may not be remiss to inform the Public, that the Compiler of the Aids to Reflection, . . . belongs to the Sect of the *Aeolists,* . . . *who can make* SHADOWS, *no thanks to the Sun; and then mould them into* SUBSTANCES, *no thanks to Philosophy*' . . .— *Tale of the Tub,* Sec xi" (*AR [CC]* 81–82). The conclusion to *Aids* opens with Coleridge foretelling the denunciations—"Visionary Ravings, Obsolete Whimsies, Transcendental Trash"—that his volume will call forth from some "anonymous" critic, perhaps one asked to review the work "beforehand," just as Hunt's *Examiner* had engaged Hazlitt to write an anticipatory 'review' of *The Statesman's Manuel* (383).

These outbursts corroborate Lucy Newlyn's study of the anxiety of reception among Romantic-era writers in *Reading, Writing, and Romanticism: The Anxiety of Reception* (2000); and Coleridge's raillery against the hostility, party spirit, and abusive power of anonymous criticism resembles attacks made against the practice since the late eighteenth century—sometimes in periodicals themselves (Keen, *Crisis* 125). If unexceptional in this regard, Coleridge's complaints reveal his belief that *Aids* was entering a middle- and upper-class print network whose machinery of evaluation was primed to shred his volume for its defiance of the common sense preached in Paley's popular textbooks.

Halfway through explicating his distinction between Reason and Understanding (*AR [CC]* 216–36), Coleridge inserts a massive footnote, pages long, on the mental passivity encouraged in the literary market. He regrets that his differentiation between Reason and Understanding will be lost on the reader who says, "'I take up a Book as a Companion, with whom I can have an easy cheerful chit-chat . . . In our leisure hours we have a right to relaxation and amusement'" (228). Here Coleridge seems to have in mind the mass middle-class readership he described in *The Statesman's Manual* (1816) as a "vast company . . . , whose heads and hearts are dieted at the two public *ordinaries* of Literature, the circulating libraries and the periodical press" (*LS [CC]* 38), especially the hundreds of thousands of readers of relatively cheap compilations of literature, such as the *Mirror of Literature, Amusement, and Instruction.* The writer who wishes to earn "applause" from readers with this "craving for *amusement*" must learn to "reconcile in one and the same occupation the love of Sloth and the hatred of Vacancy," and distract them from "their own permanent Being" by regurgitating "their own errors and prejudices" (*AR [CC]* 228–29). These comments are unjust to the hundreds of thousands of men and women they impugn. Yet they communicate Coleridge's sense of vast reading audiences encouraged to substitute distracted amusement for reflection, familiar opinion for active inquiry, making them vulnerable to passive acceptance of the commonsense "Materialism" that he saw dominating his age (394). While, Coleridge asserts in *Aids,* few people consciously avow materialism, almost everyone "who calls himself a Christian" regards only "sensible OBJECTS" as real (394).

In the prose written in the final two decades of his life, Coleridge conjured up nightmarish visions of reading and writing to suggest the dehumanizing impact of the mechanical philosophy that descends from Locke through Hartley to Paley, a philosophy that Coleridge believed reduced the thinking mind and active will to physiological association. In *Biographia Literaria,* Coleridge seeks to expose the logical consequences of Hartley's associationism by inviting the reader to consider the print on the page:

> [According to Hartley's] hypothesis the disquisition, to which I am at present soliciting the reader's attention, may be as truly said to be written by Saint Paul's church, as by *me:* for it is the mere motion of my muscles and nerves; and these again are set in motion from external causes equally passive . . . in interdependent connection with every thing that exists or has existed. Thus the whole universe co-operates to produce the minutest stroke of every letter, save only that I myself, and I alone, have nothing to do with it, but merely the causeless and *effectless* beholding of it when it is done. Yet scarcely can it be called a beholding . . . It is the mere quick-silver plating behind a looking-glass; and in this alone consists the poor worthless I! (1:119)

This is a dark parody of the art of reflection that Coleridge will defend in *Aids:* rather than beholding the cosmic Logos reflected in the inner man, Coleridge and his attending reader become mere reflections— "plating behind a looking-glass"—of motions rippling across the universe. Coleridge's *reductio ad absurdum* is meant to provoke the reader to reject a reductive materialism and acknowledge the experiential reality of self-conscious minds and free wills. The very printed text, as a record of deliberately communicated meanings, ought to affirm a world ordered and participated in by living intelligence, rather than by dead mechanism. If the print network, by which this "disquisition" reaches the "reader's attention," primarily circulates attitudes current in the epoch of Paley, it might also communicate intuitions of the interdependent connection of everything in Reason, the Logos that indwells humanity. To this end Coleridge will develop his rhetoric in *Aids to Reflection,* converting his text into a virtual classroom of reflection for young men.

III. COLERIDGE'S VIRTUAL CLASSROOM AND THE SPIRITUAL REPUBLIC OF LETTERS

In defining "Reason" as "the Light that lighteth every man's individual Understanding" (*AR* 218), Coleridge distinguishes it from the utilitarian rationality he saw spreading through Paley and the print market. Yet Coleridge is also redefining reason to sustain, in heavily revised form, a hope virtually consubstantial with the Enlightenment as it took hold in eighteenth-century Britain: the conviction, held most intensely by the reformist middle classes (Keen, *Crisis* 38), that the expanding diffusion of print would create a "republic of letters," a "virtual space" (37) in which readers and writers, mainly men, of every social rank could engage in rational consideration of public issues for the sake of national improvement.

The "republic of letters" has been the subject of scholarly debate for the last three decades, mainly conducted in critical dialogue with Jürgen Habermas's concept of the "public sphere" (Miles, *Romantic Misfits* 13–18). Despite their differences, scholars such as John Klancher (*The Making of English Reading Audiences* 1987), Kevin Gilmartin (*Print Politics* 1996), Paul Keen (*The Crisis of Literature* 1999), and Robert Miles (*Romantic Misfits* 2008) give us a generally coherent picture of the history and fate of this virtual republic. Nourished by an ever-expanding network of coffeehouses and reading rooms, lending libraries, and periodicals, the ideal of a republic of letters was often appealed to by middle-class writers between the early and late decades of the eighteenth century. In the 1790s, it began to lose favor as an achievable goal as the French Revolution and ensuing Napoleonic Wars induced intense government censorship, promotion of lower-class and artisan counterpublics by radicals such as John Thelwall, and political and ideological divisions within bourgeois print culture itself. If reformist and Dissenting bourgeois writers and journals were the most ardent champions of the republic of letters, even eighteenth-century upper-class conservatives could embrace the ideal (Keen, *Crisis* 41), as the following passage from the *Gentleman's Magazine* of 1797 indicates:

> The republic of letters, like every well ordered community, has differing degrees of established rank . . . Every member of it, however obscure, possesses the most unbounded right to discuss with perfect freedom the opinions and reasonings of every other: but in the exercise of this right, all men are bound to observe the rules of decency. Obscure men owe deference to established reputation . . . (qtd. in Miles, "Trouble" 324)

This review censures John Thelwall (an "obscure" man) for challenging Edmund Burke (one of "established reputation"), and affirms assumed rules of conduct in the republic of letters. Participation in the republic requires deference to the rules of rational discourse, and those who have set them—in this case the conservative establishment, but in other cases the reformist middle classes, in opposition to radical counterpublics that were claiming "the power of reason and the authority of the reading public" for themselves (Keen, *Crisis* 138). "Reason," then, was the watchword at the borders of the virtual republic of letters, used to determine who set the terms of discussion and who had to obey them. The ideal of an overarching republic, containing the whole nation of readers, became untenable by the century's end, as differences intensified over whose rules of "reason" counted and as countering "publics" proliferated. Yet in the early nineteenth century, middle- and upper-class periodicals such as the *Edinburgh Review* (1802), *Quarterly Review* (1809), and *Blackwood's Magazine* (1817) were still making general appeals to a broad, "cosmopolitan ideal of the republic of letters," a standard of rationality and supposed fair-mindedness that they used to present their openly political and mutually exclusive views as self-evident and foundational to the health of the nation (Keen, "Politics" 109).

The fate of the "republic of letters" informs Coleridge's sustained criticism from *The Statesman's Manual* through *Aids* of appeals to some shadowy "READING PUBLIC" (*LS [CC]* 36). He felt early nineteenth-century authors and periodicals were using the term "public" to shape divided hosts of readers "into personal unity by the magic of abstraction" (*BL [CC]* I:59), creating an imaginary personification they could address as "a supreme and inapellable Tribunal of intellectual Excellence" (*AR [CC]* 229). Such apparently deferential appeals to a shared rule of reason within the republic of letters, were, Coleridge argued, attempts to put in the mouth of an actually non-existent national community of readers the "decisions of its invisible ministers," anonymous reviewers and periodical journalists (*BL [CC]*

1:59). Coleridge had himself partaken in the dissenting effort to reform society through the republic of letters when, as a young radical Unitarian, he launched his periodical the *Watchman* (1796), only to witness his liberal middle-class readership rapidly diminish over ideological differences when his arguments became specific (Klancher 37–38; *BL [CC]* 1:179–87).[5]

When writing *Aids,* then, Coleridge was convinced that the ideal of a republic of letters had already foundered on competing claims to rational authority and that it had since devolved into personifications of a "Public" by writers and periodicals who wished to present their factious views as universal and unquestionable. Yet he did not abandon reason, nor did he suppress all hope of its illumination of the print network. His vision of an inwardly grounded, Christian Neo-Platonic republic of letters is an effort to imagine shared recognition of a level of reason deeper (and higher) than any given political rationality or utilitarian goal: the reflectively intuited ideas of the Logos. Coleridge saw this republic anticipated in the less expansive print culture in which the Cambridge Platonists had thrived "prior to the Glorious Revolution," a period when, he believed, religion had been vigorously contested in print and in person (Canuel 95) under a shared commitment to reason as the 'candle of the Lord,' a reflection of divine truths (Hedley 297).

Mark Canuel pushes his case too far when he suggests that Coleridge's admiration of this past ideal makes him resist the "attempt to imagine *any* uniformity in religious belief" (93).[6] In the years in which Coleridge was articulating his ideal of a spiritual republic of letters, he disparaged the "enfeeble[ment]" of "religion" by Dissenting groups, such as the Unitarians, in which he had once vocally participated (Kitson 167; *AR [CC]* 208–9n). Furthermore, the political and ideological coercion that troubles every invocation of a republic of letters—someone sets the rules for "rational" discourse and identifies violators—surfaces in Coleridge's sneers at the supposedly shallow and materialist mass reading public, and in his attempts to recruit a spiritually enlightened cadre of Anglican middle- and

---

5. In *Biographia Literaria,* Coleridge claims that a satirical essay against national fast days lost him "nearly five hundred . . . subscribers at one blow" (Bate and Engell think Coleridge exaggerates the number of readers who dropped the paper over this essay [*BL [CC]* I:185 n.3]); and in the following two numbers, attacks on "French *psilosophy*" (Coleridge's term for "shallow philosophy") drove away "all my Jacobin and Democratic Patrons" (*BL [CC]* I:184–85).

6. In his chapter on Coleridge, Canuel focuses on the *Watchman* and *The Friend,* devoting only a few short paragraphs to *Aids* and *On the Constitution of the Church and the State* (120–21): in *Aids,* Coleridge insists on the centrality of beliefs such as the Trinity (and so the divinity of Christ), indwelling of the Holy Spirit, Redemption through Christ, and Baptism, even as he recommends respect for those of differing opinions (*AR* 208–13n.).

upper-class men to reform print culture. Yet in stressing Coleridge's theoretical resistance to all censorship and penalization of beliefs (see *AR [CC]* 209–13n), Canuel highlights Coleridge's astonishing confidence in *Aids* that self-reflection, in voluntary submission to ideas and principles derived from an indwelling Logos, will inevitably lead to religious, social, and political cohesion, as well as advancement in all branches of the arts and sciences (Hedley 194–211). In place of a non-existent homogenous "public," and in reaction to empiricist attitudes circulating in the print market between anonymous authors (periodical reviewers) and faceless readers, Coleridge attempts in *Aids* to lay the groundwork for a revitalized, spiritual republic of letters.

In this context, the subtitle—*In the Formation of a Manly Character*—does more than specify the young male audience of university students and future clergy to whom Coleridge directs *Aids*. (At one point, Coleridge seems to anticipate an audience wider than these men, addressing "my Lay Readers of both sexes" [*AR [CC]* 332].) Over the course of the eighteenth century, professional middle-class writers had fused their Christian values with the ideal of a republic of letters, redefining manliness as moral authority manifested in public service and authorship rather than the sport, military prowess, and wealth associated with the gentry (Keen, *Crisis* 83). The *Analytical Review* (1790), for example, praised Joseph Priestly for his "manly" feat of studious scientific inquiry, supporting his recommendation to "men of fortune" to shake themselves out of their "sensual pleasures" through similar pursuits (qtd. in Keen, *Crisis* 93). As late as 1818, John Hunt's radical journal, *The Yellow Dwarf*, protested that the government permitted "just so much literature as can exist without the aid of manly knowledge" (*The Popular Radical Press* II:254).

In *Aids,* Coleridge retains the association of "manly" with energetic, revisionary thought and conduct, but redirects the primary effort of this ethical striving from public to interior spaces. Thinking of 2 Peter 1:5, "giving all diligence, add to your faith virtue; and to virtue knowledge" (AV), Coleridge tells his reader that the Greek word translated *virtue* actually means "*manly energy*. . . . and not virtue, at least in the present and ordinary acceptation of the word" (*AR [CC]* 18). The "manly character" he would encourage in readers derives from strenuous reflection on Christ (the Logos) within the truest self, which requires aligning "the WILL (the *Man*hood, *Vir*tus)" with "the Light of Reason in the WILL itself [i.e., the dictates of conscience]" (260). If Coleridge's audience is to graduate from the instruction of *Aids* to impact society, they will need to pursue the "manly" labor of conforming to the true person in Christ, the inward reflection of the Logos that provides the potential for spiritually reformed debate and exchange within the virtual space of the republic of letters.

Coleridge initiates university and seminary students into this "manly" labor by way of personal lessons on reflection in the virtual classroom of his text. "We are in the silent school of Reflection, . . . the secret confessional of Thought" (*AR[CC]* 84), Coleridge remarks to his reader, identifying the virtual meeting place of the text as at once the most individual of spaces—the confessional of thought each must enter for himself—and potentially the most communal—shared between author and reader by virtue of the Logos present to each. From the moral principles and spiritual truths discovered in this virtual space, any empirical community "out there" must take its growth. In *Aids,* therefore, Coleridge makes a fresh intervention into a widespread contemporary effort—shared by the form of Romantic lyric he partially invented and the nineteenth-century novel whose rise he foresaw and dreaded[7]—to address the reader in ways that distance the site of reading from the anonymous, uncontrollable print market. Coleridge moves his audience from "THE READER" greeted anonymously at the bookstall (3), to the reading individual confronted without the generalizing article—"READER!" (9), to "You" (9), the person simultaneously located in a particular place and in the virtual space of the reflective classroom.

To create this impression of a virtual classroom, Coleridge mediates into print forms of rhetoric he may have used when running an actual weekly tutorial for young men between 1822 and 1827 at the Royal College of Surgeons, a sort of postgraduate seminar in which he intended to assist students "in the formation of their minds" by expounding ideas that would make their way into *Aids* (R. Holmes, *Darker Reflections* 524). Throughout *Aids,* Coleridge addresses his imagined reader as a "Pupil" (85) who "has taken me as his temporary guide on the straight, but . . . difficult way of religious Inquiry" (250). As if pausing in the midst of a lengthy lecture to ensure his pupil's engagement, he interrupts long aphorisms with apostrophes and sermonic calls to attention ("Observe, Reader!" [278]; "Do you . . . aim at Dignity of Character? . . . I conjure you, O youth! turn away from those who live in the Twilight between Vice and Virtue" [63]). Or he refers to *Aids* almost as a textbook being used in a seminar, directing

---

7. Garrett Stewart has demonstrated that novelists' apostrophes and second-person addresses to the reader were part of "the effort of nineteenth-century fiction to reprivatize . . . an overgrown commonwealth of reading within an undeniable sales economy" (9); and Mark Jones has argued that Romantic lyrics, especially Coleridge's own early poems, generally aim to "publiciz[e] private reflections" for "a relatively elite readership" (105), thereby creating a guarded form of private, reflective discourse for a print market that was policed by the government and generative of uncontrollable responses to one's publications.

his tutee's pace and focus ("I earnestly entreat the Reader to pause awhile, and to join with me in reflecting on the preceding Aphorism" [198]). At other times, he anticipates the reader's responses, as if they were engaged in a classroom discussion. ("I will now suppose the Reader to have thoughtfully re-perused the Paragraph containing the Tenets peculiar to Christianity, and . . . I should expect to overhear a troubled Murmur: How can I comprehend this? How is this to be proved?" [202].) Even as Coleridge singles out the reader as an individual pupil, he includes the reader in a classroom of initiates, "those who have had the patience to accompany me so far on the up-hill road to manly Principles" (245). Personally addressed and yet included in a virtual community of dedicated inquirers, the reader is encouraged to imagine the act of reading *Aids* as an individual and simultaneously interpersonal journey into the republic illumined by the Logos.

Not long after his disquisition on Understanding and Reason, Coleridge includes an aphorism and footnote on a "permanent Learned Class" (*AR [CC]* 295), which reveals that the virtual classroom of *Aids* is the training ground for the clerisy he will describe in *On the Constitution of the Church and State* (1829). This "Learned Order" will consist of "three Classes": original thinkers "employed in adding to the existing Sum of Power and Knowledge;" clergymen, educators, and middle-class professionals scattered through the kingdom "whose office it is to diffuse through the community at large" guiding moral and spiritual truths; and those who will instruct this second, professional class "in Schools, Halls, and Universities, *or through the medium of the Press*" (*AR[CC]* 295; emphasis mine). Here is the nascent vision of a reformed print network, a spiritual republic of letters irradiated by the Logos, which motivates Coleridge's method of address in the virtual school of reflection.

IV. THE PRODUCTIVE FICTION OF COLERIDGE'S ADDRESS TO THE READER

Coleridge's address to his reader aims to evaporate print and paper. Reading a text gives way to a surreal form of inward yet immediate conversation with a tutor amidst a classroom of seekers: "We *are* in the *silent* school of reflection" (*AR [CC]* 84; emphasis mine); "let me be allowed still to suppose the Reader present to me" (84); "To . . . my Pupil or Junior Fellow-student, I continue to address myself" (304). Yet the very title "Reader" confirms that Coleridge and his "Pupil" are not present to each other: should the

"Reader, who has consented to submit his mind to my temporary guidance . . . , *exist only in my imagination,* let the bread [i.e., these meditations] float on the waters! If it be the Bread of Life, it will not have been utterly cast away" (304; emphasis mine). This is a typically Coleridgean display of self-pity over predestined neglect by a society of the shallow, but here Coleridge also acknowledges the voluntary hallucination his rhetoric seeks in a reader, the confusion of print with presence, of reflective reading with shared reflection. Simultaneously, he makes a veiled prophecy of reception for an actual reader to fulfill, disguising within a scriptural allusion (Eccles. 11:1) the circulation of *Aids* through the print network ("let the bread float on the waters"), as well as a reader's conscious submission to the delusion—the identification of reading with communion—by which *Aids* will mediate "The Bread of Life" (Jesus, the Incarnate Logos; cf. John 6:35). For he immediately follows the caveat about his imagined reader by continuing the virtual seminar: "Let us pause a moment, and review the road we have passed over" (304).

Coleridge asks the initiated reader to sustain such "willing suspension of disbelief for the moment" (*BL [CC]* II:6) as a means of acquiring the reflective art that responds to intuitions of the Logos. As he explains, Descartes' conception in the *Geometry* (1637) of "Bodies as differing from equal portions of Space only by figure and mobility" enabled him to "submit the various phenomena of moving bodies to [the] geometrical construction" by which physics represents the forces of nature. Yet, Coleridge claims, when Descartes declared this *"Fiction of Science"* a *"truth of fact,"* concluding that the human body and all physical reality were simply matter governed by the mechanical laws of physics, he abolished "a World *created* and filled with productive forces by the Almighty Fiat" and left behind "a lifeless Machine whirled about by the dust of its own Grinding" (*AR [CC]* 400–401). This is the fiction of a purely mechanical universe refined in the eighteenth century and reinforced by print culture and utilitarian society in the nineteenth. Coleridge acknowledges that this fiction of science has come to seem common sense: he holds that the average English Christian believes his "Mind" is some immaterial abstraction, the mere negative "opposite of Bodies" out there in the real, solid, visible world (394). In *Aids,* Coleridge aims to show that this work-a-day assumption is indeed a fiction, and that the printed book bearing his words, and the reader holding that book, are sustained by dynamic forces ultimately flowing from the Logos.

Coleridge published *Aids* (1825) a few years after high-profile public controversy over vitalism, the supposed existence of a life force, had been aroused by his friend John Abernethy, who from 1814–19 had published his public lectures on the subject to the Royal College of Surgeons (R. Holmes, *Age of Wonder* 308–9, 317–18). At stake in the contentious public debate over Abernethy's vitalist ideas (themselves drawn from an anatomist praised by Coleridge, John Hunter), was the question of whether some positive and formative power—was it material or immaterial?—animated living things, and whether this force was the same as the human soul (317). Abernethy's view—that an invisible "physiological life force" was superadded to matter to give it life and that the intelligent human mind might in turn be superadded to this vital force (309)—was immediately attacked by his former protégé, William Lawrence. In his 1816 public lectures at the Royal College and in his 1819 *Natural History of Man*, Lawrence insisted on the materiality of the brain (331) and maintained that the physical development of the human body could be observed in an unbroken continuum "from an oyster to a man" (qtd. in R. Holmes, *Age of Wonder* 312). Soon influential literary journals such as the *Edinburgh Review* and *Quarterly Review* were closely following and publicizing the caustic debate between Abernethy and Lawrence.[8]

Coleridge extends the vitalism controversy in the conclusion of *Aids* when he praises "John Hunter" for dealing a "mortal blow" to the "dogmatism of the Corpuscular [atomistic] school" (*AR [CC]* 395). Hunter and chemists such as Hans Christian Oersted represent for Coleridge an "increasingly *dynamic* spirit of the physical Sciences" (395). Denise Gigante has traced this dynamic spirit through European Romantic life sciences, aesthetics, and poems that portray art and nature as organic forms developed by a living power from within, and that resist the vision in Enlightenment science of "the universe" as a "machine" built up from "already articulated parts" (9). The distinction between mechanical empiricism and vitalism is, for Coleridge, analogous to his distinction between "fancy," which combines "fixed and dead" parts in allegories without an animating spark, and the "*vital*" power of "imagination," which echoes the "eternal act of creation in the infinite I AM," generating symbols that unify parts into living wholes (*BL [CC]* 1:304). Coleridge's organicism and vitalism thereby resist rigid versions of what Charles Taylor calls "the buffered self, and the world it . . . built" (Taylor, *A Secular Age* 314). Partially enabled by Enlightenment science, this is a modern sense of selfhood as "buffered," protected and sharply distinguished, from an outer world disenchanted of its own meanings and intentions—good or malevolent non-human things

---

8. Marilyn Butler provides an incisive and entertaining account of the public controversy surrounding the Abernethy-Lawrence debate in her introduction to Mary Shelley's *Frankenstein* (ix–li).

and powers, such as spirits—to become the material on which the self exercises instrumental reason in pursuit of its goals (540). From this angle, Coleridge and other Romantic-era vitalists aspired to a partial re-enchantment of the world, "the threat—or sublime possibility, depending on perspective—of an intangible living power with its own agency and formative purpose" (Gigante 38–39).

Coleridge defends vitalism in part to reenchant the lifeless machine that he believes many contemporary readers have come to substitute for a world sustained by vital forces that exceed profit margins and utilitarian ends. As indicated by the well-known definition of imagination quoted above, Coleridge furthermore gives vitalism a strong theological spin, in defiance of the "paradigm change from a Christian cosmology to a world of self-shaping matter" that Gigante discerns in "Romantic life science" (29).[9] Denying a physiological life force, in *Aids* Coleridge claims that an "invisible Energy" (*AR [CC]* 398) is dynamically at work in the visible world, a principle by which "all things strive to ascend" into a greater state of individuation that is fully achieved in the self-conscious human soul (118). He identifies this energy with "productive forces" sustained in nature by "the Almighty" and recognized in the human mind as ideas of Reason (400). Coleridge anticipated this position in his manuscript "Theory of Life" (1816) and *The Friend* of 1818 (*Friend [CC]* I:563, I:497n.2), articulating it most fully in his 1820–23 draft for the *Opus Maximum,* where he constructed "a vitalist system of theology" (L. Wright, "The Divine Ideas" 57): "What then is the ground of this coincidence between . . . the laws of the sensible world and the ideas of the pure intellect? The only answer is that both have their ultimate ground, and are ultimately identified in . . . the Supreme Reason [Logos] that constitutes the objects which it contemplates and then by the powers thus constituted, viz. the divine Ideas [the "productive forces" in the above quote from *Aids*], gives being to the whole phenomenal universe" (*Op Max [CC]* 163–64).

By invoking vitalism in *Aids,* Coleridge suggests that some in the scientific community are sensing the insufficiency of eighteenth-century mechanical empiricism and are on the verge of intuiting the Logos. We indicate, Coleridge argues, a whole greater than "paper, ink, and differently combined straight and curved lines" when we call an "Edition of Homer" the "Iliad" (*AR [CC]* 397), and the same must be true of the eye with which we read the book, since it and the rest of the body can be materially reduced to fluctuating combinations of "Carbon and Nitrogen,

---

9. Although Coleridge is central to her argument at many stages, Gigante is curiously silent about the explicitly theological orientation of his vitalism.

Oxygen and Hydrogen, Sulphur, Phosphorus, and one or two Metals and Metallic Bases" (396). When we say human "Body," therefore, we confess that there must be a "distinct and individualizing Agency that by the given combinations [of matter] utters and bespeaks its Presence" (397). In a passage that dramatically reverses the nightmare of automatic writing in *Biographia Literaria,* Coleridge claims that reflecting on the very printed text of his volume leads to the same intuition of Reason that the new "*dynamic* spirit of the physical Sciences" (*AR [CC]* 395) is beginning to affirm:

> The characters, which I am now shaping on this paper, abide. Not only the forms remain the same, but the particles of the coloring stuff are fixed, and, for an indefinite period at least, remain the same. But the particles that constitute the *size,* the visibility of an organic structure are in perpetual flux. They are to the combining and constitutive Power as the pulses of air to the Voice of a Discourser; or of one who sings a roundelay. The same words may be repeated; but in each second of time the articulated air hath passed away, and each act of articulation appropriates and gives momentary form to a new and other portion . . . [S]uch is the flesh, which our *bodily* eyes transmit to us; which our *Palates* taste; which our Hands touch. (397–98)

Coleridge is not at this moment "shaping" characters "on this paper"—nor, as his analogy to a "Discourser" half tempts readers to imagine, is his "Voice" audible. Yet his text implies that the fiction of immediate address is truer to the world in which readers read than the mechanical fiction challenged by vitalism. If Coleridge's rhetoric—"The characters, which I am *now* shaping"—falsely identifies his pen's ink with the publisher's fixed print and then evaporates the solidity of the latter, this fiction approximates a world where in fact nothing is fixed, where particles are in "perpetual flux," held together by a "constitutive Power," an "invisible Energy," that renders the material blur into "the flesh, which our *bodily* eyes transmit to us; which our *Palates* taste; which our Hands touch." For Coleridge, this "invisible Energy" ultimately radiates from the Logos. Fittingly, his phrase alludes to the first epistle of St. John: "That which was from the beginning, which we have heard, which we have seen with our eyes, which we have looked upon, and our hands have handled, . . . the Word of life" (1 John 1:1). Wishfully drawing on dynamic science, Coleridge suggests that the medium of print culture, the printed text, can enable not only his fiction of a virtual classroom but also an intuition of the Word he desires readers to find within themselves.

V. THE CLERISY AND THE SPIRITUAL REPUBLIC OF LETTERS

Coleridge's rhetoric is aimed at reforming into a spiritual republic of letters the very print network through which he now solicits his intended audience of young educated men who hope to enter "the Ministry" or serve as "Instructors of Youth" (*AR [CC]* 6). The virtual classroom of *Aids* (1825) is a preparatory school and model of instruction for the ideal alliance of ministers and educators that Coleridge calls the "clerisy" a few years later in *On the Constitution of the Church and State* (1829). Through a system of national education, this learned coalition will inculcate in the wider populace the reflective awareness that *Aids* attempts to cultivate in the clerisy's future leaders. The long-term result, Coleridge implies, will be the transformation of the mass media into a medium through which British citizens would become aware of themselves as a community united by the intuitive moral and spiritual truths articulated in *Aids*.

As I note above, Coleridge included an aphorism and footnote in *Aids* pointing to the clerisy as the goal of his virtual school of reflection (*AR [CC]* 295). Yet a vision of the clerisy was taking shape in Coleridge's mind since at least the 1809 *Friend*.[10] By *On the Constitution of the Church and State,* he could offer a full exposition of the clerisy, arguing that his treasured idea was anticipated in the Church of England, the institution in which he hoped it would be realized. In principle, Coleridge believed, the clerisy could comprehend "the learned of all denominations," that is, from all the arts, sciences, and professions (*CS [CC]* 46). Its centers of intellectual conservation and discovery would be the ancient universities, whose fellows were then still ordained in the Anglican Church (L. Wright, *Coleridge and the Anglican Church* 196). The universities would send forth Anglican pastors and school teachers into every parish, charged with ensuring that each citizen experienced what Coleridge had championed in *Aids:* "the harmonious development of those qualities and faculties that characterize our *humanity*" (*CS [CC]* 43) and that "qualify" each person to be

---

10. Coleridge's first use of the *term clerisy,* as far as I know, is in his 1818 "Lectures on Principles of Judgement, Culture, and European Literature" for the London Philosophical Society. In the March 13 lecture, he says that the "clerisy," a body of reflective men of letters, gradually disappeared after the 1688 Revolution, so that "literature in general began to be addressed to the common miscellaneous public" (*Lects 1808–1819 [CC]* II:236). Yet the idea of a national learned class dedicated to moral reflection and right reason had been with Coleridge long before he fully expressed it in *Church and State.* Klancher argues that Coleridge was attempting to form a reading audience of learned professionals through the publication of the 1809 *Friend* (152). Coleridge approached *The Statesman's Manual* (1816) with similar ambitions.

"the free subject of a civilized realm" (*CS [CC]* 74). Coleridge clarifies that whereas "Christianity, or the Church of Christ" (55), is not national and looks to Christ as its head, the clergy of the Anglican Church are part of a national institution and properly swear loyalty to their king. In theory, such a "National" Church, or clerisy, need not even be Christian: "religion . . . is not the essential constitutive end of" the education they ought to provide for the nation (45). Yet by what Coleridge calls "a blessed accident, a providential boon" (55), Christianity is the creed of England's national church, and efforts to "separate" the clerisy's ministry from their civilizing influence, he says, would lead to "great and grievous . . . evils" (57).

Many a reader of Coleridge's explanation of the clerisy in *Church and State* has probably recalled Byron's quip about *Biographia Literaria* (1817): "I wish he would explain his explanation" ("Dedication" to *Don Juan* 2.16). Coleridge does not condescend to explain how, in nineteenth-century Britain, free academic inquiry, a broad civic and humanistic education, and Anglican devotion could be coordinated within one national system, especially at a time when every scheme for national education was withering under the heat of religious sectarian debate. Yet as Stephen Prickett suggested some time ago, Coleridge's idea of the clerisy is just that—an *idea,* a set of principles meant to inspire and guide reform, not a practical instruction manual ("Idea of the Clerisy" 273). Furthermore, this idea "exists under" necessary "tension": it resists tidy institutional and functional definitions, since "each function, the National and the Christian," is distinct from, and yet "supported by, the other" (269).

The heterogeneous nature of Coleridge's clerisy reflects his response to the process, diversely played out in modernizing societies, that sociologists have called "differentiation." Differentiation refers not to widespread decline and privatization of religious belief and practice (which did not happen in nineteenth-century Britain), but to emerging distinctions between religious institutions and other spheres of society, such as the market place, mass media, and professions (Casanova, "The Secular" 61). Although Coleridge believed that in principle the clerisy included "the learned of all denominations" (*CS [CC]* 46), he knew that profitable practical sciences and professions—such as "law, medicine, &c."—had long ago "detached themselves" from the Church and were now financially independent (50). He also recognized that this process of differentiation from the Church had extended to non-theological and non-practical dimensions of humanistic learning, so that these pursuits had no extensive national "institutional home" (Kaiser 70). Guided by his sense that the humanities are institutionally homeless, Coleridge slants his account of the clerisy in

Church and State to emphasize the Anglican Church's duty to establish a public humanistic education system rooted in "those fundamental truths, which are the common ground-work of our civil and our religious duties" (*CS [CC]* 48). He envisions a body of educators straddling theology and the humanities, the classroom and the sanctuary, and differently diffusing through both offices those "fundamental truths" he feels are essential to civil society.

More precisely, the elusive role Coleridge gives to the clerisy in *Church and State* is determined by his critical view of the mass media, which he felt was expanding to fill the vacuum created by the differentiation of modern society, and as a result had become the primary influence on national imagination. How exactly Coleridge believed the clerisy should relate to the media remains a hazy subject in scholarship. As Anne Frey observes, "Coleridge at times includes the press—because of its role in distributing knowledge—in the clerisy, but at other times he complains that the press has become too involved with partisan and mercantile interests" (Frey 31). Coleridge did waver in his views, but I believe that comments he made in the last two decades of his life point to a coherent position that *Church and State* helps clarify. He eventually confined the clerisy to the university scholars, clergy, and parish teachers of the Anglican establishment because he believed Britain required an independent ethical and humanistic body that could contest the influence of a commercialized and sectarian mass media. Rather than simply restraining the press, however, the clerisy was to effect its reformation. Journalists and editors trained and guided by the national clerisy would one day extend the clerisy's teaching into the mass media that was increasingly shaping how Britons imagined their membership and responsibility in the nation. British citizens would become aware of themselves as a spiritually and ethically united community through the very media that—in Coleridge's opinion—currently threatened to undermine their freedom.

Coleridge is not dealing with syllabi, so he does not clarify what the clerisy would teach. Since Coleridge promoted Bell's Anglican education system (*Friend [CC]* II:165), however, we can assume that he thought the clerisy should supplement subjects such as literature, history, and what early twentieth-century U.S. educators used to call "civics" with classroom instruction in theology and the Anglican catechism. The most *crucial* responsibility of the clerisy in offering this instruction would not be to train citizens in distinct disciplines and skills, but to accompany explanation of the "laws and rights" to which British citizens are "entitled" (*CS [CC]* 44) with the awakening of what Coleridge called, in language directly echoing *Aids,* "the potential divinity in every man" (*CS [CC]* 52)—each person's intuitive but latent knowledge of a "responsible will" and the "ultimate" ethical "ends" toward which it is to be directed (123). As explained above, Coleridge believed such intuitive knowledge derived from God's indwelling divine Reason, and that humanistic education and Christian devotion could diversely testify to it. These "ultimate ends" could not be *proven* by experience, but conviction of them was innate and often tacitly guided the organic growth of "customs" and "familiar sympathies" in one's national society (*Friend [CC]* II:83): "free agency," Coleridge asserted in *The Friend,* "is a *fact* of immediate consciousness" (I:509). Unless citizens could be brought to feel and trust such ingrained ethical principles, Coleridge believed, a commonwealth would have no moral guide.

C. S. Lewis, in *The Abolition of Man* (1943), a series of lectures about the need to reform British education, in many ways retains the vision of education that Coleridge hoped the clerisy would follow. Lewis contends that national education in the humanities should use classic literary and learned works drawn from many cultures, but especially Western, to cultivate in students from an early age the *right* virtuous feelings, convictions worth following whether or not they lead to practical gain: loyalty to family; respect for elders; treatment of people as ends rather than means; sacrificial devotion to the freedom of one's country; submission to legal authority. Perhaps even more confidently than Lewis, Coleridge himself believed, as he remarks in *Church and State,* that all branches of learning, especially "moral science," could bring students to contemplate "the supernatural in themselves" and from this to consider a "superhuman" power, so that humanistic study would naturally "lead to religion, and remain blended with it" in the thought and practice of British citizens (*CS [CC]* 44).

The clerisy should instill a shared ethical and religious frame of interpretation by which each person might become convinced of his or her moral responsibility within the national community. For Coleridge, the national community, or state, is not essentially a territory, governmental structure, or body of people, but an idea shared by its members: "The State," he wrote in his notebook, "is actual only in" this common "Idea. The Idea is the Reality of the State, yea, *is* the State" (qtd. Calleo 77). Starting from idealist convictions, then, Coleridge anticipates the view of national community that Benedict Anderson famously reaches as a historical materialist in his book *Imagined Communities* (1991): nations are not concrete entities but discursively constructed imagined communities existing in the minds of their members. Well before writing *Church and*

State, Coleridge had become convinced that the most potent influence on national imagination was the rapidly expanding mass media, which he felt was becoming the central interpretive authority in the vacuum created by the differentiation of modern society. Coleridge summed up his view of this process in a remark made in 1832 near the end of his life: "There have been three silent revolutions in England: 1. When the Professions fell off from the Church. 2. When Literature fell off from the Professions. 3. When the Press fell off from Literature" (*TT [CC]* I:285).¹¹ Here Coleridge describes his view of how differentiation impacted the clerisy: the practical and profitable professions "fell off" from the Church, thereby distancing themselves from guidance by reflective branches of learning unrelated to commerce ("Literature"), and such scholarship in turn lost influence on the primary modern medium of national discourse and information, the periodicals and newspapers of "the Press." If Henry Nelson Coleridge can be trusted, Coleridge made this remark only a few weeks after asserting that "The Clerisy of a Nation—its learned—" maintain its sole "points of rest" and "harmony" (*TT [CC]* II:164; April 10, 1832).

The expansion of the modern mass media as a medium of national imagination and self-understanding, then, was a vital stimulant to Coleridge's desire for "points of" interpretive "rest" and "harmony" provided throughout Britain by the clerisy. Here Coleridge again anticipates Benedict Anderson, who has argued that national imagination in Europe and the Americas was empowered by the expansion of newspapers beginning in the eighteenth century: reading the morning paper with the knowledge that it was being encountered at roughly the same time by thousands, and later millions, of other readers, encouraged people to imagine themselves within a vast web of individuals simultaneously pursuing varied occupations and aspirations within a common national storyline (24, 35). Similarly, in the 1809 *Friend,* Coleridge observed that expansion of the press disseminated and standardized national consciousness: "Newspapers, their Advertisements, [their reports of the] Speeches in Parliament, Law-courts, and Public Meetings, Reviews, Magazines, [and] Obituaries" have made possible a "diffusion of uniform opinions" and "Fashions in

---

11. As Coleridge grew older, he increasingly refuted "getting and spending," believing that commercial and utilitarian interests were overtaking British society: he would, in 1827, for instance, lament "the present dedication of all ranks from the cradle to the Coffin to the fiend Mammon . . . It has taken away the Life of England, and put a bustling drudging Death in it's [*sic*] place" (*CN* V:5697). This is what Coleridge saw as the inevitable consequence of the rise in commercialism after the 1688 Revolution, the disappearance of a learned class (the clerisy), and literature in general being addressed to "the common miscellaneous public" (*Lects 1808–1819 [CC]* II:236).

things external and internal" so as "to render evanescent, the distinctions between the enlightened Inhabitants of the great city, and the scattered Hamlet" (II:28). While Anderson's claim that print capitalism was foundational to the rise of popular national consciousness has been discredited (Van Young 41, 59; Thompson 63), his and Coleridge's view that the mass media has decisively shaped national imagination, especially among the middle classes and elite, remains convincing.

For all Coleridge's complaints against newspapers and periodicals, he himself was a lifelong contributor to them, and he not only granted their vital role in spreading the idea of a British national community but also saw them as necessary to the freedom and progression of modern nations. In the 1809 *Friend,* he argued that the strength and wisdom of English law owed more to "the good sense and generous dispositions diffused by the Press . . . than to any other single cause" (II:60). Even the humblest British citizen, Coleridge remarked in the same publication, is becoming so used to "the stirrings of Mind" excited by the printed page that he or she can never again "be treated or governed as a Child" (II:86). The only "Upholder and Judge" of national safety and progress must now be "Intellect and Thought," and they must be freely circulated (II:86).

Yet Coleridge worried that the national community imagined through early nineteenth-century British print culture was becoming shallow and factious. Thinking about the widespread influence of the press on national consciousness in the 1809 *Friend,* Coleridge remarks: "I have fully persuaded my own mind, that formerly MEN WERE WORSE THAN THEIR PRINCIPLES, but that at present THE PRINCIPLES ARE WORSE THAN THE MEN" (II:28). As he argued in *Church and State,* Coleridge felt that the mass media was fueling pressure groups and financial interests that were increasingly setting the agenda of government (*CS [CC]* 67–68), thereby overturning the balance of permanence and progression he considered necessary to good government and civil life in favor of finance and commerce (Calleo 111). In his own contributions to periodicals and papers, Coleridge portrayed these mass media in a state of decline: he asserted that most journalists were out to flatter the "half-instructed many" (*Friend [CC]* II:87), and consequently they adopted styles he criticized in the 1811 *Courier* (Sept. 21) as feeding a general "antipathy" to "close thinking" through "skipping, unconnected, short-winded, asthmatic sentences," even as they trained readers to disparage difficult writings as "'*heavy stuff, metaphysical jargon,*' &c" (*EOT* II:306). As noted earlier in this chapter, Coleridge feared that print culture was encouraging Britons to prioritize calculating, self-interested prudence over trust in ideas and principles of Reason.

For Coleridge, then, "The Press is indifferently the passive Instrument of Evil and of Good" (*Friend [CC]* II:60). If journalists and reviewers continued to feed readers' complacent self-interest and indifference to the fundamental principles necessary to moral and civic life, Coleridge warned with increasing urgency after 1810, Britain's expanding print culture would pave the way for exploitation. Under the same freedom of press that made it impossible for despots to ignore public opinion (*EOT [CC]* I:330), a national society was even now threatening to arise in which non-negotiable convictions, such as the immorality of treating people as things or mere units of production, would become negotiable in the name of practical expediency and the supposed general good of "society" in the abstract (*Friend [CC]* II:326). For example, Coleridge argues in *Church and State*, utilitarian public policy is now regularly substituting "the wealth of the nation (*i.e.* of the wealthy individuals thereof, and the magnitude of the Revenue) for the well-being of the people" (*CS [CC]* 68). "Even the genuine maxims of expedience," Coleridge remarked in the 1809 *Friend*, are unlikely "to be perceived or acted upon by those who have been habituated to admit nothing higher than Expedience" (II:85).

The only hope for a free press to sustain a free people, Coleridge came to believe, was national education, and he implies how he envisioned the clerisy accomplishing this mission in a letter to Rev. James Gillman written in the margins of an 1830 edition of *Church and State* (Table 1, below). In the letter, Coleridge portrays his idea of the state using his favorite logical scheme, the Pentad, placing "The Press," which he is careful to identify as "the ideal Press," at the center of a polarity: the ideal press is the "Mesothesis," the indifferent or medial point, between the "State"—understood as the government—and "the Church" (*CS [CC]* 233). Coleridge's point is that the British nation, composed simultaneously of the state and the church, could achieve the synthesis of these identities through an ideal press, acting out on a social scale what the "Crown," head of church and state, does in one person. This Pentad for the nation, with the press at the center, can be put into dialogue with the "Pentad of Operative Christianity" with which Coleridge intended to preface his essay on biblical hermeneutics, *Confessions of an Inquiring Spirit* (Table 2, below).

This second Pentad illustrates the dialectical process by which God, in Coleridge's view, reveals truth to the Christian community. "The Holy Spirit" occupies the same mediating position as "the Press" does in the Pentad for the Nation. In Coleridge's theology, God's "Holy Spirit" works through the divine Reason indwelling each believer to coordinate his or her subjective experiences with the objective history and scriptural revela-

TABLE 1. PENTAD FOR THE STATE*

	a. State (Prothesis)	
b. State (Thesis)	c. the Press (Mesothesis)	d. the Church (Antithesis)
	e. the Crown (Synthesis)	

The State (i.e., the *Nation*—n.b. NOT the People) is the Prothesis: *including* <both> the *State* in its *thetic* sense, *and* the Church, the antithesis of the latter; while the Crown, or ideal King, is the *Synthesis* of the *b.* and *d.* = State and Church; and the ideal Press the mesothesis.

*Adapted from Coleridge's letter to the Rev. James Gillman, written in the margins of *On the Constitution of the Church and State* (1830, 2nd ed.) (*CS [CC]* 233).

TABLE 2. THE PENTAD OF OPERATIVE CHRISTIANITY†

	PROTHESIS Christ, The Word	
THESIS	*MESOTHESIS* Or "The Indifference"	*ANTITHESIS*
The Scriptures	The Holy Spirit	The Church
	SYNTHESIS The Preacher	

†Adapted from *Confessions of an Inquiring Spirit*, ed. Henry Nelson Coleridge (1840, 1st ed.). x.

tion of Christianity, and to unite him or her in a confessing community: "the Spirit is the source of community" in the Trinity and in Christian life (Barbeau 127). The same Pentad portrays "the Preacher," the local member of "the clerisy," as the one who, following the Holy Spirit also at work in his parishioners, leads them in right interpretation of the Bible and creeds (L. Wright, *Coleridge and the Anglican Church* 219).

Coleridge's two Pentads—of the nation, with the press at the center, and of Christianity, with the Holy Spirit at the center—suggest what he thought would happen if the clerisy were realized through the Anglican Church, and Britons were brought up in a system of education that awakened them to the ethical and spiritual truths inwardly affirmed by God's Spirit and outwardly elaborated in humanistic study and congregational worship. Journalists and editors trained under the clerisy would eventually transform Britain's burgeoning print network into a spiritually illuminated republic of letters. Although operating outside the institutional and financially independent Anglican clerisy, these members of the "ideal Press" would extend the influence of the official clerisy through the nation's most popular and wide-reaching channels of information.

These reformed members of the press would help achieve within modern, differentiated British society the coordinated role Coleridge envisioned the clerisy serving in pre-modern England, when the Church, professions, and literature were not evolved into distinction. The popular press would become almost a secular—as in extra-ecclesiastical—national scripture, a medium through which members of the national community would be kept attuned to the guidance of the Spirit and the "ultimate ends" of their civic responsibility, all mediated through commentary on the nation's economic, political, and social life. As Coleridge dreamed in *The Statesman's Manual:* "it would be a wise method of sympathizing with the tone and spirit of the Times, if we elevated even our daily newspapers and political journals into COMMENTS ON THE BIBLE" (*LS [CC]* 35). Through such cooperation of the clerisy and press, or rather, through a press trained into civic responsibility by the clerisy, throughout Britain would spread "the spirit which . . . can blend and harmonize the most discordant Elements—. . . the spirit of a rational Freedom diffused and become national, in the consequent influence and controul of public opinion" (*Friend [CC]* II:66). Freedom of thought and press would combine with cultivation of each person's ability to reflect on first principles, grounding society's ongoing development in the reconciliation of "PERMANENCE and . . . PROGRESSION" (*C&S [CC]* 24).

This, I believe, is the mission for the clerisy implied in Coleridge's published prose including and following *The Friend* (especially *Aids*), his notebook entries and marginalia, and his comments in *Table Talk*. Philip Connell has helped dispel the notion that Coleridge's clerisy was imagined in simple antagonism to "THE COMMERCIAL SPIRIT," the world of finance and commerce (*LS [CC]* 168; Connell 127). We might further recover the complexity of Coleridge's clerisy by questioning the traditional impression that he dreamed of this intellectual class simply because he wished to ward off the evils of the mass media and mass-market literature. Coleridge's clerisy has, with justice, been seen as motivating an elitist and reactionary strand of nineteenth-century social criticism, exemplified in the work of Matthew Arnold (who is discussed in chapter 3), which lamented the poverty of bourgeois values and the vacuity of popular culture (Connell

282–83). At various points in this chapter, I have foregrounded the class and gender bias of the social idealism that informs Coleridge's clerisy. Yet I have argued that Coleridge's idea of the clerisy was, for all its ideological limitations, also a creative effort to envision a dynamic interaction between religion, civic values, and education in a differentiated society, and by this to ensure the freedom and progress of the people alongside the expansion of the mass media—in particular by helping the nation achieve the ethical and spiritual community that this media could uniquely facilitate.

VI. GRADUATES FROM COLERIDGE'S VIRTUAL CLASSROOM—AND OUR CLASSROOMS?

The burden of this chapter is that Coleridge's rhetoric in *Aids* constructs a virtual classroom meant to be the training ground for the clerisy, the body of educators and ministers that he imagined might one day establish literal classrooms that would extend to the rest of the population the reflective awareness cultivated in *Aids*. This would eventually lead to the formation of a divinely illuminated republic of letters, especially in the case of the mass media, which, in the hands of journalists and editors trained by the clerisy, would become a widely-circulating platform for imagining a popular version of the virtual community invoked in *Aids:* through such a reformed media, British citizens could envision themselves in a spiritually and ethically united national community. Early responses to Coleridge's *Aids* by young religious liberals in the 1820s and 1830s indicate that they perceived the connection between its intimate school of reflection and this wider clerical mission.

Coleridge opened *Aids* with an apostrophe to his "Fellow-Christian!," asking the reader to judge "for or against" the book by answering a question: "Has it led you to reflect? . . . If your conscience dictates an affirmative answer . . . , declare this too aloud, and endeavour to extend my utility" (3). In 1832, an anonymous reviewer of *Aids* for *Fraser's Magazine* (John A. Heraud) answered Coleridge's request, adding his praise to that of other young intellectuals in England and New England[12]:

---

12. In addition to lengthy treatments of the impact of *Aids* on Victorian-era intellectuals by Charles Sanders, Reardon, and Tod E. Jones, see Beer's pithy accounts in his introduction to *Aids* for the *Collected Works* and in his *Romantic Influences* (147–74).

> Yes, old man! with right gladness of heart will we make this endeavour
> ... O how much is owing to thee by the greatest and brightest of minds
> which now shine down upon the republic of letters—kings and priests
> over a people of kings and priests, or a people who should consist of such.
> (*Critical Heritage [1970]* 586)

In his apostrophic reply and his spiritually renewed commitment to "the republic of letters," Heraud indicates that he has caught the animating spirit of *Aids,* Coleridge's vision of a transformed print culture supported by reflection on "'*the* man *in* the man,'" "our proper humanity" to which we can "return" by divine "aid" (*Critical Heritage [1970]* 593). Heraud anticipates what Christopher Kent has identified as the expansion of a "higher journalism" in Victorian "reviews, the superior magazines, and the quality newspapers . . . between 1850 and 1875" ("Higher Journalism" 181). Kent suggests that this learned, literary journalism, much of it practiced by "fellows or ex-fellows from Oxford or Cambridge," constituted an extension of "the Coleridgean idea of the clerisy" (189). In Kent's view, mid-century Oxbridge educated barristers and fellows who practiced high-level journalism as an avocation, rather than as a trade upon which their livings fully depended, partially realized Coleridge's advice in *Biographia Literaria* that authors should remain respected members of society by joining established professions, even as, on the side, they contributed their genius and guidance to the republic of letters (182).[13] Yet Coleridge's mature mission for the clerisy and media was aimed not merely at promoting high discourse through respectable publications; it included transforming the nation's mass media into a medium of unified national imagination, and of ethical and spiritual reflection on national affairs.

Among the Victorian high journalists Kent includes the Anglican theologian, educator, and social reformer Frederick Denison Maurice, to whom the next chapter of this study is dedicated (190, 192). I believe Maurice was one of several young religious liberals in the early nineteenth century to catch the wider implications of Coleridge's *Aids*. As the recognized leader of the Cambridge "Apostles" in the late 1820s, Maurice advocated ideas he found in *Aids* in ways that transformed this close-knit coterie of undergraduates into the audience of future ministers, educators, and authors that Coleridge imagined addressing in his print-mediated school of reflection. Soon after, Maurice continued evangelizing for Coleridge as editor of

---

13. Curiously, Kent focuses on Coleridge's suggestive advice to young authors in *Biographia,* and leaves unmentioned Coleridge's extended address to young men in *Aids* and explicit treatment of the clerisy in *Church and State.*

The Athenaeum (1827–28), teaming up with Sterling to promote Coleridge's views and defend the Sage from hostile reviewers (C. Sanders 187–89). He became determined to bring Coleridge's method of reflection into his work as a member of the nation's clerisy, one of "those who are called to the work of teaching" others to recognize through self-reflection and reading "that which is fixed and eternal, which belongs to man as man" (*Kingdom of Christ* I:7). If properly instructed in this art, Maurice came to believe, persons in Britain's working, middle, and upper classes would recognize their common membership in the Logos as part of "a Universal Society for man as man" (*Kingdom* I:11). Through popular journalism, lectures, sermons, and the creation of the Working Men's College in 1854, Maurice promoted practices of reading that he believed would transform even the most apparently degraded and socially disconnected forms of print communication—such as newspaper advertisements—into media through which Britons of different classes and sects could imagine themselves in a national Christian society.

Coleridge never suggested extending the clerisy's attention to such a wide range of mass media, and he would have probably had qualms about Maurice's willingness for Anglicans to share the labor of popular education with unbelievers, and to learn from working people as well as teach them. Yet Coleridge's vision of the clerisy, in addition to revealing conservative and coercive tendencies in his thought, is also adaptive and aimed at developing a free and just national community by establishing a learned body capable of reforming the influence of the mass media. Maurice, for all his own paternalism toward the working classes, helps us recognize this fact through his more participatory, reform-minded approach to forms of education that could enable social and moral consensus in a mass-mediated society.

Coleridge's *Aids*, then, provided Maurice, Heraud, Sterling, and other young intellectuals who early came under its spell not only with a means of resisting "infidelity" but also with a method of adapting to the rapidly emerging world of mass print. Reflectively used, *Aids* encouraged them to believe, the print network could facilitate a national spiritual community illumined by the Logos. The otherwise untenable eighteenth-century hope in diffusion of literature as a means to enlightened public agreement could be salvaged on radically new—and, one might say, radically old and Platonic—terms.

By the end of the nineteenth century, *Biographia Literaria* took the place of *Aids to Reflection* as the most influential prose work by Coleridge, and that legacy remains powerful, making *Aids* seem relevant only to the few who are sympathetic to Coleridge's brand of Christian Neo-Platonism, or who have wearied themselves mapping the maze of his religious philosophy. There is, however, a surprising parallel between the needs *Aids* addressed in its first, middle-class, educated readers and those addressed in a meeting place uploaded onto *Second Life,* a virtual online world: an Anglican cathedral in which congregants scattered across the globe attend services and hold interactive Bible studies through their digital avatars. Amid a bewildering and accelerating proliferation of texts, the print age that has after many permutations blended into our information saturated digital age, Coleridge's *Aids* offered its devoted readers not only hope in a divinely sustained national community but also a method for converting their virtual world of text, the print network, into a space for the new spiritual republic.

Coleridge's and Maurice's dreams of national spiritual community are now unconvincing, and it would be easy to assume their sense of clerical calling is likewise simply outdated. Yet with the loose phrase "critical thinking," circulating through the websites of humanities departments and vigorously defended by public intellectuals such as Martha Nussbaum, humanities scholars retain a shadowy sense of clerical mission: the feeling that they ought to instill habits of reflection and scrutiny that extend beyond a single profession or practical application, and that are essential to individual and public life in a free society.[14] Perhaps we could consider this vague sense of vocation more carefully by consciontiously asking ourselves and our students how the texts we teach offer wisdom for present life.

At the conclusion of a chapter on Coleridge, it is fitting to ask how this sense of mission could shape the ways we engage Romantic-era texts with our students. In a class on Romantic poetry, we might pause to wonder why Blake, living under the 1795 Gagging Acts and network of Home Spies, concluded in 1798 that "Nothing can be more contemptible than to suppose Public RECORDS to be True" (*Blake's Poetry and Designs* 485), and then appreciate how Blake gave such convictions imaginative force when depicting Urizen's suppression of eternity's vital dissent under iron codes of law. Being careful to avoid undue influence, we—especially those of us in the United States—might take the less familiar step of asking students whether we can learn from Blake when watching and reading today's mainline news. We might suggest interested students "google" the

---

14. Martha Nussbaum, in *Not for Profit* (2010), frequently identifies "critical thinking" as the primary contribution of the humanities, arguing that this capacity is essential to the preservation of democracy and is in danger of utter neglect by current models of education that prioritize economic profit (20–26, 41–54, 88–94).

Habbush memo, Ayad Allawi, and "Agent Curveball," and later ask those who do how responsibly the consolidated U.S. media has reported on the manufactured justification of a war that has, according to major surveys, cost over one million Iraqi lives.[15] In a mass-mediated world often perilously lacking in spaces for the "critical thinking" some of us still profess to teach, we would do well to apply Coleridge's belief that humanistic instruction should cultivate civic responsibility—in part by allowing Romantic-era texts to encourage students' critical analysis of the ways public opinion and state actions are represented in the mass media.[16]

---

15. In 2007, a survey conducted by Opinion Research Business, a leading independent polling group in Britain, concluded that between 946,258 and 1.12 million Iraqis had died as a result of the war (L. Baker, "Iraqi Conflict Has Killed a Million Iraqis: Survey," *Reuters* [Jan. 30, 2008]).

16. Talal Asad argues that corporate mainline media contradict widespread belief that liberal democracies are based on "direct-access" participation. "*The mass media,* increasingly owned by conglomerates and often cooperating with the state, mediate the political reactions of the public and its sense of guarantee and threat . . . The media are not simply the means through which individuals simultaneously imagine their national community; they *mediate* that imagination, construct the sensibilities that underpin it" (*Formations* 4–5). Issued through a consolidated mass media, "coverage" of public debate, elections, state actions, and global affairs never just "informs" or "reflects" public opinion; it also manufactures images of how the public has reacted and, in effect, helps set the terms on which it can react.

CHAPTER 2

F. D. MAURICE'S UNIVERSAL SOCIETY

National Spiritual Community in a Sectarian Print Culture

In 1848, just over a week before the February Revolution drove Louis Phillipe from his throne, Frederick Denison Maurice (1805–72), the English clergyman and educator, called on worshippers at Lincoln's Inn Chapel in London to redeem Britain's own threatened national unity. "How," he asked, "can we look round upon the people whom we habitually feel to be separated from us by almost impassible barriers" of class and "faction," and "then teach ourselves to think that it in the very highest exercise of our lives these are associated with us; that when we pray, we are praying for them and with them . . . ?" (*Prayer-Book and Lord's Prayer* 284). In encouraging his Victorian audience, composed largely of middle-class professionals, to "teach" themselves "to think" that they are united in social life and prayer with other Britons across class and sect, Maurice locates Britain less in a physical space than in an actively imagined national community that rests in the back of the mind, even "when we pray."

Maurice published this sermon in May, one month after many in the middle and upper classes had been unnerved by the April 10 gathering of Chartists on Kennington Common. In the "Advertisement" to the volume, he hopes that the words he first offered to his congregation can, through the medium of print, still answer "the thoughts which are most likely to be occupying us at this time" (*Prayer-Book and Lord's Prayer* 282). Maurice invites his readers to see themselves in a nation—"us"—united by anxious "thoughts" about its unity and future in the wake of the Chartist gathering, extending to them through print the request he first made of his congregation: to consider themselves part of the "Our" supposedly cutting across boundaries of class, faction, and individual location that every recitation of the "Our Father" claims for the nation (*Prayer-Book and Lord's Prayer* 285). Between this idealized vision of Christian Britain and the minds of its members, Maurice early came to believe, there were "almost impassible barriers" of class and sectarianism, which he spent his career as a journalist, preacher, and educator laboring to break down (*Prayer-Book and Lord's Prayer* 284). Although Maurice was convinced that Britain's national identity was providentially ordained, in promoting his vision of its spiritual unity he confronted how much its realization had to rely on educated acts of imagination, on cultivated mental images of the collective in which one's daily and social life took place. Lectures, sermons, periodical essays, and serialized stories that Maurice wrote across his career grudgingly but consistently point to Britain's continuously expanding print culture as a crucial stimulant and medium for imagining the nation. He came to see the very print media he criticized for dividing Britons as the means by which the British public might at last awaken to its spiritual unity. Only then, Maurice argued, would Britain be able to redress the sectarianism, ruthless competition, and transformation of persons into things that he believed attended the expansion of industrialism and print capitalism.

When analyzed from this perspective, Maurice's work as a theologian, journalist, and educator acquires fresh significance. Normally studied for his contributions to theology, social reform, and adult education, Maurice also unexpectedly anticipates and revises Benedict Anderson's influential claims in *Imagined Communities* (1991) about the relationship between national consciousness and media: (1) a nation is not an empirical entity, but a discursively constructed community imagined as limited to a finite territory and composed of members who see themselves progressing simultaneously through history; (2) national communities should be studied in terms of the media that make them imaginable.[1] Arguably print-based media were most decisive for circulating and debating images of national community in nineteenth-century Britain. Certainly Maurice, as so many others in his day, felt this was the case. Maurice is also one of many nineteenth-century authors who fail to support the opposition between national consciousness and religious forms of imagined community that

---

1. In the introduction to this book, I discuss the historical and theoretical limitations, but abiding explanatory power, of Anderson's thesis about the connection between national consciousness and print capitalism.

Benedict Anderson has implied in his account of nationalism, and which is still occasionally taken for granted in academic discussions. Maurice's career suggests that efforts by Victorian intellectuals and educators to represent Britain were in fact often inseparable from strained attempts to envision a form of Christian communion that could bind together classes and sects at the center of the empire. Maurice furthermore indicates how closely wedded nineteenth-century British accounts of the nation's spiritual unity could be to analysis of its print culture.

I. COLERIDGEAN APPRENTICESHIP: THE KINGDOM OF CHRIST IN BRITAIN

Maurice critically appropriated assumptions basic to his view of national spiritual community from his reading of Coleridge. For Coleridge, individuals in a nation can achieve a just life together only if they share certainty about guiding moral laws—such as the "sacred distinction between Things and Persons" (*AR [CC]* 140), the existence of a morally responsible but corrupted "Will" (140), and the need of a personal divine agent "present to all and in all" to assist this will in conforming to morality (77). The source of intuitive moral and rational certainty, Coleridge maintains in *Aids to Reflection* (1825), is not the sense-abstracting power that John Locke called "reason" and Coleridge calls "understanding," but the divine Reason (Christ the Logos) reflected at the deepest level of each person and discerned through self-reflection (*AR [CC]* 218). As I argued in the previous chapter, Coleridge designed *Aids to Reflection* as a virtual classroom of reflection for young men who might one day help establish a learned class, a clerisy, capable of transforming Britain's print network into a divinely illumined republic of letters.

Maurice was among the earliest graduates from Coleridge's school of reflection in *Aids,* and his background prepared him to take to heart Coleridge's emphasis on an inner witness to spiritual and moral truth that surpassed, and yet was reflected in, the limited concepts and systems created by human understanding. As Vidler observes, Maurice's family provided him with "a closer and larger acquaintance with the [religious] sects and parties of his time than almost anyone else can have had" (82). Sustained religious tensions in his family—between a liberal Unitarian father and a mother and sisters pledged to Baptist and Evangelical forms of Calvinism—were so severe that members sometimes resorted to writing letters to each other rather than speaking (Brose 12–13). As Maurice later wrote to his son, this experience made him long for "an agreement" between different persuasions "without destroying diversities" (qtd. Allen 65). While the family controversy was reaching its height in the early 1820s, Maurice was reading Coleridge (Allen 68), and his later comments indicate that he seized on Coleridge's distinction of universal reason from individual understanding: this assured him of a fundamental unity resting beneath the battle lines of sectarians who grasped only portions of the whole truth (*Kingdom of Christ* I:7–8).

As the recognized leader of the Cambridge Apostles in the late 1820s, Maurice "defended Coleridge's metaphysics . . . against the Utilitarian teaching" then "prevalent" among the "cleverer" students (*Life* I:176), transforming this society of undergraduates into the audience of future ministers, educators, and authors that Coleridge had sought in *Aids* (Allen 58, 79–80). Maurice continued promulgating Coleridgean views as editor of *The Athenaeum* (1827–28) (Allen 77–78). In 1842, Maurice explained his debt to Coleridge's *Aids*:

> [*Aids*] has led me . . . to the practical conclusion, that those who are called to the work of teaching must cultivate and exercise their understandings, in order that they may discriminate between that which is factitious and accidental, or belongs to our artificial habits of thought, and that which is fixed and eternal, which belongs to man as man, and which God will open the eyes of every humble man to perceive. (*Kingdom* I:7)

In 1833, after converting from Unitarianism to Anglicanism and resolving to seek ordination in late 1828–29 (Brose 28–35), Maurice wrote "the truth is that every man is in Christ; the condemnation of every man is, that he will not own the truth . . . Separate from Christ, I am separate from every one of my brethren" (*Life* I:155). He saw himself as a member of the nation's clerisy, one of "those who are called to the work of teaching" others to recognize through self-reflection "that which is fixed and eternal, which belongs to man" as a member of Christ.

By 1836, when writing his most important work on the place of Christianity in national life, *The Kingdom of Christ* (1838; 2nd revised ed. 1842), Maurice had come to believe that persons in the working, middle, and upper classes could be led to recognize their membership in what he called the Kingdom of Christ, "a Universal Society for man as man" (*Kingdom* I:11). Imperfectly witnessed to by the universal Christian Church—most faithfully (it so happened) in the sacraments, creeds, and institutions of the Anglican Church—this universal society was always intended for humanity by God, manifested in the incarnation of Christ its King, and meant to be realized distinctively within the life of each nation (Vidler 72, 162–65). It rested upon the immanent presence of Christ, the Logos, in and to all persons, and its necessity was felt and demonstrated in every system of thought and development in human history (Morris 67–71). For Maurice, the nation-state was not an arbitrary human construction, but a providentially developed form of society in which people were to practice the self-sacrificial service and community that was at the center of God's life and that had been revealed most fully in Christ's incarnation (Neville 71–72).

Since the Reformation, Maurice argued in *The Kingdom of Christ,* there had been a struggle in Christendom between "Protestantism," the protection of national self-determination from domination by a transnational Church, and "Catholicism," the resistance to efforts by states to divide their subjects from a universal spiritual society in Christ (Morris 89). In the modern era, Maurice hoped, God would reconcile the two tendencies, and because of the position providentially given it, the Church of England stood the best chance of realizing within Britain, and demonstrating to other nations, the desired balance between universal Christian society and its distinct national expressions. Furthermore, the Church of England's Articles and sacraments testified, against warring religious parties within and without its pale, to comprehensive principles of membership in Christ's universal society, which transcended rigid systems of doctrine aimed at excluding others (89–92). Adapting Coleridge's view that the light of Christ was within every man but imperfectly reflected in human history and the limited systems created by human understanding, Maurice arrived at his own theology of national identity (Morris 41–43).

Maurice's theology of nationhood can be understood as an idiosyncratic response to pressures felt by many Britons, especially English Anglicans. Linda Colley has forcefully argued that the popular British identity forged between the early eighteenth and nineteenth centuries depended on the image of a Protestant nation blessed by God to defend liberty against continental antagonists, especially the French (18)—a national "Other" at first imagined as idolatrous and Catholic, and, after 1793, as atheistic and immoral (McLeod, "Protestantism" 46). The Act of Union with Catholic Ireland (1800), the overthrow of the continental dragon at Waterloo (1815), and Catholic emancipation (1829) threatened this sense of Britishness (Colley 322–24). Massive popular and elite pressure to end slavery in 1833, following on the heels of the slight expansion of the electorate in 1832, demonstrated the widely-felt need to preserve Britain's self-image as the world's defender of true religion and freedom, even if the net impact of such proclamations of holy liberty was conservative, giving ideological fuel to imperial expansion, and allowing elites to disregard efforts for reform at home by redirecting attention to liberation abroad. As Colley observes, "Great Britain was still Israel, and its crusade against slavery was just one more vital proof and guarantee of its supremacy among the nations. British gun-boats sailed under God's protection because they carried out God's work" (360). Despite the bitter domestic unrest of the "hungry forties," momentum was given to a shift from the notion of England as a Protestant elect providentially delivered from Catholic oppression to narratives about imperial Britain's unique appointment to bear spiritual and civilizing light around the world (Wellings 165). Maurice participates in this Victorian reconstruction of national identity when he asserts the unique position offered to the Church of England to assist its "neighbours . . . in realizing the blessings of their own" positions within the universal society of Christ (*Kingdom* II:329).

Maurice could sound quite imperialistic when articulating this mission for "Englishmen," whose tasks included "taming the savages of the antipodes"; but when he insisted that this missionary imperialism should establish unity between "distinct" nations that differently expressed the "universal Church," he effectively made the purpose of the British Empire its own dissolution (*Kingdom* II:329). Maurice was being consistent with the principles announced in *The Kingdom of Christ* when thirty years later he urged Cambridge undergraduates to combat "the lust of imperialism," asking them to hope "that we have been permitted" by God "to educate nations which are to have a great future of their own," and to resist "all miserable ambition for the spread of our own speech or our power" that would frustrate this "high calling" (*Social Morality* 176–77). Paternalistic to be sure, Maurice's theological sense of British nationality differed sharply from familiar Victorian assumptions that Britain's destiny would be fulfilled through colonization and expanding markets (Wellings 167). It also reflected Maurice's "deep unease about the" actual "absence of social" and spiritual "cohesion" at the center of the empire, and his profound need to believe that Britons would discover their unity "in the Christian Church" (Morris 99).

Maurice fully developed these views by 1836, when he began *The Kingdom of Christ*, but he was approaching them while working as a journalist and editor in London in 1827–28, and he had formed them fairly firmly by 1832 (Morris 53). Even when writing from a more politically radical and theologically undefined perspective as a young journalist, Maurice cultivated his own Coleridgean viewpoints, defending the inherent identity of nations and the need to reform society by "look[ing] within for the higher principles of" moral and spiritual "existence" ("Scott" 218). Yet during these formative years in London, Maurice confronted the ways in which periodical journalists and other authors were building conflicting imagined communities for British readers—print-mediated communities that required the conceptual displacement of others.

II. GREAT RESPIRATORS: PERIODICALS AND EXCLUSIVE PRINT-MEDIATED COMMUNITIES

Throughout his career, Maurice was anxious about the tendency of newspapers and periodicals to rely on prejudices about other groups to instill readers with a sense of shared identity. As he remarked in a public lecture on newspapers given in 1852, "a newspaper which speaks to us the notions and phrases of one school or party is a Respirator. We get our own breath returned to us again" (*Friendship of Books* 89). Even if we aim for fair-mindedness and dip into journals aimed at opposing reading audiences, the "sharp sayings and well-seasoned jokes" such publications use to mock our own views will "send us forth spiteful," "quite certain" that our opponents are "wrong," and "less willing to admit than we were before that there may be wrong in us" (89–90).

As a young journalist working out these convictions in the late 1820s, Maurice became sensitive to the ways that each major sect and political group in the early nineteenth century was gaining its specialty newspapers, periodicals, advertising venues, and publishers, continuing the formation of distinct reading audiences that John Klancher has so influentially analyzed in the Romantic period (*The Making of English Reading Audiences* 1987). Several scholars have argued that nineteenth-century readers began to imagine themselves in a vast national community of individuals leading distinct lives as they read the news at relatively the same time, and that novelists directly encouraged this form of imagined community (Colley 220, 364–65; Anderson 24–36). As Maurice saw the situation in the 1820s, however, the imagined national community of British readers was being conceptually divided into mutually exclusive audiences, or publics, by the periodical organs of parties. As Josef Altholz has remarked, it "became the rule" in nineteenth-century Britain "that every movement, every school of thought, every sect, and every party had to have at least one periodical organ of expression" (1).

In 1828, Maurice served as editor and journalist for a new literary magazine, *The Athenaeum*, and in a series of "Sketches on Contemporary Authors" he criticized sectarianism in print culture, identifying it as "one of the greatest afflictions of humanity" ("Southey" 66). Maurice's first literary sketch reviews the career of Francis Jeffrey, editor of the *Edinburgh Review*, the first of the great quarterlies that appeared at the beginning of the nineteenth century offering to help professionals and upper-class readers learn how to judge the otherwise "anarchic state" of the crowded literary market (Keen, "Politics" 109). Maurice acknowledges Jeffrey's success in influencing the "literary feeling and opinion" of his intended audience—a triumph that soon provoked others to rush into the field and create the familiar distinctions between Whig readers of the *Edinburgh Review*, Tory readers of the *Quarterly Review*, and reform-minded readers of the *Westminster Review* ("Jeffrey" 49). Seeking to distinguish the tolerant mindset cultivated by his own fledgling *Athenaeum* from that encouraged by Jeffrey's established Whig review, Maurice argues that Jeffrey inaugurated a form of journalism that is "always based upon the narrow system of a particular sect" (49).

Maurice contends that Jeffrey's periodical aims to transform members of the upper and middle classes into a loyal and paying readership by convincing them that they share an identity rooted in their self-interest and party allegiances, which means ignoring "what is demanded from us by God, our consciences, and society": "[The *Edinburgh Review*] scarcely contains a page which does not attempt to depress, either by contemptuous silence, grave argument, or flippant ribaldry, every emotion and principle that spreads itself beyond the narrow circuit of our external and personal interest" ("Jeffrey" 49). For Maurice, Jeffrey has popularized a form of print-mediated imagined community nourished by sectarianism, and this is ultimately because of his empiricist, utilitarian "indifference" to the Coleridgean vision Maurice seeks to promote in the *Athenaeum*, according to which print is a medium for awakening readers to "those nobler moral and religious propensities . . . of our nature" needed to achieve "wide and permanent good" in the national community (50).

Robert Southey, Maurice claims in his next sketch, is now a Poet Laureate who sings for the Tories, but he has nevertheless caught in his poems—not his prose—exactly what Jeffrey lacks: an "unsectarian Catholicism of religion," a sense that God "breath[es] into all men a capacity for higher than earthly things," and a "feeling of brotherhood with all mankind" ("Southey" 65). Yet Southey is a man of his times, Maurice laments, and instead of promoting a Coleridgean vision of print as a medium for national spiritual community, Southey has written prose under the "perpetual consciousness that he is the gladiator of a sect or a party" (65). Identifying absolute perfection of government with the British State and the only lawful and good religion with the Anglican Church, Southey lashes out "against all from whom he differs": "He hates Roman Catholics, he hates Calvinists, he hates Unitarians, he hates Frenchmen," and "he believes that the Edinburgh Review is possessed by Satan" (66). Guaranteed to remain a "popular author" as long he lives, Southey fuels the formation of exclusive imagined communities on either side of the issues he takes up: "The Edinburgh Review has uniformly dealt him hard and unjust measure; and all his political opponents have" returned "the blows which he has shewn the example in afflicting" (66).

By his own account, Maurice defended "Wordsworth's poetry" as earnestly as Coleridge's metaphysics when he led the Apostles (*Life* I:176), and his sketch of Wordsworth for the *Athenaeum* indicates that the poet won his praise for showing "the mode in which it is really useful and wise to combat . . . unchristian sectarianism" ("Wordsworth" 114). Almost "all his works," Maurice claims, "make men look within for those things in which they agree, instead of looking without for those in which they differ," emphasizing "the powers and the tendencies" in us all "that are in communion with the divine nature" (114). Wordsworth's poetry resists sectarianism in general, and prejudiced representations of the poor in particular: his verse has encouraged "the instructed classes" to recognize "the power and tenderness of that [divine] spirit who lives as strongly . . . in the sod-built hut, as among primates, and kaisers, and the conclaves of emblazoned aristocracies" (113–14).

Here Maurice raises a subject that would increasingly occupy him in later journalism and published addresses: how print-mediated imagined communities, or publics, encouraged among middle- and upper-class readers required the exclusion or false representation of the poor and working classes. Jeffrey's *Edinburgh Review* and Southey's vitriolic prose are manifestations of a general tendency in early nineteenth-century print culture to coordinate readers' loyalties "with our own individual selfishness" ("Wordsworth" 114). The "vagrant act and the standing army" keep "the poor . . . out of our way," and this social enclosure is fortified by "speeches" made "in praise of . . . commercial competition" without mention of the "children" laboring in "cotton mills" to sustain the production;

writers of verse and fiction cover "the men and women of instructed society" with "the varnish of refinement"; and authors of chivalric tales "deify misanthropy" by exalting "the rude warriors of the middle ages" (114).

When in 1848 Maurice looked back on this period of his life, he felt that authors at that earlier time appealed to readers' sense of "national" identity only by giving "great heed to the boundaries and divisions of classes": "We had our novels for the aristocracy, our novels for the middle class, our novels about low life, each affecting to give glimpses of what passed within a world quite unknown to those who lay beyond it" (*Politics for the People* 2). Maria Edgeworth might have been one of the novelists Maurice had in mind in this comment, as indicated by his 1828 discussion of Irish literature for *The Westminster Review*. In the article, Maurice acknowledges Edgeworth's success in creating "admirable specimens of Irish gentility," but he believes she fails when attempting "to describe the situation of the Irish people," giving readers only "some notion that her poor fellow-countrymen are deficient in sundry articles of clothing and cleanliness—that the pig is an admitted parlour-boarder, and the middleman an occasional visitor of their cabins" ("National Tales of Ireland" 423).

III. SAINTLY SECTARIANISM: MAURICE VS. THE RELIGIOUS PERIODICALS

If Maurice early criticized the formation of reading audiences along exclusive party and class lines, by the time he began developing his theology of nationhood in 1836, he had identified the religious press as the most potent agent of sectarianism. The Tractarian controversy erupted in 1833, a year after Maurice had solidified his national theology, and a year before he was ordained in the Church of England. The emergence of Tractarianism did more than anything else to provoke the media warfare between the High (Tractarian, Oxford Movement) and Low (Evangelical)[2] church

---

2. *The Tracts for the Times* (1833–41) gave the Tractarians their popular name, but after midcentury the label *Oxford Movement* became more common and is now standard. Many followers at this time preferred the term *Anglo-Catholicism*, which Newman himself had used in his Tractarian phase (R. Chapman, "Nomenclature"). The term *High Church* sometimes was, and still is, employed to include Anglicans who sympathized with the Tractarians' high views of Church authority and liturgy, but who did not identify themselves as Tractarian or Anglo-Catholic (Blair, *Form and Faith* 19). I follow the practice of most religious historians in using *Evangelical* with a capital *E* for the party within the Church of England, and *evangelical* without a capital for the diverse evangelical movement within and without the Church of England.

parties that was to characterize religious polemics in and out of the Anglican Church for the rest of the century (Morris 56–57). From the beginning, the conflict was a print-culture sensation, and it concentrated on perceived threats to the nation's spiritual community. The Evangelicals often appealed to the still powerful sense that God had protected the British nation from Catholic oppression since 1588, ordaining it to be a representative of liberty and right religion. After Newman and other Tractarians left the Church of England for Rome and the Peel administration increased funds for the Catholic college of Maynooth in Ireland (1845), evangelicals[3] in and out of the Church formed the Evangelical Alliance (1846), whose publications starkly portrayed the Tractarian threat to national identity: "The Romish anti-Christian apostasy is manifestly occupied in putting forth new . . . efforts to obtain dominion and power" (qtd. Schlossberg 176).

For their part, the Tractarians took their cue from John Keble's 1833 "National Apostasy" sermon and the ensuing *Tracts for the Times* (1833–41): with the repeal of the Test Acts (1828), Keble claimed, Parliament had embarked on a mission to destroy the English confessional state. As Keble and fellow Tractarian Isaac Williams would argue in sermons and tracts published in the 1830s and '40s, the Mechanics' Institutes (1821), Society for the Diffusion of Useful Knowledge (1825), and even the interdenominational British and Foreign Bible Society (1804) were combining their influence to spread "a feverish thirst after knowledge for its own sake," and a faith in the power of reading governed by private judgment rather than the supervision of the Church (Keble, *Sermons* 54). Print culture and Parliament were cooperating to erode the unity of the Church of England and restrict its spiritual guidance of the nation. To rescue Britain from antinomian infidelity, argued leaders such as Newman, Keble, and Hurrell Froude, the Anglican Church had to reassert its independent apostolic authority and Pre-Reformation heritage, even at the price of disestablishment (Morris 57).

By the mid-1830s, strife between Tractarians and evangelicals in and outside the Church was being stoked by the religious periodical press. Increasing fourfold in number by 1825, comprising about 20 percent of the total number of journals, and outpacing the sale of all other magazines, religious periodicals were becoming the mainstay of reading, communication, and propaganda for religious groups—and these publications were often firmly divided along partisan lines (Altholz 2, 10, 12). The first

---

3. See previous note.

periodical to attack the Tractarians was the *Record* (founded 1828), an influential evangelical paper known for its assaults on other church parties (Altholz 18). By 1843, *The Christian Remembrancer,* a periodical for the High Church, could state that "the lines are strongly and decidedly marked" in the battle between Evangelicals and the High Church, and that every man must choose a side (qtd. Schlossberg 194).

Maurice launched his attack on the religious periodicals, particularly the *Record,* in the first edition of *The Kingdom of Christ* (1838), berating them for fueling sectarianism, especially among the clergy who would direct others in imagining their place in a British spiritual community (Brose 127; *Life* I:243-44). Maurice targeted this clerical audience in his next major attack on the religious press, "Reasons for Not Joining a Party in the Church" (1841; hereafter cited as "Reasons"). Earlier that year, Newman had published his controversial Tract 90 for *Tracts for the Times,* in which he asserted that the Thirty Nine Articles could be reconciled with Pre-Reformation doctrine, and for which he was censured by the Hebdomadal Board at Oxford. Hearing of the censure, Dr. W. F. Hook, the Vicar of Leeds, issued a pamphlet titled "On the State of Parties in the Church" in which, despite strong points of disagreement with Newman, he pledged himself to Newman's side and declared that the Oxford censure only confirmed what seemed unavoidable: the Church of England was a divided body, and it was the duty of every priest to choose a party, the Low (Evangelical) or High Church (Tractarian).

Hook's announcement that "*it is absolutely necessary for us to range ourselves on one side or the other,*" substantiated Maurice's fear that battles lines proclaimed by the religious press were becoming entrenched in the minds of Anglican clergy (qtd. by Maurice, "Reasons" 2). Within a month, Maurice answered Hook with "Reasons," pointedly addressing this public letter to Samuel Wilberforce, then Archdeacon of Surrey. Wilberforce was becoming known for his opposition to parties in the church, but Maurice feared that Wilberforce would soon become regarded as a leader of another contingent, the "No Party" party—and that his own name was already being attached to such a group by fellow clergy (*Life* I:239). By addressing the letter against church parties to Wilberforce, Maurice indicated that even rallying around the No Party flag would be a mistake, since it would promote in print yet another image of public religious communion defined by exclusion of others—in this case by "common dread of the Liberals, the Evangelicals, and the High Church school" (I.239).

In calling for a standoff between High and Low Churchmen, Maurice argues in "Reasons," Dr. Hook has recycled "Popular catchwords" circulating through the press. These labels obscure the real nature of the conflict, and compel clergy and their congregations to divide their allegiance between principles that can in fact only be properly understood and applied when they are held together by a united national religious community (pars. 10–11). A better distinction than Low and High Church, Maurice suggests, would be between *"Anglo-Catholic"* and *"Those who hold the peculiar doctrines of the Reformation"* (par. 10). Each, he argues, grasps something of the whole truth. If those often derisively labeled "Low Church" emphasize the "personal" nature of faith, the "sense of" individual "relationship to God," then those of the Anglo-Catholic position witness to a principle necessary for realizing one's "individual . . . salvation": the "law of our fellowship, the duties growing out of that fellowship, the manifestation of God, the unfathomable mystery of His being and unity" (par. 11). Protestantism, an emphasis on personal experience of God, cannot remain vital without the support of Catholicism, an emphasis on institutional and sacramental growth into a society ordered by God. Hook and a majority of clergy and their followers, Maurice fears, have forgotten this perspective, which he defended in *Kingdom of Christ* as "*the actual position [of] the English Church*" (par. 12)—and the religious press depends for its survival on ensuring that they continue to forget it.

Probably thinking of periodicals such as *The Record,* Maurice claims that the Evangelical school of the Church originated with great "spiritual strength" in the eighteenth century, but has since shriveled into an automated "party" system of sectarian meetings, councils, and mass-distributed publications (par. 14). Although some of its "pious" leaders still wish to acknowledge their fellowship with other Anglicans, the Evangelical "*system*" itself "has become a newspaper, cheap book, lecture machinery; not for propagating certain principles, but for attacking and slandering those who are supposed not to hold them, or to hold others different from them" (par. 14). Dr. Hook's letter confirms that publications such as *The Record* and *Tracts for the Times* have convinced many ministers that they must arrange their flocks on either side of a battle between the Evangelical party and the Tractarians. As a result, the Anglo-Catholic school is coming to resemble its Evangelical rival:

> Why is it more shocking to read advertisements in a religious newspaper, about a[n Evangelical] clergyman who will preach justification by faith alone, for six weeks at the sea-side, than to read letters and leading articles in a fashionable newspaper [e.g., the Tractarian sponsored *British Critic*] about the Sacraments? Why is the quack machinery of the age less offen-

sive, when it is employed in support of "Catholic Consent," than when it is used to support the principles of the Bible? (par. 14)

Rather than regarding sacramental signs of grace, the authority of Christian tradition, and justification by faith as complimentary principles in a shared national Church, Maurice worries, Anglican clergy are becoming accustomed to regard the phrases *Sacrament, Catholic Consent,* and *justification by faith alone* as shibboleths—printed symbols of the hostile imagined religious communities to which they must pledge themselves and their congregants. To sustain the energy of party allegiance—and circulation rates—periodicals such as *The Record,* the *British Critic,* and the *Christian Remembrancer* are encouraging clergy to believe "that we are sent into the world to rob other men of their principles, and not to defend our own" (par. 15). In truth, Maurice's anxiety was probably exaggerated: many who purchased *The Record* lamented its harsh tone toward other denominations and Church parties (Altholz 18), and if Tractarian and Evangelical (as well as Nonconformist) leaders did often imagine themselves in sharply opposed communities, parishioners—at least in rural areas—do not seem to have shared their hostility (Knight, *Nineteenth-Century Church* 33). "Reasons for Not Joining a Party in the Church" is less reliable as a measure of widespread social tensions than of Maurice's own deepening conviction that religious publishing was enforcing the mental backdrop of a nation composed of mutually exclusive religious sects.

A few years after "Reasons," Maurice issued another public letter, "On Right and Wrong Methods of Supporting Protestantism" (1843), in which he again identified religious periodicals as a major threat to national spiritual unity, this time explicitly linking the divisive imagined communities encouraged by such periodicals to class divisions in the "hungry forties." As with the earlier pamphlet, Maurice was goaded into print by warfare between the Evangelicals and Tractarians. In 1843, Edward Pusey, a leading Tractarian theologian and priest, had been suspended from preaching at Oxford by university authorities for unspecified heretical tendencies in one of his sermons on the Eucharist. In November of that year, Lord Ashley (later seventh Earl of Shaftesbury) presided at a meeting that resolved to pressure the Duke of Wellington, the Chancellor of Oxford, to silence the Tractarians entirely (Brose 163). Ashley was a prominent MP known for his strong Evangelical commitments and his efforts to improve the education and labor conditions of workers. (He had just secured passage of the Mines Act of 1842.) Maurice addressed his letter directly to Ashley, arguing that suppression of the Tractarians would only exaggerate into a party platform their "worst" and most un-Protestant "tendencies," which would drive "the Evangelical clergy" to form even "more of a party" subjected "to the yoke of the religious newspapers," and as a result "frustrate" any united effort to address "the welfare of the working classes" ("Right and Wrong" 20).

In "Right and Wrong," Maurice applies to socio-economic classes the distinction he made in "Reasons" between the Protestant emphasis on the individual's direct relationship to God, retained by Evangelicals, and the Catholic stress on duties and relations within a society ordered by God, retained by Anglo-Catholics, or Tractarians (4). To the individual and Protestant focus, he argues, "the middle class" has been committed since the nearly simultaneous "rise of the trading class, and the proclamation of Wickliffe's doctrine" (4). In Maurice's view, Nonconformity is an extreme extension of this principle: "Mere Protestantism . . . constitutes the very idea of dissent" and "is the religion of the middle class in its highest power, if that class be meant to exist apart from both the others" (5).

Among the upper classes, by contrast, the Catholic principle, a "faith which connected itself with . . . social relations," had always been "most operative" (9), degenerating by the early nineteenth century into the old High (and dry) Church, whose adherents defended established Anglican authority and liturgy out of mere "antiquarian and traditional homage" (10). This narrow High Church mindset had been entrenched among the aristocratic classes at Oxford before the rise of the Tractarians there, who in the 1830s began to insist that the forms of the Church were "shams and delusions" unless they were "the witnesses of an actual connection between man and the invisible world, of an actual fellowship between man and man" (10). In this the Tractarians recovered the "great principle of a social faith, the principle that we exist in a permanent communion which was not created by human hands," a fundamental tenet in Maurice's own vision of a national religious community centered on the Anglican Church and established by God (10).

Combining renewed devotion to the sacraments and priestly authority with "severe doctrines of self-discipline" and "a very sincere sympathy with the actual miseries of the poor," the Oxford Movement's social faith began to awaken young members of the aristocracy, clergy, and professions to "the cause of their fellow-creatures" (11). Yet devotion to the Catholic and social principle of faith, Maurice concedes, has for many upper-class converts to the Oxford school been mixed with nostalgia for "the state of things in which the priest, the landlord, and the retainer, were the only elements of society," thereby justly exciting the disgust of the middle classes (12). Furthermore, publications such as *The Tracts for the Times* have revealed a sectarian spirit in teachers and leaders of the movement, who have been unable to defend truths connected to a social faith, such as "apostolical succession," without harshly condemning "those who were without" such principles; and who have risked "*catholicis*[ing] the church" only by "treaten[ing] to *unprotestantise* it," denigrating the principle of an individual faithful relationship to God that the Reformation rightly championed (12).

The speeches and writings of those who wish to defend evangelical Protestantism, Maurice argues, have made a parallel error, converting individual relationship with God and salvation by faith into "mere symbols of our difference from Rome, . . . or else our hatred of Oxford and its Catholic school" (13). As before, Maurice links the reinforcement of mutually exclusive Christian communities in the nation to the religious periodical press. "Our religious newspapers and magazines" are "degrading Protestantism" into an identity defined by resisting and attacking the positions of others, Maurice contends, and, he (hyperbolically) claims, as a result "a school for religious scandal is opened in every town and village; men employ themselves in the house of God in observing the tones and gestures of their pastors, that they may report something evil of them in the next week's newspaper" (13). Newspapers such as *The Record* and *Nonconformist* (1841) are contributing to a destructive tendency Maurice believes always present in English society—for the upper class to identify "the social religion" as "the whole" of Christianity, and the middle classes to cling to "the individual religion" as "the whole," thereby disabling the unified faith they might develop by working with each other (14).

Should this continue, Maurice claims, each class will refuse to cooperate in their service to the rest of society, and the physical distress and lack of education among the working classes will eventually lead to a revolution that will mean "the certain destruction of both" the middle and the upper classes (14). For all Maurice's criticism of distorted and prejudiced representations of the lower classes in his early essays for *The Westminster Review* and *The Athenaeum*, he here assumes a thoroughly paternalistic attitude. Unless, Maurice warns Ashley, the individualizing principle defended in the Protestantism of the middle classes and the social faith of the upper classes can "act together and harmoniously upon them," the "lower orders" will "be left without any faith of their own"; instead, their "Magicians" will "produce a counterfeit" of "either form": "of Catholicism in Socialism;

of Protestantism in the assertion of individual will" (15). Only a form of education that results from the collaboration of clergy from the individual and social schools can avert social chaos by removing from the "hearts" of the laboring classes "the deep sense of separation and alienation from their fellow men on the one hand," and "the consciousness of personal degradation on the other" (16).

In approaching education as the panacea for the misery and class conflict of the 1840s, Maurice follows the path of many earnest Victorians concerned about the social unrest of the day (Brose 165). Ultimately, he arrives at what Raymond Williams has called a "paternal system" of communication: a ruling minority regards the majority "as having many of the characteristics of children, . . . as being in many ways unfortunate and ill-equipped," and plans, on its terms and schedule, to use a network of communication and education to teach the underprivileged to improve their minds and situations ("Communications and Community" 24). Maurice unconsciously extends the imagination of community through exclusion that he condemned as a young journalist, portraying working-class leaders as only capable of playing the role of Pharaoh's sham "Magicians" next to the prophetic clerisy of the wealthier classes allied with the Established Church, who are to be responsible for safeguarding and controlling the dissemination of God's message about Britain's true religious and social identity.

Even so, Maurice reveals his growing conviction that print-mediated sectarian religious communities deepen class divisions and contribute to the suffering of the poor. As a result, in this pamphlet he focuses more intensely than in his earlier writings on the ways journalists and writers reinforce sectarianism and class bias through the forms of community that they invite readers to imagine. The "great aim of the religious newspapers," Maurice asks Ashley to recognize, "is to keep the evangelical clergy from co-operating with their brethren" (17). Evangelical papers attempt to sustain their partisan readerships by threatening "Evangelical clergymen" with the label of "Papists or Puseyites" if they "take part" with those of the Oxford school "in the work of educating their countrymen" (18). The "noisy journalists" on the Oxford side likewise produce "diatribes against Luther," sneering "at modern protestantism" (19). By helping to suppress the Tractarians at Oxford, Ashley will increase the intensity and appeal of their mockery of Protestantism, even as he drives Evangelical clergy further into the party mentality fanned by religious newspapers, thereby frustrating efforts to educate the working classes and overcome the nation's socio-economic divisions.

IV. CRISIS OF NATIONAL IMAGINATION: *POLITICS FOR THE PEOPLE* (1848)

As the public letters of 1841 and 1843 reveal, even when promoting reconciliation between classes and church parties under the aegis of the Anglican Church, Maurice identified mass-produced literature and habits of reading, not the Church, as one of the most powerful influences on the ways Britons were imagining themselves in community. In fact, he came to believe religious periodicals were forcing Anglican clergy into sharply opposed camps, in effect dictating the Church's teaching and policy. Maurice grudgingly admitted that print culture could imprint in the back of readers' minds an image of Britain divided into irreconcilable sects between which they must choose.

Maurice acknowledged this power in early May 1848, when he helped launch a cheap weekly paper, *Politics for the People*. Barely lasting two months because of poor circulation, *Politics* had a negligible impact on the artisans and middle-class professionals Maurice and his fellow contributors hoped to reach.[4] The paper nonetheless represents an important step in Maurice's attempt to convince diverse British readers of their membership in a divinely established spiritual society. *Politics* emerged in response to concerns Maurice shared with fellow clergyman Charles Kingsley and London barrister John Ludlow for the working poor and the class tensions most recently evidenced by the gathering of thousands of Chartists at Kennington Common on April 10, 1848. In his contributions to *Politics* and the Christian Socialist movement it inspired, Maurice strove to apply his vision of national spiritual community to his local community in West End London. Later known for its culture and wealth, in Maurice's day parts of the West End seemed to be in decay, with homes of the affluent next to streets of intense poverty. As many contemporary writers observed, the neighborhood's skilled craftsmen and garment workers were being threatened by the growth of "sweated" shops, which made them

---

4. *Politics* did, however, lead to meetings—which began in 1849—between Maurice, others involved in the venture, and workers in London. These gatherings fueled the brief Christian Socialist movement, which, in Maurice's mind, was essentially traditional in motivation and aim: he hoped to stabilize (rather than restructure) current class relations, ground the nation's social unity on orthodox Christian values, and inspire the Anglican Church to be the main agent of reform in education, sanitation, and labor relations through the ministry of its local parishes (Morris 150). Nonetheless, Maurice was persuaded to support progressive economic measures, such as establishing (and himself sacrificially funding) several workers' cooperatives, because he believed they agreed with his vision of a national community sustained by mutual service, rather than selfish competition (143).

sympathetic to Chartism and "working-class radicalism" (Morris 151). With nearly a third of such skilled laborers out of work by the summer of 1848, and the rest on reduced hours and wages, it is hardly surprising that in the wake of the Chartist petition in April loud gatherings and processions continued in the West End (152).

In *Politics,* Maurice admits the success of the popular press in responding to these workers' political concerns: the political instruction that workers desire, he argues, "comes forth generally through Sunday newspapers, and such like organs of popular feeling," rather than through the many competing initiatives then afoot to educate the poor, especially those of the Anglican Church (*Politics* 196). Maurice probably had in mind Chartist papers such as *The Northern Star,* or popular Sunday papers such as *Lloyd's Weekly Newspaper,* which relied on a low price and moderate expressions of sympathy for Chartism to secure a relatively wide circulation among working-class readers (Altick 343–45). By distributing *Politics for the People* on a weekly basis and at a cheap price (one penny), Maurice and his associates tried to turn affordable news into a channel of communication with frustrated workers in London's West End. In the "Prospectus" to the first issue, Maurice announces that the paper will take up "questions" most recently and powerfully addressed by Chartism, "such as the Extension of the Suffrage; the relation of the Capitalist to the Labourer; [and] what a Government can or cannot do, to find work or pay for the Poor" (*Politics* 1).

Maurice's rhetorical strategy in *Politics* is confused. On one hand, he aims the "Prospectus" at middle- and upper-class readers, and talks past a potential working-class readership, when he states that he and his fellow contributors hope "to cultivate in ourselves and in our countrymen" a true "sympathy" for the "miseries" of the laboring class (1). On the other, he appeals in the same section to radicalized workers, arguing that "a Living and Righteous God is ruling in human society," which is "the rich man's warning," the "poor man's comfort," and a guarantee that a modified version of the revolutionary trinity—"Liberty, Fraternity, Unity"—is "intended for every people under heaven" (1). The "Prospectus" concludes with a direct address to the "WORKMEN OF ENGLAND," which is unusual in admitting that the papers' authors—identified as middle class (they belong neither to the laboring nor to the "richer classes")—must be educated by their working-class readers: "Many of you write clearly and nobly; you can tell us what you are thinking and wherein we have mistaken you . . . You are in contact with the realities of life; you can help to make all our studies and thoughts more real" (2).

The undecided tone of the paper—at once addressed to members of more affluent classes and to potentially radicalized workers—probably contributed to its low circulation. Yet this indecision also reflected the attempt to transform cheap weekly news, a proven success with (at least artisanal) working audiences, into a means of inviting readers to acknowledge their membership in a national spiritual community that included every class. This might have also influenced the decision to avoid proper names: all the authors wrote under pseudonyms, giving the impression that the paper was open to the views of any contributor earnestly in search of the spiritual unity and cooperation the nation needed. If the paper's middle-class authors and their target readers from the working and higher classes were not discovering their God-ordained unity in churches, chapels, taverns, or gentlemen's clubs, then they might be encouraged to imagine that fellowship through the printed page. In contributing to *Politics*, Maurice effectively conceded the point made by John Ludlow in a letter sent to him two months before they began the paper: "the great daily teacher of mankind in modern times is not the pulpit, but the press" (qtd. in Christensen 62).

In a letter sent to Ludlow shortly before beginning *Politics*, Maurice assumed their potential working-class readers had a general "indifference to religion," a view Ludlow shared (*Life* 1:461). It was typical of Victorian clergy, civil servants, and politicians to remark on the irreligion of the working classes (C. Brown 18–30), even though, as Hugh McLeod has demonstrated, before and after Chartism many working-class radicals grounded their politics in Christianity (McLeod *Religion and Irreligion* 39–42) and generally held "some form of Christian belief" (36). Nevertheless, even if many might have considered themselves Christians, London workers attended church much less often than other groups in the nation (McLeod 32), and Maurice, then a preacher at Lincoln's Inn with a congregation mainly of lawyers and local professionals, might have confused this trend with unbelief or indifference. Partly the result of limited knowledge, the assumption that workers were alienated from Christianity might have also been ideologically useful. In presuming the religious indifference of working-class political culture, and then reflecting on solutions to class tensions from a middle-class Anglican perspective, *Politics* contributes to widespread interpretive strategies developed in the wake of Chartism, by which middle- and upper-class commentators ignored "any genuinely Christian motivation" in radical activists, since this might legitimate demands for immediate, far-reaching changes to the "public order" (Groth Lyon 228). To the degree that this is true of *Politics*, the paper founds communication on selective silencing, broadcasting a vision of spiritual unity by denying workers their own spiritual motives and vocabularies.

Within these limits, Maurice and Ludlow were nevertheless atypical in addressing their working-class readers as responsible individuals capable of articulating their own ideas, and in printing those readers' critical responses. In a series of articles on "The Suffrage," Ludlow proclaims his desire "for Universal Suffrage," the central reform advocated by Chartists (*Politics* 10). Yet he immediately qualifies his statement, insisting that the vote should be extended gradually, and only to those who prove themselves to be morally responsible; the Chartists failed this test, he argues, when they gathered on Kennington Common in defiance of the Queen's prohibition of the meeting (10). Granting the vote to those who force their agenda through "a monster meeting" rather than appealing to the law (11), Ludlow contends, would be like trusting "a child or a mad-man" with "a razor," or granting "a book" to "an unlettered savage" (10).

In a letter printed immediately after Ludlow's final piece on suffrage, a watch-case-joint finisher—Joseph Millbank (Christensen 98–100)—signs himself "One of the wicked Chartists of Kennington Common," and expresses respect for the "soul-earnestness" of the paper, even as he condemns its harsh judgment of Chartism, and reclaims the appeal to "Liberty, *Equality*, and Fraternity" (*Politics* 45, emphasis mine) that Maurice had modified to "Liberty, Fraternity, Unity" in the "Prospectus" (1). Millbank's friend and coworker, Thomas Shorter (Christensen 98–100), also contributed a letter, declaring himself "A Working Man, but no Chartist," and criticizing the paper's unjust identification of all Chartists with the few thousand who gathered at Kennington (*Politics* 63). Shorter rejects Ludlow's moral test for suffrage as "worthy of but little notice," characterizing it as an old excuse trotted out by the fortunate to maintain exclusive privileges. The point could as easily be made against them: are not, he asks, "the tradesmen, as a body," more "ignorant than the working classes," helped as the latter now are by "great facilities" for obtaining political knowledge (63)? The "facilities" Shorter has in mind are presumably the Mechanics' Institutes.

Published just before the periodical stopped, one letter by a craftsman admires the spirit of the paper but is unsurprised by its impending failure: having in mind contributions authored by Maurice, the letter suggests that "if the writer . . . were to work up the principles he has to teach in other and more attractive forms, his work would find numerous and thankful readers of all classes" (224). Ironically, an appeal through "more attractive forms" is just what Maurice seems to have attempted. In the paper's second number, he introduces the first of a series of "Dialogues in the Penny Boats," the steamboats that ferried Londoners up and down the Thames for a cheap price. Penny steamers were in fact not an ideal setting for conversation, at least according to Henry Mayhew's later interviews with musicians who loudly played on the boats for money (III:184). Maurice, however, represents the ferries as classless salons, where "free and pleasant intercourse" can occur between "people of all sorts" (*Politics* 19). Posing as an anonymous contributor, Maurice stages dialogues between himself and various penny-boat riders about the nation's socioeconomic tensions. In the first dialogue, Maurice converses with "a Templar, a Silk Mercer" and "a Coalwhipper," and their discussion points to the need to replace a spirit of ruthless "competition," which is justified by political economy, with respect for mutual service across class divisions, which is required by "God's law" (21).

Circulating through London, charging a penny, and providing a medium of communication between members of otherwise separated and estranged classes, the penny boats become an analogy for the kind of virtual communicative space, or public sphere, Maurice hopes his penny weekly will offer. To promote a public sphere outside the sectarian and class-restricted spaces projected by many periodicals, Maurice invites readers to imagine themselves overhearing conversations on the mobile and economically accessible decks of penny boats—rather than the fashionable churches and chapels workers tended to regard as middle- and upper-class territory, or the pubs at the center of male working-class culture (McLeod, *Religion and Irreligion* 23–25).

Maurice prefaces the second penny-boat dialogue by parodying the sectarian divisions into which he thinks readers will automatically try to fit *Politics for the People*. He recounts the contradictory responses to the paper that he has supposedly heard from a range of passengers on the penny steamers, from "doctors of divinity" to "reporters of newspapers" and middle-class "ladies" (*Politics* 81). "I am told," he informs the editors, that in each number of *Politics* "you have fallen" into "the fanatical extremes of ultra-Chartism, ultra-Toryism, and ultra-Moderation" (81). Straining to pigeonhole the paper politically, these readers have also labored to pin it to a single audience religiously. "Mr. Johnson" believes the editors of *Politics* are "mere creatures of the bishops," while "Mrs. Dorothy Snooks" affirms they have "bitter ill-will against the clergy"; others observe one day that the writers of *Politics* address "working-men as if they were babies," but on the following day contend that the authors "deliberately shoot" over their "reader's [sic] heads" (81). Maurice portrays London readers as incapable of encountering printed literature without instantly straining to fit the writers and themselves into the antagonistic parties that their previous exposure to mass print culture has trained them to identify with Britain's public sphere. Readers, in this account, instinctively imagine themselves in a nation of sects.

In the ensuing penny-boat dialogue, Maurice tries to model the free intercourse that he believes is needed to reform and spread education, the solution he most arduously championed for the nation's socioeconomic tensions. Discussing the need for such an education, the anonymous narrator—Maurice—and his friend Wilkinson, who has just graduated from Oxford, encounter an intelligent carpenter, also an associate of Maurice's. The West-End artisan is reading "one of the cheap Radical papers," the type of publication that Maurice and his associates hoped to imitate and counteract through *Politics* (82). Wilkinson immediately asks the carpenter whether he understands politics, admitting that he doesn't himself. "Why, sir," the carpenter answers, "that was just what the man in this article is saying of you gentlemen," and at Wilkinson's request he reads the following from his paper: "[teaching only about events hundreds and thousands of years old, the colleges of the privileged] *send forth men utterly unfit to cope with the questions which are occupying our hearts; men who will enter parliament . . . by cajoleries and bribes, who will talk plentifully, (for they learn to talk,) but will not utter one new thought, or help us one step in the removal of any practical grievance*" (82).

Wilkinson laments that universities are not adding instruction about the present to study of the past, but he inadvertently indicates another way of redressing the blindness of educated elites to grievances of the disenfranchised majority. Asked to consider whether he and his classmates were interested in the stirring events connected with the 1848 revolutions in France, Germany, and Italy, Wilkinson replies: "'Prodigiously, for a few days, . . . but the interest dies out, because we do not connect it with anything permanent—no one explains to us what these miracles signify'" (82). Maurice (the narrator) observes that only when Wilkinson's knowledge of the past, until now "lying as dead lumber in your mind," is activated by desire for "active service" in response to "the necessities of our time," will he search after the "permanent . . . principles which lie hidden in" the "facts" of the past and present (83).

Maurice is, heavy-handedly, steering this young Oxonian toward a Coleridgean school of reflection. The right education will teach Wilkinson to recognize those abiding "principles" that underlie the facts of history and reveal the necessity of "a Universal society for man as man" (*Kingdom* 1:11), a spiritual fellowship to be realized distinctively by each national community. Yet in a way Coleridge would probably have resisted, Maurice encourages this potential member of the nation's clerisy to learn from the lower classes he will instruct, extending the principle of "reciprocity" so loudly praised in commercial "trade" to greater "freedom in exchanging the treasures which God has committed to the *minds* of different men in this community of ours" (*Politics* 83). The immediate reference for "this community of ours" is London, specifically the West End: the carpenter came aboard "at Waterloo-bridge" (81). Yet Wilkinson and the carpenter clearly also stand for the nation's educated elite and working classes, each of whom can teach the other. Wilkinson must draw from his privileged knowledge of history principles that apply to the health of all nations, helping to alleviate the "confusion and narrowness in our handicraftsmen," who, as the carpenter observes, are pressured by the radical press and the demands of their occupations to forego reflection as they grapple with the "evils that oppress" them (83). Yet only if Wilkinson is willing to learn about the difficulties faced by men such as the carpenter will he feel compelled to search through the "dead lumber" of facts and knowledge stored in his mind for those "principles" that will guide him in contributing to "the different experiments" afoot for addressing the nation's socioeconomic crisis (83).

Staged in the penny-boats, whose circulating decks temporarily force members of different classes out of their distinctive territories into a common space, Maurice's dialogues are a virtual experiment in the "free, unreserved, honest" communication between classes he thinks must occur to reform the universities and produce an expanded version of Coleridge's clerisy. The middle-class "writers" of *Politics,* poised between "the rich" and "poor," hope to lead the "upper classes" in confessing their injustices to working people, "whom we have injured by our ill doings," so that laborers will "believe us when we tell them that we have that [education] which will do them good" (83). For all his insistence on dialogue and mutual education, however, Maurice adheres to a "paternal" system of communication. At no point does he imply that the underprivileged should help manage the nation's media and institutions of education. Unlike Ludlow, Maurice never aligned himself fully with a plan to redistribute socioeconomic roles and resources. Tellingly, in this dialogue Wilkinson—the Oxonian—is named, while the carpenter is known only by his occupation. Maurice's "dialogues" in *Politics* are, of course, not really dialogues but his effort to put his ideas into the mouths of imagined workers.

In the next penny-boat dialogue, Maurice informs readers that he and the carpenter now regularly meet on their commutes and "have many opportunities of intercourse" (154). Even as Maurice again turns the penny-boat into an example of the open public sphere needed to reform education and class tensions, he reminds readers of sectarian obstacles. The previous Wednesday evening, he and the carpenter were talking on a penny-steamer when a party of gentlemen boarded who had just "been present at a meeting on the subject of Education" (154). In the recounted dialogue, one of these gentlemen, a shrill-voiced young churchman, argues that the Anglican Church should supervise national education without government supervision; another, "somewhat effeminate" and conceited, contends for state education (154); and a third, a Nonconformist, breaks in supporting "Voluntaryism," or the entrustment of national education to competing private societies, largely to protect religious freedom (155). "'And so, gentlemen,'" observes the carpenter, "'while you are fighting about these beautiful words of yours,—Church, State, Voluntary Principle,—and settling who is not to teach us, our sons are to become vagabonds, and our daughters harlots'" (155).

Maurice's carpenter ventriloquizes a tenet of faith widespread among the Victorian upper middle classes, according to which the poor suffered from lack of wisdom, rather than from systematically enforced economic disparity. Maurice again reveals the paternalism underpinning the open public sphere that he invites readers to imagine; but he also proceeds to single out the media's role in preventing the "mutual reverence" and "understanding" between sects necessary for lasting educational reform (157). The ability to see the worth in another side's principles and practical efforts at educating the poor is precisely what "our party writers, religious and political," aim "to destroy" (157). Despite calls for cooperation from an elderly clergyman, a teacher in the ragged schools, and a government inspector of schools who are also riding the penny-boat, the young Churchman, State defender, and supporter of Voluntarism return to shore ready for battle. The Churchman, Maurice speculates, left "very eager to get a report of the meeting he had been attending, and a leading article of his own about it, into a High Church newspaper;" and the Voluntary hurried "to enrich the columns of one of the Dissenting journals, with remarks on the promising split between the two great enemies of Educational Freedom," even as the "State disputant was on his way to a political dinner" (156). Even if conversations resembling those "reported" in *Politics* could actually take place, Maurice suggests, some participants would ensure that they were remediated to the public through sectarian venues.

Maurice did try to practice in life the open communication he modeled through the penny-boat dialogues: he and others associated with *Politics* followed up the dissolution of the paper by engaging in ongoing dialogues with artisans at the Cranbourne Coffee Tavern in the West End (Christensen 99). These conversations arguably led to Maurice's temporary but crucial support of cooperative workshops for skilled workers beginning in late 1849 (131–34); his confused promotion of Christian Socialism the following year (he was no socialist); and his establishment of the Working Men's College in 1854. While Maurice always insisted on the need for direct engagement with the disadvantaged and institutional solutions to their physical and educational needs, beginning especially with *Politics*, his publications stress the power of the printed page. Even more crucial than systematic reforms to education or the contents of periodicals, he suggests, is the promotion of strategies of reinterpretation and imagination by which the millions of texts already circulating through the nation can become means for British readers to awaken to membership in a national Christian community. Maurice tries to promote such reading practices in one of his most substantial contributions to *Politics*, a serialized novella called *Recollections and Confessions of William Milward*.

In the tale, William Milward describes his eventual movement, after the economic downfall of his farming family, to retail work in London and to Owenite socialism, a cluster of ideas that was especially attractive to West-End skilled workers when *Politics* was being published. By the 1830s, Robert Owen's communitarian socialism had been widely popularized among the working classes, particularly his doctrines that moral character was formed by circumstances and not the will, and that model communities should be set up in which production and property were cooperatively owned (Claeys *DNB*). Owen's Universal Community Society of Rational Religionists, with its journal *New Moral Order* and over sixty local chapters dedicated to spreading socialist principles, achieved influence great enough for the 1839 *Westminster Review* to remark that Owen's hatred of capitalist competition seemed to be "the actual creed of a great portion of the working classes" (qtd. ibid.). By 1844, the Society had run out of funds and effectively come to an end, but the 1848 revolution in France and disillusionment with Chartism seem to have revived commitment to Owenite socialism—minus Owen's antipathy to religion—among artisans, especially in London (Christensen 222).

Maurice's story is a rather heavy-handed effort to help West-End workers attracted to Owenism, and members of the middle and upper classes suspicious of such ideas, recognize the principles of fellowship and mutual service buried amidst socialism's "errors"—and then to see that the Church will best guide society in realizing these principles. At the end of the novella, Susan, William's pious Anglican wife, dies in a hospital bed in London, after having lived a hard life and endured slander—including from William—for her commitment to disadvantaged and fallen women.

In a deathbed sermon resembling those popularized through Victorian novels and religious periodicals, Susan exhorts her socialist husband and an attendant clergyman:

> The poor people in cellars and garrets . . . know that there is a hell about them . . . If you [priest] do but tell them that there is a heaven, and that it is God's pleasure that they should possess it; if you will tell them that Christ is as near to them as the Devil, and stronger than he, they will not, dearest William—they will not be the slaves of their circumstances . . . I am speaking—God is speaking—to both of you. Show my husband, sir, that there is a society [the Church] which has the love of God and man for the root of it, and I know he will not live for any other. (*Politics* 272)

Susan declares what William realizes in hindsight was always true about his socialism: "[Upon becoming a Socialist,] I began to think, to act, to resolve, to consider what I could do to alter society; I was claiming the power of a creature who is not the mere slave of circumstances" (175). Maurice engineers his story to illustrate the point he would soon argue in a letter to Ludlow. Socialists, although apparently "worshippers of circumstances," bear "witness for the power of the will to regulate . . . circumstances" and to the intuitive knowledge that humans are meant to live in fellowship (*Life* II:7). Susan and William, joined in marriage by the Anglican Church despite Owenist antipathy to both institutions, and reconciled through Susan's dying speech, anticipate the potential marriage between workers' desire for a society of cooperative fellowship and the leadership of the Anglican Church, whose mission is to proclaim God's intention for such a society to be realized in each nation.

The story also turns upon conspicuous scenes of reading. After marrying and moving to London, William and Susan have a son, who soon dies, perhaps from an illness caused by the poor sanitation criticized elsewhere in *Politics for the People*. One evening shortly thereafter, William is reading the newspaper, and coming across an advertisement for a socialist lecture, tells Susan that he will attend. Again pointing to the potential marriage of Christianity with the socialist demand for fellowship, Susan defies the typical Victorian division of reading activities voiced by William—"I thought the Bible was for women, the newspaper for men" (262)—by insisting that she keeps up with debates about social ills, and that she wishes to accompany William to the lecture. Taking the paper, Susan's eye falls on "the list of births," and she exclaims "My poor, dear lady!" when she reads that "the Honorable Mrs. Merton" has had "a boy still-born" (262). Before marrying William, Susan had been the maid of Mrs. Merton, then Miss Newbolt, "a young lady of large property" who later married Mr. Merton, a politician who uses religion and politics merely to further his own interests (176). William mocks Susan's pity for the affluent Mrs. Merton, dryly commenting that with "horses, and carriages, and the park, and the opera, and their fashionable preacher on Sundays, what signifies a baby?" (262). "Surely," Susan protests, "rich people have hearts as well as we," arguing that "what we have felt"—the loss of their own son just a month earlier—"should make us feel for them" (262).

The debate between William and Susan suggests that even commonplace sections of the newspaper, such as lists of births and deaths, can be a mass-distributed daily reminder of the collective in which each Briton exists. The "Honourable Mrs. Merton" is socially and economically removed from William Milward, a retailer, and even further from his socialist friend, the mechanic Edward Harmer. While they will rarely, if ever, occupy the same physical space, these disparate members of the nation might be prompted by newspaper lists to remember losses and hopes shared by poor and rich alike—the deaths of children, for instance. Even as Susan models this imaginative and sympathetic reaction to traces of other lives in newspapers, she concedes William's point that being "just to our own class and the miserable people below us" might require losing the good opinion of people who move in the high society of the Honourable Mrs. Merton; yet she insists that "love" of "our fellow-creatures" cannot—without self-contradiction and harm—be motivated by "spite" of other social groups (262).

Maurice implies that if the artisanal and affluent members of the West End—and, by implication, of Britain—truly wish to redress the problems discussed at socialist meetings such as the one William finds advertised, then they must learn a new way of reading their daily papers. They must learn to find in even such seemingly miscellaneous and trivial lists reminders of a community of suffering and hope that defies the boundaries set up by sects and parties, divisions that are often reinforced by articles in the same periodicals. Maurice thereby partially confirms the account of national imagination offered by Benedict Anderson. The expansion of newspapers beginning in the eighteenth century, Anderson claims, helped European readers imagine themselves linked to hosts of unnamed citizens in nations moving through secular time. If newspapers, as Ludlow observed to Maurice in the letter quoted earlier, were vying with the pulpit to instruct the populace, they might also seem to offer "a substitute for morning prayers" (Anderson 35). Opening the paper each morning, each reader is well aware that the ceremony he performs is being replicated simultaneously by thousands (or millions) of others of whose existence he is confident, yet of whose identity he has not the slightest notion . . . What more vivid figure for the secular, historically clocked, imagined community can be envisioned? At the same time, the newspaper reader, observing exact replicas of his own paper being consumed by his . . . neighbours, is continually reassured that the imagined [national] world is visibly rooted in everyday life. (Anderson 35–36)

By staging such an act of national imagination within a novella circulating through a weekly paper, Maurice also supports Anderson's claim that newspapers can be viewed as a form of "fiction" (35). Newspapers sustain the belief also affirmed by nineteenth-century novelists when they weave lives from across a social spectrum into an overarching plot: one's national society should be imagined as a vast web of individuals simultaneously pursuing their diverse occupations and aspirations. Novels, Maurice claims in an article on "Fraternity" printed in the opening pages of *Politics for the People,* have recently nurtured the capacity of readers to imagine the worth and emotional quality of the lives of Britons from different social classes. If, in reaction to the first French Revolution, novelists championed nationalistic "English feelings" and reinforced social divisions by aiming their novels at class-specific audiences, since that time "Mr. Dickens" has emerged at "the head of a company" of novelists that "has been most earnest and pertinacious in asserting a common humanity with every dweller in St. Giles's" (3).

Dickens self-consciously advocates this formation of imagined fellowship in *Hard Times* (1854), itself published serially in *Household Words,* when—rather unrealistically—he portrays factory workers using Coketown's public library after work: "These readers . . . wondered about human nature, human passions, human hopes and fears, the struggles, triumphs and defeats, the cares and joys and sorrows, the lives and deaths, of common men and women! They, sometimes, after fifteen hours' work, sat down to read mere fables about men and women, more or less like themselves, and about children, more or less like their own" (53; ch. 8). Through Susan's and William's reading of the newspaper and their ensuing discussion, Maurice, who had himself published a novel in 1834 (*Eustace Conway*), recommends that the habits of imagination nurtured by reading novels be transferred to other columns in the periodicals in which novels were often serialized. Read as details in a novel, obituaries and birth lists become opportunities to "wonder" about the "human hopes and fears," the "lives and deaths," shared between "common men and women" of all classes.

V. READING LESSONS: EDUCATING THE NATIONAL IMAGINATION

Like Anderson, then, Maurice stresses the decisive role played by modern media, such as novels and newspapers, in forming a sense of national community. Unlike Anderson, he does not see this formation as essentially secular or secularizing. Instead, in his novella in *Politics for the People*, he promotes reading habits that can cultivate an image of a national fellowship that is waiting to be realized in Britain, and that is enacted in the worship and sacraments of the Church of England. This approach characterizes Maurice's later work, especially sermons and lectures delivered in the 1850s and 1860s to working-, middle-, and upper-class audiences, mainly in London. In these addresses, Maurice articulates what could be called a social theology of print culture and reading that is rooted in his understanding of history.

When writing about history in and after *The Kingdom of Christ* (1838), Maurice's methodological assumption was that God's providential goodness—aimed at bringing all humanity into the universal society of Christ—was to be sought in the vicissitudes of human history (Morris 67). In a short note on modern history in *Politics for the People,* Maurice claims that all "history is the record of [God's] education": in all its developments, even those reported "in the newspapers," "I think He is educating the human race, that He is educating my nation, that He is educating me" (113).

Just as, for Coleridge, ultimate moral principles must be intuitively recognized by Reason and cannot be demonstrated by experience, so for Maurice belief in God's providential and educative ordering of history must be presumed before it can be traced. In "The Divine Interpretation of History," a sermon preached in London in 1851, Maurice asserted flatly that "the student of history" must "start from the belief that there is an absolute Will to all good—an eternal Truth, a living Person—at the foundation" of the universe (*Sermons on the Sabbath-Day* 102–3). God, Maurice asserts, has always been indicating through the rise and fall of nations the universal kingdom of Christ, a kingdom governed by the law of "self-sacrifice," which "is and must be the only ground upon which human society can stand" (119). Yet as soon as "we begin to seek for light" in "the course of the world's history," he concedes, "[we] know what darkness covers" it, and the "farther we advance the thicker and heavier the mists become" (104). A prior conviction—that God is witnessing to the kingdom of Christ in which modern nations are meant to partake—is the condition of historical interpretation, rather than its clear result, and this principle must often be assumed in the face of troubling evidence. Maurice's view of history as the field of God's providence explains why he could be so adaptive, regarding workers' cooperatives and the growing addiction of Britons to periodicals as new means for realizing divinely intended fellowship—and yet so conservative, insisting that the nation's existing social orders and institutions (the aristocracy, division of capital and labor, constitutional monarchy, and Established Church) should be reformed, but were nonetheless God-ordained.

Near the end of his career, Maurice applied this view of history in his 1865 lecture "On Books," delivered to the Leicester Literary and Philosophical Society. In the lecture, he conducts a sweeping review of the history of books and reading, ranging from the ancient Library of Alexandria to Victorian novels, to demonstrate that divinely ordained disasters come upon societies "when books are more thought of than human beings; when they have accumulated, and men have been hidden" (*Friendship* 49). Although the burning of the Alexandrian Library erased many ancient works forever, Maurice argues, "the great living books" of antiquity, such as "the poems of Homer," have survived all conflagrations, demonstrating that through the fire God was purging the dross from ancient wisdom so that what remained might contribute to the light He is always shedding on the kingdom for which humanity is truly destined: "what discovers to us no truth of nature and no principle of God's government, what serves only to encourage pride and feed controversy, had better cease to exist" (49). The "law" that governed the fate of "the MSS. in the Alexandrian Library," Maurice claims, also "applies to the printed books in the Vatican or the British Museum," and books will continue to "rise and fall, live and die, by the same law in the reign of Queen Victoria as in the reign of King Alfred" (59). In the present day, Maurice concludes, as British production and consumption of print reach levels unknown in all previous societies, it remains truer than ever that books "may be light or heavy, the penny sheet or the vast folio; . . . [but] if they do not assist to make us better and more substantial men, they are only providing fuel for a fire larger, and more utterly destructive, than that which consumed the Library of the Ptolemies" (69).

As this apocalyptic conclusion suggests, Maurice in his later lectures and sermons combined confidence in divine direction of the history of reading and print media with growing fear that print culture was segregating Britons mentally and socially. In an 1858 sermon for Lincoln's Inn Chapel, he wonders if this splintering process will be inevitably accelerated by the increasing speed and reach of mass communications (thinking, perhaps, of the augmentation of print through telegraphs): "Are we to live in an age in which every mechanical facility for communication between man and man is multiplied ten-thousandfold, only that the inward isolation, the separation of those who meet continually, may be increased in a far greater measure?" (*Sermons in Lincoln's Inn* V:24). Occasionally sounding very much like today's critics of the social alienation enabled by smartphones and social media, the mature Maurice worries that immersion in a world of texts and mass communications is causing Britons to lose sight of their social relations, rendering them incapable of moral life together, even as they "meet continually" in their anonymous circulation through urban streets, stock exchanges, and factories. Taken together, Maurice's addresses of the 1850s and 1860s reveal a productive contradiction. On one hand, he is perhaps more alarmed than ever by the contribution of print culture to social fragmentation; on the other hand, he labors to detect in the very elements of print culture that he critiques signs that God is providentially moving British readers toward a sense of their national spiritual community.

Maurice's perplexing attempt to represent a centrifugal force as ultimately creating centripetal motion characterizes one of his most creative—and strained—efforts to guide an audience's reading. In 1852, a few years after the dissolution of *Politics for the People* and two before the foundation of the Working Men's College, Maurice delivered a lecture in South London "On the Use and Abuse of Newspapers." Even as Maurice criticizes newspapers for inflaming party spirit (*Friendship* 89) and threatening to destroy "our intellects and our characters" by asking us to "live [only] in the moment that is passing" (85–86), he is determined to believe that newspapers are within the providence of the God "who orders times and seasons" (93). The tremendous proliferation and influence of newspapers, he concludes, is actually a testimony to the national community they endanger: "Their diffusion is a sign that there is far more association and fellowship among the members of the community than there was of old; they are a sign that each one of us has an influence, and responsibility, which did not belong even to great men who went before us" (93).

In 1852 it was timely and political to argue for the contribution of newspapers to making "us a hearty and united nation" (94). Access to and use of newspapers was a subject of national controversy and class tension. The year before Maurice's lecture, Parliament had convened a select committee to hear arguments for and against abolition of the "taxes on knowledge"—the stamp tax, paper duty, and advertisement duty that were designed to keep the lower classes from purchasing papers (Altick 348). In addition, the class bias of the major papers was on display in January of the year Maurice gave his lecture, with *The Times* leading a charge to condemn the Amalgamated Society of Engineers for threatening to strike after their employers introduced systematic overtime and piece-work pay (Christensen 252). Probably as a result of his regular meetings with artisans from the West End, the type of workers most likely to read newspapers (Altick 342, 355), Maurice is aware that "some of my friends" in the working classes "complain that they have no newspaper which expresses their feelings, and makes known their wants" (*Friendship* 92). He reveals the middle- and upper-class composition of his audience, and his paternalistic view of the nation's "means of communication" (R. Williams, "Means" 50), when he concludes that "the working men" should not "seek for some special organ for the utterance of their own thoughts," since this will spread to working-class readers the sectarianism with which periodicals have already infected other classes (92). This remark seeks to brush to the wayside of history, or simply forget, the radical laboring-class press doggedly fighting for survival in 1852, when the once-great Chartist newspaper, *The Northern Star*, was coming to an end with the movement it supported. Maurice does appear to sanction abolition of the taxes on knowledge when he says that workers "may be sharers" in "all" the "good to be got out of the newspaper literature which exists" (93). Yet if, as advertised in the title of the talk, Maurice wishes to convert the present "abuse" of the news into a national "use," he clearly believes the middle and upper classes should control production of the news. He seems content that workers learn to use earnestly "the little time that they can give to reading," so that "five minutes of honest study" will be "worth days and weeks of flimsy newsmongering study" (85–86).

Despite these signs of typical middle-class paternalism, Maurice differs from attitudes that seem to have been widely shared when he recommends methods of reading newspapers. Although Maurice offers advice for reading leading articles, police and law reports, war correspondence, and coverage of parliamentary debates, he devotes his most creative attention to the "sheet . . . which contains the Advertisements" (72). Maurice can still speak of a single sheet or set of sheets containing a printed list of notices. Although the number of advertisements in papers began to rise sharply in the 1830s and 1840s after reductions to the advertisement tax in 1833 (R. Williams, "Advertising" 173), until spurred on by the development of "'monopoly' (corporate) capitalism" in the 1880s and 1890s (177), newspaper advertising remained "of a classified kind," restricted by cautious editors to specified sections and "still widely" regarded as undignified—a sign of inferior goods—"in many kinds of trade" (173). Recognizing that his audience expects him to "pass over" the culturally insignificant advertisement page "without notice," Maurice decides to begin with this page, and considers it more closely than any other section of the paper (72).

This is a step Coleridge would never have taken. In *Biographia Literaria,* he included advertisement reading in a list of the worst examples of the "*kill-time*" pursued by the reading masses (*BL [CC]* 1: 48–49n). Again, Maurice's greater flexibility in responding to mass media seems to proceed from a conservative source: his theological assumption that through all the contingencies of human history signs of God's divine support of Christ's kingdom can be traced. If in *The Kingdom of Christ* Maurice early acknowledged the importance of the rites of the Anglican Church in bearing witness to this universal society, in his later sermons and lectures he follows a strategy that first surfaces in *Politics for the People*. He labors to show that even the most apparently degraded, insignificant, and socially disconnected forms of exchange and communication in print culture might become means through which people habitually encounter their common humanity and membership in a national society under Christ.

Advertisements mass mediate a society of strangers, one in which the rapid exchange of things replaces relations between people. Yet, seen from the right imaginative angle, the ad page becomes an aid to reflection on the spiritual community it threatens to occlude:

> [The advertisements page] is a curious and motley assemblage; *that* at least we must feel,—a great heap and chaos of things, that are somehow helping to make up this world in which we are dwelling. Might not we stop just for a moment or two to think of that, to recollect what a number of wants and wishes are set down here, and what a number of persons are trying, each in his own way, to gratify them? (72)

"Take, for instance, the simplest case of a cook or a housemaid wanting a place": perhaps she "has a mother and sisters dependent" on her "earnings," and has applied to "one family after another," determining, "as a last resource, . . . to run the risk" and the price "of 'the paper'" (72–73). As in the newspaper reading scene in *Politics for the People,* Maurice advises his audience to treat the seemingly least personal and interesting details in a newspaper as if they were outlines for moving passages in a novel, imagining the human aspirations signified by the print-mediated exchange of commodities and services.

Reinterpreted through a novelistic imagination, the ad page becomes a unique medium of insight, a vision of a spiritual collective deeper than the print and market matrix it supports:

> If you looked down upon [London] from the top of St. Paul's, or of the Colosseum in the Regent's Park, you would not have such a panoramic view of the streets and houses as you have in a large sheet of advertisements. *There* you see the outsides of the houses and some indistinguishable figures walking about in the streets; *here* you have a glimpse into the insides of them, some little hint of what these people are walking about for, of some of the thoughts that are going on in their hearts. (73)

This sense of connection to countless lives, Maurice insists in language that anticipates Benedict Anderson's, paradoxically depends on the feeling of being one of countless "threads" in "a very complicated web" of strangers (74). Precisely because readers "do not know who these people are" behind the advertisements, in wondering about the "secret history" of an ad, they transcend "petty, prying, vulgar curiosity" about "the circumstances or the schemes of" immediate "neighbours" (73), and instead become conscious "of *some* fellow citizen, *some* fellow-creature of ours" (74).

When coupled with the novelistic effort to "[b]ring before yourselves just a few of the disappointments, and wearinesses, and temptations, that have come to some three or four out of the numbers that are stating their wants day after day" in the ads (73), readers' perception of themselves in a society of strangers might become recognition of themselves in a national community bound together by struggles that cross class boundaries and that require spiritual and moral resources transcending the products advertised. Generally in "one corner of" the advertisement page "one finds the Births, Marriages, and Deaths," the list that inspired William's and Susan's debate in *Politics for the People,* and that might become for readers a "memorial of the people we never saw or heard of set before us day after day, in the midst of all these homes and shops, these chairs and tables and millinery" (75). Making their way through the most apparently dull and impersonal section of the paper in this manner, readers might conclude that "we are not" simply "threads" in a web, that "we are" not "parts of a puzzle" that "might fit each into the other if each that has need of something could just find out the other who has that something to supply." They might feel instead "that we are human beings, with all kinds of sorrows and joys, and contradictions and sins, . . . with the sense of having something very great, and mysterious, and immortal, about us" (74). The advertisement page can mediate to reflective readers an intuition of the body of Christ, the "something very great, and immortal" within "human beings" whose individual "sorrows and joys" reflect a common "contradiction" of aspiration and degradation. "There must be something else than" the circulation of goods, or the circulation of ad sheets promoting them, "to bind us together, and make us live together and work together, as men are meant to do" (74). Maurice here proposes a sacramental understanding of media and print culture, with newspaper advertisements pointing to the communion ultimately signified and enacted, for him, in the Eucharist.

To suggest that the national imagination facilitated by mass media arises at the expense of religious imagined community, Benedict Anderson quotes Hegel as saying "newspapers serve modern man as a substitute for morning prayers" (35). Maurice lands near this remark, but out of essentially theological convictions and in the hope of a religious national community. Every opening of the morning paper, he might say, could become a national prayer breakfast.

VI. CONCLUSION: ILLUMINATING CONTRADICTIONS

Maurice ultimately produces a social theology of media, reading, and national community, attributing an almost sacramental role to print culture in the providential awakening of Britons to their national spiritual unity. Yet Maurice's theology of media is sustained by contradictions. Without wavering in his faith in the Anglican Church as God's providential agent for forming Britain into a united spiritual community, Maurice tacitly concedes that the sense of spiritual fellowship formed in churches and chapels must now also, and perhaps primarily, be cultivated in mental spaces imagined through the printed page. Maurice elaborates his vision of national community, then, through a creative response to the very print culture that seems to challenge his fundamental premises. He also, as a result of his paternalistic assumption that workers were unable to share ownership of the means of communication or envision their place in the national community without supervision, replicates the imagination of community through exclusion and misrepresentation that he condemns throughout his career.

In an 1863 address to artisans and clerks (J. F. C. Harrison 3–4) at his Working Men's College, Maurice exposes the contradictions inherent in his theology of media and national community, even as he demonstrates the degree to which his vision continued to be informed by Coleridge's ideal of a spiritual republic of letters. Maurice compares two ways of thinking about learning, acquisition and illumination. Warning against the "acquisition" view, which associates knowledge with property, inheritance, capital and—therefore—the exclusive rights of the privileged, Maurice advocates for the Coleridgean view that true knowledge is "light," illumination.

> If knowledge comes to us as light comes to us, it can never be third-hand or second-hand knowledge. The sun is very, very old; but he is new to me every time I welcome him . . . And again, it does not in the least interfere with the illumination which I receive from him, that tens of thousands of others are illuminated by him at the same instant . . . [A]s to imparting or diffusing it, what I can do in that way is to invite all I know to leave their close houses and enjoy it with me; or to let it into their houses when that is possible. (*Friendship* 260–1)

Likening the "imparting or diffusing" of knowledge to a light that illuminates "tens of thousands . . . at the same instant" as they voluntarily "let it into their houses," Maurice seems to naturalize, and transform into an instrument of God (who is symbolized by "the sun"), the "mechanical facility for communication" that he had feared would accelerate the sectarianism and isolation of Britons in the 1858 sermon mentioned earlier (*Sermons in Lincoln's Inn* V:24). Underpinning Maurice's confidence that not only the classes in the Working Men's College but also the "diffusion" of print outside its walls might communicate such light is his Coleridgean assumption that "the Eternal and Infinite . . . discovers Himself [to us], and in discovering Himself helps us to see what we are, what our relations to our fellow-creatures are, what we are to seek, and what we are to hate" (*Friendship* 273). The media forms Maurice so often regards as centrifugal forces might in fact be God's means of drawing the nation together. Furthermore, Maurice's portrayal of learning—as the reception of light— might tacitly reinforce a paternalistic model of knowledge. Working people are on the receiving and internalizing, but not the producing, end of the communication system.

Maurice's formation of the Working Men's College (1854) demonstrates how distant his vision could be from those he was striving to inspire with a sense of their membership in a national community held together by

Christ. For Maurice, the College, firmly separating itself from all sectarian parties in the debate about national education, was ultimately meant to help working men see their "common interest" with other classes in "a Son of Man" (*Learning and Working* viii). Maurice hoped to instill in workers the belief "that the order of society, like the order of nature, was not created by us for our convenience . . . ; that we are all its subjects; that it asserts itself; that it avenges itself; that we are humbly and devoutly to ask what its demands of us are, and whence we can obtain the power for fulfilling them" (117).

Taught from this perspective, Maurice believed, classes in history, literature, political science, and ethics would counteract the idea widespread among some proponents of national education "that poor people were sent into the world to work for *them*, and that all which had to be considered was, how they might be made into the handiest tools" (*Learning and Working* 9). Resisting the tendency of Mechanics' Institutes to restrict working people's education to knowledge deemed useful for their labor and social advancement, Maurice asked whether because "our works are so much greater than those of our forefathers, we must be content that our men should be less intelligent, less human" (46). All subjects should be tested by their capacity to "make men know that they are persons" and not things (121), rather than the principle spreading like a "disease" through society that "the acquisition and the accumulation of" money "is the purpose for which men are to live and die" (87).

Ironically, the very subjects in which Maurice and his fellow founders placed greatest hope—history, literature, law, and politics—were those least attended by workers when the College opened: instead manual laborers attended those classes, such as mathematics and grammar, that they felt would advance their socioeconomic positions, and this pattern remained constant throughout Maurice's presidency of the College (J. F. C. Harrison 58–62). Once again, in trying to educate working people about their membership in Britain's spiritual community, Maurice seems to have replaced those he sought to help with his own image of them. Without any apparent sense of irony, in the lectures delivered to support the College, he had claimed that there was nothing in factory work that was in itself "unfavourable to . . . learning," and that it might even "be a vast advantage" (*Learning and Working* 76), since "factories" were among the "gifts of God," part of the providential orchestration of Christ's kingdom in Britain (100).

Although often contradictory in theory, and sometimes fruitless in practice, Maurice's efforts to help his contemporaries imagine their national spiritual community are illuminating. They anticipate more recent studies of nationalism by indicating how greatly modern national imagination depends on media; they also suggest how conflicted and indirect the relationship can be between experiments in promoting media-based national and religious consciousness and the ways people and groups actually imagine and practice community. Most importantly for the argument of this book, Maurice, in promoting Britain's spiritual collective, seems to have devoted so much attention to how readers consumed print—and how they might be taught to consume it—precisely because he, for all his desire to do so, could not correlate popular national consciousness with any single existing religious institution. Accounts of reading and efforts to induce practices of reading, Maurice encourages us to think, were a central means by which nineteenth-century authors and educators conceived and tried to spread the image of a coherent spiritual community for a nation increasingly and obviously divided between class interests and a multiplicity of religious—predominantly Christian—allegiances. That Maurice himself, for theological reasons, might have wished to underemphasize the mediated construction of national imagination makes his lifelong analysis of this process all the more compelling.

CHAPTER 3

ARNOLD'S POETIC NATIONAL CHURCH

Anarchy and the Charming Force of Poetry

In the last two chapters, I have examined efforts by Samuel Taylor Coleridge and one of his most creative disciples, the theologian Frederick Denison Maurice, to envision and enable a national print-mediated spiritual community. Working after the collapse of the eighteenth-century ideal of a rational, egalitarian republic of letters (see the introduction and chapter 1), Coleridge and Maurice did not think readers and writers recognized universal standards for the "public use of their reason" in the kind of rational-critical debate Habermas has associated with the ideal of the public sphere (Habermas 27).[1] Coleridge and Maurice instead located the source of consensus in the witness of the conscience to permanent truths about God and humanity, which each Briton could recognize through reflective reading. They each hoped for a united Christian community under the aegis of a tolerant Anglican Church. Yet both reluctantly concluded that British citizens would ultimately awaken to their spiritual unity through reading rather than the services of the Church of England and its competitors. This recognition, even if sometimes avoided or refuted in their

---

1. As Michael Warner points out, Habermas never pretends that this ideal of public reason was actually realized in print culture or discussions in coffeehouses and taverns, or that there ever existed a "unitary public" by which it could be practiced; instead Habermas treats it as an "imaginary" ideal (Warner, *Publics and Counterpublics* 55), which, although containing "emancipatory potential," was contradicted by the very "organization" and "ideology" of "bourgeois society" (46).

explicit arguments, propels Coleridge's and Maurice's most creative and idealistic attempts to guide British readers' interpretations of their mass-mediated world.

In the second half of this book, I turn from nineteenth-century apologists for a spiritually reformed republic of letters, such as Coleridge and Maurice, to a range of poets and commentators who imagined national congregations formed by the private reading of widely circulating poetry, beginning with the creation and reception of *The Christian Year* (1827) by the Anglican priest and poet John Keble. Any discussion of connections between poetry, religion, and national imagination in nineteenth-century Britain immediately calls to mind Matthew Arnold, popularly misremembered as prophesying that poetry would replace institutional Christianity as the source of modern social unity and character formation. Arnold is also frequently linked to Coleridge and Maurice in a line of Anglican thought that Victorian commentators labeled "Broad Church" by the middle of the century, and which included a very "broad" range of individuals who advocated for religious tolerance and a liberal attitude toward modern learning within the Church of England.

In this chapter, I claim that these ways of categorizing Arnold's stance on poetry and religion—as a program for setting up literature in place of religion, or as part of a "Broad Church" movement—should be tempered by another. Arnold can be grouped with Coleridge and Maurice as a more heterodox, but no less earnest, apologist for the transformation of Britain's print network into a medium through which readers of all classes and ideologies could imagine themselves in a Christian community spanning the nation. This way of putting Arnold, Maurice, and Coleridge into dialogue, I think, better illustrates their common concerns than a "Broad Church" label that was invented after Coleridge's lifetime (T. Jones 205), that Maurice rejected along with all party labels (*Life* 1:239), and that Arnold earned less for the ultimate drift of his religious prose than for points of agreement between his views of Church-State relations and those of his father, Dr. Thomas Arnold, and his friend, A. P. Stanley (T. Jones 248, 281). Theologically, Coleridge and Maurice have many points in common; they share few with Arnold. Yet all three share anxiety over the swift expansion of print culture and of non-elite reading audiences, and the support these developments seemingly lent to sectarianism, class tensions, and the decline of the Anglican Church's political and social influence. In response, they all variously envision establishing, through reading, an imagined national Christian community in the minds of Britons.

After *Culture and Anarchy* (1869), Arnold developed his program for "culture" by arguing for reformed yet strengthened national commitment to the Bible and worship services of the Church of England—not as repositories of doctrine, but as shared forms of ethical "poetic" language capable of binding together the British reading public in an emerging mass-mediated democracy. Less obviously, he also appropriated for this cultural project the theological authority of the orthodoxy he challenged. Denying inspired authority to the Bible or the Church, he transferred it to men of culture who were to discern the operation of the laws of perfection; determine the poetic forms and public rituals by which these laws would be honored or dishonored; and, occasionally, sanction state coercion to help Britons slough off their class-bound identities and uncover their "best selves."

I. THE REPLACEMENT THEORY, ANARCHY, AND ARNOLD'S POETIC NATIONAL CHURCH

"Most of what now passes with us for religion and philosophy will be replaced by poetry" (CPW IX:161–62).[2] So proclaimed Matthew Arnold in an essay, later retitled "The Study of Poetry," introducing the influential anthology *The English Poets* (1880). Ignoring the qualifiers in Arnold's statement, later commentators have often transformed it into a prophecy that poetry and its academic study would replace institutional religion in modern society. So firmly associated is this idea with Arnold that it has recently been dubbed "the Arnoldian replacement theory" (Kaufmann 616). This caricature of Arnold's ideas was useful to apologists for the study of English literature in the 1920s and 1930s, including members of the 1921 Newbolt Committee, who promoted English poetry as a means of spiritual grace and national unity (Mathieson 69–77), and literary critics such as F. R. Leavis, who touted literature (particularly poetry) as a humanistic antidote to the evils of industrial mass society (Eagleton 27–29). Arguments for or against the validity of a so-called "Arnoldian replacement theory" therefore risk perpetuating a misinterpretation of Arnold's views bound up with self-justifying narratives about the value of academic literary study and criticism (Kaufmann 614–24).

---

2. All quotations of Arnold's prose are from *The Complete Prose Works* and are cited in the text in the following format: (CPW volume: page).

Yet Arnold, in "The Study of Poetry," does not say that "religion" in general will be replaced by poetry, but "most of what now passes with us for religion," or Christianity as it was then popularly understood: a metaphysical system of "dogma[s]," such as the divinity of Jesus, that is supported by miraculous "evidences," such as the resurrection (CPW IX:161–62). In the 1870s and 1880s, Arnold argued that this form of Christianity would vanish before the advance of modern knowledge, and that the Bible and Christian worship should be retained as "poetry." Although Arnold did promote biblical writings, such as Isaiah, which were originally composed as poetry in the sense of writing distinguished from prose, when describing the Bible and liturgy as "poetic" he has in mind a more general sense of beauty and emotional power. As Arnold asserts in *Literature and Dogma* (1873), the old forms of Christian worship and the Bible use "literary, not scientific language; language *thrown out* at an object of consciousness not fully grasped, which inspired emotion" (CPW VI:189). This "language of figure and feeling" is better equipped than that of "literal fact and science" (VI:189) for grasping human beings' deepest experiences of a transcendent force for good at work in them and the world, popularly called "God" (Livingston 90–94).

Arnold therefore advocated transforming the Church of England into a national mediator of a shared "poetic" language that was best suited to inspire ethical self-formation and a harmonious collective life. He was compelled to advance a central role for the Church of England in British national imagination at the moment when that Church had lost most of its privileged ties to the British state, and when the mass reading nation imagined (and feared) by middle- and upper-class writers throughout the century seemed immediately in view. William McKelvy aptly summarizes the process by which the Church of England had, by the early 1870s and especially by 1880, lost most of its exclusive connections to education and public life: "In the 1760s, conformity with Anglican doctrine (expressed by the Thirty-Nine Articles) was deeply involved in civic rights and access to national institutions ranging from municipal and government offices to the ancient English universities and the primary professions; by the 1880s, (non)conformity with those same doctrines had negligible consequences" (*English Cult of Literature* 29).[3]

By 1867 for urban areas, and by 1884 for the rest of Britain, the franchise had been extended to males in the lower middle classes and a sizeable

---

3. See my introduction for a brief review of the legal changes that stripped the Church of England of most of its official influence over British political, social, and intellectual life by 1871.

portion of those in the laboring classes,[4] both of which tended to gravitate to Nonconformity (McLeod *Religion and Society* 24, 35–37, 62–63). The price of many newspapers and periodicals steadily fell and their circulation widened after the repeal of the last of the "taxes on knowledge" in 1861, reaching more artisans and members of the working classes (Altick 354–64). Provision for national elementary education across England and Wales was established after 1870, becoming compulsory through age ten by 1880 (Lawson and Silver 314, 322).[5] Britain had become a functionally non-confessional state presiding over an expanding reading nation that seemed increasingly pluralistic in religious allegiances after a century of inter-Christian battles in print and politics, and whose future public opinion and policy promised to be determined by the middle and lower classes. As an Inspector of Schools since 1851, Oxford Professor of Poetry from 1857–67, and regular commentator on national education and Church-State relations by the 1860s, Arnold kept in close touch with these developments. Although he supported secular, state-funded education, Arnold felt the central dilemma of the 1870s and 1880s was how the English Bible and a national Church were to become forces of moral and emotional unity at a moment when an enfranchised nation of readers was on the horizon, and when religion seemed more than ever a matter of public debate and individual consumption in a competitive print market.

The chief agents of anarchy, for Arnold, were middle-class evangelicals, especially Nonconformists. In *Culture and Anarchy,* Arnold (in)famously warned of middle-class Dissenters' dangerous combination of anti-intellectual moralism, or "Puritan . . . Hebraising," with blind faith in individualism and economic gain, or "Philistinism" (CPW V:243). Arnold was anxious about the immense "machinery of ideas and agencies by which . . . evangelical piety dominated" Victorian "public culture" (C. Brown 36), particularly the vast media industry fueled by Nonconformists such as Edward Miall, who ran the disestablishmentarian *Nonconformist* news-

---

4. The 1867 Reform Act nearly doubled the electorate in England and Wales, adding another 938,000 voters to the existing 1,056,000, and giving "working class voters in the towns a majority whilst most of the new country voters were members of the middle class" (Hostettler 282); an extension of the 1867 provision (all householders, lodgers, and occupiers paying £10 rent/year) in the 1884 bill and 1885 Redistribution Act enfranchised most agricultural laborers, tripling the electorate (Everett). Yet the distribution of votes was unequal across the United Kingdom: after the 1884 Reform Act, 2 in 3 men in England and Wales could vote, 3 in 5 in Scotland, and only 1 in 2 in Ireland (Cook 68).

5. In 1872, Scotland anticipated the 1880 Elementary Education Act by more thoroughly bringing elementary education under state boards and making attendance compulsory (Lawson and Silver 322).

paper, and after whom Arnold coined the term *"Mialism"* to describe the highly politicized and publicized form of Dissent he felt most threatened Britain's stability and progress.

As a result of their moralism and sectarian politics, Arnold contended, the middle classes were failing to win influence over the lower classes who would soon determine Britain's democratic future. Most distressingly, the Puritans' "unlovely present[ation] of Christian dogma and practices" was driving "the lower classes" from "Christianity" (CPW IX:154). Arnold shared with most Victorian middle-class commentators an exaggerated fear of widespread working-class disaffection from Christianity (McLeod, *Religion and Irreligion* 36; *Religion and Society* 6–7), which would allegedly deprive the working classes of their best guide to "conduct," and so fuel their hasty pursuit of self-interest through riot and revolution (CPW VI:362–63). *Literature and Dogma* (1873), Arnold's best-selling work in the nineteenth century, issues a warning: "This is what everyone sees to constitute the special moral feature of our times: *the masses* are losing the Bible and its religion . . . This promises, certainly, if it does not already constitute, a very unsettled condition of things" (VI:362–63). In his religious prose, Arnold identifies three elements that combine to create this "unsettled condition": an Anglican Church whose clergy preach submission to the wealthy elite (CPW VIII:71); a "Puritan" middle class whose sectarianism and moralism are dominating print culture and politics; and an expanding readership of enfranchised artisans who, under the influence of secularist publicists such as Charles Bradlaugh (VI:148), are preparing to throw off restraining allegiances to the Bible and Christianity.

The antidote Arnold proposed to anarchy was transformation of the middle classes into a force that would supply "an ideal to ennoble the spirit of the nation and keep it together" (CPW II:25). A primary medium for this transformation, Arnold preached with increasing determination after becoming a school inspector in 1851, was well-rounded, humanistic, and state-supported education, eventually extended equally to all, but at first running through secondary school for the middle classes and primary school for the working classes. In language borrowed from the Puritans he sought to convert, Arnold hoped this education would bring about a new birth in individuals, causing them to die to their "old, untransformed self" limited to "the ideas and wishes of the class to which" they belonged, and raising them into their *"best self "* (CPW V:134–35) whose qualities Arnold identified with "culture," or "the ideal of a human nature harmoniously perfect in all points" (V:188). This combination of moral conviction, intellectual flexibility, and love of beauty would be created only by "the disinterested and active use of reading, reflection, and observation" (CPW VI:204). Arnold, of course, entrusted secular poetry with a major role in this process of formation, arguing in his reports to the Education Department for its power to "elevate and humanize" working-class children (*Reports on Schools* 17). As he puts it in "The Study of Poetry" for a middle-class reading audience, lines from great poetry should be internalized "to interpret life for us, to console us, to sustain us" in ways that rise above dogmatic controversies and sectarian politics (CPW IX:161).

Yet Arnold campaigned with equal intensity in the 1870s and 1880s for an inclusive state Church that would lead the nation's divided population in rehearsals of Christianity as a unifying, morally transformative body of poetic language and ritual. Dissenters and the working classes had to be persuaded to embrace the established Church, reconceived not as a Society for the Promotion of Christian Knowledge, but as "a great national society for the promotion of what is commonly called *goodness*" (CPW VIII:65). In the words of "The Study of Poetry," Arnold felt the "strongest part of our religion to-day is its unconscious poetry" (IX:161). St. Paul's language about death to sin and resurrection, for example, had been distorted into rigid Protestant formulas about atonement and justification by faith, obscuring its nature as imagistic, emotional language that conveyed—and could in turn motivate—the struggle of conforming to Christ as humanity's ideal ethical exemplar (Livingston 163–64). Recovered consciously *as* "poetic" language, as passionate and approximate rather than propositional language, the words of the Bible and the liturgy could fulfill more powerfully and widely the goal Arnold set for poetry written by Wordsworth and Milton—that of "form[ing] the soul and character" by "suggest[ing] . . . high and noble principles of action" and "inspir[ing] the emotion so helpful in making these principles operative" (*Reports on Schools* 200–201). Arnold therefore likened a Church of England clergyman "to a school inspector" and "public functionary" (CPW VI:129). Performing the ethical poetic language of the Bible and liturgy in a future national Church tolerant enough to win back and temper the Dissenters, Anglican ministers would call citizens to die to their ordinary selves and enter "into one harmonious and truly humane life" as a nation (CPW IX:6). In the 1870s and 1880s, Arnold repeatedly justifies his more familiar advocacy of secular culture and national literary education as aids to the larger project of promoting the rise of a reformed and public Christianity:

> I am persuaded that the transformation of religion, which is essential for its perpetuance, can be accomplished only by carrying the qualities of flexibility, perceptiveness, and judgment, which are the best fruits of letters,

to whole classes of the community which know next to nothing of them, and by procuring the application of those qualities to matters [of religion] where they are never applied now. (VIII:149)

Arnold, then, outlined a theologically "demystified" version of Coleridge's program for the clerisy discussed in chapter 1: the establishment of a national Church and public humanistic education system that could direct and synthesize the reading and reflection of an increasingly democratic, differentiated, and pluralistic reading nation. Alongside these institutions, and incrementally expanded by them, would labor a cultural and moral "righteous remnant" of every class distinct from the "unsound" majority, its members "placed at many points, and operating in many directions" to purify, leaven, and "reform" the "State" and its "community" (X:149).

Measured against political philosopher Charles Taylor's concept of "the immanent frame," Arnold's program for reading and a poetic National Church can be seen as a strategy for adapting to emerging conditions of social imagination and public life in the modern North Atlantic world. Medieval Western Christendom distinguished sharply between "secular," or immanent, this-worldly affairs and the Church's "religious" institutions and disciplines aimed at the transcendent reality of God and eternity. Taylor argues that this distinction paved the way for a gradual reversal of emphasis after the seventeenth century, according to which "the 'lower,' immanent or secular, order is all that there is," with the "first unambiguous assertion of the self-sufficiency of the secular" coming in the radical phases of the French Revolution ("Western Secularity" 33–34). Taylor portrays rising insistence on the self-sufficiency of the secular order as the formation of an "immanent frame," a sense of the world as working of itself and impersonally ordered without reference to God or a transcendent realm. Fitted to the immanent frame is the modern "buffered self," a selfhood imagined to generate meaning and purpose within the individual mind, which is strongly "buffered"—or barricaded, and so potentially disengaged—from an "outside" world, understood to operate by "merely" physical cause-and-effect (*A Secular Age* 35–42). Rather than fitting into cosmically mandated social orders, modern buffered individuals are imagined to act instrumentally and rationally within the immanent frame to construct "societies designed for mutual benefit" according to supposedly natural social "laws" (542).

In conformity with the immanent frame, Arnold could in 1877 summarize his position as the defense of "the natural truth of Christianity" (CPW VIII:153). Christianity rests upon "a law of things which is found in conscience, and which is an indication, irrespective of our arbitrary wish and fancy, of what we ought to do" (CPW VI:190). Like the natural laws of society and individual rights, the law of conduct is a fact of immanent experience, what Arnold calls its "scientific" or "experimental" basis (Livingston 99–104). Within this experience of moral law is God, or as Arnold puts it, "the Eternal Power, not ourselves, that makes for righteousness" (CPW VI:373). That definition comes from *Literature and Dogma*, where Arnold offers a more impersonal version for the scientifically minded, "*the stream of tendency by which all things seek to fulfill the law of their being*" (VI:189). Properly interpreted, the Bible and forms of Christian worship will cease to catalyze sectarian warfare and instead acquire for Britons "the force and charm of poetry" (VIII:334)—a sentimental magic capable of binding the modern buffered self to an inwardly experienced eternal power for good, without obvious recourse to supernatural authority or dogmas that challenge the bounds of the immanent frame. Aided by "poetic" language and ritual, individuals will emotionally grasp and enter, for their own and society's good, Jesus' "method" of inward reflection and "secret" of death to egoistic impulse, by which cooperation with the moral stream of tendency is achieved in a spirit of tolerant "sweet reasonableness" (300).

Arnold's strategy for defending Christianity's experiential authority through its poetic language and forms ultimately participates in a liberal vision of religion's proper contribution to social morality within the immanent frame:

> [In this view] the essential impact of good religion takes place *in foro interno:* on one hand, it generates the right moral motivation; on the other, by remaining within the mind and soul of the subject, it refrains from challenging the external order. So pubic ritual can be an essential element of this "rational" religion only if it can help by celebrating public order or by stimulating inner moral motivation. (Taylor, "Western Secularity" 35)

Arnold, with his stress on poetic language as the natural medium of religion and moral truth, and his defense of a Church-State establishment, does not tidily fit into this rational liberalism. Yet his literary interpretation of the Bible and liturgy ultimately point in much the same direction, prioritizing inward effect and displays of public order. Since Arnold's vision of the English Church is functional rather than doctrinal, he can often claim, as in *St. Paul and Protestantism* (1870), that it must first achieve "the union of Protestants" in "England," but then expand to "comprehend Roman Catholics" (CPW VI:107). With "formularies" that poetically express Christianity's moral "truth . . . so as to suit and unite the English nation," the "Church of England" stands to exert its greatest initial attraction at home (VIII:94). Yet it might be coordinated with a "purged" form "of Catholicism" in Ireland (VIII:334), and, until a more comprehensive unity becomes possible, with Presbyterianism in the established Church of Scotland (VIII:344)—and, just possibly, an Established Church of Wales (Murray 347).

Arnold's vision of a poetic National Church is centered on England, with his treatments of Ireland, Scotland, and Wales often arising as necessary afterthoughts in reaction to religious and political strife that threatens English supervision over the British archipelago. He never theorizes how the various church establishments he imagines really are to cooperate in promoting an imagined community for British readers. Furthermore, his argument for unity within England under the Church of England ultimately rests on almost magical faith in its poetic forms to charm Dissenters and workers back into the fold. In the next section, I turn to the influences upon, and power dynamics within, Arnold's faith in the charm of Anglican poetics.

II. KEBLE'S GODSON AND THE POETIC DISCIPLINES OF THE CHURCH OF ENGLAND

Arnold's faith in the forms of Anglicanism to unify English Protestants, and eventually contribute to the unity of the British reading nation, curiously extends the views of poetry and religion held by John Keble, Arnold's godfather and predecessor as Oxford Professor of Poetry, and the Anglican priest and poet to whom my next chapter is devoted. Keble and other Tractarians set the terms for widely circulating discussions of poetic and religious form throughout the century. For the Tractarians, poetry did not "supplant . . . religious worship, but . . . religious worship and devotion in all its forms was frequently read as poetry" (Blair, *Form and Faith* 35), with these poetic qualities providing a "precondition for expression" of faith and "an embodiment of God's law and order at work" (36–37). By the middle of the century, this widely diffused High Church discourse had helped to give a broad "cultural significance" to "Anglican ritual . . . and its creation of communal, national identity" (86), an environment in which "the impact of the renewed engagement with religious form in Anglicanism was inescapable" (122).

Arnold strongly disapproved of the reverence for patristic doctrine, priestly authority, and sacramental theology among Tractarians and the High Church movement they inspired. He also resisted High Church "insistence on retaining the controversial forms of the Book of Common Prayer," such as the rubric for the burial service and the Athanasian Creed, "without alteration" (Blair, *Form and Faith* 130). For this reason, earlier commentators have tended to portray Arnold's views of poetry and religion in stark "contrast" with Keble's (apRoberts 68n), tracing the main influence on Arnold's ideas to German Historicism and its treatment of religion as myth (216–38). Yet Arnold owes a discernable debt to High Church poetics in his promotion of the Anglican liturgy and English Bible as powerful poetic means of disciplining the imaginations and emotions of English readers. If Arnold's theological relationship to a coherent "Broad Church" party is tenuous, he and figures such as F. D. Maurice, Benjamin Jowett, and Arthur Stanley share vulnerability to the charms of High Church poetics (Blair, *Form and Faith* 171–73). Works by all these figures evince tension between varieties of "liberal ecumenicism and . . . a strong belief in the efficacy and affective power of the time-honoured, traditional, repetitive forms of Christianity in general and the Church of England in particular" (176).

Tractarians and High Churchmen "tended to emphasize the identity of worship with poetry, as a regulated and repetitive form capable of creating heightened emotional effects" (Blair, *Form and Faith* 87). Similarly, Arnold prioritizes Anglican forms out of his belief that their regularity and familiarity enable them to discipline and raise the emotions of worshippers. In "A Psychological Parallel" (1876), Arnold denounces "all radical change in the Prayer Book" on the grounds that its language "has created sentiments deeper than we can see or measure. Our feeling does not connect itself with *any* language about righteousness and religion, but with *that* language" (VIII:135). As Keble's godson, Arnold was taught to repeat lyrics from Keble's *The Christian Year,* and Keble's emphasis on adherence to a steady rhythm is evident in Arnold's own work (Blair, *Culture of the Heart* 166). Daniel Kline has demonstrated the impact of *The Christian Year* on Arnold's juvenilia, as well as the commitment to reserved expression through regular poetic form that Arnold seems to have imbibed from his year at Winchester Grammar School in 1836 (151), and from his exposure to Keble's essays on poetry (148, 152–54).

Arnold's personal attachment to Anglican forms of worship and devotion seems to have been so great that he persuaded himself they could reassert their binding force upon all Englishmen (and, eventually, all Britons). As late as 1883, in his lecture on "Emerson" during his tour of America, Arnold famously recalled the impression made upon him by Newman's preaching when he was an undergraduate at Oxford: "he seemed about to transform and to renew what was for us the most national and natural institution in the world, the Church of England. Who could resist the charm of that spiritual apparition, . . . in the most entrancing of voices, breaking the silence with words and thoughts which were a religious music,—subtle, sweet, mournful?" (X:166). Paired with his recollections of the "daily worship and prayer" at Littlemore to which Newman welcomed undergraduates (X:166), Arnold's nostalgic portrait of Newman is suffused with longing for the familiar forms, the spoken "religious music,"[6] with which he still seems to connect "the most national and natural institution in the world, the Church of England." Arnold himself not only regularly attended church but also used the Prayer Book as a guide for personal reflection throughout his life. Shortly after completing *Culture and Anarchy* as a book, and while meditating on the direction of his future work as well as the recent death of his son Tommy, Arnold wrote a letter to his mother. His sense of purpose arises largely from the alignment he discovers between events in his life and the reading directions of the Prayer Book:

> Tommy's death in particular was associated with several awakening and epoch-making things. The chapter for the day of his death was that great chapter, the 1st of Isaiah [where Isaiah laments Israel's misunderstanding of religion and predicts a saving remnant]; the first Sunday after his death was Advent Sunday, with its glorious collect ['Put upon us the armour of light, now in the time of this mortal life'], and in the Epistle the passage which converted St. Augustine [Rom. 13:8: 'Owe no man anything but to love one another: for he that loveth another hath fulfilled the law.']. All these things point to a new beginning . . . (*Letters* III:305)

Through the Prayer Book's structuring of his emotions and his personal application of scriptural and liturgical texts, Arnold comes to see himself as

---

6. Pointedly, Arnold turns Newman's *speaking* voice into a "religious music," in keeping with the disdain he always held for popular hymn singing, and perhaps suggesting his support of the plainsong that the High Church revival had (controversially) helped make familiar to many Victorian Anglican worshippers (Blair, *Form and Faith* 96–101, 115).

a latter-day Isaiah who must put on the armor of cultural light in his fight to rescue religion from its popular misunderstanding (Isaiah 1 and the collect) and inspire a saving remnant to give it "a new beginning" in Britain as a force for national ethical life (Romans 13:8).[7]

Arnold might be seen as a heterodox and selective inheritor of High Church poetics at a late stage in the evolution of the reading nation. He remains guided by a sense of poetry as at once highly emotional and formally regular and regularizing, and of religious forms as broadly "poetic" in this sense. Arnold's persistent defense of firm classical structures in secular poetry was arguably influenced by Keble's championship of restrained and regular poetic form (Kline 155), and it dovetails with his later apology for the regularity and solemnity of Anglican liturgy. Arnold's classicism and support of Anglican forms appear to be partially motivated by the desire to retrain social dissent and unrest. In this again Arnold's commitment to poetic and religious forms resembles that of Tractarian and High Church authors. A central text of the early Oxford Movement was Hurrell Froude's *Remains* (1838), a posthumous collection of letters and journals edited by Newman and Keble. In it, Froude compares social customs to liturgical forms:

> I consider that, if the forms of *society* are calculated to make each individual feel his proper place with reference to others, and to help us in acting right in this relation,—it cannot be absurd to keep up *religious* ceremonies, which may be witnesses to us of the presence of the great King, and of the way of acting and thinking which suits our relation to him. (qtd. in Blair, *Form and Faith* 26)

For Froude, social traditions enforcing class distinction are analogous to inherited liturgical forms in that they both induce proper humility before a superior (God, aristocrats). Nicholas Murray provides a telling summary of similar tendencies in Arnold's thinking about poetic form and social order:

> Just as in his social and cultural criticism he would seek to impose a centralising narrative of coherence and a firm cultural authority on the 'multitudinousness' of mid-Victorian England, so in his aesthetic theory he was [even by 1848] firmly convinced of the need for a classical architecture in the poem to counter its tendency to run riot, to glut itself on the richness of local detail. (89)

---

7. I draw from Ruth apRoberts' excellent discussion of this letter, 176–77.

Murray's metaphor—"tendency to run riot"—nicely captures the slippage between Arnold's abhorrence of political enthusiasm that runs riot in the streets and his disgust at supposedly riotous expressions in poetry and worship, evident in his condemnations of dissenting hymns such as Wesley's "My God, I Am Thine" in *Literature and Dogma* (1873) (VI:191). The last great Chartist demonstrations of 1848, which Arnold worriedly observed while working in London as a young man (*Letters* 1:101; A. Harrison 9–11), early impressed into his imagination a vision of Britain threatened with self-destruction by its unruly working classes. Twenty years later in *Culture and Anarchy,* Arnold warns that the fever for "doing as one likes," the worship of individualism in a *laissez-faire* society, has spread beyond the middle-class Philistines and infected "immense numbers" of the laboring classes, whose passion for pursuing self-interest through mass agitation will "increase . . . anarchy and social disintegration" (CPW V:123). Arnold began work on lectures that would become *Culture and Anarchy* only a year after witnessing the 1866 suffrage demonstrations that erupted into public vandalism in Hyde Park and Chester Square (Honan 341). In a passage from the original conclusion to *Culture and Anarchy,* judiciously removed in the second edition, Arnold prefaces his condemnation of "monster-processions in the streets and forcible irruptions into the parks" by praising a remark in one of his father's early letters (V:223): "'As for rioting, the old Roman way of dealing with *that* is always the right one; flog the rank and file, and fling the ringleaders from the Tarpeian Rock!'" (V:526). The Tractarian Tory Hurrell Froude lends support to an almost neo-feudal order, while Arnold envisions an ultimately democratic and tolerant society. Yet in pursuing their divergent social ideals, both seek in religious poetics an analogy for the formal restraints needed to regulate, and suppress, multitudinous emotion in individuals and in the nation.

III. THE BINDING POWER OF THE ENGLISH BIBLE

Arnold's unorthodox High Church poetics are central to his campaign against anarchy in an increasingly media-saturated and polarized Britain. Beginning with *St. Paul and Protestantism* (1870), Arnold points to "Puritan" *sola scriptura* hermeneutics as the greatest obstacle to a united British Christian community. Narrowly committed to *sola scriptura,* Dissenters have ignored the Bible's literary and historical qualities, transforming it into a proof text in which they discover confirmation of their own favorite doctrines, such as justification by faith alone. The result, as Arnold puts it in *St. Paul and Protestantism,* is "a machinery of covenants, conditions, bargains, and parties-contractors, such as could have proceeded from no one but the born . . . man of business, British or American" (CPW VI:14). Agreement with these doctrines has become for Nonconformists the "biblical" basis for joining or protesting the established Church, a situation exacerbated by related treatment of the Bible as a policy book for "church-polity and church-management" (VI:122). Since a hierarchy of bishops, a State-Church establishment, infant baptism, and priestly vestments are not prescribed in the New Testament (96, 114), *sola scriptura* hermeneutics empower widely publicized demands by Dissenting MPs and papers such as *The Nonconformist* "that the State . . . frame its legislation" in ways that avoid favoring the Church of England (116). The result, in Arnold's view, is a cycle of inter-Christian print battles that repulse the skeptical working classes and prevent the middle classes from assuming the role Arnold believes is theirs: to lead the way in appropriating the Bible as a shared "poetic" language that can inspire Britons to rise from class-based identities into tolerant, better selves in a shared national Church founded on supposedly natural Christian ethical truths.

St. Paul and Protestantism (1870) and *Literature and Dogma* (1873) were and remain Arnold's best-known efforts to rescue the poetic charm—and therefore, for him, unifying ethical power—of the Bible from the Puritans and win the Puritans to his cause. Yet his less familiar promotion of the book of Isaiah between 1872 and 1883 offers a more concentrated, and arguably more concrete, illustration of the ways in which he hoped the "poetic" style of a specifically English Bible would bind together various classes of British readers. For this reason, Arnold's work on Isaiah is arguably "a suitable crown of his career" (apRoberts vii). In 1871, Arnold began a corrected edition of the Authorized Version of Isaiah chapters XL–LXVI for working and lower middle-class children in the national elementary school system that had just been established by the 1870 Elementary Education Act (VII:412). Titled *A Bible-Reading for Schools: The Great Prophecy of Israel's Restoration (Isaiah, Chapters 40–66),* and published in 1872 at a relatively low price (1 s.), Arnold's biblical textbook was designed to redress neglect of poetry recitation and study in the elementary schools. While Arnold also promoted classics of English poetry for these literary lessons (*Reports on Schools* 163), in the 1872 preface to his *Bible-Reading* text of Isaiah he argues that "the Bible . . . would naturally be the great vehicle for carrying" into these schools "the power of letters," or that "side [of education] which engages our feelings and imagination" (VII:499–500). Arnold observes that working-class children are unprepared to comprehend classical allusions in poetry by Shakespeare or Gray, but that they have from an early age been made conversant "with the forms, fashions, notions, wordings, allusions, of the Bible" (VII:503). Engaging working-class children with well-selected and annotated biblical texts would expose them to "the real power of letters" that upper middle-class and upper-class students experience through "great works" of Greek and Latin literature at the "leading secondary schools" (VII:500–501).

Yet Arnold recognized that the 1870 Act made this task difficult, since the government had abolished state inspection of religious instruction after decades of debate and controversy over the issue (*Reports on Schools* 143). Arnold's 1872 preface to *A Bible-Reading* is riddled with anxiety over the political and religious conflict that could be stirred up by adopting his textbook and by his decision to follow biblical criticism in regarding the last twenty-seven chapters of Isaiah as a work written by a "deutero-Isaiah" at least 150 years after the composition of the first thirty-nine chapters (VII:414, 504–5, 510–11). Convinced in the late 1870s that his work on Isaiah had made little impact (VII:413), Arnold seems to have fully conceded by 1880 that state-funded elementary study of the Bible as literature remained politically impossible, and that recitation and (he hoped) study of English poetry would need to fulfill the mission he had claimed the Bible could accomplish in elementary schools.[8]

Nevertheless, Arnold published an expanded and more expensive edition of *Isaiah XL–LXVI* for general readers in 1875, followed in 1883 by articles about, and a corrected edition of, the first half of Isaiah, *Isaiah of Jerusalem*. Whether seeking an audience of educators and working-class students, or addressing a "general reader" likely to come from the middle and upper classes (VII:59), Arnold retains his faith in the power that Isaiah, and the Authorized Version of the Bible more generally, can exercise over English readers. In the 1875 preface, Arnold defines this "power" as the capacity of a "great national monument like the English Bible" (VII:66) to so "entwine" itself with the "feelings and memories" (VII:59) of English readers that it forms deep, half-conscious bonds of national community enlivened with the sense of an "ideal" future (71). This charming poetic power of the Authorized Version, Arnold hopes, can become

---

8. In his "General Report for 1880" on the schools under his supervision, Arnold argued that memorization, comprehension, and recitation of English poetry be made "part of the regular work of" elementary "school[s]" (205), even as he deliberately left "out of view religious instruction" (*Reports on Schools* 210).

"a force of the utmost magnitude" for binding together a reading nation teetering on anarchy (X:556).

For this reason, when amending the Authorized Version Arnold is concerned to preserve the "style" of "the English Bible" (VII:60), whether for school children in 1872 or for a general middle- and upper-class audience after 1875. Arnold sees himself competing with an ecclesiastical effort in the 1870s to render the Authorized Version more acceptable for nineteenth-century British readers. In 1870, a year before Arnold planned *A Bible-Reading*, the Anglican Church had commissioned a revised Authorized Version meant to be more faithful to the original texts. A Revised Version of the New Testament appeared in 1881, followed by the Old Testament in 1885 (VII:414). In prefaces to his editions of Isaiah XL–LXVI, Arnold concedes that it would be a great advantage if the correctors produced a "universally accepted" revision (VII:51), but he also implies that "the learned divines now at work at Westminster" should learn from his effort to preserve the seventeenth-century style that is no longer "*in the air*" (VII:60). By 1883, in articles preparing the way for his edition of *Isaiah of Jerusalem* after the appearance of the Revised New Testament, Arnold firmly asserts his literary authority, observing that the "revisers seem to me to have been insufficiently aware" of the "force" of the Authorized Version's style, and "of its importance" (X:557). Were their version to be forced upon the nation at the expense of the old, "a blow would be struck at religion in this country far more dangerous to it than the hindrances with which it has to contend now—beer-shops, Dissent, Ritualism, [and] the Salvation Army" (X:557). In their quest for interpretive accuracy, the Canterbury commission has neglected the affective force of the "*English* Bible," whose style has "fixed" itself "in the English reader's mind" (VII:60). Arnold, by contrast, labors to preserve "*the character of the diction*" and "*the balance of the rhythm*" that have ordered and colored English readers' (and hearers') imaginations and memories over the last three hundred years (61).

Arnold's fight to preserve the rhythm of the Authorized Version recalls his arguments, in school reports of the same years, for the unconscious operation of English poetry's rhythms upon the minds of working-class students. School children, Arnold recommends in his 1878 report, should recite and learn to understand "good poetry" because it "is formative," acting on them "by itself and in a way managed by nature," even at the level of "rhythm and diction" (*Reports on Schools* 187). Meredith Martin has recently suggested that Arnold hoped this character-building poetic education would turn these future voters and readers into "a nation intimately civilized by poetic form" (144). While Martin and most other commentators have focused on Arnold's confidence in the civilizing power of secular English poetry, I would argue that he placed even greater faith in the subconscious, disciplining force of the Authorized Version. In his work on Isaiah in the 1870s and 1880s, he defends the value of this rhythmic discipline not only for working-class children but also for the "general" English reader.

Arnold shows his concern to further the influence of the prose rhythms of the Authorized Version in his 1875 preface to *Isaiah XL–LXVI*, where he criticizes the recent emendation of Isaiah 53:8 by Thomas Kelley Cheyne, a distinguished biblical critic at Oxford, in *The Book of Isaiah Chronologically Arranged* (1870). The verse runs as follows in the Authorized Version: "He was taken from prison and from judgment, and who shall declare his generation? for he was cut off out of the land of the living; for the transgression of my people was he stricken."[9] For this "Mr. Cheyne substitutes: 'From oppression and from punishment was he taken,—and as for his generation, who considered that he was cut off out of the land of the living, for the transgression of my people he was stricken?'" While Arnold regrets the lack of "clear sense" in both cases, he condemns Cheyne's revision less for perpetuating obscurity than for sacrificing the original "fall," or rhythm, "of" the "sentence"(VII:63). Rather than "translate the verse more literally by changing its words and rhythm more radically," Arnold retains as much of the Authorized Version as possible: "He was taken from prison and from judgment; and who of his generation regarded it, why he was cut off out of the land of the living? for the transgression of my people was he stricken!" (63). Relying primarily on changed punctuation and the introduction of "who of his generation regarded it" and "why," Arnold strives to protect the basic rhythmic phrasing of the Authorized Version from Cheyne's disregard of pauses (Cheyne's dash introduces a drastic pause after the first clause and removes one after "living") and replacement of disyllabic with trisyllabic words ("oppression" for "prison").

In seeking to clarify Isaiah while conserving "the balance of the rhythm" in the Authorized Version, Arnold is as concerned with social as much as literary "balance." At stake is an inherited ordering of thought and feeling transmitted through the rhythm of "the English Bible," which has come to be felt as "English," rather than simply the destruction of a stately seventeenth-century cadence (VII:64). Arnold's prefaces to Isaiah seem surprisingly High Church when they stress the "poetic" quality of

---

9. I use Arnold's quotation, in which he makes—probably accidental—changes of punctuation, replacing a colon after "judgment" and "living" with a comma and semicolon, respectively.

the Authorized Version, and when they connect inherited rhythmic forms to the salutary regulation of individual and social passions. Yet Arnold separates rhythmic and social forms from dogmatic ones, hoping to create a clarified English Bible capable of uniting doctrinal diversity within established and emotionally binding rhythms. He argues that his Isaiah could be used by "the adherent of any school of Biblical interpretation or of religious belief" (VII:66). "Nothing would be so gratifying to me," he remarks, "as to find that a reader had gone from the beginning chapters to the end without noticing anything different from what he was accustomed to, except that he was not perplexed or thrown out as formerly" (66). Arnold's goals would be best achieved if readers of all classes were to remain unconscious of his changes, not "noticing anything different" as the familiar rhythms and diction insensibly blended in their minds with a clearer understanding of the text.

Arnold pursues this strategy of cloaking revision under familiar forms in the popular (cheaper, at 2s6d) and abridged version of *Literature and Dogma* (1883). In the concluding sections of the book, where he warns that the masses are becoming disenchanted with the Bible, Arnold strings together quotations from Isaiah and Jeremiah to show that their great prophecies foresee a society of justice that can only be realized by a Christendom purged of its "false . . . theology" (CPW VI:397). Within this cluster of quotations, Arnold includes a phrase from his own altered version of Isaiah 32:5 in his then forthcoming *Isaiah of Jerusalem* (1883), changing the Authorized Version's "The vile person shall no more be called liberal, nor the churl said to be bountiful" to "The vile person shall no more be called noble, nor the worker of mischief said to be worthy" (VII:97). Arnold's substitution of *noble* for *liberal* might be amusingly self-protective. Yet it might also permit the largely middle-class audience of this popular edition of *Literature and Dogma* to associate Isaiah's prophecy with a transition—free from "worker[s'] mischief"—to a more democratic society after the deterioration of a superficially "noble" aristocracy, a transition that Arnold had been publically predicting since "Democracy" (1861) (II:8).

Arnold concludes this collocation of prophetic quotations in *Literature and Dogma* with Isaiah 60:20, silently replacing the Authorized Version's "The Lord" with "The Eternal" in the verse "The Eternal shall be thine everlasting light, and the days of thy mourning shall be ended" (VI:397). In coordination with Arnold's parallel revisions to Old Testament passages throughout *Literature and Dogma* (eg., VI:203–4), this slight adjustment pulls the proclamation of Isaiah 60:20 further into the immanent frame, quieting the reference to a transcendent anthropomorphic deity and supporting Arnold's argument that the natural truth of Christianity, the law of "righteousness" best fulfilled in Christ, will "prevail" in British and world history (VI:397). Arnold creates a prophetical pastiche that clothes his vision of a distantly reformed Christian Britain in rhythms and wording of the English Bible that have bound themselves to "a thousand sentiments and associations" within English readers' minds (X:556).

Together, *Literature and Dogma* and Arnold's work on Isaiah indicate his faith in the charming force of a slightly clarified Authorized Version to inspire "the mind" of readers with a social "ideal" worth treasuring and pursuing (CPW VII:71). This helps explain Arnold's decision to select Isaiah XV–XLVI as the first portion of the Bible to extract, clarify, and recommend to school children and (later) a general audience. These last chapters of Isaiah, Arnold claims in his 1875 preface, "mark the very point where Jewish history, caught in the current of [the Persian emperor] Cyrus's wars and policy, is carried into the great open stream of the world's history, never again to be separated from it" (VII:53). These passages gain their "most striking" character from "Cyrus's attack on Babylon and contemplated restoration of the [exiled] Jews" to Israel (VII:67). The latter half of Isaiah therefore owes its stirring qualities to ancient imperialism, which propelled the poet-prophet beyond local Jewish concerns into a vision of "the world's salvation" (67). For Arnold, this means Isaiah's prophecy of redemption can be lifted from its Jewish context and applied to "universal history," so as to nourish confidence in all classes of British readers in the "'good time coming,' for which we all of us long" (71). The fluidity with which Arnold links the cosmopolitan influences of imperialism to the binding charms of the English Bible indicates the ease with which his apologies for the Bible's regulating poetic force can bleed into support for the worldly force required to pull recalcitrant subjects into "the great" progressive "stream of the world's history." Only seven years after publishing *A Bible-Reading* (1872), Arnold expressed his hope that British troops might thoroughly subjugate the Zulus and speedily extend the spread of English influence for the good of humanity's future civilization (Murray 294–95).

In the passage from his preface to Isaiah quoted above, Arnold alludes to "The Good Time Coming" (pub. 1846) by Charles Mackay, a poet often associated with Chartism (M. Sanders 260–66). He thereby signals his hope that the Authorized Version of Isaiah, when emended for accessibility, will momentarily "extricate" laboring-class readers from their mental and physical "misery" as their spirits are "animat[ed]" and consol[ed]" by visions of a better future (CPW VII:72). "If but for a certain number of readers this could happen, what access would they thus gain to a new life, unknown to them hitherto! what an extending of their horizons, what a lifting of them out of the present, what a suggestion of hope and courage!" (71–72). In this formulation, Isaiah's majestic prophecies would replace hope in an abstract heaven with belief in a better humanly constructed society of the future; but they would also replace direct political action by the working classes with patient contentment with an indefinite sense of forward momentum. Arnold here arguably practices what he condemned in an 1876 lecture on "The Church of England," when he accused Anglican clergy of "preaching submission" to the laboring classes "and reserving transformation in general for the other side of the grave" (CPW VIII:71). This dimension of Arnold's faith in the enchanting power of the English Bible nearly justifies Eagleton's caustic remark that Arnold relied on great literary works, such as the exhilarating final chapters of Isaiah, "to place in cosmic perspective the petty demands of working people for decent living conditions or greater control over their own lives" (22).

This is not to say that Arnold, in evangelizing for a "poetic" reading of the English Bible, was seeking an opiate for the masses to ensure preservation of the status quo. Early and late in his career, Arnold defended democracy (CPW II:7) and socio-economic equality as necessary goals (IX:157–60), lambasted the plundering of the poor under *laissez-faire* industrial capitalism (V:213–16), and strove—to a greater degree than most of his latter-day critics—to improve the affordability (*Reports on Schools* 3), instructional quality (103–6), teaching materials (119), and facilities of public education for all (79–81, 216). He feared police states and hated the use of force for its own sake (Honan 341). Nevertheless, while Arnold aimed his campaign to restrain anarchy with the enchanting power of the Bible at a tolerant and equal future, he could be uncomfortably willing to sanction violent state power as an aid to this onward progress, as revealed in his comments about Hyde Park and wars with the Zulus. He stressed patient, disciplined, riotless movement toward national perfection, motivated by the reading nation's expanding collective imagination, rather than by mass demonstration or political strife. The magnificent visions of Isaiah's later chapters should lift readers, especially of the lower classes, from "'stingy selfishness . . . which makes us so sensible of [our] crosses'" into contemplation of the forward "career of our race as a whole" (VII:72). At best, Arnold confesses in his 1883 articles leading up to *Isaiah of Jerusalem,* only an elect remnant of any class of readers will awaken to the true import of Isaiah's prophecy of "the reign of Immanuel," the enlightened Christendom of the future; and it is this "upshot of history on a vast scale," not a call for "change to appear to-morrow," that they "must oppose" to "the perversities of the day" (X:566).

IV. LITURGY AND NATIONAL IMAGINATION

The campaign Arnold mounted in print in the 1870s and 1880s to revise the Authorized Version and extend its influence complements his championship of Anglican liturgy in the same years. For Arnold, establishing the Anglican liturgy as a shared, ethical "poetic" language for a mass-mediated nation begins less with practice in the sanctuary than defining and defending this liturgy's affective power in print. He undertakes this task through a series of essays in the 1870s and 1880s.[10] Appearing in *Macmillan's*, *The Contemporary Review*, and *The Fortnightly*, distinguished literary journals noted for avoiding sectarianism (Altholz 34) and catering to an educated middle- and upper-class readership (Altick 359), these essays are Arnold's attempt to commend a reformed national liturgy to a relatively informed and open-minded audience.

In one such essay, "A Last Word on the Burials Bill" (1876), Arnold focuses on the Anglican burial service. Prior to reforms in 1880, burial services in Church of England graveyards had to be performed by Anglican priests according to the Book of Common Prayer—a fact deeply resented by Nonconformists, since nearly all countryside graveyards in England were Anglican. In the "Burials Bill" essay, Arnold resists those who wish to permit all religious groups to conduct burials in Anglican graveyards with their own ministers. Arnold takes as his initial target an article recommending reform in the *Times* (January 17, 1876), which concludes: "An Englishman has a right to worship in the style he thinks truest and best, just as he has a right to dress as he likes, to select his own acquaintances, or to choose his own pursuits. Let the Dissenting minister . . . enter the churchyard, and have his own say over his own spiritual son or daughter" (qtd. in CPW VIII:87).

Using this quote to recall the philosophy of "Doing as One Likes" that he attacked in *Culture and Anarchy* (1869), Arnold portrays the burial reform effort as yet another invitation to anarchy from Liberal politicians

---

10. "A Psychological Parallel" (*Contemporary Review* [November 1876]), "A Last Word on the Burials Bill," (*Macmillan's* [July 1876]), "Irish Catholicism and British Liberalism" (*Fortnightly Review* [July 1878]), and "A Comment on Christmas" (*Contemporary Review* [April 1885]). All were collected and reprinted in various books during Arnold's lifetime and are in volumes VIII and X of *The Complete Prose Works*.

and newspapers, such as *The Times,* who seek favor with Dissenters. The "Burials Bill" essay reveals the deep congruity between Arnold's unorthodox High Church confidence in the poetic charms of Anglican liturgy and his belief in the nonsectarian state's power to discipline citizens' bodies, rituals, and collective actions into exhibitions of public order. Arnold portrays burial rites as "a kind of schooling" for citizens in the "pure, noble, and elevated" styles of speech and procession that preserve an image "of national character" (VIII:91). The regular forms of the Anglican rite will facilitate exemplary public performances of a body politic that resembles a well-ordered poem, restraining unruly emotion and subordinating local concerns to the unity of the whole. For such a purpose, the Church of England was in fact founded, with its Prayer Book and services designed "to satisfy the whole English people," so as to include "Catholics and Protestants in a compromise between old and new" (VIII:95). The "Church of England, in offering its formularies to Englishmen, offers them with the recommendation that here is truth presented expressly so as to suit and unite the English nation" (VIII:95).

On the road to a more comprehensive British Christian establishment, Wales and Ireland might, like Scotland, be permitted their own national church establishments, Presbyterian and Catholic respectively. If only these "large and well-known bodies of our fellow Christians" were to be reckoned with in England, the "burials question" would be entirely different: Catholic liturgical uniformity and Scotch Presbyterian observance of solemn "silence" turn burial rituals into presentations of "deliberate public consent" (VIII:96). Yet in England, Arnold claims, one finds "one hundred and thirty-eight" Dissenting sects (VIII:96), each of them accustomed, after half a century of widely publicized religious debate, to exalt the principle of free opinion into self-assertion for its own sake, as seen in the well-known mantra of the *Nonconformist* newspaper: "the dissidence of Dissent and the Protestantism of the Protestant religion" (VIII:95).

Arnold trades on clichés that had been circulating for at least a century through middle- and upper-class Anglican print culture about the ignorance, narrow-mindedness, and barbarity of dissenting sects (Blair, *Form and Faith* 145). Alongside (for Arnold slightly) more respectable bodies such as Presbyterians and Baptists, there are "Ranters, Recreative Religionists, and Peculiar People" (VIII:96). The Anglican rite's purpose of nurturing "deliberate public consent" (VIII:96) would, Arnold claims, be destroyed by "ignorant and fanatical little sects . . . parad[ing] themselves" through "churchyards" (97) with their spontaneous "speech-making and prayer-making" (104). Such spontaneous speech-making, it would seem, could all too easily cultivate a habit of assembling, ranting, and "doing as one likes" in public spaces, whether in churchyards or in Hyde Park.

With a few moderate reforms,[11] the Anglican burial service could enable the state to transform burials into exhibitions of national spiritual and ethical unity (or at least toleration), even as differences of theology among the living would be reserved for "private places" (VIII:91). Then, despite all variations of belief and skepticism among individuals, the Prayer Book's declaration that "'We commit his body to the ground in the sure and certain hope of the resurrection to eternal life'" could "affirm our sure and certain hope, that for *man* a resurrection to eternal life there is" (104). That is, this liturgical poetry could be accepted as "certain" in a more literal sense by those still clinging to hope of an afterlife, and by those "certain" of the sense for which Arnold argues in works such as *Literature and Dogma:* the ethical resurrection into new moral life through identification with Christ's example, and, eventually, the kingdom of God realized in just societies on earth. Leaving witnesses to sort out their theological responses in private, the British state could forge a public liturgy that represented English people to themselves as a national society passing together from birth to death in hope of a better future, without riot and with apparent consensus.

Arnold's apology for the enchanting force of Anglican liturgy in this and related articles is therefore also a justification for the regulative power of the modern non-confessional state over its citizens. As Talal Asad observes, "the modern nation-state seeks to regulate all aspects of individual life—even the most intimate, such as birth and death—[and] no one, whether religious or otherwise, can avoid encountering its ambitious powers" (*Formations* 199). A reformed but regularized Anglican liturgy extends the work of Arnold's ideal State, defended in *Culture and Anarchy* (1869) as the "organ of our collective best self," and therefore empowered "to deal . . . stringently" with social and cultural anarchy (V:136) in order to move each individual citizen toward an ever-receding goal of "human nature perfect on all its sides" (V:99). Arnold dreams of a non-confessional State encouraging, as he puts it in *Culture and Anarchy,* "a certain ideal centre" or standard for literature and religion for a divided mass-mediated nation in which each "section of the public has its own literary organ" (V:147),

---

11. For example, existing bans on unbaptised children, suicides, and the excommunicated should be removed from the Prayer Book rubric (VIII:102); hymns popular among Dissenters and Anglicans—though "bad music and bad poetry" that hurt those who "take pleasure" in them (104)—should be permitted, and the prescribed Scripture reading shortened to permit their inclusion (105); Dissenters should be allowed to hold "silent funerals" (107).

and in which ideologically opposed audiences of middle- and working-class readers are poised to determine Britain's democratic future. In the 1870s and 1880s, then, Arnold promotes a national Christian liturgy to further his vision of the "*State*" being "*of the religion of all its citizens, without the fanaticism of any of them*" (V:193).

This treatment of liturgy is bound up with tensions in the relationships that Arnold imagines between religion and culture. On one hand, Sebastian Lecourt has observed, Arnold has liberal faith in a culture that will "produce invisible consensus without violence" (475); on the other, Arnold struggles with the "moment of normative violence" implicit in his desire to establish the public meaning of religion by placing it under the (state-enforced) authority of culture (473). Lecourt briefly connects Arnold's hope for nonviolent cultural consensus through broad exposure and learning to Arnold's admiration of the Church of England as an institution that could "absorb as many different groups as possible in the hope that as they mingle they will each contribute something valuable while checking each other's errant peculiarities" (471). Yet to show the value Arnold sets on the "sheer internal diversity" of the Church of England, Lecourt quotes a passage from *Culture and Anarchy* whose normative violence emerges on the level of liturgical conformity rather than doctrinal consent. Here Arnold praises the established "Church" as one "which is historical as the State itself is historical, and whose order, ceremonies, and monuments reach, like the State, far beyond any fancies and devising of ours" (Lecourt 471; CPW V:239). Within an accommodating Church of England, Evangelicals might bump up against High Churchmen and force each other into a degree of theological toleration; but the Peculiar People, Ranters, and members of Nonconformity's 136 other sects, Arnold suggests, should be recognized as individualistic threats to the "forms for expressing the inexpressible . . . which have commended themselves most to the religious life of [the] nation" (V:239). Written in anxious awareness of a reading nation that seemed to be losing its normative center, Arnold's later essays on liturgy and ritual defend in specific and energetic terms the normative violence implicit in his earlier praise of the Church of England's "order, ceremonies, and monuments."

Here Arnold's poetics again recall those of Tractarians such as Hurrell Froude. For both, religious forms are "poetic" because they inspire emotion to flow within restraining channels, and this reserve forms a desirable analogy with order in British society. Arnold also follows Tractarian and High Church writers in asserting the continuity between ancient Catholic and Anglican forms of worship, and resting the superiority of Anglican forms on this claim. In the "Burials Bill" essay, he asserts that the "Anglican burial service" is not only considered "acceptable" by "the great majority of Protestants" but also "taken, almost every word of it, from the Catholic offices of religion, the old common worship of Christendom" (VIII:100). Arnold's primary concern when defending the Catholic lineage of the Anglican liturgy is its potential effects on national imagination. In the "Burials Bill" essay, he recommends bringing the Prayer Book's arrangement of scriptural lessons for the burial service into conformity with "the Catholic offices for the dead," since the "unknown arranger of these old lessons has simply followed the instinct of a true critic" in selecting passages whose brevity makes them "clear and impressive"—and leaves time for Dissenters and Evangelicals to add hymns to the service (VIII:105). At the close of the article, Arnold observes that "unity and continuity in religious worship are a need of human nature," so that a "Catholic Church transformed"—freed from dogmatism—"is, I believe, the Church of the future" (VIII:110). Arnold reasserts this claim in "Irish Catholicism and British Liberalism" (1878). The "Christianity of the future will be the form of Catholicism" because its forms "symboliz[e] with the force and charm of poetry a few cardinal facts and ideas"—about ethical rebirth through identification with Christ's example—"on which our race could lay hold only by materializing them" (VIII:334). Although the "Church of England" will, because it "kept in great measure the traditional form of Catholicism," endure as a national representative of this "great impersonal artist whom we can only name Catholic Christendom" (VIII:342), the Established Church of Scotland will follow other "Puritan Churches" to the grave, its theological "false science" falling away before criticism to reveal the "most dismal performance ever invented by man" (VIII:344).

The force with which Arnold makes this prediction in his late essays reveals the normative violence behind his advocacy of Anglican liturgy (he envisions the extirpation of most existing styles of Christian worship in the United Kingdom), as well as the tension between the universal reach and particular basis of a reformed Church of England. He bases his support of Anglican liturgical forms on their "consecrat[ion] by use and sentiment" (VIII:104), their offering of supposedly universal Christian moral truth to "Englishmen" in forms that "suit and unite the English nation" (94). Such forms manifestly did not suit the English "Puritans" or "fanatical little sects" who drew Arnold's mockery (VIII:97), and who collectively made up Britain's religious majority. To facilitate the Christian moral unity of the British reading nation, Arnold requires forms whose pull of sentiment and habit are binding. Yet this drives him to present as universally attractive a selective version of the liturgy endeared to him by growing up as the son of Thomas Arnold, a beloved master of Rugby and ordained Oxford don.

Similarly, at the end of the "Burials Bill" essay, Arnold rests his faith in the eventual turn of English public opinion against Dissent and to the state-funded "Catholic" liturgy on "*the ancient and inbred integrity, piety, good nature, and good humour of the English people*" (VIII:110). Quoting Edmund Burke's "A Letter to a Noble Lord" (1796), Arnold recycles clichés about English reasonableness, honesty, and simplicity rooted in literature of the English Reformation (Carruthers 2) and still popularly linked to Protestantism at the time (McLeod, "Protestantism" 56). This vaguely Protestant English identity sorts oddly with Arnold's Catholic-Anglican poetic revival, which risks appearing too close to the "vehement rites" of late-century Anglo-Catholic ritualism he had anxiously condemned in *Literature and Dogma* (VI:361). Arnold's poetic National Church is founded on sentiments he never persuasively locates beyond his own elite background and idiosyncratic adoption of High Church poetics.

V. "RELIGION" IN THE MAKING OF A NATIONAL READING PUBLIC

To define the role of a reformed National Church in a mass-mediated nation, Arnold also labors to establish the boundaries of "*the* public" in Britain, the "unitary space" imagined to overarch and contain, in the form of valid "public opinion," all the various mass-mediated audiences in a national community (Warner, *Publics and Counterpublics* 116). Arnold therefore represents himself as defending "the public life of the nation and the main current of its thoughts" (CPW VIII:334). This stance encourages one-sided representations of benighted Puritans and skeptical artisans, among others, as audiences who resist the authentic stream of national consciousness, which is tacitly defined by Arnold's own Anglican, Oxonian background. Yet Arnold portrays members of these classes, subcultures, and counterpublics as *already* part of the "main" national community. They simply need to be trained to recognize this fact with the aid of burial services guarded from the freaks of private fancy, poetry recitation exercises in national schools, and heightened appreciation of the charms of the English Bible. Arnold here reproduces the misrecognition constitutive to "public speech": it "lies under the necessity of addressing its public as already existing real persons" (Warner, *Publics and Counterpublics* 114). His frequent expectation of his reader's consent—his gestures to what "any one who weighs the matter well" will realize (CPW VI:381)—results from his efforts to confirm and enlarge, through strangers' positive reception of his texts, the membership of the public whose existence he has assumed beforehand.

Arnold, then, joins other apologists for print-mediated spiritual communities examined in this book in ultimately locating Britain's spiritual communion in an ideal reading public rather than in institutions or locations. As Warner observes, modern mass publics are understood and present themselves as "a multicontextual space of circulation, organized not by a place or an institution but by the circulation of discourse" (118). Arnold imagines national Christian community as ultimately the product of readers and circulating texts, even if its production needs to be guided by cultural critics, public rituals in a National Church, national education, and the state's "stringent" repression of unruly dissent (CPW V:136). For the time being, of course, Arnold's ideal public exists only in his printed words, by which clergy, educators, and policy makers might be inspired to construct it.

The national reading public Arnold proposes depends on securing the role and meaning of religion in public discourse. "Religion," Arnold claims in *Literature and Dogma*, must mean "simply either a binding to righteousness, or else a serious attending to righteousness," so that "the right antithesis to both ethical and religious, is the same as the right antithesis to practical: namely *theoretical*" (CPW VI:176). This definition of religion permits Arnold to portray "propositions about the Godhead of the Eternal Son" as "theoretical," and therefore paradoxically "opposed to propositions which are religious" (VI:176); it enables him to be "quite sure" that "Israel" began with no "metaphysical conception," whether "the monotheistic idea" or "the pantheistic idea," but "a moral perception of a rule of conduct not of our own making, into which we are born, and which exists whether we will or no" (241–42). Language about the death and resurrection of Christ should be recovered as a "poetry of life" expressing "that which we hope, augur, imagine," and thereby kept from invading the critical territory of "science," whether literary or physical (212).

By drawing the language of divine agency, sacrificial atonement, and crucifixion inside the immanent frame, Arnold performs a containment act in more than a merely theoretical sense. On this model, the cultural critic and the elect who heed him will dismiss appeals to transcendent beings or realities in favor of confidence in an inward "perception of a rule of conduct" that can be clarified through criticism and practical experience. This has the effect of invalidating a supernatural source of authority that might inspire opposition to the social order and its regulation by secular power—whether this opposition assumes the form of radical nineteenth-century laboring-class leaders and poets claiming the support of God's will and Scripture (Groth Lyon 228; M. Sanders 35), or of Dissenters asserting that the Bible does not endorse Christian ministers becoming state servants. Arnold here justifies Talal Asad's suggestions that the "concept of the secular cannot do without the idea of religion" (*Formations* 200), and that proponents of a liberal public sphere often limit toleration to a certain "*kind* of religion" imagined to "play a positive role in modern society" (183). In promoting a supposedly tolerant public sphere for Britain, Arnold requires a public Christianity that will relinquish its absolute theological claims while remaining a strong advocate for a "law of conduct" rooted in immanent experience. This law has the advantage of falling under the rule of criticism and policy while eluding the grasp of political religion.

In this dimension of his thought, Arnold is an early and idiosyncratic exemplar of "what could be called a 'Hegelian secularism,'" a line of thought that Michael Scherer claims "has been gaining ground recently" (624). By this Scherer means the willingness of scholars to follow the spirit of Hegel's *Lectures on the Philosophy of History* (1825–26) in showing how "a specifically Christian religious tradition" helped "prepare . . . secular reason, and thus the continuity between this tradition and modern secularism" (624). Scherer points to Habermas' *Between Naturalism and Religion* (2009), where Habermas suggests "that secularists should continue to learn from . . . and preserve the unique reserve of moral insight particular to religion (or at least religion in the 'Judeo-Christian' tradition)" (625).

Arnold's own endeavor to establish a role for public Christianity in a reading nation depends not only on a strategic redefinition of valid "religion" but also on selective appropriation of elements of Christian theology under new names. Throughout his biblical and cultural criticism, Arnold derisively turns the Jewishness of the Bible and its authors into a symbol of dangerous provinciality, or Hebraism, a tendency in any group of people, such as middle-class Puritans, to become locked in their "narrow, rigid, sectarian, unintelligent, [and] impracticable temper, their heads full of some impossible politics of their own" (CPW IX:18). Presenting his biblical exegesis as an attempt to rescue from Hebraic fanaticism the "poetic" expression of a universal "law of our being" (VI:242), Arnold redirects attention from the absolutism of his own claim to discern such an eternal law. Arnold and other cultural elect will cooperate with the only "infallible Catholic Church," or "the whole human race, in its onward progress" (VI:161), guided in their ministration by critical tact "insensibly" formed in their "mind" as if it were the mysterious gift of an unacknowledged Holy Spirit; spread through state-supported schools and churches, this tact will lift others into a more humane—more human—society, "without any turmoil of controversial reasonings" (VI:168). Arnold's displeasure is, as it were, God's. Not only Arnold, for example, but "God . . . is displeased and disserved by men uttering such doggerel hymns as: *Sing glory, glory, glory, to the great God Triune!* And: *Out of my griefs Bethels I'll raise!* and: *My Jesus to know, and feel his blood flow, 'tis life everlasting, 'tis heaven below!*" (VI:409–10). One day "we shall" all "surely come" to feel the same, even the Puritans (410). In the meantime, Arnold often implies that he does not mind the state enforcing what men of culture hear God telling them.

VI. OTHER NATIONAL CONGREGATIONS OF POETRY

Representations of Arnold as a replacement theorist have made it difficult to appreciate the religious definitions and theological claims on which his program of "culture" depends. Arnold's project of culture, in the 1870s and 1880s, requires not the rejection of institutional Christianity but a sustained attempt to delimit and defend its normative and emotional power over a national reading public, and a less obvious recovery of its theological authority for the regulation of that reading public by critics and the state. Slowness to see Arnold in this light has been accompanied by relative scholarly neglect of another set of practices in nineteenth-century Britain that connected the reading of poetry to participation in a Christian community. John Keble's *Christian Year* (1827) set the precedent for a new type of lyric sequence that imaginatively aligned the private time and space of reading with the public time and space of institutional worship. This mode of poetry, and the way of reading it encouraged, extended in unexpected directions, taking in works as diverse as Tennyson's *In Memoriam* (1850) and Christina Rossetti's *Verses* (1893).

Arnold presupposes a cultural center of interpretation, which is to be fostered by critics of culture among the reading public and supported by the state through the national Church and public education. The poetic phenomenon that I describe above and follow in the remaining chapters of this book arises in the late 1820s from a related motive: Keble's attempt to extend the imaginative and moral discipline of the Anglican Church over the (to him) dangerously unguided private reading of Britons. Yet the very success of *The Christian Year,* which crosses institutional, sectarian, and (according to many nineteenth-century commentators) class barriers, turns the mode of poetry Keble initiated into a medium through which poets and commentators of competing religious and political backgrounds can represent private reading as a means of participation in a national Christian, and generally Protestant, community that resists, overcomes, or eludes the sectarian divisions elsewhere reinforced in print culture.

PART 2

VIRTUAL CONGREGATIONS AND PRINTED POETIC CYCLES

CHAPTER 4

JOHN KEBLE'S *CHRISTIAN YEAR*

Private Reading and Imagined National Religious Community

The Christian Year (1827), by the Anglican priest and poet John Keble, is known to scholars of nineteenth-century British literature for being hardly read today but avidly reread throughout the nineteenth century. A series of devotional lyrics organized around the Book of Common Prayer, *The Christian Year* was the century's poetic blockbuster, going through 158 editions before its copyright expired in 1873 and setting what might be a world record for the number of editions produced in its author's lifetime[1]; by the century's end, at least half a million copies had been sold and nearly every literate Victorian household would have had one (G. B. Tennyson 226–27). Allegedly read by members of all classes, *The Christian Year* appealed to many readers outside the Anglican Church, and abundant citations in novels, poems, letters, and essays indicate that it was impressed into the memory of nearly every nineteenth-century author.[2]

Yet why might *The Christian Year* have been so well received? And how might this astounding reception relate to Keble's design of the col-

---

1. At least this seemed to be the case in 1927, when the *Times Literary Supplement* suggested that "with its ninety-five editions in thirty-nine years," *The Christian Year* "is probably a world's 'record'" for the most editions of a work sold in an author's lifetime ("Note on Sales" 492).
2. In addition to G. B. Tennyson's discussion in *Victorian Devotional Poetry* (226–32), see Blair's survey of responses to *The Christian Year* in her "Introduction" to *Keble in Context* (7–9), "John Keble and the Rhythm of Faith" (129–30), and "Keble and *The Christian Year*" (607–8, 616–21).

lection? In answer to the first question, Kirstie Blair has noted that *The Christian Year*, in "the decisiveness of its formal, measured" affirmation of faith, offered great spiritual "security" to generations of Victorians ("The Rhythm of Faith" 147). Indeed, the religiously soothing, reassuring effect of Keble's poems was widely praised in the nineteenth century.³ As for Keble's design of the volume, critics have most often focused on questions of theology and aesthetics, affirming or questioning the poetry's agreement with Tractarian ideals and poetics that Keble later explicated in his lectures and essays.⁴ Here I take another approach to these questions about the intent and influence of *The Christian Year* by analyzing the collection's intervention in nineteenth-century print culture. In this, I build upon recent work by scholars such as William R. McKelvy, who has persuasively argued for Keble's participation through *The Christian Year* in contemporary discussions about "the promise and peril of becoming a nation of independent readers" (*English Cult of Literature* 142). The immense popularity and wide reception of *The Christian Year*, I argue, are in part explained by the fact that to a degree unrivalled by any other single collection of poetry, it provided a means for imagining private and domestic acts of reading as ways of participating in a print-mediated, national religious community. *The Christian Year* gained its capacity to exercise this influence from the fluid connections it invited between involvement in a worshiping community and private reading, as well as from the typological significances it encouraged each reader to find in an unknown, mundane life pursued amidst a host of similarly anonymous believers and compatriots. In this way, I will claim, *The Christian Year* enabled overlooked religious versions of the imagined national communities described by Benedict Anderson in his well-known work on the interdependence of nationalism and print capitalism.

---

3. A journalist for the *Daily News* (April 2, 1866) joined many in identifying the immense influence of *The Christian Year* with the religious assurance it encouraged at a time when Christian orthodoxy seemed to face challenges to its authority: "His religious verse was eminently that of a satisfied mind, one resting in the assurance of truths which, for it, are beyond question, and in the spiritual relationships and duties accepted as of divine appointment . . . and this habit of mind may have, more than is commonly suspected, to do with the merits which have recommended 'The Christian Year.' . . . It is remarkable 'The Christian Year' has gained steadily in favour during the rise and progress within the church of schools of thought that have tended to unsettle old forms of faith" ("The Late Rev. John Keble" 2).

4. Did, this scholarly discussion asks, *The Christian Year* anticipate and popularize Tractarian ideas such as analogy and reserve (G. B. Tennyson 69–71, 93), or have these concepts been too hastily read into the poetry in hindsight (Edgecombe 17)? I side with the first opinion, but I believe that the consistency between Keble's position in *The Christian Year* and later Tractarian writings was due to persistent anxiety over print culture as well as—perhaps as much as—theological tenets.

I believe we can also understand Keble's construction of the volume in terms of print culture. Both of the qualities contributing to the devoted reception of *The Christian Year*—its provision of a typological understanding of daily life, and its coordination of private reading with communal worship—were shaped by Keble's resistance to what he, together with others who later joined him in the Tractarian controversy, regarded as the potentially corrupting impact of print culture upon the spiritual character of the nation. Yet *The Christian Year* far exceeded any of Keble's discernable aims. Despite Keble's stated attempt in his "Advertisement" to bring British readers' daily thoughts under greater Anglican discipline, the wide interdenominational circulation of *The Christian Year* enabled religiously and politically opposed British journalists, churchmen, and educators to imagine competing versions of a national, non-sectarian religious collectivity formed by the act of reading devotional poetry.[5]

I. "A FEVERISH THIRST AFTER KNOWLEDGE FOR ITS OWN SAKE": KEBLE, PRINT CULTURE, AND POETRY

In the prefacing "Advertisement" to *The Christian Year,* Keble stresses three points that suggest the intervention he thought his volume would make in nineteenth-century print culture. First, he emphasizes that daily behavior as a member of a faith community ("practical religion") is determined at least as much by "discipline," by routinely formed "thoughts and feelings," as by a core set of teachings, or "a sound rule of faith." The special value of the Book of Common Prayer, he observes, is its ability to support belief by conditioning habits of feeling and thought. Second, Keble, known to friends for his "aversion to" periodical "reviews" (R. H. Froude I:190), assumes that the efficacy of the Prayer Book has been undermined by the explosive growth of print culture. At the turn of the century, Wordsworth, Keble's poetic hero, had asserted in the "Preface" to *Lyrical Ballads* (1802) that the mushrooming print market and increasing circulation

---

5. This is not to deny strong claims made for *The Christian Year* as part of a transatlantic Anglican culture by nineteenth-century American Episcopalian Tractarians such as George Washington Doane, Bishop of New Jersey. Doane published the first American edition of *The Christian Year* (1834) and was also instrumental in redefining Wordsworth's poetry as a united *corpus* that sustained a High Church vision of Christian community (see Potkay 106–17 and Blair, "Transatlantic Tractarians" 291–97).

of periodicals ("the rapid communication of intelligence") were creating a "craving for extraordinary incident" and a "degrading thirst after outrageous stimulation" (Wordsworth I:128). In his "Advertisement," Keble implies that similar causes are acting upon the minds of readers in his day to render them insensitive to the ministrations of the Prayer Book. Its "sober" and "*soothing*" inculcation of a devotional mindset ill suits readers who are driven by "a morbid eagerness" for "excitement" and are itching to satisfy their "unbounded curiosity." Third, in ways he does not explain, Keble says he has designed *The Christian Year* to remedy this breakdown in reception by cultivating the kind of emotional and mental habits the Prayer Book disciplines—Keble will have achieved his goal if his collection helps "any person" conform to the "thoughts and feelings . . . recommended and exemplified in the Prayer Book."

These three points build on and anticipate related arguments in Keble's early periodical essays, sermons of the 1820s and 1830s, Oxford lectures on poetry (1832–41), and the entries he contributed to and helped formulate for *The Tracts for the Times* in the 1830s and 1840s. Keble's "Advertisement" suggests, therefore, a strong agreement between the intended effects of *The Christian Year* and the views of print culture, poetry, and religious discipline that Keble and fellow Tractarians expressed in works preceding and following the collection's publication. Tracing these connections indicates that *The Christian Year* was published in reaction to tendencies that Keble felt were encouraged in readers by the rapid multiplication and circulation of printed literature.

In 1823, by which time Keble had completed most of the poems that would become *The Christian Year,* and two years before he resolved to publish them (J. Coleridge, *Memoir* I:117), he gave a sermon at Oxford University. He warned his academic audience that they were living "in an age and nation, characterised perhaps beyond all others by a feverish thirst after knowledge for its own sake" (*Sermons* 54). If the wide dissemination of printed works, especially among those "of large intellectual attainments" (such as those in his audience), has fed a craving for knowledge, it does not seem to have encouraged reverence for sacred truths or a desire to lead holy lives. Therefore "it is a point of sound wisdom to be less sanguine, than first impressions would make us, about the success of plans for the general diffusion of knowledge: even of that which is most truly called *Christian* knowledge" (54).

Keble no doubt had in mind efforts such as those by the Whig politician Henry Brougham, who by 1823 was a decade into his campaign to found a national school system and would soon begin energetically supporting channels for diffusing knowledge among the working poor. Helping to found the British and Foreign School Society in 1814, planting and publicizing Mechanics' Institutes by 1824, and then in 1825 setting up the Society for the Diffusion of Useful Knowledge to distribute cheap literature on the arts and sciences among the poor, Brougham represented a vision of the reading nation staunchly resisted by Keble. Keble, like many other Anglican clergymen and politicians, abhorred groups such as the (largely Nonconformist) British and Foreign School Society for their desire to limit the religious component of education to the Bible, cut off from Anglican liturgical worship, catechism, and discipleship (Chadwick I:346). For similar reasons, he would have opposed the Society for the Diffusion of Useful Knowledge as an effort to "usurp ecclesiastical authority" by spreading faith in the power of reading itself, freed from church guidance (McKelvy, *English Cult of Literature* 131).

Yet Keble's antipathy to these projects reveals more than evidence for his theological conservatism or his quite obvious "opposition to the spirit of democracy" (Rowlands 46). Proposed and existing plans for expanding undogmatic study of the Bible and diffusing cheap literature without ecclesiastical guidance were dangerous, in his view, because of the disposition they encouraged toward knowledge and its communication through print. They were spreading an infection to the working classes that a steady supply of reviews and news had already transmitted among the middle and upper classes—the "feverish thirst after knowledge for its own sake," whether secular or "that which is most truly called *Christian*."

In 1823, then, Keble was setting himself against the print-stimulated "unbounded curiosity" and "morbid eagerness" he would denounce in his "Advertisement" to *The Christian Year*. Originally committed to posthumous publication, Keble might have been pushed to publish his poems by the discernable effects, in relatively elite circles, of overconfidence in readers' independent judgments and the transmission of knowledge through print. 1825, the year Keble resolved to make *The Christian Year* public, was also the year that controversy erupted in print among Anglican clergymen, intellectuals, and some middle- and upper-class readers of quarterly reviews over current German biblical criticism and John Milton's treatise on Christian doctrine, then for the first time published to reveal the poet's Arian heresy (McKelvy, *English Cult of Literature* 133–37). Hailing from the homeland of Protestantism, modern German biblical criticism seemed to confirm for Keble and others the danger that Milton, it was now clear, long ago courted when he set out to read the Bible for himself: longstanding Protestant faith in the individual believer's ability to discern the truths of Scripture was resulting in open heresy and undermining church authority. Now nineteenth-century print culture was amplifying such misplaced trust in private judgment among elite readers, and plans were well in motion to diffuse the error among the lower classes. As Keble would announce in the "Advertisement," something needed to be done to discipline private reading and bring it into greater conformity with the "thoughts and feelings . . . recommended and exemplified in the Prayer Book."

Before publishing *The Christian Year*, therefore, Keble had developed strong suspicions that the rapid transmission of printed works was spreading incredulity toward ancient church authority, worship of knowledge as a value in itself, and confidence in one's own judgment as a reader at the expense of mediating ecclesiastical disciplines. The right-wing, Tory politics that inform this attitude are clear.[6] Yet for Keble, and for those Tractarians he inspired, anxiety about print culture always centered first and foremost on the threat it posed to the nation's religious self-conception. For this reason, in 1838 Keble addressed the Anglican Societies for Promoting Christian Knowledge and the Propagation of the Gospel in Foreign Parts, warning them of the dangers of selling "all sorts of well-meaning books, which are at all likely to find general acceptance" (*Sermons* 249). Even these established missions and publishing arms of the Church risked deepening the "enchantment" of "a literary and refined age" with the "secular power," or social capital, of knowledge accumulated without the guiding discipline of the Church (237). Increasingly, Keble would claim in 1847, "no one of us is safe from being called on, at any moment, to exercise something like a judgment of his own, on matters" of faith "which in better times would have been indisputably settled for him" (*Sermons* i–ii).

In this light, the well-known Tractarian code of "reserve," which stresses that believers should only gradually be let into the mysteries of Christianity through a process of moral preparation in liturgical worship and pastoral discipleship, seems as much a strategy for resisting perceived excesses of nineteenth-century print culture as an effort to recover patristic tradition.[7] Tractarian reserve is probably a codified outgrowth of attitudes toward print culture that Keble had already firmly established when deciding to

---

6. It is hardly surprising that amidst clamor for parliamentary reform in 1831, with pro-reform newspapers steadily reporting speeches and petitions "from all over the island" (Colley 343), Keble should preach another sermon at Oxford, warning of the "daily diffusion of . . . irreverence and insubordination" through "the popular channels of information" (*Sermons* 116).

7. McKelvy comes to a similar conclusion in his chapter on *The Christian Year* (*English Cult of Literature* 142).

arrange *The Christian Year* for publication. The clearest articulation of reserve is in numbers 80 (1837) and 87 (1840) of *Tracts for the Times*, titled "On Reserve in Communicating Religious Knowledge" by Isaac Williams. Williams became Keble's devoted disciple after meeting him in 1822, and Keble's influence on his tracts is well attested (Blair, "*The Christian Year*" 618). Williams's defense of the principle of Reserve is buttressed throughout by attacks on the "indiscriminate distribution of Bibles and religious publications" (Part 1:70) and the habit of "discuss[ing] the most sacred subjects in the daily periodical" (Part 2:47); he concludes with a warning about trusting growth in piety to "the bad instruments of the world (such as the daily periodical)" rather than to "Sacraments and prayers, and a good life" of service to "the poor" (Part 2:125).[8]

For Williams, the modern British "impatience at any book being held back from any person, as too high and sacred for them" (Part 1:63) is a transmogrified development of the post-Reformation view that religion consists of saving knowledge communicated through sermons and individual Bible study rather than of habits of mind and feeling trained by church liturgy and formularies for regular self-examination, repentance, and prayer (Part 1:72–73). Keble has a similar perspective in Tract 89, "On the Mysticism Attributed to the Early Fathers of the Church" (1841). He opens by criticizing the Reformation for initiating too exclusive an identification of religion with beliefs and their reasoned analysis (1), and he praises the typological interpretations of Scripture by the early fathers as an ingrained hermeneutic, "an instinctive skill" that was "train[ed]" through long practice and submission to "Ecclesiastical" discipline and tradition (40). The typological reading of Scripture, according to which the laws, events, and people of the Old Testament are anticipations (types) of Christ and His dispensation, "was not this or that writer's . . . invention, but it was from the beginning habitually inwrought into the thoughts and language of the Catholic Church" (40). Learning to see as the patristic writers, to find Christ in every part of Scripture, and even to discover in objects of daily life types of spiritual realities, is not a matter of memorizing "set statements" (151), but of acquiring "by degrees their practised eye" (40). And this means following "the same devout observances which we know they kept up" (40), that is, "repentance, devotion, and self-denial" (134).

In this way, Keble and Williams anticipate recent attempts to revise the standard academic treatment of religions as systems of belief. Building on the work of anthropologist Talal Asad (*Genealogies of Religion* 1993),

---

8. I annotate the two installments of Williams's "On Reserve" as Part 1 and Part 2.

the Romanticist Colin Jager has stressed the need to reconsider the paradigm for analyzing religion that the Reformation helped make possible and that became increasingly entrenched after the later eighteenth century (Jager, *The Book of God* 203, 254–55): identifying religion with belief in a set of propositions, which can be studied in abstraction from believers' lived contexts, at the expense of attending to habits, sensibilities, and postures disciplined within institutional contexts (201–15). Similarly, Keble and Williams emphasize that a religious view of the world and fidelity to a spiritual community are engendered by devotional routines and engrained ways of interpreting texts and circumstances.[9] Both writers assume that ecclesiastically mediated mindsets enable the "wise or simple," and even those unable to read, to discern the typological meanings of Scripture (Keble, "Mysticism" 135–36), and of "the visible creation" (I. Williams, Part 2:27). These typological habits are being challenged by the nation's progressive immersion in print, since this is encouraging a contrasting disregard for ancient forms of knowing, the assumption that knowledge is a good in itself, and overconfidence in one's private judgment as a reader.

These views inform Keble's earlier meditations on poetry in "Sacred Poetry," an essay that appeared in *The Quarterly Review* shortly after he decided to publish *The Christian Year*. Driven by the commercial demand for works of "mere literature" rather than devotional books, the majority of authors, "who write for money or applause," will be "carried" away from devotional subjects "by the tide of popularity" (*Occasional* 96). Those who do wish to write religious poetry will therefore most often either shrink from the "mockery and neglect" that their "retired thoughts" stand to face from indiscriminate reviewers (96), or sensationally declaim on Christian truths, neglecting reserve toward holy things to satisfy a public accustomed to having "the most sacred subjects" discussed "in the daily periodical" (I. Williams, Part 1:47).

For this reason, Keble holds up the author of *The Faerie Queene* as the preeminent "sacred poet of his country" (*Occasional* 107), as opposed to

---

9. Keble consistently stressed the role of mental and emotional habit in the Christian life, as opposed to mere dogmatic instruction. Emphasizing this point in his "Advertisement" to *The Christian Year* and Tract 89, Keble also did so in his lifelong service as a pastor in rural Hursley. As Maria Poggi Johnson has observed, Keble's parochial sermons "assume but do not insist on a basic grasp of the Christian creed. Rather they are designed to foster in their hearers habits of thought, which, if they take sufficiently deep root, will form a thoroughly Christian mind, even as ingrained moral habits constitute a virtuous character" (417). The two major resources on which Keble drew when trying to inculcate such devout mental habits in his parishioners were the same that I argue he emphasizes in *The Christian Year*: "the cycle of the liturgical year and the typological method of scriptural exegesis" (417).

Milton, whose Arian conclusions had been exposed as the consequence of his unmediated approach to the Bible—an approach that also distinguishes the bold and free treatment of scriptural subjects in *Paradise Lost* from their indirect treatment in the allegory of *The Faerie Queene*. Spenser, through his veiled allusions to Christian virtues "and the doctrines of sacred writ" (101), intuitively practiced the principle of reserve that Keble and Williams were later explicitly to defend in opposition to the trends of nineteenth-century print culture. In fact, Keble claims, in training readers in the "habit of looking at things with a view to something beyond their qualities merely sensible" (99), Spenser is helping them develop that "practised eye" ("Mysticism" 40) upon which the "comparison of the Old Testament with the New" depends (*Occasional* 100).

Poetry that trains habits of interpreting texts and the world as types of spiritual realities is for Keble the best agent for curing the infections spread by overindulgence in print culture—the "feverish thirst after knowledge," overconfidence in private judgment, and dismissal of ecclesiastical guidance.[10] In Tract 13 for the 1833 *Tracts for the Times*, "Sunday Lessons: The Principle of Selection," Keble argues that typological interpretation of Scripture, individual Christian experience, national history, and the surrounding world is a fundamental discipline trained by the Prayer Book's coordination of readings from the Old and New Testaments (2, 10–11). *The Christian Year* can be understood, therefore, as an attempt to translate into the private reading of poetry the typological disciplines of the Prayer Book and Church fathers (or Keble's versions of them).

II. TRAINING A "PRACTICED EYE": TYPOLOGICAL DISCIPLINES IN *THE CHRISTIAN YEAR*

In *The Christian Year*, Keble extends typology from the study of Old Testament anticipations of Christ to the interpretation of all reality according to a principle of "analogy." Keble held that material things, from sunlight to the fall of autumn leaves, provided a system of signs that could dimly show forth the qualities of God, illustrate each Christian's experience, and correspond with the spiritual truths revealed in Scripture and guarded by

---

10. Keble would later affirm that poetry, "traced as high up as we can go [to the Scriptures themselves], may almost seem to be God's gift from the beginning" as a means of "training God's people" in "supernatural knowledge" ("Mysticism" 185).

the Church. This form of analogical interpretation, Keble would argue in "On the Mysticism Attributed to the Early Fathers of the Church" (Tract 89), was practiced in the Bible itself (162–86), consistently applied by the early fathers (151–62), and intended by God (144, 171). The poem for "Septuagesima Sunday" in *The Christian Year* rehearses natural types discussed by the early fathers in the form of accessible devotional poetry. In Tract 89, Keble gives examples of natural types or analogies used by St. Basil (330–c. 379) and St. Ambrose (c. 340–397) in their meditations on the six days of Creation:

> Proceeding to [their interpretation of] the works of the fourth day [Gen. 1:14–19], we have another set of well-known symbols. The Sun, the greater light, is our LORD; the Moon, the lesser light, the Church . . . The Saints are stars in this mystical heaven, as . . . seen in a passage from St. Basil. ("Mysticism" 155–56)

Declaring material reality a "book" that imparts "heavenly truth" to "Pure eyes and Christian hearts" at the opening of "Septuagesima Sunday" (1–4), Keble follows with types drawn from St. Basil and St. Ambrose:

> The Moon above, the Church below,
>   A wondrous race they run,
> But all their radiance, all their glow,
>   Each borrows of its Sun.
>
> The Saviour lends the light and heat
>   That crowns his holy hill;
> The saints, like stars, around his seat,
>   Perform their courses still. (13–20)

In a footnote Keble links the last two lines to Daniel 12:3: "[Many shall awake to everlasting life, and] they that be wise shall shine as the brightness of the firmament; and they that turn many to righteousness, as the stars for ever and ever" (AV[11]). Ensuing lines follow this pattern of scriptural annotation, as do many others throughout *The Christian Year*, repeatedly directing readers to scriptural passages in order to give the impression of a complete network of types in the Bible waiting to be associated with objects of the material world. "Sin" might forbid "us to descry / The mystic heaven

---

[11]. All references to the Bible are to the Authorized Version.

and earth within" the world (41–43), and the reader might find Keble's typologies far-fetched. Yet should she or he adopt the prayer modeled at the poem's end, the spiritual vision of the divine presence anticipated in the rhyme—"see" / "Thee"—might be progressively made possible through the formation of a new "heart": "Thou, who hast given me eyes to see / And love this sight so fair, / Give me a heart to find out Thee, / And read Thee every where" (45–48). Keble attempts to instill the "practised eye" of the early fathers in British readers through his devotional verse, and this "remediation"[12] of traditional practices reflects his belief in disciplined habits of reading, carried out in submission to unstated principles of exegesis safeguarded by the early church. In so doing, he aims to inculcate (his reconstruction of) ancient typological disciplines through the very spread of private reading that he feared threatened to undermine the nation's religious identity.

Despite Keble's fears about Britain's growing obsession with reading, much of this reading activity had in fact prepared readers to welcome his attempt to cultivate typological habits of mind. George P. Landow has noted the general familiarity of nearly all nineteenth-century British people with typological modes of thinking as a result of the tremendous amount of (spoken and printed) sermons, tracts, biblical commentaries, devotional literature, and hymns produced throughout the century, largely by evangelicals (15–22). Widespread acquaintance with typological methods of interpreting the Bible and the world partly accounts for the favorable reception of *The Christian Year* among evangelicals,[13] and for the remark of *The Morning Post* (April 7, 1866) just after Keble's death that there "is scarcely a volume of sermons, or religious essays, by writers of this genera-

---

12. I borrow this term from Bolter and Grusin, who use it to describe the formal logic by which new media refashion prior media forms (273). While typological exegesis early relied on texts, Keble is here attempting to refashion this tradition through the particular media form of printed poetry, and the practice of privately reading it.

13. In the October 1866 issue of the *Evangelical Magazine*, the Rev. J. S. Bright approvingly quotes from Keble's "The Twenty-third Sunday after Trinity" to illustrate his own typological explication of "Autumn" (633). Bright advocates a view of nature that in many ways agrees with Keble's in "Septuagesima Sunday": "The world . . . , notwithstanding its sin and sorrow, is the temple of the Divine presence, and full of the richest beauty for those who have eyes to see and ears to hear" (629). Bright, like Keble, assumes that interpreting nature and texts for spiritual types is natural: "[In autumn] the days begin to shorten, as if to veil somewhat the fading beauty of the year, and men begin unconsciously to moralize . . . Serious passages of Scripture recur to the memory, and then the sad confession of the ancient church comes home to the heart: 'We all do fade as a leaf, and our iniquities, like the wind, have taken us away.' . . . [Yet by the] mental law of contrast. . . . , humble and obedient souls may realize the blessedness of Him of whom it is said, 'His leaf shall not wither, and whatsoever he doeth shall prosper'" (632).

tion, which has not enriched its pages with precious thoughts from 'The Christian Year'" ("London" 4).

Keble was also in good company when encouraging the extension of biblical typology to all of reality. Childhood exposure to the reading and preaching described by Landow seems to have motivated writers and artists throughout the first half of the nineteenth century to apply the typological exegesis developed for the Bible to all facets of nature, secular history, and daily life. In *Past and Present* (1843), Thomas Carlyle extends his youthful training in biblical typology to read all of secular history as a grand universal scripture, employing "a prefigurative pattern" that evokes "the Second Coming" to suggest that British industrialization will providentially lead to a "new savior" figure, "the Captain of Industry" (Sussman 15, 17). John Ruskin, rigorously schooled in evangelical interpretation of biblical types, argues in the first two volumes of *Modern Painters* (1843–46) that artistic fidelity to the facts of nature and history will reveal God's attributes and the inherent spiritual significance of each physical phenomenon (Sussman 10–12). These principles inform *Stones of Venice* (1851–53), in which Ruskin interprets Venetian history and architecture as a fall—from integrated religious sensibility to prideful sensuality after the Renaissance—that prefigures the alienated consciousness and impending divine punishment of the English people (25–30).

Members of the early Pre-Raphaelite Brotherhood (active from roughly 1846–54) were directly influenced by Ruskin and Carlyle, and shared their conviction that "no matter how apparently trivial, each fact in the phenomenal world is meaningful if only read rightly" (50). For all the obvious differences of descriptive precision and psychological subtlety, the early version of Dante Gabriel Rossetti's poem "My Sister's Sleep," published in *The Germ* (1850), agrees with *The Christian Year* in affirming that "every where we find our suffering God, / And where He trod / May set our steps" ("Wednesday before Easter" 57–59). In Rossetti's poem, the speaker and his mother attend to his dying sister on Christmas Eve, and the brother's observations of the hushed scene suggest intricate correspondences between the scheme of Christian salvation and the smallest domestic details. Even the needles his mother sets on her worktable when she rises to announce the arrival of Christmas Day signify, as they accidentally form a cross, the passage from death to life charted by Christ after his birth upon which the sister's impending entry into the next life relies: "Her needles, as she laid them down, / Met lightly . . . / 'Glory unto the Newly Born!' / So, as said angels, she did say; / Because we were in Christmas-day" (W. Rossetti, *The Germ* 38–39, 41–43).

Yet Keble differs from these later Victorians by insisting on scriptural and ecclesiastical parameters for typological interpretation. The early Pre-Raphaelite Brotherhood, in agreement with Carlyle and Ruskin, believed that unbiased "scientific" observation of natural and historical fact could uncover transcendent meanings and the providential design of history (Sussman 41). Despite insisting on the undistorted representation of history and nature, Carlyle and Ruskin in their historical and cultural criticism, and the early Pre-Raphaelites in their paintings and poems, indicated typological patterns only by relying on the "unacknowledged principle" of "shaping . . . fact into formal parallels with traditional" Christian "iconography" (15). Pre-Raphaelites such as Holman Hunt also resorted to inscribing Scriptural texts on the frames of their paintings to help viewers interpret the otherwise obscure typological meanings of finely rendered details (74). In *The Christian Year,* however, Keble assumes that every detail of reality acquires typological significance only if read according to a shared text in the first place. In *The Christian Year,* then, he relies on nineteenth-century British readers' general familiarity with typological interpretation to inculcate a "practised eye" adept at reading personal and national life in terms of scriptural typologies mediated through ecclesiastical tradition and Anglican devotional disciplines.

Keble's view of the threat print culture posed to national religious community informs the frequent typological connections in *The Christian Year* between the history of ancient Israel and that of present British Christianity, a good example of which appears in "Thursday before Easter." As so often in *The Christian Year,* the poem takes its departure from the biblical lesson assigned for the day by the Prayer Book, in this case the prophet Daniel's supplication to God to show mercy to his people, then scattered abroad with their city Jerusalem in ruins, and the prophecy of terrible judgment and eventual restoration that Daniel receives in response through the angel Gabriel (Dan. 9). After paraphrasing Daniel's prayer in the first stanza, Keble continues:

> Oh for a love like Daniel's now,
>   To wing to Heaven but one strong prayer
> For God's new Israel, sunk as low,
>   Yet flourishing to sight as fair,
> As Sion [Jerusalem] in her height of pride
> . . . .
>   'Tis true, nor winter stays thy [the new Israel's] growth,
>   Nor torrid summer's sickly smile;

> The flashing billows of the south
>   Break not upon so lone an isle,
> But thou, rich vine, art grafted there,
> The fruit of death or life to bear,
> Yielding a surer witness every day,
> To thine Almighty Author and his steadfast sway.
>
> Oh grief to think, that grapes of gall
>   Should cluster round thine healthiest shoot!
> . . . .
> Even such is this bad world we see,
> Which, self-condemn'd in owning Thee,
> Yet dares not open farewell of Thee take,
> For very pride, and her high-boasted Reason's sake. (9–32)

If "God's new Israel" is the Christian church in general, the poem concentrates particularly on the Anglican Church, the representative of the "rich vine" (alluding to Jesus' description of his followers as branches on a vine in John 15) that the British Empire has transplanted across "flashing billows of the south" to every "lone . . . isle." Yet from even this "healthiest shoot" of Christ's vine are springing "grapes of gall," a bitter yield of "high-boasted Reason" and "pride" nourished by the diffusion of knowledge for its own sake. This malady only evades detection because the desire to benefit from their connections to the Established Church keeps shut the mouths of those actually committed to skeptical private judgment. Keble maintains typological connections of this admonitory kind throughout *The Christian Year*. Later, in the poem for "Eighteenth Sunday after Trinity," he connects the reading for the day, Ezekiel 20 (where God says he will judge disobedient Israel by bringing them a second time into the wilderness) to the present Anglican Church, dwelling in a "desert where iniquity / And knowledge both abound": its members thirst after knowledge for its own sake while disregarding spiritual discipline (3–4).

The title of "Thursday before Easter" of course directly ties it to the Thursday before Christ's crucifixion, so that the phrase "grapes of gall" would not fall idly on readers schooled in the Bible (as most nineteenth-century readers were): it alludes to the "vinegar . . . mingled with gall" mockingly offered by Pilate's soldiers to Christ when he was thirsting on the Cross (Matt. 27:34). Not only Daniel's prayer and the state of Israel in his time but also the mockery of Christ by the Roman government become ominous types fulfilled in modern Britain; and, should the reader turn to the other lesson for the day (John 13), she or he would meet with an earlier figure who had not "Yet" dared to take "open farewell" of Christ: Judas, privately contracted to hand over his master for silver, sitting at Jesus's last meal with the disciples. Following the coordinated typological disciplines of Keble's poems and the Prayer Book through *The Christian Year,* a reader arrives at a composite image of nineteenth-century Britain, its fidelity to God tested by its very power, wealth, and remarkable dissemination of knowledge in print.

For each reader who "find[s] assistance from" *The Christian Year* in this form of typological discipline, Keble's purpose of bringing readers' "thoughts and feelings into more entire unison" with the Prayer Book is at least partially fulfilled according to the terms of his "Advertisement." As Keble would remark later in Tract 13 (1833), "Sunday Lessons: The Principle of Selection," he believed the Prayer Book's schedule of scriptural readings was especially suited to keep alive such typological warnings for each member of the nation, however uneducated, enabling worshipers to perceive intuitively the prophetic correspondences between ancient Israel's waywardness and judgment and "the circumstances of civilized and Christian Europe, especially those of our own country, during the comparatively few years which have passed since the arrangement of the Prayer-Book" (6). Those readers, especially Anglican, who took to heart the typological admonitions of poems such as "Thursday before Easter," might find themselves in the position recommended by Charlotte Yonge, the famous novelist and disciple of Keble, when she later commented on the poem in *Musings over "The Christian Year" and "Lyra Innocentium"* (1872): "Would that we [like Daniel] could pray with the same might of love for our own Israel, now sunk as low as Daniel's, though outwardly . . . fair and prosperous" (114).

If so, such readers would be primed to engage in another discipline recommended in this poem and throughout *The Christian Year*: applying scriptural events and persons typologically to one's individual experience. As Landow has shown, perceiving the fulfillment of scriptural types within one's own life was a practice common to all nineteenth-century church parties, so that many readers who had followed Keble thus far in "Thursday before Easter" might be prepared for the turn to individual application at its close (33, 48–50). If "far and wide / Men kneel to Christ . . . , / Yet rage with passion, swell with pride," the speaker asks, "Have we not still our faith to seek?" (33–36). No, he insists, rather than abandoning the ailing Anglican Church, readers ought to realize the model set for them in Daniel, who could face the "Dark . . . future" foreseen for his Israel (41) only because he was "Nam'd to be heir of glory" (46)—the angel delivering his visions promised that he would "stand in thy lot at the end of the days" of judgment (Dan. 12:13). "So then," Yonge concludes in agreement with the poem's recommendation, "to us in these latter times, the only balance for the fearful glimpses we get of the course of this world, is attention to secure our own salvation" (115–16).

By coupling these typological disciplines with emphasis throughout *The Christian Year* upon the reserved, private, self-effacing religious devotion that the Tractarians would later defend in their prose, Keble introduced a quality into the collection that accounts for much of its tremendous popularity. *The Christian Year* enabled readers to convert their anonymity and isolation in a socially fractured, urbanizing nation into a sign of significant membership in spiritual community. As J. R. Watson has recently remarked, "Keble is at his best . . . when he is describing a certain style of Christian living—reverent, influenced by the doctrine of Reserve, withdrawn from the hurly-burly of nineteenth-century eagerness and excitement" (333–34). Victorian commentators agreed when assessing the wide interdenominational appeal of *The Christian Year,* and it was perhaps this quality, in addition to its simple meter and stanzas, that recommended the opening poem, "Morning," to hymnists when they incorporated it into the public worship of many denominations. The "secret . . . of Rest below" (60), the poem counsels, is known by those who in the "trivial round, the common task" (53) have learned "in all [things] to espy / Their God" and "themselves deny" (43–44). Attaining the practiced eye that "hallow[s] all we find" in "our daily course" as types of God is a matter of quiet self-discipline (29–30), ideally guided by the "timely" use of the Prayer Book's formulary for morning prayer recommended to private readers by this poem: "Oh! timely happy, timely wise, / Hearts that with rising morn arise [to God]!" (17–18).

Many poems in the collection portray such anonymous, self-denying, mundane discipline as a typological fulfillment of the most momentous events and lives in sacred history. "Wednesday before Easter," for example, asks readers to see in their isolated and unappreciated inner conflict a mysterious impartation of Christ's own lonely agony in Gethsemane, a moment remembered in the week of the Church calendar that provides the poem's title. Quoting Christ's words in Gethsemane in the epigraph ("Father, if thou be willing, remove this cup from me: nevertheless not my will, but thine, be done" Luke 22:42), the poem claims that "To the still wrestlings of the lonely heart / He doth impart / The virtue of His midnight agony" (63–65). In lines from "St. Thomas' Day" later approvingly quoted and italicized for readers of the Congregationalist *Eclectic Review* (Hood 436), Keble's speaker calls out to a world of anonymous readers, asking them to find in their personal struggle with belief in the Resurrection a typological echo of St. Thomas' difficulty in accepting the testimony of the first witnesses, and to await their own heavenly experience of the resurrected Christ's answer to Thomas:

> Is there, on earth, a spirit frail,
>   Who fears to take their [the first witnesses'] word,
> Scarce daring, through the twilight pale,
>   To think he sees the Lord?
> . . . .
>   Read [the story of St. Thomas in John's Gospel] and confess the
>   hand divine
> That drew thy likeness here so true in every line.
> . . . .
>   Soon will He [Christ] shew thee all His wounds, and say
> "Long have I known thy name—know thou my face alway." (57–60,
>   63–64, 71–72)

Perhaps unwittingly, Keble tempts readers to equate the lines of Scripture with "every line" in his poem, so that "the hand divine" that "drew" the typological link between Thomas and later conflicted believers also sanctions Keble's lines. In a poem widely praised by contemporaries, "St. Matthew's Day," Keble presents the former tax collector as a type of all urbanites, surrounded by the absorbing bustle of commerce, threading their way through a "crowded loneliness" of "ever-moving myriads" (22–23), and barred from the sky by smog. Like Matthew, who dwelt in the city and thrived on what the religious of his day condemned as dirty business, nineteenth-century urban readers and businessmen can still feel a divine call and blessing:

> There are in this loud and stunning tide
>   Of human care and crime,
> . . . .
>   Who carry music in their heart
> Through dusky lane and wrangling mart,
>   Plying their daily task with busier feet,
> Because their secret souls a holy strain repeat. (25–32)

In lines that mildly resemble Wordsworth's then unpublished portrayal of London's alienated masses in *The Prelude,* Keble assures readers that the heightened sense of anonymity created by urban, industrializing society can actually be converted into a worthy discipline: the reserve forcibly trained by routinely passing nameless faces can be voluntarily adopted rather than despondently endured. Throughout *The Christian Year,* in fact, Keble gives the impression of what might be called a community of the isolated, one that implicitly involves the anonymous reader and Keble as distant poet, each of them engaged in private prayer and reflection by way of the poetry. At the end of "St. Matthew's Day," the speaker adopts a voice that *The Christian Year*'s almost instantaneous popularity soon helped readers recognize as Keble's, despite the retiring country parson's refusal to put his name on the title page: "oh! if even on Babel [the city] shine / Such gleams of Paradise, / . . . Shame on us, who about us Babel bear, / And live in Paradise [the countryside], as if God was not there!" (72–73, 78–79). After describing the unnoticed, repressed spiritual struggle among the anonymous "myriads" living in "crowded loneliness," the Keblean speaker, alone in his countryside retirement, pauses to be admonished by their good example. Fictively overheard by any given reader of *The Christian Year,* the solitary authorial speaker represents anonymous individuals, simultaneously carrying out their overlooked lives across the nation, as members of a Christian community. Such lines drew unanimous praise from Victorian commentators of every denomination. "The children of 'the nameless family of God' kindle in him a deep enthusiasm, such as most poets have reserved for earth's great heroes," observed William Shairp in an essay that originally appeared in the *North British Review* (337), a journal associated with an institution deeply opposed to the Tractarians, the Free Church of Scotland (Altholz 92–93).

Especially as *The Christian Year* began "to be met with in every form, at every place—between one shilling and two guineas" (Hood 428), the sense of being one among the hundreds of thousands of its nameless readers could confirm one's sense of membership in a national community of the daily faithful, each of whom was pursuing a parallel life of unexpressed spiritual hopes and uncertainties. Perhaps with little to no exaggeration, *The Morning Post* (April 2, 1866) could claim that the "announcement of the death of" the "venerated author of 'The Christian year,' will cast a gloom over the Easter festivity of many a household in this country" ("John Keble" 5), and *The Times* (April 6, 1866) could more moderately affirm that "everywhere throughout this empire are hearts and households to which the news will come like a far distant sound, more felt than heard" ("The Late John Keble" 5).

III. "OUR ANNUAL STEPS": PRIVATE READING AND NATIONAL RELIGIOUS COMMUNITY

The Christian Year, then, was designed to bring private readers into conformity with modes of thought and feeling trained in the Prayer Book, specifically by inculcating the "practiced eye" of disciplined typological interpretation, and by modeling reserved, ecclesiastically ordered devotion. By these means, Keble aimed to counteract nineteenth-century print culture's stimulation of a "feverish thirst after knowledge for its own sake" and celebration of private judgment unhindered by the Church's oversight. Yet, as I have argued, Keble's poems quickly exceeded the scope of his strategy for curing the infectious spread of indiscriminate reading. *The Christian Year* became one of the century's most powerful and popular means for imagining private devotional reading as participation in a national and imperial religious community of nameless individuals, each simultaneously leading unremarked lives of private aspiration and inner strife in their disparate social stations.

The Christian Year thereby provided a religiously inflected version of the form of imagined community described by Benedict Anderson in *Imagined Communities* (1991), his study of the interdependent rise of nationalism and print capitalism. After the later eighteenth century, Anderson argues, growth in periodical and novel reading increasingly enabled middle- and upper-class readers to imagine themselves joined to countless other anonymous individuals in a nation progressing through secular time—time charted by the secular calendar rather than providentially arranged (24–36). That is, this form of national imagination was stimulated by the very forces of print culture that Keble and Williams set out to subdue and discipline. *The Christian Year* thereby enjoyed a somewhat paradoxical existence: strategically arranged to align private reading with the ecclesiastical calendar and Prayer Book, its capacity to project a national religious community derived at least in part from a potentially competing, secular way of conceiving the temporal unity of the nation.

Landow aptly summarizes the typological view of time and history recommended in works such as *The Christian Year:* "Before Christ, all recorded Old Testament events served as a lens converging upon His appearance; after His death and resurrection, all things simultaneously point backwards towards His earthly life and forwards to His second coming" (40). For this reason, invoking one well-known type communicates a whole view of history and the world as "completely ordered" by "God's plan" (40).

Keble held that a typological mindset, when trained by ecclesiastical discipline, embraces not only events of biblical history but also all facets of the natural world, daily life, and national events. In his ideal scenario, Britons of every class would come to see their individual spiritual trials and hopes as shared in a larger community of faith that stretched backward and forward through providential history—a history in which each fact and event was reassuringly interwoven in a web of divinely ordained interdependency, however difficult or impossible it might be to apprehend all the connections.

By contrast, Anderson claims, newspaper and novel reading helped stimulate a type of national imagination in which one was joined to others by a "transverse, cross-time" form of "simultaneity," marked "not by prefigurement and fulfillment, but by temporal coincidence, and measured by clock and calendar" (24). In the 1820s, newspaper circulation rose to a level previously unattained, and Sunday newspapers far outpaced dailies, reaching an aggregate of about 110,000 copies a week and penetrating into mass middle-class, artisanal, and, to a lesser degree, working-class audiences (Altick 329). Taking up an increasing portion of Sunday afternoon reading, periodical publications were becoming an alternate, non-ecclesiastical means of imagining oneself as part of a national community progressing through time.

Sir David Wilkie provides an example of this form of press-mediated national imagination in his painting *Chelsea Pensioners Reading the Gazette of the Battle of Waterloo*, which thousands of men and women lined up to see when it was first displayed at the Royal Academy in 1822. Set on Thursday, June 2, 1815, when the British and Allied victory was first officially announced, the painting portrays a street scene in London near Chelsea Hospital, a home for invalid and retired soldiers. A miscellaneous crowd—dancing women, shabbily dressed workers, people straining out of windows, and soldiers from Scotland, Wales, Ireland, and England—listens attentively as a Chelsea pensioner reads the account of the victory in the *Gazette* (Colley 364–65). This is an idealized image of the British national collective, united for a moment across classes and ethnicities on June 2, 1815, by their simultaneous print-mediated awakening to a great national event. The figures in the painting, of course, stand for unseen millions to whom the news is being conveyed by periodicals like the *Gazette* through private or group readings. Since, until the 1850s, provincial newspapers often relied on central London news, it became possible to imagine a nation of nameless, private readers (and hearers of newspapers read aloud) all receiving word of national events at relatively the same moment in secular, calendrical time. This capacity was early increased by innovative techniques to communicate news almost instantly—for example, outlining front pages in black to mark royal deaths, a sign that even the illiterate could immediately decipher, and printing the most sensational headlines on placards affixed to mail coaches (Colley 220).

As Anderson notes, the nineteenth-century rise in novel reading also contributed to this ability to envision oneself in a massive collection of anonymous individuals participating simultaneously in a national society. To take just one example from the middle of the century, Dickens solicits this form of imagination when he emotionally centers *Bleak House* (1853) on Jo, an impoverished orphan in London connected only by coincidence to a web of characters who for long stretches of the novel do not know each other. Dickens transforms Jo's miserable death into a protest against the economic injustice, elite indifference, and urban squalor that threaten to tear apart the interdependency of British society. "Dead, your Majesty. Dead, my lords and gentlemen. Dead, Right Reverends and Wrong Reverends of every order. Dead, men and women, born with Heavenly compassion in your hearts. And dying thus around us, every day" (734; ch. 47). The page of Dickens's novel suddenly becomes a virtual national parliament or meeting house. The assembly is formed by a vast host of readers from every social order (or at least from the middle classes and up), who for the most part are unknown and invisible to each other, and who, in the act of reading, are called both to judge the ruling elites and exercise "Heavenly compassion," asking themselves if they stand guilty of their suggested indifference.

While Anderson implies that this secular, non-typological view of temporal unity was coordinated with the incremental erosion of religious belief, there was in fact no general decline of Christianity in nineteenth-century Britain. Religious participation experienced high growth between 1800 and 1840, and then continued to grow at a more moderate pace until 1910 (Currie, Gilbert, and Horsley 23–29); and historians such as Linda Colley have amply demonstrated the persistent and popular link in this period between British nationalism and Protestantism. Anderson, then, is most helpful if understood as describing the contribution of periodical and novel reading to a process by which it became possible, without any necessary decline in religious beliefs (or even the abandonment of typological thinking[14]), for nineteenth-century readers to imagine themselves

---

14. Landow and Korshin have demonstrated the degree to which novelists throughout the century depended on forms of typology to create, define, and foreshadow the qualities and actions of their characters (Korshin 226–45; Landow 97–99).

linked by temporal coincidence and a finite national destiny, rather than primarily by the seasons of the church and God's typological arrangement of history.

However, *The Christian Year* resisted its readers' total immersion in this form of imagined national community, not only by promoting typological interpretation of history and daily life but also by orienting private reading around participation in the seasonal worship of the Church. Poems in *The Christian Year* regularly reinforce the confusion between their private reception and involvement in a worshiping community by aligning the two in the time of reading. "Sunday next before Advent," taking its title from the final day in the Church's calendar, addresses readers as members of a congregation that has completed the ecclesiastical year, calling them to account for their spiritual progress: "Now through her round of holy thought / The Church our annual steps has brought, / But we no holy fire have caught" (13–15). The phrase "her round of holy thought" seamlessly blends the annual cycle of public worship with the interior cycle of reflection it might stimulate—and with the time of reading, if one is reading *The Christian Year* according to schedule. When commenting on the poem later in the century, Yonge assumes that repeated perusal has made such connections habitual for Anglican readers: "alas! how often have we felt how little our advance" over the Church year "since the last time" this poem "formed and expressed our sense of failure" (272). Readers in and out of the Anglican Church would have experienced the merger of private reading with public worship as *The Christian Year* was incorporated directly into services, whether by transforming select poems into hymns or by reading and commenting on poems from the pulpit in place of a Sunday sermon (J. Coleridge, *Memoir* I:157).

At the same time, the fluid connections that *The Christian Year* invited readers to make between private reading and membership in a worshiping community allowed Keble's poems to be powerfully informed by the capacity Anderson describes for imagining a national community of individuals progressing simultaneously through secular time. This is apparent in "Monday in Easter Week," reportedly a favorite among nineteenth-century readers (Yonge 128). The poem opens by calling on the analogical mode of interpretation disciplined throughout the volume, sustaining an elaborate comparison between prayer and a "new-born rill" (1) that swells, as it gathers force and meets with other streams, into the "bulwark of some mighty realm," bearing "navies to and fro / With monarchs at their helm" (10–12), until the comingled waters "in the wide sea end / Their spotless lives at last" (19–20):

> Even so, the course of prayer who knows?
>   It springs in silence where it will,
>   Springs out of sight, and flows
>   At first a lonely rill:
>
> But streams shall meet it by and by
>   From thousand sympathetic hearts,
>   Together swelling high
>   Their chant of many parts. (21–28)

As in "Septuagesima Sunday," Keble appears to be mediating patristic exegesis to British readers through the habit of private reading. Later, in his 1841 tract on "Mysticism," he quotes St. Ambrose, who drew upon various scriptural verses to conclude that God intended us to find an analogy between streams, each taking their separate start and ending in a common sea, and the conversion and congregational prayer of Christians:

> It is a true similitude, which is commonly made of the sea to a Church, first receiving or swallowing by all its porches certain waves of people entering in long array, then in the prayer of the whole congregation sounding as with refluent waves, when in harmony to the responsories of the Psalms an echo is made, a breaking of waves, by the chanting of men and women, of virgins and children. (153–54)

Keble completes the patristic analogy near the end of the poem, when he describes "Gentile spirits" "daily" pressing "through Christ's open gate" (47–48). Yet he reworks the analogy in two ways that keep his poem open to the form of national imagination analyzed by Anderson. First, Keble turns the analogy toward Britain; second, Keble describes "a chant of many parts" that none of its mortal participants can hear. Keble's lines—"bulwark of some mighty realm, / [That] Bear[s] navies to and fro / With monarchs at their helm"—recall the address of the Thames to Windsor forest in Pope's nationalist pastoral by that name ("half thy Forests rush into my Floods, / Bear *Britain's* Thunder and her Cross display, / To the bright Regions of the rising Day" [385–88]), as well as James Thomson's "Rule, Britannia" (1740), early converted into a patriotic song still roared out at concert halls and soccer matches:

> When Britain first at heaven's command,
> Arose from out the azure main,

> This was the charter of the land.
> And guardian angels sung this strain:
>
> 'Rule Britannia, rule the waves,
> Britons never will be slaves.' (1–6)

According to Yonge's 1872 commentary (129) and earlier remarks in periodicals ("John Keble," *Month* [1866]: 444), there was a literary rumor that Keble was thinking of the sources of the Thames and Severn rivers when composing his lines. Of course, Keble comes nowhere near Thomson's nationalist strutting. His stanza form gently recalls the long measure used by Thomson and many hymnists, even as it shortens the lines metrically (from 4-4-4-4 to 4-4-3-3) in an aural and typographical concentration obedient both to the governing analogy—the gathering of many streams of prayer into one "chant"—and to the quiet, restrained private devotion recommended in the poem: the "course of prayer" cannot be charted by those who pray, for it "springs in silence where it will, / Springs out of sight, and flows / At first a lonely rill." If Keble's poem unobtrusively suggests that the "thousand sympathetic hearts" are British by alluding to Britain's mighty commercial and military waterways, these prayers are only part of a mightier influx of praise and supplication from throughout the Christian church. The allusion at the close of the poem to "perils brav'd" by "veterans" (55–56) might have unavoidably recalled for Keble's first readers recent glories in the Napoleonic wars, and later readers might have thought of many other overseas campaigns waged by the British as *The Christian Year* continued its reign; but such nationalist triumphs are hinted at only to be devalued and to set off the far greater triumph, achieved through prayer, over conquered "Gentile spirits" now pressing into "Christ's open gate" (gates held open, perhaps, by the imperial spread of the Anglican church).

In view of the private-public nature of reading *The Christian Year*, these lines could easily take on additional resonances as they became a "first love" among "those who have known the 'Christian Year' from childhood" (Yonge 128). Prayers, springing silently out of sight from a "thousand sympathetic hearts," each nameless to the others, yet coordinated simultaneously, as it were, into one "chant of many parts"—this is yet another image of the fusion between domestic reading and public worship solicited throughout *The Christian Year*. In "Trinity Sunday," for instance, the time and space of private reading strangely slide into the time and space of corporate, seasonal worship within a virtual church building: "Along the Church's central space / The sacred weeks with unfelt pace / Have borne us on from grace to grace. / . . . And now before the choir we pause. / [Where we overhear a hymn of] Three solemn parts [that] together twine / In harmony's mysterious line" (10–12, 21, 28–29).

When in "Monday in Easter Week" Keble invokes another discipline instilled throughout *The Christian Year,* the discovery of scriptural types fulfilled in present Christian lives, he interestingly draws on the New Testament story of two individuals, praying alone and unknown to each other, yet coordinated in their meditation by the providence of God. Acts 10, which provides the epigraph for Keble's poem, tells of Cornelius, a Roman centurion attracted to Judaism, who receives a message "about the ninth hour of the day" (10:9) from an angel while praying in his villa at Caesarea. The angel tells him to send men to Joppa, about 40 miles away, to obtain St. Peter, who will instruct Cornelius spiritually. "On the morrow, as they went on their journey, and drew nigh unto the city, Peter went up upon the housetop to pray about the sixth hour" (10:9), receiving a vision from God in which he was commanded to eat previously unclean things, which the narrative later reveals is a sign of the Gentiles' inclusion in Christian salvation, as Cornelius and his household gladly receive Peter's message and are baptized (10:25–48). Keble seems simply to repeat the story, but certain details have been altered:

> Unheard by all but angel ears
>   The good Cornelius knelt alone,
>   Nor dream'd his prayers and tears
>   Would help a world undone.
>
> The while upon his terrac'd roof
>   The lov'd Apostle to his Lord
>   In silent thought aloof
>   For heavenly vision soar'd.
>
> Far o'er the glowing western main
>   His wistful brow was upward rais'd,
>   Where, like an angel's train,
>   The burnish'd water blazed.
>
> The saint beside the ocean pray'd,
>   The soldier in his chosen bower,
>   Where all his eye survey'd
>   Seem'd sacred in that hour.

> To each unknown his brother's prayer,
>   Yet brethren true in dearest love
>   Were they—and now they share
>   Fraternal joys above. (29–48)

In Acts, Cornelius and Peter pray at different hours of the day (the "ninth" and "sixth" respectively), and on different days: Peter is found praying by Cornelius' men "on the morrow" after he sends them to Joppa. Keble, however, blurs these distinctions, allowing readers to imagine Cornelius praying "while" Peter, far away on his terrace overlooking the Mediterranean, is also meditating, "each unknown to his brother's prayer" and each "Unheard by all but angel ears" and God. Keble transforms Cornelius not only into a type of all the Gentiles, including his present readers, who will flow into heaven through Christ's gate, but also turns Cornelius, together with Peter, into a type of scattered individuals, simultaneously praying alone and unknown to each other, yet mysteriously coordinated into a network of prayer by God.

At least some Victorian readers reread Acts under the influence of Keble's poem. In her commentary, Yonge agrees that an outstanding example of God's integration of disparate, simultaneous prayers is found in "Cornelius . . . praying in his villa at Caeserea, . . . *at the same time*" as "the ardent simple hearted Apostle, at Joppa on the house-top," was "praying to know his Lord's will," each "perfectly ignorant of the prayer of the other" (129; emphasis mine). Readers attuned to the massive circulation of *The Christian Year,* and also familiar with its use as "a book for each individual, found in every room, companion in travel, comfort in sickness" (J. Coleridge, *The Guardian* [April 11, 1866]: 372), might recognize in Keble's presentation of Corenlius and Peter an anticipation of their own reading activity as faithful individuals scattered throughout a nation and empire—a prefiguration ultimately made possible, according to the poem, by God's superintendence of history, the basis of Christian typology. The fusion of private reading with communal worship throughout *The Christian Year* thereby left the collection's use open to the imagined simultaneity in secular time to which periodicals and novels accustomed nineteenth-century readers. Yet in the imagined national religious community enabled by *The Christian Year,* the network of print, by means of which individual Britons could conceive of themselves in a nation of anonymous compatriots simultaneously leading separate lives, is sublimated into a network of prayer, its channels providentially interlinked from above.

On April 11, 1866, a week after Keble's death, the High-Church newspaper *The Guardian* published a letter from an anonymous reader commemorating the author of *The Christian Year*. The correspondent reveals the influence of Keble's volume in the way he imagines a national religious community. He opens by alluding to Acts 13:36—"David, after he had served his own generation by the will of God, fell on sleep, and was laid unto his fathers" (AV)—to transform the Psalmist into a type of Keble, even as he transforms Israel into a type of Britain: "Your next number will record the laying to rest of the great psalmist of our Israel, who having 'served his own generation by the will of God, has fallen on sleep'" ("John Keble" 371). Included in a series of letters sent from different corners of the nation to commemorate Keble and *The Christian Year*, this act of typological interpretation takes for granted the sense of membership in a nation of individuals simultaneously progressing through secular time that was stimulated by the regular circulation of newspapers such as the *Guardian* ("Your next number will record the laying to rest . . ."). In ways Keble could never have predicted, *The Christian Year* had provided a means for adapting a typological vision of Christian history and community to the secular, non-ecclesiastical time by which readers were becoming accustomed to clock the nation's imagined life.

IV. CONCLUSION: (RE)IMAGINING NATIONAL RELIGIOUS COMMUNITY THROUGH *THE CHRISTIAN YEAR*

While Keble intended *The Christian Year* to bring British readers under the moral and imaginative discipline of the Anglican Church, conceived not as Protestant, but as a branch of the true Catholic Church, his collection quickly became a means not only for Anglicans but also for those outside the Established Church to conceive of an imagined national religious community. This is perhaps clearest in the many attempts made by nineteenth-century journalists, educators, and clergymen to account for the influence and popularity of *The Christian Year* after Keble's death on March 29, 1866. Writing for *The Contemporary Review*, William Lake, an Anglican clergyman liberal in politics and connected with leading Broad Churchmen, provides a typical example of how commentators built on the interdenominational circulation of *The Christian Year* to imagine a national, non-sectarian religious unity formed by reading devotional poetry:

> We may reckon amongst the best signs of [the] Age . . . , the fact that poetry, so pure and unworldly, should be, far above any other that can be

named, the constant companion of every class of thoughtful Englishmen and Englishwomen,—a true 'Eirenicon' [an attempt to make peace], in which, spite of all differences of thought and feeling,—

> "Reconcilèd Christians meet,
> And face to face and heart to heart,
> High thoughts of holy love impart,
>   In silence meek or converse sweet." (337)

Quoting from "St. Mark's Day" in *The Christian Year,* Lake performs the act of imagination made so habitual by Keble's collection: he describes private reading ("constant companion of every class of thoughtful Englishmen and Englishwomen") as participation in a national religious community ("Christians meet, / . . . face to face and heart to heart"). For Lake, by piercing denominational divisions through private reading, *The Christian Year* outlines a fundamental, non-sectarian Christian unity for the nation, providing, as it were, a virtual meeting place that no single church party could hope to offer. One might expect such a reading from a clergyman with Broad Church affinities, but similar assertions were widely made after Keble's death by writers in Dissenting periodicals. In his denomination's quarterly review, James Harrison Rigg, a Wesleyan Methodist minister and educator, observed: "Very remarkable and very beautiful is the unanimity of affectionate admiration and regret with which the intelligence of Mr. Keble's decease has been responded to by Christian men of every denominational colour. The *Nonconformist* has vied with the *Guardian* [High-Church newspaper] in its tribute to his merits as a sacred poet and his goodness as a man" (403).

In *Culture and Anarchy* (1869), Arnold would poke fun at the narrowness of the *Nonconformist* simply by quoting its motto, "The Dissidence of Dissent, and the Protestantism of the Protestant Religion!" (V:101). Yet even this newspaper strained to present the enjoyment of *The Christian Year* "among all cultured men and women" ("Ecclesiastical Notes" 261) as a sign of a generally Protestant nation, with room for different religious camps—a vision that Keble had himself apparently only imperfectly understood: "In almost everything that relates to Church life and outward Christian worship on earth he was opposed to us . . . [But] Keble is to the Christian Church what Tennyson is to all of our own age . . .—the poet of lofty spirituality. We wish he had not so often sung in such sectarian dress, but we have always forgotten the dress when we have heard the song" (262).

As the *Nonconformist* journalist shows, envisioning the interdenominational national community indicated by *The Christian Year* did not mean surrendering conviction of the superiority of one's own ground. In fact, demonstrating sensitivity to *The Christian Year* could be a way of pointing out the spiritual narrowness of other religious groups in the nation. Immediately after rebuking Keble's confinement to the establishment, the *Nonconformist* casts aspersions on Scotch Presbyterians for refusing "to read a line of Keble's," a sign of the Puritanical "idolatry of most Scotchmen" ("Ecclesiastical Notes" 262). Similarly, a journalist for the Jesuit-run *Month* builds on the familiar connection between Keble's poems and a generally Protestant national community, arguing that "its thousands of readers" ("John Keble" 441) have underappreciated the "great movement towards antiquity and Catholicism, which was originated by the *Christian Year*" (445). The *Month* critic resolutely links *The Christian Year* to its author's later involvement in *Tracts for the Times* and the Anglo-Catholic movement it sparked—which, this critic and the *Nonconformist* author would agree, threatened the "Protestantism of England" (446). *The Christian Year*, the *Month* author continues, has in fact proven so attractive to Protestants precisely because Keble's "poetic fancy and devotional feeling invested Anglicanism with beauties and graces which did not really belong to it" (451). By following "hints contained in the Prayer-Book" Keble was unconsciously drawing on the ancient majesty belonging to Roman Catholicism, so that "the royal attributes of the Spouse of Christ" seemed to belong "to the Communion" he adored (451). *The Christian Year* itself becomes an emblem of Britain's spiritual condition: despite the intentions of its author and the conscious beliefs of the majority of its readers, it has revealed Protestant Britain's unconscious desire for the beauty of the Catholic Church.

When commemorating Keble's *The Christian Year*, then, ideologically disparate journalists, educators, and clergymen felt empowered by the collection's influence to imagine conflicting versions of a national religious community that the law had by then increasingly made a reality,[15] and

---

[15]. Over the thirty years preceding Keble's death, the Established Church had lost most of its civil power and exclusive political patronage from the British state. The two major periods of public debate and legislative reform leading to this situation were the late 1820s and the 1850s (1828 repeal of the Test Acts; 1829 Catholic Relief Act; 1854 admission of Dissenters to Oxford and Cambridge; 1857 removal of divorce from ecclesiastical control; 1858 admission of Jews to Parliament; the relative freedom from prosecution for blasphemy by 1860). Despite the increasing disassociation of Anglicanism from civil life, there remained a strong popular and official connection between the life of the nation (and empire) and Christianity in general: national days of prayer and fasting, for example, were still being declared by the state in the latter part of the century. Chadwick lucidly discusses these issues in *The Victorian Church* (I:476–91; II:427–39).

about which Keble was prophetically anxious in his 1833 "National Apostasy" sermon: a generally Christian Britain in which the Anglican Church was "henceforth to stand, in the eye of the State, as one sect among many" (*Sermons* 127). This act of imagining a non-sectarian (but generally Protestant) religious community for the nation by means of *The Christian Year* was compatible with attempts to privilege one's own ecclesiastical camp within the national spiritual collective—or, in the case of Catholic writers, to argue that devoted reading of *The Christian Year* showed the unconscious longing of Britain for the Church it had forsaken.

The Christian Year might have ultimately proved so popular and resonant with the life of the nation because it provided a flexible means of imagining a link between a national community secularly timed by clocks and periodicals, and a cross-denominational community of anonymous, faithful readers united by basic piety and a generally Christian typological code for interpreting national and daily life. Considering Keble's anxiety over "popular channels of information" such as periodicals and newspapers (*Sermons* 116), it is a little ironic that late into the century these publications remained important agents in sustaining readers' fluid associations between *The Christian Year*, the Church calendar it defended, and the secular temporal journey of the nation. Many newspapers and journals published weekly and monthly calendars that synthesized central events in national history, the Church seasons, and the deaths of outstanding national figures. In constructing the nation's calendar, simultaneously secular and sacred, *Reynolds's Weekly Newspaper*, left-leaning, cheap, and with a fairly wide circulation that penetrated the working classes, cooperated with *All the Year Round*, launched by Dickens and catering to a wide but respectable middle-class audience. Sandwiched between events such as "The Fifth Sunday in Lent" and "Slave Trade Abolished," both journals regularly included "John Keble died, 1866" ("Calendar for the Week" 4; "Calendar for 1895" 58). No one needed to add that he was the author of *The Christian Year*.

CHAPTER 5

TENNYSON'S "NEW CHRISTIAN YEAR"

In Memoriam and the Minimum of Faith

When *In Memoriam* was released to the public in 1850 after its seventeen-year incubation, Tennyson was showered with praise—and censure. Within months the poem brought him the laureateship (*Memoir* I:334). It just as quickly drew rebuke from reviewers whose orthodoxy was offended. A critic for *The English Review*, a quarterly catering to those wanting High Church Toryism without extreme Tractarianism (Altholz 26), itched for a birch when reading lyric 33, where Tennyson seemed to suggest that a "faith" still "fix[ed]" to traditional and orthodox "form[s]" was childish and feminine, yet worthy of toleration by educated males "Whose" rarified "faith has centre everywhere" (33.4, 3):[1] "Really," declared the outraged reviewer, "we could find it in our hearts to whip this self-conceited rhymester" ("New Poetry" 74). For *The English Review* critic, lyric 33 reflects Tennyson's disregard for traditional Christianity and his complacent satisfaction with a bland compromise adopted by a "very numerous class" of "good folks, if we may so call them," who retain "a general sense of God's existence and His goodness from that Revelation which they nevertheless ignore," simply "because they have been taught" to believe these things,

---

1. All citations of *In Memoriam* are from the edition by Susan Shatto and Marion Shaw (Clarendon Press, 1982). I refer to separate sections of the elegy as "lyrics" (e.g., lyric 33), and in citations give the number of the lyric followed by line numbers within it (e.g., 33.4).

"and because it is pleasant to hold them; and as for the rest, they simply 'let it go'" ("New Poetry" 73).

Until quite recently, a number of modern literary critics have embraced versions of this interpretation.[2] Viewed from this angle, as a poem that appealed to Victorians content to "let go" of traditional doctrines and forms, *In Memoriam* seems poised to obtain the devotion Kirstie Blair has recently shown it gained among liberal Anglicans eager to reconcile their Christian faith with modern learning and toleration of diversity in theology and worship. As Blair persuasively argues, *In Memoriam* not only was shaped by "emerging Broad Church liberalism," but probably also "helped to codify a sense of what it meant to be 'broad' in religion" (*Form and Faith* 174). Less expected is the (then) Anglo-Catholic[3] Coventry Patmore's claim only five years after *In Memoriam*'s publication that with it Tennyson "has gained the hearts of the best thinkers of all the denominations of Christianity" ("Maud" 503). Patmore's assertion seems credible given the frequency with which *In Memoriam* was quoted by British Anglican and evangelical ministers in their sermons (Ryan 120), and by authors and journalists of every sect and sort throughout the century.[4] During the same years that *In Memoriam* was being publicly linked to the writings and lectures of theologically liberal Anglicans such as F. D. Maurice and F. W. Robertson (Blair, *Form and Faith* 168–76), the elegy was also being recognized for its religious power by commentators from directly opposed groups, such as conservative Anglicans, Anglo-Catholics, and Nonconformists.

These heterogeneous appeals to the religious significance of *In Memoriam* converged in claiming the poem as a witness to fundamental intuitions about a God of love, the immortality of the soul, and the providential guidance of nature and human history. These intuitions were presented as necessary for human life by commentators and critics from a number of opposed Christian affiliations, and by some who located themselves on the margins of Christian faith. As the theistic but skeptical Cambridge philosopher Henry Sidgwick put it when reflecting on the mid-century importance of *In Memoriam*, Tennyson's elegy seemed to reveal "the inde-

---

2. As Kirstie Blair notes, Herbert Tucker perpetuated this view in his short essay "The Fix of Form: An Open Letter." Yet Blair suggests that lyric 33 actually evokes deep doubt as to whether faith can survive without form, seems to argue for the need of form, and expresses envious admiration for the supposed greater ease with which women accept traditional faith (*Form and Faith* 182–4).

3. Patmore converted to Roman Catholicism in 1864.

4. By 1861, *The Evening Herald* could observe that "no modern poem is more frequently quoted" than "'In Memoriam,'" and praise Moxon and Co. for issuing "an Index to it" (5).

structible and inalienable minimum of faith which humanity cannot give up because it is necessary for life" (*Memoir* I:303). Sidgwick was content to limit *In Memoriam*'s significance to its facilitation of this minimal commitment. While the writer for *The English Review* condemned *In Memoriam* for encouraging such doctrinal minimalism, many evangelical, Anglo-Catholic, Nonconformist, and liberal Christian contemporaries perceived this quality of the poem as a service. For them, Tennyson confirmed a bedrock of faith within the human soul, below which doubt could never plummet, and on which more explicit, public forms of Christian confession could be raised.

While for many Victorians *In Memoriam* pointed to a "minimal" faith in the inner reaches of individual experience, it also inspired nearly all commentators—even the critic for the 1850 *English Review*—with a sense that the journey Tennyson traced through his "hopes and fears . . . as to a Providence and a life beyond the grave" somehow involved them and represented their society ("New Poetry" 72). This sense of almost involuntary inclusion could, as in the case of *The English Review*, inspire resentment. Yet it could also provoke a call to build orthodox Christian commitments upon the inalienable spiritual convictions that *In Memoriam* signaled within the nation; and it could enable a sense of shared spiritual experience that the poem was felt to make newly articulate for nineteenth-century British readers. Reading, analyzing, and quoting *In Memoriam* quickly became for a surprisingly wide range of Victorians a way of understanding their sense of place in the nation's spiritual landscape. *In Memoriam*, in other words, offered an important medium for mid-century upper- and middle-class British readers to imagine their spiritual relationship to strangers across their society in ways that exceeded strict denominational boundaries—even if that meant imagining themselves part of a disciplined Christian community within a more acquiescent mass reading public that was too easily enchanted with the apparently watered-down faith of *In Memoriam*.

The personal quality of *In Memoriam* was powerfully public, seeming to ground spiritual truths in inward experience while prompting readers to imagine their spiritual place in a national community. In this and the next chapter, I consider this paradoxical impact. *In Memoriam* owed its power over readers not only to Tennyson's standing as "our greatest living poet" (Lewes 64) but also to the fact that its testimony to inward truths was intimately structured by public religious and cultural forms. As a result of the echoes and remnants of "creeds" running throughout its lines, the "doubt" expressed by *In Memoriam* could, in the words of the poem, seem "honest," and the "faith" it arduously pursued could feel persuasive (96.11–12). The same "honest doubt" and reformed hope could, for this reason, strike some readers as dangerously enticing or in need of greater orthodox discipline.

In chapter 6, I study in greater detail the range of forms and structures vital to *In Memoriam*'s presentation of inward spiritual experience—including church bells, the Christian calendar, the Nicene creed, biblical language and authority, domestic seasonal rituals, hymns, corporate prayer, typological interpretations of nature and daily life, and even metrical forms. Setting the stage for this analysis, the present chapter primarily conducts a reception history, asking why many contemporaries intuitively compared *In Memoriam* to *The Christian Year* (1827), a best-selling collection of devotional lyrics by the Anglican priest John Keble organized around the Book of Common Prayer. As discussed in chapter 4, in defiance of Keble's own designs, his volume became a popular medium for turning private poetry reading into a means of virtual participation in a national Christian community that transcended denominational and sectarian boundaries. *In Memoriam* became for a relatively wide spectrum of mid-century Victorian middle- and upper-class readers what *The Christian Year* had been and still was for a perhaps larger and more socially diverse readership: a confirmation of membership in a Christian community with strangers from across one's society. Tennyson's *In Memoriam* could thus strike some readers and critics as a new, updated *Christian Year*.

My approach to *In Memoriam*, especially in this chapter on reception history, could strike some literary scholars as emphasizing thematic elements at the expense of sensuous textures and semantic ambiguities. Yet most Victorian commentators were preoccupied with the dimension of *In Memoriam* that feels "sermonic" to modern critics—the degree to which its drama of doubt confirms (or not) basic conviction in a God of love, the immortality of the soul, and the action of divine providence. Reviewers for evangelical magazines such as *Leisure Hour* often glossed over the intricacy with which Tennyson's song registers a "contradiction on the tongue" (125.4) as it negotiates doubt and faith at the level of sound and syllable. Such commentators were nonetheless attentive, as recent critics often are not, to the potential for bringing Tennyson's poem into conversation with the spaces, rhythms, and words of communal worship, and with the massmediated nature of Victorian religious imagination. Without neglecting the nuances and soundscapes of *In Memoriam*, in prioritizing its reception by Victorian religious audiences, I necessarily omit much of what could be observed about its intensity of doubt and aesthetic subtlety. Instead, I highlight how reviewers and readers used *In Memoriam* when imagining their religious communities and the spiritual character of their nation, and I scrutinize the features of the poem that encouraged their appropriations.

The striking difference between *In Memoriam* and *The Christian Year,* as Victorian reviewers and commentators noticed when praising or censuring Tennyson's poem in comparison with Keble's, is the degree to which *In Memoriam*'s testimony of faith disguises or internalizes its public and formal supports, seeming to arise from purely private and individual resources. For this reason, some critics early and recent have expressed Alan Hill's view that the "Faith" of *In Memoriam* "is an entirely personal matter and not always explicitly Christian. Prayer is entirely private" (31). Regarded in this light, *In Memoriam* would seem to support the proposition of liberal secularism that modern nations are naturally headed on a path toward pluralism under a tolerant secular state, and that in this context religious belief and practice will recede from the public sphere, retaining a modified hold in the private life of each individual. Tennyson, such an interpretation might conclude, began to outrank Keble as the nation's great Christian poet precisely because he conceded the direction educated readers already felt polite society and politics were heading: the dismissal of doctrinal religious authority from politics and the mass-mediated public sphere, and the accompanying retreat of faith to the private conscience.

One could argue that Tennyson himself and his more theologically and politically liberal admirers supported modified versions of this view.[5] Yet the testimonies of *In Memoriam*'s Victorian readers and reviewers, as well as the structure of the poem itself, reveal a more complex situation, so that the poem defies inclusion in a simplistic story about the inevitable privatization of faith in the public spheres of modern nations. The poem follows *The Christian Year* in coordinating private spiritual experiences and poetry reading with participation in a public religious fellowship of strangers; it represents faith as at once fundamentally individualistic and fundamentally communal. Victorians of various Christian and skeptical parties felt encouraged to regard their experience of *In Memoriam* as publicly, even nationally, significant. The poem's expression of a minimal faith could therefore seem

---

5. Tennyson did not subscribe to a fully secularized state in that he always seems to have supported a state church. As for Tennyson's "personal views on formal worship," his biographies and letters dimly suggest "someone who had no objection to participating, but who did not perceive it as necessary, who was much less passionate than Maurice and other Broad Church figures about the need for *the* Church, but nonetheless agreed that a state church was necessary and had a healthy respect for the use of forms in communal and private worship" (Blair, *Form and Faith* 177). For the connection between the inward faith of *In Memoriam* and Tennyson's evolving advocacy of religious pluralism under a tolerant but broadly Christian state, see my discussion of Tennyson's late poem, "Akbar's Dream" (1892), in chapter 6.

to include them in a community of honest doubters; foretell an awakening to spiritual fundamentals as a first step toward the renewed Christian life of Britain; or require them to broadcast to their own imagined Christian communities a call for reinvigorated vigilance in the face of incipient dissolution of Christian conviction in modernizing Britain.

I. TENNYSON'S "NEW CHRISTIAN YEAR"

We will probably never know if Tennyson anticipated the comparison that Victorians made between the character and influence of *In Memoriam* and that of *The Christian Year*. Like Keble's *Christian Year*, Tennyson's *In Memoriam* unexpectedly grew into a whole from individual lyrics written over a span of years, was not at first intended for publication, and was shrouded behind the diffidence of its author (Shaw 162): both authors published the first editions of their immensely popular poems anonymously. Keble's volume was certainly familiar to the Tennyson circle by the early 1840s, though probably before (P. Scott, "Rewriting" 143), and it is reasonable to believe that Tennyson would have had *The Christian Year* in mind when using the Christian calendar as one of the major structures for his poetic cycle (P. Scott, "Rewriting" 146; Blair, *Form and Faith* 185). Tennyson's famous reticence about discussing his poetry or naming his influences renders impossible any final statement about intentional parallels between *In Memoriam* and *The Christian Year*. He never mentions Keble in his surviving letters; but then he does not often mention his own views of poetry or explain his poetic practice, and he never wrote a preface, *apologia*, or manifesto outlining his poetics (Shaw 160).

Keble was, in any case, in the early nineteenth-century air, and the poetic structure and field of expectations that *The Christian Year* most influentially spread abroad were there for Tennyson to apply in his own directions, whether or not he was conscious of a debt to Keble. For many contemporaries it seemed natural to compare the forms of imagined religious community stimulated by *In Memoriam* with those *The Christian Year* had so popularly inspired. Since *In Memoriam* appeared to sanction "honest doubt" (96.11) and sympathy for those "Perplext in faith" (96.9), many educated mid-century "broad" Anglicans, liberal Christians, and skeptical theists found in Tennyson's elegy a new *Christian Year* that could inspire them with a sense of community amidst a more traditional Christian public often suspicious of their views. Toward the century's end, Frederic Harrison, a leading positivist, was justified in observing that *In Memoriam* became "a kind of glorified *Christian Year*" for liberal Anglicans (qtd. Blair, *Forms and Faith* 185). The charismatic liberal Anglican preacher F. W. Robertson revered Keble's *Christian Year* (Blair, *Form and Faith* 175), but within two years of *In Memoriam*'s publication, Robertson could recommend it, and not *The Christian Year*, to a grieving friend as "the most precious work published this century" (*Life and Letters* II:83), calling it "the richest treasure I have had" for the support it lent to his "conviction" that "God is, and God is Love" (II:84). James Anthony Froude, the disaffected but still skeptically Christian sibling of the early Tractarian leader Hurrell Froude, recalled that for him and other skeptical young men in the mid-century, "Tennyson's . . . 'In Memoriam'" became "what the 'Christian Year' was to orthodox Churchmen" (I:311–12). The theistic but skeptical Cambridge philosopher Henry Sidgwick offered a similar testimony. For him and other inquiring young university men of the 1860s, Sidgwick remarked, "What 'In Memoriam' did for us" in the "struggle" with agnostic science and historical criticism of the Bible "was to impress on us the ineffaceable and ineradicable conviction that *humanity* will not and cannot acquiesce in a godless world" (*Memoir* I:302).

Victorians fluidly shifted between referencing *In Memoriam* and *The Christian Year* when trying to create religious solidarity with associates and print-mediated audiences. A friend of Robertson recalls being with the liberal Anglican minister when he mounted a countryside hill, and, inspired by his open surroundings, read aloud *In Memoriam*'s "Ring out, wild bells, to the wild sky" (106.1) in "solemn" tones, and then recited Keble's "Twentieth Sunday After Trinity" in *The Christian Year* (*Life and Letters* II:306–7). In that poem, Keble describes the need to retreat into nature to hear again God's promise that He is working all things together for good—a hope that Tennyson's lyric 106 differently encourages. The Evangelical Anglican minister John Richard Vernon objected to Robertson's theology, but he also paired *In Memoriam* and *The Christian Year* when promoting Christian community. In the 1868 *Sunday at Home*, a cheap evangelical weekly magazine founded by the Religious Tract Society to "supersede . . . infidel publications" among the working classes (qtd. Altholz 54), Vernon urges his audience to join him in nurturing and defending the God-given, childlike disposition needed to receive "Christ's religion" ("Quiet Thoughts" 342). As evidence for such a "*Divine instinct*" of faith (342), Vernon quotes Tennyson's famous equation of faith with feeling in *In Memoriam* ("'I have felt'" [124.16]), followed immediately by Keble's praise of "child-like faith" in "St. Bartholomew" from *The Christian Year* (343).

Nonconformists appear to have been as likely as Anglicans to connect the poetic cycles. In 1864, *The Patriot,* a Nonconformist weekly newspaper dominated by Congregationalists, favorably reviewed and reprinted excerpts from letters by a Congregationalist minister arguing for British Christian unity and the disestablishment of the Church of England. To support his call for a "deeper basis of union" in one Lord, the minister quotes Tennyson's introductory stanzas to *In Memoriam,* just after citing Keble's most frequently quoted poem from *The Christian Year,* "Evening," which by then had been adapted for hymnals by many denominations outside Anglicanism ("Letters" 75). Reflecting on the influence of *The Christian Year* after Keble's death in 1866, a journalist for *The Nonconformist* newspaper concludes that "Keble is to the Christian Church what Tennyson is to all of our own age, whether of Christ or not—the poet of lofty spirituality" ("Ecclesiastical Notes" 262). Like the clergyman in *The Patriot,* this Nonconformist commentator claims *The Christian Year* as a medium for an interdenominational community that transcends Keble's "sectarian dress" (262), even as he suggests that Tennyson's *In Memoriam* has a wider (if less doctrinally reliable) spiritual reach among readers "of our own age." A year later, in an 1867 article for the moderate Nonconformist *The British Quarterly Review,* the Congregationalist minister Braden William portrays Keble's *Christian Year* as a virtual interdenominational meeting place that shuts out the sectarian conflict of the public sphere: "through its pages of hallowed thoughts we [felt we] could hold communion with thousands of pious hearts, whose prejudices and convictions otherwise separate us most widely" (123). In the essay's introduction, Braden follows praise for "the 'Christian Year'" as a book "read and pondered" by "a large number of persons whose religious beliefs Keble could not appreciate" with the statement that the "volume stands upon our shelves in the hallowed company of the *de imitation Christi* of Thomas à Kempis, Augustine's 'Confessions,' [and] 'In Memoriam'" (97).

Coming from Nonconformists, "broad" and Evangelical Anglicans, and skeptical religious figures, these comments indicate more than a superficial perception of similarity between *In Memoriam* and *The Christian Year.* They justify the claim of an 1868 critic for *Fraser's Magazine* that "Keble's *Christian Year* and Tennyson's *In Memoriam*" are "more popular and more largely read and quoted than any other volumes of modern poetry" ("Poetical Theology" 630). Even as they pair *In Memoriam* with *The Christian Year,* and recognize the capacity of both works to inspire readers with the sense of participating in a community of strangers, these commentators often remark that Tennyson's poem is distinguished by its more diffuse penetration of the British reading public. At mid-century, when the interdenominational influence of *The Christian Year* could be taken for granted, Tennyson's *In Memoriam* made him seem for a growing number of commentators a poet who would enable readers to imagine a national spiritual community in related but potentially more relevant ways. For some reviewers, such as the *Fraser's* critic quoted above, Tennyson had demonstrated with *In Memoriam* that he, and not "the author of the *Christian Year*," should be recognized as "'our great Christian poet'" ("Poetical Theology" 636).

One source of *In Memoriam's* attraction was its adaptation of the poetic paradigm Keble unintentionally established with *The Christian Year:* a cycle of meditative lyrics structured by public religious forms that invites readers to confuse their private reception of the poems with membership in a religious community shared with strangers. Whether Tennyson intended *In Memoriam* to exert influence similar to that of *The Christian Year* will, for the reasons stated earlier, never be known. Yet many Victorians assumed this influence had been achieved.

II. THE CREED, CONFESSION, LITANY, AND DOXOLOGY OF TENNYSON

Henry Sidgwick, at the close of the nineteenth century, felt that the famous introductory stanzas of *In Memoriam* ("Strong Son of God, immortal Love") were "too completely triumphant" on the side of Christian faith, and thus not representative of the poem's complex and temporarily resolved alternation between "assurance and doubt" (*Memoir* I:304). As Shatto and Shaw acknowledge in their authoritative scholarly edition of *In Memoriam,* Sidgwick anticipated their own view that Tennyson "intended that the [introductory] stanzas should be considered separately from the sections that follow" (159).

To support their position, Shatto and Shaw ironically point to the very features that most Victorian reviewers felt supported their view of the introductory stanzas as a summarizing invitation into *In Memoriam:* Tennyson did not give the opening stanzas a distinct title, but he did print them before the inscription "IN MEMORIAM A. H. H." and assign them a different date than the ensuing sections, "1849." A reviewer of 1850 for *The Atlas,* a general newspaper with a high reputation and wide circulation, is typical of commentators before 1900 in assuming that Tennyson distinguished the introductory stanzas to reinforce their role as a comprehensive statement about *In Memoriam,* "written at a much later date, on reviewing the unpublished collection [of poems], and preparing to submit them to the world" ("In Memoriam" 379). As Bishop Wescott put it when reflecting on the reception of *In Memoriam* in the 1850s, "the Introduction . . . appeared to me the mature summing up after an interval of the many strains of thought in the 'Elegies'" (*Memoir* I:300). An 1884 author for *Sunday at Home* puts this common Victorian assumption more baldly: in the "prelude" to "'In Memoriam'" is found "the Creed, the Confession, the Litany, and Doxology of Tennyson" ("Gospel Notes" 181). When read as a statement of faith, Tennyson's introductory stanzas seem to comment on the type of religious community he imagines for his elegiac meditations—and into which he invites readers.

Just how naturally Victorians adopted this reading of *In Memoriam*, and how close it could be to Tennyson's own final designs for the volume, is indicated by the way his wife, Emily, incorporated the poem into her personal prayer book. Emily designed a book of prayers for family worship and private devotion and appears to have begun using it shortly after her marriage to Alfred.[6] The binding for her prayer book had originally contained the manuscript of *In Memoriam*, and four lines from the introductory stanzas exist in holograph only on her book's inside cover (Thwaite 3). These four lines are an early version of the stanza invoking the seemingly "human and divine" Son of God to make "Our wills . . . thine" (Intro.13–16). The draft in Emily's prayer book appears more doctrinally confident, even more evangelical, than the published version, emphasizing Christ's (or at least God's) creation of humanity, who is alone held responsible for making "sin."[7] Emily's prayer book was composed after she was familiar with Tennyson's final draft of the stanzas, so one can imagine her linking the corporate invocation of both versions of Tennyson's opening lines to her own daily attempt to make her will over to Christ through personal and family devotions.[8] In so doing, Emily would have appropriated *In Memoriam* in a manner related to the use advocated by the 1884 evangelical critic

---

6. The laid paper in the prayer book is watermarked 1855 (Shatto and Shaw 316), and Tennyson first sent a copy of *In Memoriam* to Emily Sellwood in March 1850—probably the Trial version with the introductory stanzas included (22).

7.

> Thou seemest human & divine
> Thou madest man without, within:
> Yet who shall say thou madest sin.
> For who shall say 'it was not mine.'

Quoted from the manuscript in the Tennyson Research Centre in Lincoln by Ann Thwaite in *Emily Tennyson*, where Thwaite also provides a helpful discussion of Emily's prayer book (3).

8. See Blair's related reading of Emily's prayer book in *Form and Faith* (177).

for *Sunday at Home* when he described this passage as part of Tennyson's "Creed" and "Confession," and held up Tennyson for his readers as "one whom we may follow in his reverence before sacred truth, one who will help us in the sorrows of the soul, and has something to say concerning those thoughts which, in our time, perplex and harass us" ("Gospel Notes" 180–81). Similarly, within a few months of *In Memoriam*'s publication, Charles Kingsley wrote a review for *Fraser's* exhorting young skeptics who admired Tennyson to follow the poet in embracing "the assured and everlasting facts of the proem to *In Memoriam*" ("Tennyson" 245). Readers, in Kingsley's view, should treat the rest of the poem as a shared journey through the "abyss of doubt" (245) into hard-won conviction and a Christian community of "living faith and hope" (255).

In this interpretive context, *In Memoriam* encourages the association between private reading and congregational membership fundamental to *The Christian Year*, and this suggests why the poetic cycles were so frequently linked in Victorians' minds. Indeed, Emily might have been one of the earliest readers to take this comparative devotional approach to Keble's and Tennyson's volumes. The introductory stanzas preceding the stanza drafted in Emily's prayer book famously appeal to the "Strong Son of God, immortal Love" (Intro.1). His "*face*" is hidden, but "*fai*th," in a substitutionary role stressed by alliteration and assonance, enables belief that "Thine are these orbs of light and shade [sun and moon]" (Intro.2, 5). This anticipates the day when human empirical "knowledge" of the cosmos containing sun and moon—knowledge believed to derive "from thee"—will "grow" as a "beam in darkness" until it corresponds with the intuitions of faith (Intro.21–24).

The pun—the Son of God is the shrouded Sun of God who yet remains the light of the world—is a Christian commonplace, but it was widely associated by nineteenth-century middle- and upper-class readers with Keble's *Christian Year*. *The Christian Year* opens with "Morning" and "Evening," paired poems that were designed to accompany morning and evening prayers in the Prayer Book. "Morning" turns the perennially rising sun into a type of Christ: in the words of Revelation 21:5, both "evermore" make "all things new" (19). Yet "Evening" opens by likening mortal life in the wake of Christ's departure to a journey after sunset. Christ, "that bright and orbed blaze" has now faded "from our wistful gaze," so that the mortal "traveller" seems doomed to "press" on in "darkness and in weariness" (1–2, 5–6). By the third stanza, the speaker recalls that while Christ is no longer visible, the Son's light still shines within, so long as His servants' eyes remain unclouded by sin or unbelief:

> Sun of my soul! Thou Saviour dear,
> It is not night if Thou be near:
> Oh! may no earth-born cloud arise
> To hide Thee from Thy servant's eyes. (9–12)

Tennyson, in the introductory stanzas, implores the "Son of God" to "Help thy vain worlds bear thy light" (Intro.32), where "worlds" might recall Donne in referring less to the created universe than to individuals imagined as microcosms, who "are fools and slight" (29) and require "help" to "bear" God's light (32). Tennyson, like Keble's speaker, follows with a request to be relieved of potentially clouding sin: "Forgive what seem'd my sin in me" (33).

These resonances between the opening poems of *The Christian Year* and *In Memoriam,* to borrow Tennyson's words, "never can be proved" (131.10); but we can discern the potential for the connection that Emily Tennyson and other Victorians seem to have made. In the Tennyson library at Lincoln is a copy of *The Christian Year* autographed "Alfred and Emily Tennyson," probably in Tennyson's hand (Shaw 159). Someone, probably Emily (Shaw 159), marked several poems in the table of contents, suggesting repeated reading (P. Scott, "Rewriting"143), and indicating that the copy was obtained secondhand after the Tennyson's marriage in 1850 (Shaw 159). Yet only one deliberate mark remains within the volume, again by Emily, and it singles out the final line of "Third Sunday in Lent" (Shaw 159). Praising God for his progressive delivery of "This world of Thine" from the dominion of Satan to his people (5), the poem chronicles the exodus and conquests of ancient Israel up through the conquering of "another Canaan" (31), "the 'old poetic' fields" (33) once ruled by Greece, whose "relics" now join modern poetry in surrendering to the light of Christian revelation, so that "What seem'd an idol hymn, now breathes of Thee, / Tun'd by Faith's ear to some celestial melody" (45, 47–48). "Faith" retunes "*idol* hymn[s]" from *idle* themes to the true "Heaven" and "Love" (41, 47), so that, in the final line of the poem marked by Emily Tennyson, Keble can proclaim: "There is no light but Thine: with Thee all beauty glows" (54). Perhaps, reading the copy of *The Christian Year* that was probably obtained after her marriage to Tennyson, Emily felt moved to approve Keble's line proclaiming the growth of Christ's light in the field of poesy, the field in which her husband had also recently invoked the Sun of God to shine and progressively unite faith and knowledge in "reverence" (Intro.26). "Tun'd by Faith's ear," the "celestial melody" might be increasingly heard, or, as Tennyson puts it, "mind and soul," one day "according well, / May make one music as before [in the ages of untroubled Christian faith, championed by Keble], / But vaster" (Intro.27–29).

The associative network that seems to have led Emily to mark "There is no light but Thine" in *The Christian Year* would have been readily available to other Victorian readers. Keble's "Sun of my soul! Thou Saviour dear" in the poem "Evening" was perhaps the most often quoted and familiar line in *The Christian Year,* and its connection to the Prayer Book's order for daily prayer would have it made it part of the regular mental furniture of many Anglicans. After mid-century, versions of Keble's "Morning" and "Evening" could be found in a wide range of Nonconformist hymnals, making the potential resonances with Tennyson's introductory invocation even more available.[9] Keble's opening poems might have been on the minds of many when entering the elegies of *In Memoriam* after having read the introductory stanzas.

For a broad spectrum of Victorian middle- and upper-class Christians, then, *In Memoriam* would have appeared to open with a poetic "Creed" and "Doxology" that invited them into the elegy on terms resembling those made familiar by *The Christian Year.* Private reading of poetry would seem to blend with participation in a Christian community defined by public worship and creedal confession of the light revealed in the Son of God. Readers would not need to make their way very far into *In Memoriam,* or into the introduction itself, before sensing how much less ecclesiastical and unquestioned the imagined Christian community was in Tennyson's poem than in *The Christian Year.* Yet a comparison between the poetic cycles could have felt intuitive, even solicited. This association would have been strengthened by Tennyson's decision to begin with a voice that could be communal—"Strong Son of God, immortal Love, / Whom we, that have not seen thy face, / By faith, and faith alone, embrace" (Intro.1–3). The poet first clearly introduces himself only in the ninth stanza when asking forgiveness for his apparent sins. This leaves readers to decide whether the "we" and "us" in the first eight stanzas are in the poet's voice, speaking for Britons or humanity in general, or in a collective voice, a religious community in which readers are included, and from which the poet steps forward to speak his solitary confession at the introduction's end. The ambiguity seems deliberate. This poem is a personal confession of grief, doubt, confusion, and eventual faith, but it also projects a devotional community, speaking for its potential readers and frequently allowing or encouraging them

---

9. See John Taylor Coleridge's *Memoir of the Rev. John Keble* (I:157); McCullagh, "A Collection of Hymns for the People Called Methodists," *The London Quarterly Review* (Jan. 1876): 377.

to adopt its words as their own. As Tennyson later observed in 1883, "'I' is not always the author speaking of himself, but the voice of the human race speaking thro' him" (*Memoir* I:305).

This interplay between the voices of the poet and an imagined spiritual community is fundamental to *The Christian Year*. "Morning" begins with a meditation implicitly in the poet's voice, but by the fourth stanza the poet is speaking for or perhaps with his readers: "Why waste your treasures of delight [oh beauties of the morning] / Upon our thankless, joyless sight" (13–14). The poem closes with a prayer that the intended use of *The Christian Year* alongside the Prayer Book, as well as its adoption in sermons and hymnals, would have helped Victorians feel was their own supplication, lifted up in a community with countless unknown strangers also using Keble's volume: "And help us, this and every day, / To live more nearly as we pray" (63–64). Turning to "Evening" for evening devotions or prayer, readers would first encounter an individual voice uttering *The Christian Year*'s most beloved line, a voice that would seem at once the poet's and their own ("Sun of my soul! Thou Saviour dear" [9]). They would then enter a communal prayer comprising the final six stanzas. Fluidly shifting between communal and individual voices in its opening poems and throughout its cycle of lyrics, *The Christian Year* pushes readers to imagine their individual or familial acts of reading and devotion within an unseen Christian community potentially spanning the nation. That Tennyson's introduction to *In Memoriam* does not close with a communal voice, but the poet's prayers for forgiveness of his own wandering cries, emphasizes the comparatively inward nature of the poet's opening public confession of faith, and of the ensuing poems' record of his struggle to attain that conviction.

Keble's "Advertisement" to *The Christian Year* explains that its "object" is to bring a reader's "thoughts and feelings into more entire union with those . . . in the Prayer Book." "Morning" praises readers who follow the Prayer Book in timing their prayer to their rising: "Oh! timely happy, timely wise, / Hearts that with rising morn arise!" (17–18). The six-stanza prayer concluding "Evening" echoes the order of supplications assigned by the Prayer Book to close morning and evening prayers. The entire *Christian Year* follows the Anglican Church calendar and often aligns themes of poems with scriptural readings assigned by the Prayer Book.

Aside from the three Christmas seasons around which *In Memoriam* is constructed, Tennyson avoids timing the cycle of his poem to the rubrics and calendars of institutional Christianity. Yet a large and interdenominational body of Victorian commentators anticipated the 1884 *Sunday at Home* critic in reading the introductory stanzas as Tennyson's "Doxology" and "Litany" shared with readers ("Gospel Notes" 181). Tennyson's lines enabled this interpretation by echoing the Apostles' and Nicene Creeds, which were then respectively prescribed by the Book of Common Prayer for daily devotions and Sunday services, and recited by many Non-Anglicans in chapels. Whereas *The Christian Year* takes these creeds as its assumed foundation, *In Memoriam* opens by implicitly questioning them and relocating their authority from doctrine and tradition to a faith of inward feeling. In the Nicene and Apostles' creeds so familiar to most Victorian Christians, one finds "I believe . . . in one Lord Jesus Christ, the only-begotten Son of God, . . . God of God, Light of Light, . . . [Who] was incarnate by the Holy Ghost of the Virgin Mary, And was made man" (Nicene Creed, *Prayer Book* 182), as well as "I believe in the . . . Resurrection of the body, And the life everlasting" (Apostles' Creed, *Prayer Book* 37). In Tennyson's introductory stanzas, by contrast, the "Strong Son of God . . . *seem[s]* human and divine" (1, 13), and "man" not so much affirms as "*thinks* he was not made to die" (10–11). If these creedal resonances were enough to convince commentators such as the liberal Anglican Charles Kingsley that Tennyson's poem was inviting readers into a confessional Christian community, others, such as a critic for the 1871 Wesleyan Methodist *London Quarterly Review,* felt the tentative language intimated a dangerously subjective and "sentimental" faith ("Birmingham Scepticism" 323). Indeed, the poet quickly reveals that what seems to be the Reformation tenet of *sola fide*—we "embrace" the "Strong Son of God" by "faith, and faith alone" (Intro.1–3)—is in fact a relegation of faith to the inward realm of conviction and feeling, in distinction from knowledge gained of the outer world through empirical science: "We have but faith: we cannot know; / For knowledge is of things we see" (21–22).

III. INWARD FAITH, THE SECULAR ABYSS, AND IMAGINING RELIGIOUS COMMUNITY

As Michael Tomko has observed, in these introductory stanzas Tennyson sanctions—rather than simply anxiously resists—a scientific ideology pioneered by Victorian geologists such as Charles Lyell. In *Principles of Geology* (1830–33), Lyell advocated uniformitarianism, the idea that the earth has evolved over immeasurable ages. If Lyell thereby challenged eighteenth-century Paleyan natural theology and traditional Judeo-Christian theories of the universe's evolution, he compensated for this rupture with a "consoling split of natural and supernatural" (Tomko 129). Surrendering the body and the natural world to indifferent, limitlessly complex, and violent processes studied by science, Lyell allowed room for a transcendent and hidden God above the material fray, and a secure, interior realm for religion left seemingly invulnerable to scientific intrusion (120–21). From this perspective, Tennyson's famous opening line indicates a need to split the hypostatic union, the joining of natural and supernatural through the incarnation, which is only ambivalently preserved in the creedal echo of the fourth stanza ("Thou seemest human and divine" [Intro.13]). In the poem's first line, the "Strong Son of God" is translated by apposition into the abstract "immortal Love" (Intro.1), an invisible divine Power with whom the spiritual side of humanity ("faith") hopes to cooperate, despite remaining unable to "prove" this faith according to scientific knowledge (Intro.3–4).

Tennyson's receptiveness to Lyell's provision of an inward retreat for faith was probably encouraged by his response to figures I discussed in the first half of this book: Samuel Taylor Coleridge and F. D. Maurice. As one of the members of the Cambridge Apostles, Tennyson was often exposed to Coleridge's religious philosophy in *Aids to Reflection* (1825), which Maurice had made part of the group's culture in the 1820s (Allen 58, 79–80). Tennyson was likely also impacted by Maurice's early writings of the 1830s and 1840s; read aloud Maurice's sermons for family devotions; made Maurice the godfather of the son he named after Hallam; and published a poem in 1855 defending Maurice after the liberal clergyman was dismissed from King's College for unorthodox views of eternal punishment (Blair, *Form and Faith* 167–68).

Donald Hair and Robert Ryan have respectively argued for the influence of Coleridge and the early Maurice on Tennyson's championship of spiritual intuitions and honest doubt above rigid creeds, philosophical systems, and proof-based Paleyan natural theology.[10] As I have discussed in chapters 1 and 2, Coleridge and the mature Maurice, more than Tennyson, stressed God's revelation in the historical incarnation of Christ, the concrete developments of human history, the laws of the natural world, Scripture, and the institutions and teachings of the Christian Church. They did not, as Tomko and others have often incorrectly implied, insist on inward spiritual experience divorced from knowledge of the empirical world (121, 123). Yet Coleridge's and Maurice's consistent argument for the witness within the self of the illuminating light of the Divine Reason or Logos

---

10. Donald Hair, "Tennyson's Faith: A Re-examination"; Robert Ryan, "The Genealogy of Honest Doubt: F. D. Maurice."

seems to have influenced Tennyson's focus in *In Memoriam* on presumably universal spiritual feelings and intuitions, rather than doctrines and religious disciplines, as the basis of the faith and spiritual community the poem invokes.

Lyric 36, dismissed in 1850 by the High Church *English Review* as "simply and purely blasphemy!" ("New Poetry" 76), builds on Maurice's and Coleridge's testimony to "truths and realities" of the Word, or Reason, of God reflected in the "truest *self, the* man *in* the man" (*AR [CC]* 15). For Tennyson, Christ's "human hands" wrought a "creed" whose value is not the entry of God into human flesh and history (36.10), but the creation of a "strong" inspirational "tale" (7) surpassing "all poetic thought" (12) in its capacity to combine lucidly spiritual truths already "darkly join[ed]" within "our" immaterial "mystic frame" (1–2). The *English Review* critic might have been irked by the potential note of condescension in this praise for the gospel story—which circulates among the multitude as widely as the "current coin" traded in the language of missionaries and the currency of markets (4)—over the rarified poetic thought in which, implicitly, only a few are capable of finding spiritual nourishment.

Just after condemning this passage, the *English Review* critic attributes the volume's undeniable aesthetic power to Tennyson's subtle aural persuasions: "his strain . . . creeps gently into the heart, and awakens there a low and long resounding echo" that makes "[us feel] captivated . . . almost against our wills" (77). This critic might have felt the compelling echoes that resound through lyric 36. An assonantal stream carries the "D*ee*p-s*ea*ted" (2) truths of the first lines to the "cr*ee*d of cr*ee*ds" embodied in a tale of "perfect d*ee*ds" (2, 10–11), which even "he may r*ea*d that binds the sh*ea*f" (13), and which penetrates the "roarings round the coral r*ee*f" (16) to open Pacific islanders' "wild eyes" (15). As "wide" as their astonished mouths, a reader might think, filling in the motion suggested by assonance and context ("*wi*ld[*e*]")—and made by her own mouth, should she voice the long "i" sounds in "wild eyes" (15). Lyric 36 admits the necessity of the Christian story, the popular need for Christ's "flesh and blood" to give "form" to "faith" (33.11, 9). Yet it rests this concession not on the strength of doctrine, but on the need for affective persuasion, perhaps most powerfully felt at the level of its own subtly persuasive form.

As *In Memoriam* progresses, inward faith, implicitly best articulated in the resonant language of poetry, is ideologically quarantined from the world observed by natural science. Inward intuitions of a benevolent providence that guarantees an afterlife ("Oh yet we trust that somehow good / Will be the final goal of ill" [54.1–2]) seem entirely at odds with the chaotic and cruel natural world revealed by the developing sciences of astronomy, early evolutionary biology, and, especially, geology: "Are God and Nature then at strife / That Nature [through science] lends such evil dreams?" (55.5–6). The poet increasingly affirms his "dream" of a providential God (54.17) only by virtue of feeling: "I stretch lame hands of faith, and grope, / . . . and call / To what I feel is Lord of all" (55.17–19). Communal affirmations of faith return throughout the poem: let us, the poet exhorts his readers toward the end, "lift from out of dust / A voice unto him that hears, / A cry above the conquered years / . . . and trust, / With faith that comes of self-control, / The truths that never can be proved" (131.5–10). Yet to the end, the ground of faith is intuition, as opposed to knowledge or discovery of the outer world. Lyrics such as 123 and 124 locate faith in the poet's "spirit" in opposition to the world of indifferent geological change (123.9), and appear to find the strongest answer to atheism in the "heart['s]" cry that it has "felt" a divine "Power" reigning above material vicissitude (124.15–16).

Taken together, *In Memoriam*'s firm "split of natural and supernatural" (Tomko 129), and its defense of the latter through inward conviction and "poetic thought," reflect what Charles Taylor has called the rise of an "immanent frame" for modern Western life. As discussed in Chapter 3, "immanent frame" is Taylor's term for widespread perception of the physical world as measured by secular time and impersonal cause and effect, without necessary reference to God or transcendent eternity. Complimentary to this immanent frame is the modern "buffered self," the individual mind that generates its own meanings and purposes, and is strongly "buffered"—or barricaded—from an "outside" material world that is disenchanted of non-human purposive powers and therefore subject to rational analysis and manipulation (*A Secular Age* 35–42). In locating faith "within my spirit" (123.9), *In Memoriam* encloses intimations of God and immortality in the "buffered self," and claims this safe haven for the realm of poetry, as distinguished from the secular immanent frame under the authority of natural science.

This might be what T. S. Eliot sensed in his famous judgment of *In Memoriam:* "It is not religious because of the quality of its faith, but because of the quality of its doubt. Its faith is a poor thing, but its doubt is a very intense experience. *In Memoriam* is a poem of despair, but of despair of the religious kind" (135). Eliot seems to have opposed, as more authentic, the poem's powerful and existential confrontation of an apparently godless world to the poem's groping after an inward, and in Eliot's view, safely watered down faith. Yet Eliot's words shrewdly capture a different truth. The poem's existential doubt and inward faith require each other. Doubt driven by a menacing sense of "The secular abyss to come" (76.6), a seemingly infinite and entropic extension of time and space closed to God, enables a faith by which that doubt is put into perspective. *In Memoriam,* which might deploy the term "secular" more than any of Tennyson's other poems (A. Baker 613), develops the significance of secular and spiritual realms in dialectical tension. The "Godless deep" of the secular abyss (124.12) actually provides the alienated environment in which the speaker can cultivate one modern Western way of believing. As expressed in lyric 127, the speaker learns to hear "across" the vain roar of secular time's "storm" the "deeper voice" (127.3–4) that faintly recalls Christ's in the storm of the gospel story (Mark 4:35–41), and proclaims with Julian of Norwich that "all is well" (127.20). Stripped of unique sacred "place[s]" to become a "space" in which even "worlds" seem small, the universe's secular infinity is a "deep night" exerting the pressure of vast, silent darkness (126.10–12). It forces Tennyson's speaker, with urgent attention, into the soul's spiritually resonant chapel.

The poem thereby participates in the modernizing process that sociologists call "differentiation," a separation of spheres of inquiry, knowledge, and culture once under the domain of religion from its explicit authority—a process that need not entail decline in religious belief or practice. Tennyson follows Lyell in declaring the physical cosmos the domain of professional science, while asserting his own authority as a poet who protectively relocates faith to the inward spirit: "I think we are . . . / Not only cunning casts in clay [i.e., intelligent but purely material beings]: / Let Science prove we are, and then / What matters Science unto men, / At least to me?" (120.2, 5–8). Poetry's phonotext, in defiance of all "Science" might "prove," witnesses to the disdain that materialism should rouse within (real) "men." Derisive alliteration—"cunning casts in clay"—suggests the harsh and barbaric quality of physiological reductionism. The grammar admits reliance on inward assumption rather than facts about the world "out there" ("I think we are . . . / Not"). Yet readers are paradoxically invited to turn their physical experience—of scornful pronunciation—into evidence for an inalienable conviction that "think[ing]" is an activity higher than the "magnetic mockeries" to which some physiologists would reduce the operations of the mind (3). In sonically defending manly disgust with materialism, Tennyson also reinforces the tacit gendering of divisions between inward faith and outward secularity to which *In Memoriam* often resorts, perhaps (as Charles Kingsley would with "masculine Christianity") to preempt charges of doctrinal effeminacy at the hands of journals such as the *English Review*.¹¹ Curiously, the poem frequently feminizes as amoral antagonists *both* ravenous Mother Nature who "shriek[s] against [man's] creed" (56.16) and the "'Science'" who elicits such cries when "'reach[ing] forth her arms / To feel from world to world'" (21.18–19). Science and the secular reality it defines risk sinking into mutually reinforced, and implicitly barren and lesbian, materialism unless checked by the strong spiritual revulsion voiced in poetry.

In so aggressively partitioning the physical world examined by science and the inward sphere of faith and poetry, Tennyson virtually guaranteed that *In Memoriam* would become a central reference point for opposed attempts to imagine religious community within the British middle- and upper-class reading public. Tennyson's distinction enabled the liberal Anglican Charles Kingsley, in an 1850 review, to recommend *In Memoriam* to a new generation of skeptical British males as their best chance of joining a renewed British Christian community. Not surprisingly, Kingsley emphasizes the opposition between feminine materialism and poetic inward conviction discussed above, arguing that *In Memoriam* defends in "the complicated rhythm and melody of modern times" the "old truths" of Christianity (255). By showing that "the heart of man still beats young and fresh" while respecting the authority of "science . . . in the nineteenth century" (255), the poem might encourage young doubters to turn with "the subtle artist" from an implicitly unmanly form of "cold dilettantism and barren epicurism, into something like a living faith and hope" (254). Avoiding Kingsley's claims for Tennyson's support of basic Christian "creeds" (255), later theistic skeptics such as Sidgwick could be inspired by *In Memoriam* to imagine a British and wider human community who "at this stage of human thought" had no choice but to live with the division Tennyson proclaimed between the "physical world" made "known to us through physical science" and the unassailable feeling that this "scientific view" is unable "to satisfy our deepest needs" (*Memoir* I:302–3).

A critic writing in 1871 for the *London Quarterly Review*, published by Wesleyan Methodists, arrived at an opposite conclusion in agreement with many other evangelical commentators. Reviewing a recent collection of essays by Members of the Birmingham Speculative Club, the *London Quarterly* critic concludes that *In Memoriam*, in yielding nature to agnostic physical science, has encouraged free-thinking young readers to ignore signs of a loving God in creation and view it as only "red in tooth and

---

11. Near the end of the fourth section of chapter 6, I suggest how this defensiveness relates to the homoerotic quality of *In Memoriam*, which was immediately sensed by Victorian reviewers.

claw" ("Birmingham Scepticism" 319; *In Memoriam* 56.15). For this journalist, *In Memoriam* risks driving these readers to the comfort of suicide, an action that the skeptical authors in the collection under review were already tentatively embracing as brave and sometimes necessary ("Birmingham Scepticism" 321). Tennyson's faith in "honest doubt" (310), hanging only on the vindication in lyric 124 that "I have felt" (320), is a narrow string on which to swing over the abyss of an indifferent material world, if not for the "*esprits d'élite* like Mr. Tennyson . . . and others of the broad sentimental school" (321), then at least for "the great majority of doubters" (321) who could not be brought to feel in Tennyson's "very singular manner" (320). These questioning young readers need "revealed religion and its evidences" (321). It is the duty of "the truly Christian admirers of the laureate" (310) to unify "the efforts of the whole Church" in Britain in printed "battle against" the swelling "flood of unbelief" that Tennyson's lines are ill-equipped to forestall (321). This reviewer identifies *In Memoriam* as a dangerously irresistible contribution to a division between physical world and inward faith that is supposedly beginning to circulate throughout British print culture. He uses Tennyson's lines to structure and give emotional force[12] to his call to Christian readers—in this case Wesleyan and evangelical—scattered across Britain, asking them to imagine themselves in a religious community responsible for rescuing the next generation of the reading nation from materialist despair.

In Memoriam became central to these irreconcilable efforts to imagine religious community in part because, by enshrining faith in "my spirit" (123.9), it participated in the long process by which "religion" in modern Western societies was coming to seem "more personal, more mental, and more voluntary" (Warner, VanAntwerpen, Calhoun 17). For Charles Taylor, this modern climate of belief relies upon the immanent frame and its counterpart, the buffered self. Both assume a sharp split between natural and supernatural realms, which Taylor argues arose from a series of reform efforts within Latin Christendom beginning in the late medieval period, of which the Protestant Reformation was only one key phase. Early reforms within Catholic Christendom sought "to impose on everyone a more individually committed and Christocentric religion of devotion and action, and to repress or even abolish older, supposedly 'magical' or 'superstitious' forms of collective ritual practice" ("Apologia" 304–5). Such reforms gradually eroded an "'enchanted' world . . . in which spirits and forces," such as

---

12. The author quotes *In Memoriam* at nearly every major turn of his argument (310, 320, 321, 323, 329, 330).

those "given off by love potions and relics," played a decisive "role"; and it thereby enabled the emergence of buffered selfhood, thickening the previously "porous boundary" between these forces and their impact on "our lives, psychic and physical" (302).

The unforeseen cumulative effect was the incremental "excarnation" of Christianity and Christian practice, and consequent spread, first at elite levels and then across the wider population, of the idea that "spirit" was "radically other than and potentially contrary to the body" (Warner, VanAntwerpen, Calhoun 19). By the sixteenth century, Western Christian belief was being defined in increasingly epistemological terms. The Reformation and Counter-Reformation generated explicit confessions of belief to clarify the conceptual boundaries of Catholic and Protestant forms of Christianity (Sheehan 222). To facilitate comparison of the truth values of Europe's competing forms of Christianity, scholastics—especially in England—created our modern category of "religion," understood as the package of propositions in which people consciously profess belief (P. Harrison 2–3).

For all these reasons, European Christianity increasingly unearthed faith from its position as a tacit truth and a relationship of trust that saturated spaces, objects, rituals, and social practices, and relocated it to the individual's self-conscious mental states, beliefs which one did or did not hold (McKeon xix, 33). This gradual process took a definitive shape among Protestants in seventeenth-century England, resulting in conceptual and legal distinctions between public actions and statements that affected social welfare and interior religious beliefs that were a matter of private conscience—and a strong association of the latter among Protestants with domestic and private spaces (McKeon 39–42).

By imagining a gulf between natural and supernatural, between the outer world and the convictions of the inner self, *In Memoriam* forcefully articulated a tectonic shift in the conditions of belief that had been underway for several centuries, and which was coming to feel inevitable, and even natural, to a widening portion of the British population. It would fly in the face of history to suggest that all Victorians came to regard faith as essentially inward and disembodied. This would discount the extreme importance of corporate worship and ritual practice to Victorian religious life and to heated debates in print culture over church architecture, Anglo-Catholic ritualism, and the (stereotyped) gesticulating fervor of dissenting sects in their services. Yet ideologically diverse Victorian reviewers indicate that *In Memoriam* powerfully resonated with a broad tendency, especially among middle- and upper-class reading audiences, to locate the "essence" of spirituality in an interior region of the soul.

A striking example comes from *The Dublin Review,* an ultramontane Roman Catholic quarterly founded by Nicholas Wiseman (Altholz 99), who a few months after *In Memoriam* was published became Cardinal Wiseman under the re-establishment of the Catholic hierarchy in England and Wales, a move which filled the British press with Protestant furor and fear. Not surprisingly, an 1864 commentator on "The Laureate and His School" for *The Dublin Review* portrays Tennyson as the consummate Protestant "English gentleman in the reign of Queen Victoria," characterized by his "indifference about Christian dogma" (363) and his desperate need for the "one religion appointed by God" to leaven the "sweet melancholy of the 'In Memoriam'" (371). Tennyson and his *In Memoriam* represent to this reviewer a Protestant tendency to turn "Christianity" into a "mere system of ethics," making religion "eminently subjective" and rendering incomprehensible Christ's physical suffering, Catholic disciplines for "mortification of the flesh," and "the Sacraments of" Christ's "Love" (372). Nevertheless, while chastising Tennyson's excarnated, subjective Protestant spirituality, the reviewer reveals his common ground with the laureate when he sanctifies a version of this spirituality in the realm of poetry. Declaring Tennyson a true poet, he explains "Poetry . . . is the daughter of Heaven," meant to "lead us nearer to Heaven" and "God" as it "unsensualize[s] the world of sense, by breathing into it somewhat of our own immortal spirit" (370). Rome might need to supplement this poetic spirituality with sacramental ritual and dogmatic discipline, but the reviewer takes for granted a distinction between interior immortal soul and outward material world, between an authentic breath of spirit within the self and the sensible world it must transfigure.

Like *In Memoriam,* Keble's *Christian Year* appears to have benefited from the tendency to locate faith within the soul. One popular poem, "St. Matthew's Day," was admired by commentators from many denominations.[13] It celebrates those who, amidst the impersonal bustle of the nineteenth-century secular urban world, retain a religion of the heart: "[They] carry music in their heart / Through dusky lane and wrangling mart, / Plying their daily task with busier feet, / Because their secret souls a holy strain repeat" ("St. Matthew" 29–32). Yet Keble's readers are exhorted to imagine

---

13. A representative praise is by the Congregationalist minister Braden William in the 1867 *British Quarterly Review:* 15.

cultivating this interior faith within a community that is united by inherited creeds, confirmed through regular private and corporate devotion, and reliant on a God revealed in Christ's incarnation and all the details of the natural world and daily life.

By contrast, *In Memoriam* seems to forgo "any external basis of religion" for "a spiritualized inner life" (Tomko 127). As I have already suggested, however, *In Memoriam* could deeply impact Victorian readers, and enable so many to compare it with *The Christian Year,* because it never functionally concedes that "faith and form" can be "sunder'd" (127.1–2). Tennyson's poetic cycle makes its subjective confession of faith by relying on the physical and affective persuasions of poetic form, and by making allusions to public religious forms. Angry reactions to *In Memoriam* show this as clearly as sympathetic ones. The High Church journalist for the 1850 *English Review* yearns to whip Tennyson only because *In Memoriam* gestures toward public forms of faith that make legible the subjective, private nature of its confession. Elements of *In Memoriam,* such as the introductory invocation to "our Blessed Lord," signify for this critic a "deliberate" and public "faith" into which the poet invites readers ("New Poetry" 72–73)—yet by lyric 33, the critic complains, it seems that Tennyson does not, after all, "care to fix" this faith in any "form" (33.4). This reviewer rejects the elegy's invitation to imagine himself in a community united by intuitions rather than Church teaching, to rest in "truths that never can be proved / Until we close with all we loved, / And all we flow from, soul in soul" (131.10–12). Yet the journalist can help his High Church readers discern and censure the nature of Tennyson's imagined community by virtue of public coordinates—the poem's shadowing of the Nicene Creed, and its implicit attack on the saturation of the print market by divisive High Church arguments for ancient rituals in defiance of internalized Protestant spirituality: "who would keep an ancient form / Thro' which the spirit breathes no more?" (105.19–20); "Ring out [New Year bells] a slowly dying cause, / And ancient forms of party strife" (106.13–14).

IV. *IN MEMORIAM* AND MID-VICTORIAN CONDITIONS OF RELIGION'S PUBLIC PRESENCE

In chapter 6, I examine in greater detail the way Tennyson's championship of inward faith depends on appeals to public forms. Here I claim that Tennyson's *In Memoriam* became a new *Christian Year* in part because of the very trends that Keble tried to counter with his poetic cycle. As discussed in chapter 4, Keble felt that a privatized view of religion was gaining too much of an undisciplined hold over nineteenth-century British print culture. Before publishing *The Christian Year,* Keble appears to have become convinced that a Protestant heritage that prioritized the individual's inward faith and interpretation of the Bible was dangerously combining with rising confidence in the private judgments of readers, and with increasing challenges to the political and social dominance of the Church of England. Taken together, Keble concluded, these developments meant that a British mass print culture was emerging in which the rapid circulation of texts was spreading incredulity and confidence in one's own judgment as a reader at the expense of Church authority. Keble abandoned his plans for posthumous publication, issuing *The Christian Year* to reassert Anglican influence over British readers by translating into the ever-expanding market for private reading the disciplined habits of devotion trained by the ancient Catholic forms preserved in the Prayer Book and Anglican worship.

If this strategy reveals Keble's reactionary conservatism, it also points to shared conditions of religious participation and communal imagination in nineteenth-century Britain. As explained in greater detail in the introduction, the rise of a voluntary religious establishment that respected private religious conscience intersected with a prodigious take-off in the activity of reading. This created an environment in which, especially after the 1830s, faith and religious allegiance were deeply shaped by competition for influence through the print market. In the resulting battle for religious audiences, full identification of a national Christian culture with any single Church institution became impossible, even as consumption of religion through the printed page skyrocketed. Imagining the nation's Christian community and one's own religious group with respect to that collective, or seeking potential converts, increasingly meant appealing to bonds formed by circulating texts between the inward feelings of strangers.

In Memoriam, seeming to conflate private reading with membership in a Christian community, and to testify to a "minimum of faith" within the soul, was poised to become a major religious landmark in Victorian print culture—especially after it won Tennyson recognition as Britain's laureate. In an 1855 article for the *Edinburgh Review,* the (then) Anglo-Catholic Coventry Patmore concludes that *In Memoriam* has attracted its widening interdenominational circle of admirers because of "the emphasis of feeling with which [Tennyson] has dwelt" in it "upon the simple first foundations of all possible religion, namely, a belief in a personal Deity" and in eternal life ("Maud" 503). Five years earlier, and two months after *In Memoriam* was published, Patmore had defended this view in *The North British Review*, a tolerant journal aligned with the Free Church of Scotland (Altholz 92–93). There Patmore points to *In Memoriam* in support of a triumphant announcement:

> The great elementary truths of life, which have constituted the A B C of Christian philosophy in all ages, up to the last century, were in that period so far forgotten in their vitality, and permitted to die into the most impotent truisms, that they now require to be resuscitated with a labour like that of discovery. "The head and mighty paramount of truths, immortal life in never-fading worlds;"¹⁴ [. . .] the assured result of evil in ultimate good; the dominion of man over nature and natural destiny; and all the doctrines which interpret existence [. . .] are now in process of recovery from the syncope into which they have been cast by a long period of practical neglect. ("In Memoriam" 553)

Enlightened Deism and the self-satisfied apathy of the Anglican establishment had, in the eighteenth century, permitted a "syncope," or dangerous pause of the British heart, with regard to the "A B C of Christian philosophy." For Patmore, Tennyson has rediscovered these elementary truths at the level of "intuitive evidences" within the human heart (552), and his poem promises to revive the hearts of a nation of readers, bringing each to beat in time with his own.¹⁵ *In Memoriam* appears, to Patmore at least, less a diary of the "Broad Church communicant who neither feels very much faith nor, all told, 'cares to'" (Tucker 535) than a strangely fundamentalist confession that might betoken a national revival. Even the antagonistic *English Review* critic of 1850 praises the poet's confirmation of basic spiritual longings in a form bound to become part of the reading nation's consciousness: "the hopes and fears of the poet, as to a Providence and a life beyond the grave, and his general views of human life, are all embodied in this most exquisite collection; an heirloom bequeathed to our nation, and to be treasured by it, as long as the English tongue endures" ("New Poetry" 72).

The Anglo-Catholic Patmore and the stodgier High Church *English Review* critic suggest why *In Memoriam* could, in Patmore's terms, appeal to reflective readers from "all denominations of Christianity" ("Maud"

---

14. Patmore quotes, altering punctuation, from Wordsworth's *Excursion* VI.86–87.

15. In chapter 6, I discuss the comparison Patmore invites in this passage between the revived pulse of belief and Tennyson's metrical art.

503). For both, *In Memoriam* showed that spiritual truths foundational to Christian belief sprung from the innermost intuitions of the heart, and it did so in poetry that would be cherished by "our nation" ("New Poetry" 72). Kingsley, whose liberal Anglican theology was at odds with the views of both of these commentators, could for this reason, in the same month as *The English Review* essay, celebrate Tennyson as the "deliberate champion of vital Christianity," and *In Memoriam* as "the noblest Christian poem which England has produced for two centuries" (245). Despite theological differences, these reviewers coincided in feeling that *In Memoriam* had revealed "vital" Christian convictions that were safeguarded in the depths of inner experience from shifting storms of doubt and the rancor of sects and their organs of public opinion.

Yet commentators parted ways when imagining the Christian community that should be built upon Tennyson's witness to bedrock spiritual truths. *The English Review* critic feels that Tennyson should "muster courage to believe" in a creed based on "received revelation" ("New Poetry" 73) and defended by "our Anglican branch of the Church Catholic" (65), since otherwise the faith of the nation's poet—and those he inspires—will remain too subjective, guided by poetic feeling more than conviction (74). While defending Tennyson against the charge of pure subjectivism, Patmore also warns in his 1850 article that "the rediscovered *ground-work* of the Christian faith" powerfully expressed in *In Memoriam* should never be mistaken for the whole building, and should instead be supplemented by "the full measure of Christian doctrine" ("In Memoriam" 553). Some evangelicals extended the strategy of reading *In Memoriam* as a doorway to dogmatic faith into bait-and-hook outreach events. In 1871, *The Christian Witness,* a widely circulating Congregationalist and evangelical magazine (Altholz 68–69), included a report from a missionary to Ireland who gave "readings from Tennyson" ("Stratagem" 261). He followed with "a short sermon," and concluded with a call to salvation, a reading from 1 Corinthians 15 about the resurrection of the dead, and a prayer (261).

The *Christian Witness* missionary seems to think he has been especially "crafty" ("Stratagem" 261). Yet he was giving an extreme application to a familiar stratagem. The Evangelical Anglican minister John Richard Vernon adopts a similar technique in the 1868 article for *Sunday at Home* discussed earlier in this chapter. Quoting lyric 124 of *In Memoriam* ("I have felt") to support the idea that faith is a "Feeling" (342), Vernon quickly guides his intended working-class readership to an evangelical destination. He claims that this Tennysonian feeling of faith comes from "the secret inward work of the Holy Spirit," and that whoever fails to go further and "believe in

Christ, and receive God's word," should heed the warning that "'he that believeth not shall be damned.' (These, I remind the reader, are the words of Jesus)" (342). In Vernon's interpretation—and, he hopes, that of his Sunday readers—Tennyson's poem is a public testimony to innate convictions planted within the soul by God, feelings that are meant to lead to the "creeds" (96.11) that *In Memoriam* tries to keep at arm's length, even while shadowing them in its introductory stanzas and at key junctures in its cycle of lyrics. Others, fewer in number, resisted treating the poem as a first step to joining a Christian community bound by creed. As mentioned earlier, Henry Sidgwick felt *In Memoriam* expressed an "indestructible and inalienable minimum of faith" (*Memoir* I:303) in "God and Immortality" (302), but opposed any firm connection between this intuition and Tennyson's prayer to Christ in the introductory stanzas (I:304).

Whether they were concerned to augment or restrict the influence of *In Memoriam*'s witness to a "minimum of faith," Victorian commentators from a broad range of religious positions interpreted Tennyson's testimony in public and national terms. Although not always in such a jingoistic fashion, many Victorian critics could join the 1860 writer for the moderate Nonconformist *British Quarterly Review* in celebrating "the opening poem of *In Memoriam*" as "the heartbeat of England," a medium through which an inalienable and minimal piety could be imagined and confirmed for Britain ("Les Contemplations" 98). The liberal Anglican Kingsley recommends Tennyson's elegy to young skeptics as a gateway into a vigorous yet intellectually adaptive nineteenth-century British Christian community of the future. The Anglo-Catholic Patmore imagines that *In Memoriam* is reaching discerning Christians of all denominations, a sign that the nation's heartbeat is once again timed to the "A B C of Christian philosophy," and is perhaps ready to receive the full measure of Christian doctrine. Patmore, Kingsley, the High Church *English Review* journalist, the Evangelical Rev. Vernon, and the Nonconformist evangelical missionary to Ireland all variously represent *In Memoriam* as a port of entry into more explicit forms of British Christian community.

This indicates that religious commentators found *In Memoriam* valuable for projecting the identity of their own religious subcultures or counterpublics within the British reading public. A public—whether the urbane eighteenth-century consumers of Addison's *Spectator*, modern hunters who read *Field and Stream*, the "younger generation" defined by MTV, the "American people" addressed by presidents, or the brotherhood of all believers—might be defined as "a multicontextual space of circulation, organized not by a place or an institution but by the circulation of discourse" (Warner, *Publics and Counterpublics* 118). Counterpublics are not merely subcultures, or subdivisions within a broader public. For Michael Warner, they maintain "at some level, conscious or not, an awareness of" their "subordinate status" within a "dominant" public (119), and they seek to "transform" the norms of public discourse (122). In my view, promoters and members of a subculture can fluidly shift between viewing themselves as subcultures and counterpublics, and their views of themselves do not always match their perception by members of other imagined communities. Chartists active before the 1850s were a counterpublic, both in their own opinion and in that of the dominant publics of "mainstream" middle- and upper-class Victorian Britain. The commentators on *In Memoriam* surveyed in this chapter, however, generally portray themselves as members of religious subcultures within respectable British Christian society, but shift to imagining themselves in embattled counterpublics when this enables a greater sense of shared identity and purpose.

The 1864 critic for *The Dublin Review* discussed above portrays the journal's ultramontane Catholic audience as a counterpublic that must distinguish themselves from a Protestant British reading public plagued by the "eminently subjective" and excarnated form of religion revealed in Tennyson's *In Memoriam* ("The Laureate" 372). Yet, as I emphasized earlier, this reviewer shares the sharp distinction between inner soul and outer material world fundamental to *In Memoriam*, as well as the idea that poetry joins religion in appealing to the former. He also addresses himself to educated readers who will imagine themselves part of a broader British audience that extends beyond conservative Catholics, and whose refinement enables them to appreciate *In Memoriam* as the work of "a genuine poet" (370). The *Dublin Review* critic uses *In Memoriam* to reaffirm his audience's identity as a counterpublic loyal to Rome and opposed to watered-down British Protestantism. Yet he also praises *In Memoriam*'s poetic qualities in order to assure his readers that they inhabit a subculture in polite society and the educated British republic of letters.

Similarly, evangelicals such as the critic for the 1871 Methodist *London Quarterly Review* discussed earlier in this chapter often portrayed themselves and their audiences as embattled godly counterpublics in an only nominally Christian British reading public. Yet the *London Quarterly* critic closes his article with a call for orthodox Christians to join in interdenominational battle against the skepticism being marketed to intelligent young male readers. For an 1852 critic in the High Church *English Review*, Tennyson, especially through *In Memoriam*, usefully exhibits the supposed general attitudes of "the highly-educated gentleman of the nineteenth century" ("Archer Gurney's Poems" 108). Like Tennyson, these gentlemen have "a little Christianity, not of a very strict or practical character; a little infidelity, and a good deal of skepticism" (108). The critic relies on this background of minimal commitment to bring into relief the counterpublic that he desires to form out of an overlapping body of elite readers. He opens his article by appealing to an audience of conservative, educated, High Anglicans who, unlike "the world," view all historical events as "tokens" of a "Divine will" at work according to principles discerned in "the sacred volume" of the Bible (105). Projecting counterpublics for themselves and their readers, these journalists still assume that their religious audience is a subculture within a wider middle- and upper-class British reading public, rather than sitting at its margins or challenging its fundamental norms. All of them find an indispensable point of reference in Tennyson's *In Memoriam* when imagining these communities of readers.

The Victorian reviewers I have analyzed in this chapter collectively demonstrate that Tennyson's minimal confession, in a poetic cycle that invited a reading experience loosely parallel to encountering *The Christian Year*, quickly became a spiritual center of gravity in Victorian print culture. Tennyson perhaps unintentionally reworked the alignment of private reading with Christian community that Keble had himself unintentionally put into interdenominational circulation. Yet in publishing in this form, Tennyson introduced a "New Christian Year" uniquely suited to the conceptual conditions and public presence of religious faith in mid-Victorian Britain. *In Memoriam* struck contradictory chords in a broad range of British Christian readers in the middle and upper classes accustomed to imagining their religious belonging, whether in the nation or in their denomination, in terms of inward faith shared with strangers through texts circulating in a competitive print market. By virtue of its minimal testimony, *In Memoriam* became, almost upon publication, a primary medium through and in terms of which a diverse array of commentators could imagine the religious landscape of their nation and the place of their religious subculture or—in their view—counterpublic within it.

CHAPTER 6

IN MEMORIAM'S OPEN SECRET

The Public Forms of Private Faith

For a wide array of Victorian commentators, I argued in the previous chapter, Tennyson's *In Memoriam* seemed to bear strong public testimony to an inalienable minimum of faith, an intuitive belief in God and immortality in the bedrock of the soul. Tennyson presented this minimal confession in a poetic cycle that Victorians intuitively compared with the coordination of private reading and imagined participation in Christian community made popular by John Keble's *The Christian Year* (1827). *In Memoriam* thereby became a powerful medium for middle- and upper-class readers to imagine their spiritual relationship to strangers across their society. Tennyson's "New Christian Year" rivaled and sometimes replaced Keble's, appealing to a broad spectrum of middle- and upper-class readers used to imagining their religious belonging, whether in the nation or in their Christian subcultures, in terms of bonds formed between the inner feelings of strangers by texts circulating in a competitive religious market.

Discussion of *In Memoriam* could therefore seem destined to add one more chapter to the story that earlier twentieth-century sociologists and historians took for granted: the evolution of the modern liberal state was inevitably attended by the privatization of religion, its removal from authority in the public sphere to the realm of private conviction. Yet Tennyson's elegy and its Victorian reception actually help discredit this theory, which a widening circle of scholars have now rejected or severely modified, especially in response to the work of sociologist José Casanova (*Public Religions in the Modern World* 1994). In a late-century Sunday evening sermon on *In Memoriam,* the Anglican clergyman and spiritualist Hugh Reginald Haweis claimed that Tennyson "reads" his audience "the open secret of their hearts, by showing them his own," reminding them that "he and they are no longer solitary units, but . . . belong to a whole" (91–92). *In Memoriam* resonated with so many Victorians because it staged a public confession of grief deepened by doubt when faced with the "secular abyss" of modern imagination (76.6), a seemingly infinite and "Godless" extension of time and space (124.12), in order to affirm poetry's authoritative defense of a sanctuary for faith within the soul. This affirmation was underwritten by the poem's regular allusions to public religious forms and texts, such as the Christian calendar, church bells, hymns, the Prayer Book, and the Bible. In chapter 5, I concentrated on one crucial way in which *In Memoriam* in fact depended for its intelligibility on publicly recognized religious forms: the creedal resonances of the introductory stanzas, to which High Church and evangelical writers alike quickly reacted when using the poem to imagine the spiritual landscape of their nation and their place within it.

In this chapter, I analyze in finer detail what Haweis calls *In Memoriam*'s "open secret," the way it communicates supposedly private intuitions of faith through public forms, religious and otherwise, that have been subtly internalized and psychologized. If faith in *In Memoriam* explicitly inhabits the region of mood and internal suggestion, its communicability and texture comes from a wide range of public allusions and shared forms. The creation of an individual experience silently coded by communal structures makes Tennyson's journey to faith seem "our" journey for many Victorian readers. Kirstie Blair makes a related observation about *In Memoriam,* concluding that it "liberally admits that forms are sometimes inadequate as a basis for faith, while insistently framing its own faith through form" (*Form and Faith* 189). Rather than situating *In Memoriam* within wider Victorian debates about poetic and religious forms, which Blair so ably does, here I focus on the private-yet-public configuration of spiritual experience in the poem, and how ideologically diverse Victorian readers found this configuration vital to the act of imagining themselves in spiritual community with strangers across their nation. As in chapter 5, this approach to *In Memoriam* must forgo attention to all that could be observed about the poem's remarkable—and oft-discussed—formal and semantic nuances to highlight those qualities of the poem that prompted

Victorians to apply it to divergent efforts to imagine their religious communities and the spiritual character of their nation.

By relying on internalized public forms to validate intuitive faith, I argue later in this chapter, *In Memoriam* encouraged a diffusive sense of British piety. This vaguely pious British fellowship was called upon by some to endorse repression of protest at home, and justify displays of military and imperial power abroad, as expressions of a sacred British community. In pointing to basic spiritual intuitions that supposedly eluded sectarian lines of battle, Tennyson's "New Christian Year" could for some of its apologists ironically encourage a markedly outward and physically enforced form of British sanctity.

I. CHRISTMAS AND MO(U)RNING DEVOTIONS

As demonstrated in chapter 5, between *In Memoriam*'s publication and the century's end nearly every Victorian commentator was inclined to treat the poem's introductory stanzas as the public and shareable "Creed, . . . Litany, and Doxology of Tennyson" ("Gospel Notes" 181). Readers from a wide spectrum of denominational and ideological allegiances also instantly and approvingly seized on Tennyson's organization of his lyrics around three Christmastides (lyrics 28–30, 78, and 104–5). The 1850 Nonconformist *Eclectic Review* was representative in identifying "Christmas-tide and its household rites" ("Tennyson's In Memoriam" 335) as powerful means by which Tennyson's spiritual struggle in *In Memoriam* assumed a publicly legible trajectory and connected "itself with the deepest life of the reader" (332). In his early book-length study of *Tennyson's In Memoriam* (1884), the American professor of rhetoric and former Baptist minister John Franklin Genung built on this critical tradition, using the Christmas sections as public coordinates by which to evaluate the poet's inward progression of mood and faith. When commenting on the first Christmas series (28–30), for example, Genung observes that the ringing of church bells on Christmas Eve signifies collective "gladness on the account of the august birth which Christmas celebrates," against which the "reality" of "this occasion" for the poet, "sorrow" over Hallam, emerges in sharply limned contrast (Genung 121).

Yet Genung submits his interpretation of *In Memoriam* to the poem's concluding insistence that "true" spiritual meaning and faith "dwell" beyond the reach of public religious forms in the poet's "spirit" (123.9–10), a "dream of good" (129.11) preserved from material harm even "tho' faith and form / Be sunder'd in the night of fear" (127.1–2). Only from such inner springs can Tennyson rise to faith and close his series calling upon others to look into their hearts for the same "truths that never can be proved" (131.10). Genung recognizes that Tennyson draws strength for his final proclamation of a "far-off divine event" (Epilogue.143) from the accumulated "holy meanings" of the Christmastides, during which believers traditionally remember the first and anticipate the Second Advent of Christ (Genung 88). Turning to the poet's censure of "ancient form / Thro' which the spirit breathes no more" in the third Christmas series (105.19–20), however, Genung concludes that the Christmas seasons and rites resemble the "ruin'd chrysalis" of Hallam's rotting body (82.8): they are disposable mediums through which a spirit happened to express itself before "moving on" (82.5). "The usual customs have lost their life because the *spirit* of Christmas hope has become so settled and significant that the ancient form can no more express its meaning. The cheer of this season not only eclipses the grief, but rejects all formal demonstrations of joy as unnecessary and meaningless" (Genung 175).

Genung's reading makes explicit the poetic cycle's open secret. According to this process, inward and private spiritual "joy" is defined and rendered publicly accessible by "formal demonstrations," which are then declared merely expedient. In retrospect, it can seem as if the "*spirit* of Christmas hope" were "settled and significant"—formed and intelligible—on its own. It only needed some passing representation to be felt in the material and social world of Tennyson, his family, and his readers. Christmas plays a tellingly different role in Keble's *Christian Year*. As Patrick Scott has observed, Keble focuses on a single Christmas contextualized by the full cycle of Church festivals, whereas Tennyson concentrates on this single season three times, apparently stressing its changing meaning to him rather than its place within an inherited ecclesiastical calendar beyond his personal timeline ("Rewriting" 149).

Keble's "Christmas Day" poem opens with a creative response to its scriptural epigraph, Luke 2:13, taken from the lesson assigned for that day by the Prayer Book, where Luke recounts the angels announcing Christ's birth to the shepherds. Noticing that the angel who begins the proclamation is joined by "a multitude of the heavenly host" (Luke 2:13 AV[1]) only after he says Christ will be born in a lowly manger, Keble turns this detail into a foreshadowing of Christ's dwelling within the manger of every hum-

---

1. All biblical quotations are from the Authorized Version.

ble believer's—and reader's—heart (35–36). Readers are not left to infer that this means Christ dwells in them apart from participation in a church under priestly authority. The approach of the shepherds to Christ's manger becomes, in Keble's hands, a type of priests—"pastoral spirits"—approaching "Thy lowly shrine" in an Anglican service (43, 46). Keble reflects on the present day, when readers are ideally considering his poem in sync with the Church calendar, which is meant to inspire memory of Christ's first Advent and longing for his Second Advent: "Still, as the day comes round / For Thee to be reveal'd, / By wakeful shepherds Thou art found" (49–51). Addressing these shepherd-priests tending their flocks in the night of the nineteenth century, Keble consoles their fears about "wandering" British "sheep" (56), reminding them that "the Lord" can make his manger in the "hearts" of even apathetic believers (63–64).

Keble offers an idiosyncratic interpretation of Luke's gospel and the feast of Christmas. Yet he does this as one priest speaking to other priests within the presence of readers drawn into an imagined congregation governed by priestly authority, the Church lectionary and calendar, and the divine arrangement of history that underwrites connections such as those between Christ's manger and believers' hearts. Tennyson, by contrast, illustrates through his changing reaction to three Christmastides the evolution of his and family members' grief and hope:

> With trembling fingers did we weave
> The holly round the Christmas hearth;
> A rainy cloud possess'd the earth,
> And sadly fell our Christmas-eve. (30.1–4)

> Again at Christmas did we weave
> The holly round the Christmas hearth;
> The silent snow possess'd the earth,
> And calmly fell our Christmas-eve . . . (78.1–4)

> To-night ungather'd let us leave
> This laurel, let this holly stand:
> We live within the stranger's land,
> And strangely falls our Christmas eve. (105.1–4)

The return of Christmas Eve across these poems marks a progression, often mirrored by weather, from weeping and sorrow on the first Christmastide after Hallam's death, to calm resignation, to a growing break with the past after relocating to a new home. Alongside the Christmas cycle,

Tennyson includes recurrences of the New Year (83, 106), anniversaries of Hallam's death (lyrics 72, 99) and birth (107), and the return of spring (38–39, 115–16). The coordinated impression of these cycles is a movement from resentful anger over Hallam's physical absence to acceptance of his spiritual rebirth in the next life, and therefore anticipation of "some strong bond which is to be" recovered (116.15) in that "one far-off divine event, / To which the whole creation moves" (Epilogue.143–44). The interweaving of ecclesiastical, domestic, seasonal, and personal calendars into a chord seemingly pulled through the central circle of the poet's feelings reinforces the total impression of moving from the poet's inward grief to inward faith, all the while making this motion feel collective.

For this reason, Tennyson's meditations on the second anniversary of Hallam's death in lyric 99 can seem to take place within an unseen community, forming an analogy to the coordination of private meditation with ecclesiastical cycles in Keble's *Christian Year*. The opening line recycles that of lyric 72, which marked the first anniversary of Hallam's death in early autumn: "Risest thou thus, dim dawn, again" (99.1, 72.1). The syntax of lyric 99 also recalls 72, repeating more pronouncedly the strategy of apostrophizing the dawn across stanzas through parallel subordinate clauses: "dim dawn . . . / Who usherest in the dolorous hour / With thy quick tears . . . / Who might'st have heaved a windless flame / Up the deep East" (72.1, 9–10, 13–14); "dim dawn . . . / Who tremblest thro' thy darkling red . . . / Who murmurest in the foliaged eaves . . . / Who wakenest with thy balmy breath" (99. 1, 5, 9, 13). Internal to *In Memoriam* and noticed only as (or after) a reader passes through the elegy, this verbal and grammatical repetition resembles an improvised secular liturgy, a ritual of lament that renders intelligible the poet's evolving grief from tears to calmer melancholy, as mirrored in the weather on each anniversary.

Yet the ecclesiastical time invoked by the Christmas cycle of *In Memoriam* is also quietly recalled in the refrain "Risest thou . . . again" (72.1, 99.1). The poet's grief is contextualized by the Church calendar's arrangement of the year around the first coming and resurrection of Christ, which herald the resurrection of the dead at his Second Coming. Implicitly extending the traditional Christian pun of *Sun* on *Son* that runs through *In Memoriam* and *The Christian Year* (see chapter 5), the autumn sun rises as the Apostles' Creed claims the Son has risen and the dead will one day—only to remind the poet yet "again" that his beloved friend remains where "roots are wrapt" about his "bones" (2.4). The indicative "Risest thou" shadows an unvoiced imperative ("rise thou, Hallam") as secular cycles—seasonal, diurnal, and poetic—recall ecclesiastical and biblical ones, which are then both subsumed in the personal calendar of grieving they structure. In this context, as the poet in lyric 99 relinquishes his earlier command to the autumn sun to "hide" its mockery of his longing "beneath the ground" (72.27), his gentler receptivity to the morning feels like a concession to sympathize with a public audience: "[You dawn] wakenest with thy balmy breath / To myriads on the genial earth, / Memories of bridal, or of birth, / And unto myriads more, of death" (13–16). Wherever in the globe these mourners are, "To-day they count as kindred souls; / They know me not, but mourn with me" (19–20). *Mourn* might tempt readers to recall *morn* and coin it as a verb, suggesting a private-yet-public form of mo(u)rning devotion, and turning this passage into a secular version of the encouragement offered readers by "Morning," Keble's poem on Morning Prayer, to use *The Christian Year* with the Prayer Book. As Tennyson's "Christian Year" continued, year after year, reaching a widening British (and imperial) audience, many could join Queen Victoria[2] in feeling these lines were addressed to them whenever their calendar of grief aligned with the laureate's.

The private, internal faith of *In Memoriam* is always given meaning by shared forms and calendars, but in ways that elude explicit notice of the kind Keble attracted when using an imposed ecclesiastical scheme. *In Memoriam* thereby risked accusations of heterodox vagueness, but it also more easily overleapt the denominational barriers imposed by Keble's explicit submission to Anglican forms.[3] The Nonconformist *Eclectic Review* critic's immediate sense that *In Memoriam*'s cycle of grief was "a cycle of experience common to thoughtful humanity," and that it even offered "the poetic solution of every-day problems" ("Tennyson's In Memoriam" 332), depended on the fact that "Familiar incident marks the progress of time and . . . sorrow" (334).

II. REPEAT THE SOUNDING JOY

In Memoriam resounds with church bells: twice on Christmas Eve (28, 104), again on New Year's Eve (106), and at the wedding of Tennyson's sister in the closing *epithalamion* (Epilogue.60–64). In all but the last case,

---

2. After Prince Albert's death in 1861, the Queen famously told Tennyson that "next to the Bible 'In Memoriam' is my comfort" (Ryan 120).

3. Braden William in 1867, in the moderate Nonconformist *British Quarterly Review*, lamented the "hard, mechanical, forced character" given to portions of *The Christian Year* by Keble's decision to compose poems "to celebrate the annual festivities and fasts authorized by the Prayer Book" (108).

Tennyson considers the bells' emotional and spiritual impact from outside the church, in what seems to be a solitary domestic setting within a series of lyrics reflecting on domestic seasonal rites. In lyric 28, he listens to the bells "Swell out and fail, as if a door / Were shut between me and the sound" (7–8). While marking a private separation from the communal worship and security to which the bells beckon, this and other solitary bell-listening scenes also situate Tennyson's meditations within an imagined religious and national community hearing the same and similar church bells proclaim that the Christian Year is "draw[ing] near the birth of Christ" (28.1). Allusions to the British technique of change-ringing— "Each [set of bells] voice four changes on the wind" [28.9]—link the bells to Anglican and British piety (Blair, "Church Going" 769); yet by virtue of their existence as public sound waves marking acts of worship and points in the year observed by many Christian denominations, the bell tones avoid exclusive Anglican associations in a way that allusions to activities within the church could not (Blair, *Form and Faith* 179).

This conflation of personal and communal resonances through church bells is clearest in lyric 106, where the poet, listening to bells on New Year's Eve, appears to speak both of his willingness to let the old year pass and to release Hallam to death ("Ring out, wild bells, and let him die" [106.4]), and where his personal acceptance of hope expands into a national and global vision: "Ring out the grief that saps the mind, / For those that here we see no more; / Ring out the feud of rich and poor, / Ring in redress to all mankind" (9–12). Yet even so universal and progressive a note reverberates personally. "Ring out the grief," in bidding sorrow farewell, also seems to demand it be expressed, broadcast "out" and received in sympathy by all who morn "those . . . we see no more." The poignant homophone, "wring out," concedes the tortured heart being expressed, and points to the "wild and wandering cries" of *In Memoriam* (Intro.41) also recalled in the "*wild* bells" (106.4). If "the fuller minstrel" of the better future is to arise within or after Tennyson, his triumphant song must be "r[u]ng . . . in" by first "ring[ing] out my mournful rhymes" (106.19–20). Perhaps just this alternation, or confusion, of personal, communal, and universal notes inspired the clergyman Haweis, mentioned above, to remark that *In Memoriam*'s "tones of sorrow invariably arrest; . . . they draw us in spite of ourselves; they win us and cling to us—because they reflect some of the deepest and most universal aspects of our common humanity" (92).

The church bells connect the poet's inner life to a national religious calendar, so that reading *In Memoriam*, just as reading *The Christian Year*, potentially becomes a passage into an interdenominational Christian British community. This helps explain why early reviewers such as Charles Kingsley recommended the private meditations of Tennyson as a powerful means for forging a national religious community through domestic reading:

> [The poems] are fit only to be read solemnly in our purest and most thoughtful moods, in the solitude of our chamber, or by the side of those we love, with thanks to the great heart who has taken courage to bestow on us the record of his own love, doubt, and triumph. (252)

One of the pieces Kingsley transcribes after this comment is, unsurprisingly, the peal of bells in lyric 106, a section quoted by British literary reviewers and clergy almost without intermission until the early twentieth century. Franklin Lushington—brother to Edmund Lushington whose marriage to Cecilia, Tennyson's sister, is announced by the bells in the Epilogue—focused on the echo of bells throughout *In Memoriam* in his 1850 review for *Tait's Edinburgh Magazine*. Lushington indicates both the nostalgic sense of national Christian community, and the familiarity with a wide body of related poetry, which many Victorians could be expected to bring to the bell-listening scenes of *In Memoriam*:

> That simple music, of which the associations stretch over the world—'the merry, merry bells of Yule' [28.20]—brings to the troubled spirit 'sorrow touched with joy' [28.19] . . . In spite of all the songs, good, bad, and indifferent, that have been written and sung on the subject of village bells, there is an invincible freshness in their merry peal. (Lushington 80)

Sailors in the tropics and wanderers in the Syrian desert, Lushington continues sentimentally, hear "distant notes of the church-bells of England booming through the thin air, and are changed by the magnetic influence of the illusion into unalloyed masses of poetical feeling" (80). As Lushington's comment about "all the songs" on "village bells" suggests, the bell-ringing sections of *In Memoriam* contribute to a large body of Victorian religious poems, in which speakers, usually standing outside of village churches, interpret ringing church bells as signs of an idealized British Christian community (Blair, "Church Going" 764–72, 776–77).

In lyric 28, Tennyson's "sorrow" over Hallam is almost forcefully overcome with the nostalgic "joy" revived by the Christmas-eve bells that "controll'd me when a boy" (18–19); but by lyric 104, when he has moved to a house and landscape unyoked to memories of boyhood and Hallam, Christmas-eve bells sound "Like strangers' voices," and only reinforce his view of his surroundings as "new unhallow'd ground" unsanctified by "memory" (9, 12, 10). This could suggest that the power of the Christmas bells is purely nostalgic rather than religious. Yet the bells' role in keeping the British public timed to the Christian Year, itself designed to recall Christ's first Advent and anticipate his return, is essential to the inner spiritual development charted by *In Memoriam*. In lyric 104, the poet laments the absence of nostalgic joy in the bell's peal, but his loss is framed within the traditional message that the bells carry over from the first line of lyric 28 into the first of 104: "The time draws near the birth of Christ" (28.1; 104.1). Repetition of the sounding joy empowers memory of the "holy morn" that "shone when Hope was born" (30.29, 32) to resurface in lyric 105. Here the poet demands an end to all domestic rites and songs at Christmas Eve so that the church bells' annual reminder of hope might echo without distraction in his mind: "Be neither song, nor game, nor feast; No dance, no motion, save alone / What lightens in the lucid east / Of rising worlds by yonder wood. / . . . Run out your measured arcs, and lead / The closing cycle rich in good" (105.22–25, 27–28). The "arcs" of the sun and other heavenly bodies seem "measured," timed by Providence to a "cycle" closing in a new Advent, because the poet's heart has been trained by the bells' recurrent strain. Prepared by an inherited Advent hope that has yearly worked its way inward, in the next section the poet can call with authority on the bells of New Year's Eve to usher in a new millennium of enlightened Christianity: "Ring out the darkness of the land, / Ring in the Christ that is to be" (106.31–2).

Bells next ring at the wedding of Cecilia Tennyson to Edmund Lushington in the Epilogue. In commemorating this marriage, Tennyson also relinquishes his desire for an earthly connection to Hallam. Now surrendered to the world of spirit, Hallam can be recovered as a "noble type" (Epilogue.138) of an oddly spiritualized "crowning" future "race" (128) that is destined to calm Nature's atheistic "shriek" (56.16) by learning to read her "open book" of knowledge (132), and to enter the great consummation in "God," the "far-off divine event, / To which the whole creation moves" (143–44). This vision itself requires quietly turning Cecilia's wedding (and resulting impregnation) into a naturalized version of the biblical use of marriage as a type of the union of Christ with the Church at creation's redemption: their child will himself be "a closer link / Betwixt us and the crowning race" (127–28). After Cecilia and Edward take their vows, Tennyson hears church bells as a member of a congregation within a church service unobtrusively governed by the Book of Common Prayer.[4] No longer listening on the outside, he is within a religious community from which the resounding joy—of the bells and his lines—reaches ears outside the walls and seems to shake dead forms of creation into life in token of what is to come: "overhead / Begins the clash and clang that tells / The joy to every wandering breeze; / The blind wall rocks, and on the trees / The dead leaf trembles to the bells" (60–64).

III. THE SACRED HEART(H) OF NATIONAL WORSHIP

For reasons explained in chapter 5, *In Memoriam* could seem a "New Christian Year" to a broad spectrum of middle- and upper-class mid-Victorians because they were used to imagining their religious national belonging as based in bonds between the inner intuitions of strangers sustained by texts circulating in a competitive, voluntary religious market. *In Memoriam* participates in the sanction these developments gave to a familiar Victorian habit of conceiving of national religious community in terms of family devotional life. Evangelicals were most vocal in tying family devotions and Sunday afternoon religious reading to national welfare, but their views were shared by many middle- and upper-class Christians (Landow 21). This conflation of national and domestic devotion was set in motion in England in the sixteenth and seventeenth centuries by Protestant stress on the priesthood of believers and emphasis by the Toleration Act (1689) on the conscientious nature of religious belief (McKeon 34–43).

These associations motivated the nearly universal praise Victorian reviewers lavished on poem 30 of *In Memoriam*. Lyric 30 looks back on the Tennyson family's Christmas Eve rituals through the poet's isolated meditations at dawn on Christmas morning. He recounts how they sat in a circle and spontaneously broke into a song resembling a hymn. The Tennyson family in poem 30 could offer a parallel, rather than a counter, to the worship service taking place in the churches whose Christmas-eve bells have been ringing in the immediately preceding poems (Blair, *Form and Faith* 179–80). The likelihood that many Victorian readers would have viewed poem 30 in this way is indicated by a call for British Christian unity from a

---

4. Lines 54–56 allude to the Form of Solemnization of Matrimony and Genesis 2:24: "The 'wilt thou' answer'd, and again / The 'wilt thou' ask'd, till out of twain / Her sweet 'I will' has made you one."

Congregationalist minister printed in 1864 by *The Patriot*, a Nonconformist newspaper. The minister cites *The Christian Year* and *In Memoriam* in support of his ecumenical message, and follows quotations of these poetic cycles known for their wide circulation among British households by asking the nation to imagine itself as a Christian family. Only when resting in "the one Father God, and the one Brother Christ" will "the union" of British "Christians . . . resemble that of a family in its filial and fraternal relations" ("Letters" 75).

Formal features of lyric 30 invite a response on these terms. Haunted by the sense of Hallam's "mute Shadow" (30.8), the family goes about their household rites with a "vain pretence / Of gladness" (6–7) until they fall into a silence. Their sense of shared agony compels them to join hands and seek relief in singing "A merry song we sang with him [Hallam] / Last year" (15–16), perhaps a Christmas carol, before beginning a gentler shared confession: "'They rest,' we said, 'their sleep is sweet'" (30.1). Laced with allusions to Scripture readings assigned for the Burial of the Dead by the Book of Common Prayer,[5] the family's alternations between singing, silence, and collective confession begin to seem less a spontaneous invention than a private memorial service for Hallam tacitly guided by known religious (Anglican) forms. The Prayer Book reading to which their words directly allude is the announcement of blessed rest for those who die in Christ (Rev. 14:13), and in the order for the burial service this verse is sandwiched between collects and Scripture readings emphasizing "hope in the Resurrection to eternal life" (*Prayer Book* 238). On this subtle absorption of public religious forms into a private and voluntary ritual the Tennyson family's return to song in the next stanzas depends: "Our voices took a higher range; / Once more we sang: 'They do not die'" (30.21–24). As discussed earlier in this chapter, Keble had based his poem for "Christmas Day" on the scripture reading assigned for that day by the Prayer Book (Luke 2:1–15), and Tennyson less explicitly does so in lyrics 28–30. One verse from that reading, the announcement to the shepherds in Luke 2:14,[6] resounds in the Christmas bells in poem 28, which ring out "Peace and goodwill, goodwill and peace, / Peace and goodwill, to all mankind" (28.11–12).

---

5. "I heard a voice from heaven saying unto me, Write, Blessed are the dead which die in the Lord from henceforth: Yea, saith the Spirit, that they may rest from their labours; and their works do follow them" (Rev. 14:13).

6. "And suddenly there was with the angel a multitude of the heavenly host praising God, and saying, Glory to God in the highest, and on earth peace, good will toward men" (Luke 2:13–14).

Combined with the dual focus on Christ's first and second comings stressed by the traditional Advent season, this network of connections provides the background support for the poet's isolated, present-tense song on Christmas morning at the close of lyric 30. Having recounted his conflicted anticipation of Christmas in lyric 28, and his family's Christmas rites and impromptu memorial service in lyrics 29–30, the poet turns to the awaited Christmas dawn with his own morning hymn: "Rise, happy morn, rise, holy morn, / . . . O Father, touch the east, and light / The light that shone when Hope was born" (30.29–32). This echoes Keble's famous "Morning" in *The Christian Year:* "New every morning is the love / Our waking and uprising prove" (21–22), so that "while we pray . . . / New thoughts of God, new hopes of Heaven" enter our minds (26, 28). Once again, Tennyson seems to have "timed" his thoughts to the public religious forms his inward confession of faith requires, and yet, time after time, downplays.

IV. FAITH IN THE BEAT

The metrical form of Keble's "Morning" encouraged its adoption as a hymn by many congregations in and outside Anglicanism (see chapter 4): its four-line tetrameter stanza loosely resembles the common measure and long meter regularly used in hymns. The same is true of *In Memoriam*'s famous stanza, whose influence was so immediate and widespread that the 1864 Catholic *Dublin Review* could assume its adoption by periodical and newspaper poets was common knowledge ("The Laureate" 383). Although some Victorian commentators, such as a contributor to the 1863 *Illustrated Times,* recognized that Tennyson had not actually invented the stanza (J. H. F. 27), everyone continued connecting it to *In Memoriam*. In 1867, *The Christian Witness,* a widely circulating Congregationalist and evangelical magazine, reviewed *The Inner Life* (1866) by the Rev. William Tidd Matson. Written in what the reviewer calls "the 'In Memoriam' stanza,'" *The Inner Life* described stages in an evangelical spiritual awakening ("Notices of New Books" 236). *The Christian Witness* reviewer notes that "sections of the poem would make exquisite hymns" (236). This advice was followed, and several poems from *Inner Life* soon entered Nonconformist hymnals (*The Puritan* 486).

As *The Christian Witness* reviewer indicates, the "'In Memoriam' stanza" invites comparison with the hymn tradition. Many modern critics have noticed that Tennyson's stanza recalls the ballad stanza (Barton 15–16), to which hymn stanzas are also akin, but Victorian religious responses to *In Memoriam* were more deeply informed by the stanza's proximity to the hymn. The alternating rhyme (A–B–A–B) and metrical pattern (4–3–4–3) of most hymn and ballad stanzas implies a forward movement of thought or narrative. But Tennyson's stanza of full tetrameters (4–4–4–4) and embracing rhymes (A–B–B–A) indicates a mirroring pattern less clearly related to progress, and, as early readers noted,[7] it is therefore more easily turned to expressing *In Memoriam*'s "wandering" (Intro.41), "Short swallow-flights of song" (48.15). Poised between the popular tradition of the hymn and the meanderings of individual inner life, the connotations of Tennyson's metrical frame are suited to his internalized use of public religious forms. Evangelical writers of poems in the "'In Memoriam' stanza" with titles such as *Inner Life* seem to have picked up on these possibilities—as did the *Christian Witness* critic who recommended *Inner Life* for congregational singing.

From this perspective, the unplanned family rites in lyric 30 reference not only the Book of Common Prayer but also the interdenominational practice of hymn signing. Pauses enforced by the stanza breaks in this section align the reader's negotiation of lines with pauses the family makes between their songs, statements of belief, and more impassioned singing. "We gambol'd," the poet recounts,

> . . . making vain pretence
> Of gladness, with an awful sense
> Of one mute Shadow [Hallam] watching all.
>
> We paused: the winds were in the beech . . . (6–9)

The reader has also "paused" in the gap between lines 8 and 9, which are on either side of a full-stopped ending to the second stanza. The family then "Sat silent, looking each at each. / [stanza break] Then echo-like our voices rang" (12–13). Again, the reader momentarily sits silent with them in the gap between stanzas—especially if this reader is sitting while reading the poem alone or aloud to family and friends—before proceeding to the account of how the family sang the "merry song we sang with him"

---

7. Kingsley, for example, observed that "the second and third lines" gave an impression of "the . . . self-restraint required by such deep themes," even as "the mournful minor rhyme of each first and fourth line always leads the ear to expect something beyond, and enables the poet's thoughts to wander sadly on, from stanza to stanza and poem to poem, in an endless chain" (252).

the previous Christmas Eve (15). The pattern continues, exaggerated by enjambment, between this and the next stanza:

. . . A merry song we sang with him
Last year: impetuously we sang:

We ceased: a gentler feeling crept
Upon us: surely rest is meet:
'They rest,' we said, 'their sleep is sweet,'
And silence follow'd, and we wept. (15–20)

As expected, the reader again pauses with the family, while they weep, between their corporate confession and their passage into the rousing hymn in the next stanza: "Our voices took a higher range . . ." (21). Crossing, yet again, the stanzaic gap between the family's hymn recounted in the next two stanzas and the poet's private, present-tense hymn in the final stanza ("'From orb to orb, from veil to veil.' / [stanza break] Rise, happy morn, rise, holy morn" [28–29]), the reader might feel a shared significance in the private family ceremony and the poet's concluding solo. The reader has been singing with them, as it were.

The recurrent rhyme scheme and steady beat of *In Memoriam* were as important to its public religious meaning as its partial affinity to the hymn stanza. As discussed in chapter 5, when reviewing *In Memoriam* in 1850 for *The North British Review*, a moderate journal associated with the Free Church of Scotland, Coventry Patmore claimed that Tennyson's poem signaled a reawakening within Britain to innate spiritual truths residing within the depths of the soul: "A fact that is vividly suggested by the book is, that . . . the A B C of Christian philosophy," including tenets such as belief in immortal life "are now in process of *recovery from the syncope* into which they have been cast by a long period of practical neglect" ("In Memoriam" 553; emphasis mine). Patmore compares this awakening to recovery from a "syncope," a term describing both a dangerous pause in the heart's action and the subtraction of a syllable or letter from a word to make it fit a meter. This relies on an association between the heartbeat and poetic rhythm that runs through Victorian prosody and poetic practice.[8] For Patmore, because of Deism and apathetic Anglicanism, in "the last century" the modern British heart ceased beating to shared convictions of a divine design in the cosmos and in

---

8. See chapter 2 of Blair's *Victorian Poetry and the Culture of the Heart*.

human experience (553). Yet, Patmore asserts, we can now hear the beat of belief reviving through the spiritual stethoscope of Tennyson's disciplined verse in *In Memoriam*.

Earlier in the review, Patmore explains his grounds for faith in Tennyson's metrical testimony. He draws an analogy between the reconciliation of "life" and "law" in "the New Testament" and the "superinduction of metre" on "language," suggesting that the difference between mature and slavish metrical practice is parallel to that between pharisaical devotion to the letter of the law and sensitivity to its spirit (533). At first imposed from without, when worked into a poet's heart through long discipline, genuine metrical laws become an internal guiding spirit rather than a box of techniques to be inflicted on language, much as God's divine moral law is written in the human heart rather than found in blind and rigid obedience to external rules. Patmore praises Tennyson for writing with the laws of English meter in his heart, thereby upholding the "faith" of readers that every "variation" from his regular metrical pattern is "suggested" by the authentic "emotion to be expressed" (534). Tennyson's mastered measure means that readers can discern and share the emotional rhythms communicated in his lines, and feel that they are universal to the "inner world of man" (551). The quickening pulse of faith in Tennyson's lines can be experienced as the reaffirmation of the "A B C of Christian philosophy" at the level of undeniable human instinct.[9]

Patmore connects *In Memoriam* to a tradition then strongest in High Anglicanism, but felt well beyond it, which saw regular metrical and verse forms as a sign of secure faith in God's laws, a reassurance that "God's ordering presence" is "always already at work" (Blair, *Form and Faith* 186). While deploring Tennyson's theological deficiencies, the 1850 reviewer of *In Memoriam* for the High Church *English Review* admires the way Tennyson's "strain . . . creeps gently into the heart, and awakens there a low and long resounding echo" ("New Poetry" 77). This reviewer also singles out (77–78) as particularly beautiful Tennyson's well-known (albeit ambiguous) description in lyric 5 of the "sad mechanic exercise" of composing "measured language" as an anodyne to intense emotional pain (5.7, 6). As High Church readers would know, this view of the calming, restraining force of metrical composition had been articulated by Keble in his lectures on poetry, and served as an underlying principle for *The Christian Year*.

---

9. For a detailed discussion of Patmore's verse practice and theory of metrical law, their theological burden, and their relationship to the metrical theory of Gerard Manley Hopkins and other late Victorians, see my "Patmore, Hopkins, and the Problem of the English Metrical Law" (2011).

Poem 96 was probably one of the passages Patmore had in mind when he admitted in 1855 that he "regret[ed]" some "careless" theological "expressions" in *In Memoriam* (503). Ironically, this poem subliminally rests its claim to credence on the regular metrical beat admired by Patmore. As Robert Ryan has noted (128), the poem turns on the unexpected injunction to "Believe me" in the midst of a description of perplexed faith:

> . . . one [Hallam] indeed I knew
> In many a subtle question versed,
> Who touch'd a jarring lyre at first,
> But ever strove to make it true:
>
> Perplext in faith, but pure in deeds,
> At last he beat his music out.
> There lives more faith in honest doubt,
> Believe me, than in half the creeds. (5–12)

The poet, defending the virtue of Hallam's honest doubt, implicitly directs his demand to believe in him to the reader as well as to the woman addressed in the poem, who is probably Emily Sellwood, soon to be his wife. Once the question of our trust in the poet is raised, a secondary meaning surfaces in the language describing Hallam's battle with doubt. If Hallam began airing his painful questions with "a jarring lyre" but learned to "beat his music out" through patient striving and "good deeds," so, too, has the poet of *In Memoriam*, who has earlier in this elegiac sequence written terrified poems about "Nature, red in tooth and claw" (56.15) before arriving at this confident solicitation of his readers' trust. The "music" achieved by Tennyson is felt in the lines, and the "good deeds" by which he "beat[s]" it "out" are displayed in the iambic regularity that keeps this very statement in good measure: "At *last* he *beat* his *mu*sic *out*" (10). In concluding lines describing Hallam's heroic victory over doubt, the regular meter provides continuity across breaks that correspond with uncertain moments in the trial of faith:

> He faced the spectres of the mind
> And laid them: thus he came at length
>
> To find a stronger faith his own;
> And Power was with him in the night,
> Which makes the darkness and the light,
> And dwells not in the light alone (15–20)

Between line 15 ("He faced the spectres of the mind") and its completion in line 16 ("And laid them") the enjambment momentarily keeps a reader hovering over the conclusion, even as the meter carries her on. Across the "length" of space between the spiritual warfare of this stanza and the "stronger faith" discovered in the next stanza, the reader must then venture, momentarily unsure of where she is heading; but the steady beat, affirmed by alliteration ("To find a stronger faith"), confirms the destination was in the greater scheme of things. Once reached, the lines add biblical weight to the measured iambic progress over the gap, confirming a Divine presence enduring through light and dark.[10] This passage through doubt to higher faith could describe Tennyson as much as Hallam (Ryan 128), a connection suggested by allusions backward and forward to lyrics 54 and 124, in which Tennyson describes himself as a child crying in the night of doubt who eventually realizes a divine fatherly power has been stretching down to him through the dark. The poet has been carried by God, but perhaps also by the (at first) weary "mechanic exercise" of "measured language" that carries readers with him over uncertain pauses between religious questioning and its evolving resolution (5.7, 6).

The steady metrical persuasion of passages such as lyric 96 might explain the note of anxious attraction sounded by the 1850 critic for the High Church *English Review,* who ridiculed this section as "mischievous language" waiting to be "caught up as the catchwords of unbelievers" ("New Poetry" 76). Immediately after this attack, the critic admits that Tennyson's ability to create "a strain" that "creeps gently into the heart" leaves readers of *In Memoriam* "captivated, . . . enchanted, almost against our wills" (78). By quietly appealing to the equation of metrical order with faith in divine control familiar in High Church circles, Tennyson might have made his request to "Believe me" particularly vexing for such readers.

Another High Churchman, Manley Hopkins (father of the poet), used his 1851 review of *In Memoriam* in *The Times* to concede Tennyson's mastery of "rhythm" and verbal "music," while suggesting this stylistic dexterity "seduce[s]" the poet into unguarded inanity: a reader, Hopkins concludes in a veiled sneer, can be "sure of a sweet sound, though nothing be in it" (8). Hopkins' insistence on vapidity beneath the seductive music betrays his need to suppress subjects in the poem to which he is "painfully" aware its "sweet . . . verses" are attached, such as the "amatory tenderness" of Tennyson for Hallam, which for Hopkins has produced the poem's

---

10. "If I say, Surely the darkness shall cover me; even the night shall be light about me. Yea, the darkness hideth not from thee; but the night shineth as the day: the darkness and the light are both alike to thee" (Psalm 139:11–12).

exaggerated "wailings" and "exclamation[s]" of quasi-theological devotion "border[ing] on blasphemy" (8). Catching Tennyson's tacit comparison of his addresses to Hallam with those of Shakespeare to the young man of his sonnets ("nor can / The soul of Shakespeare love thee more" [61.11–12]), Hopkins suggests "that floating remembrances of Shakespeare's sonnets have beguiled Mr. Tennyson" (8). Tennyson's friends were also nervous about his devotion to Shakespeare's sonnets, which had become "a standard Victorian" signifier of "male homoerotic passion" (Nunokawa 432), and Manley Hopkins was not the only reader to regard homoeroticism as one of *In Memoriam*'s most disturbing open secrets (427).

Jeffrey Nunokawa argues that Tennyson's elegy actually strains to affirm a widespread Victorian narrative, strongly connected to the public schools of the upper and upper-middle classes, about homoeroticism as a tutelary phase through which young men pass (and then forever relinquish) on their way to mature heterosexual love (Nunokawa 429, 436). In this reading, *In Memoriam* admits and gradually allays the poet's fear that "Hallam's death left him . . . permanently arrested at the stage of schoolboy love" (434). If so, this quality of the poem gives Manley Hopkins the opportunity to imply that the laureate's stylistic allurements, unchecked by manly reflection and a devout "conscience," are both a sign and stimulant of his tendency to follow "floating remembrances of Shakespeare's sonnets" into erotically regressive and theologically damaging "laments" for "a lost companion of his school, or college, or maturer days" (8). The 1850 *English Review* critic might also imply a connection between undeveloped schoolboy passion, dangerous metrical persuasion, and theological error when declaring his desire "to whip this self-conceited rhymester" for unorthodoxy (74).

As suggested in chapter 5, Tennyson tries to forestall this kind of criticism when he represents the phonotext of *In Memoriam* as a medium for voicing manly outrage against the collusion between a feminized materialist science and the feminized nature that its caresses have transformed into a shrieking enemy of faith. These High Church critics differ strongly from Patmore when aligning the metrical and spiritual qualities of *In Memoriam*. Yet they agree with Patmore in identifying the poem's power, for good or ill, with the way it channels subjective expressions through a metrical form that carries strong public and religious associations (in this case, the High Anglican tendency to find faith confirmed in regular verse). For them, the experience of reading *In Memoriam* often seems one of being lulled by enchanting strains *despite* oneself—and fearing that others might be drawn in unwarily.

V. A NATIONAL SCRIPTURE

In chapter 4, I discussed the powerful appeal of Keble's *Christian Year* to a practice also cultivated by countless Victorian sermons and Sunday reading materials aimed at all denominations: the art of discerning how biblical people, events, and images prefigured and made sense of one's own daily life and surroundings (Landow 33, 48–50). The reception history of *The Christian Year* indicates that for many it gave this typological habit a fresh application: it convinced readers of many denominations that Keble's poetic cycle included them in a far-flung community of anonymous individuals who were simultaneously pursuing humble lives of devotion. As a result, Keble's poems could, especially among Anglicans who used them daily alongside the Prayer Book, come to seem a necessary supplement to Scripture, and even to acquire some of the Bible's sacred status. As mentioned in chapter 4, in "St. Thomas," Keble turns the difficulty experienced by the apostle in believing in the Resurrection into a type of his readers' present doubts: "Read [the story of St. Thomas in John's Gospel] and confess the hand divine / That drew thy likeness so true in every line" (63–64). Unintentionally, Keble tempts an equation of the lines of Scripture with "every line" of his own poem, so that "the hand divine" that "drew" the typological connection between Thomas and later struggling believers also blesses Keble's lines. As my analysis of the many testimonies to Keble's "sacred" influence in chapter 4 would suggest, readers took the accidental hint.

The Christian Year, then, derived a quasi-scriptural aura by contributing to what Paul Korshin has called "the typology of everyday life," the result of a tendency beginning in the sixteenth century to extend habits of discerning typological prefiguration and fulfillment in the Scriptures to every aspect of human experience (370). As Korshin demonstrates, during the eighteenth and nineteenth centuries, many British prose writers, novelists, and poets gave typological patterns from Christian tradition flexible and non-doctrinal application, using them to reveal and foreshadow characters' qualities and actions, or to suggest generalized spiritual meanings in natural objects and the incidents of daily life (226–45, 268, 388, 399–400). Next to these more psychologized, internalized forms of typology, Keble's ecclesiastical, traditional, and biblically restricted framework could increasingly strike some readers as mechanical, especially if they were unsympathetic to the Oxford Movement he helped to inspire.

While granting that *The Christian Year* deserves reverence since it "has been so long a household book with many of us" ("Poetical Theology"

631), an 1868 critic writing for *Fraser's Magazine* criticizes Keble's volume for bending reality to a time-bound theology, and praises *In Memoriam* for appealing "to those deeper thoughts and desires which form the permanent basis of human character" (623). Turning to Keble's best-known typological reading of the natural world, "Septuagesima Sunday," the *Fraser's* critic sanctions Keble's view of nature as a book that reveals its creator. Yet he resents Keble's "system of pulling Nature to bits, like a Chinese puzzle, and assigning each bit its appropriate meaning" (632), represented by lines such as "The moon above, the church below, / A wondrous race they run, / But all their radiance, all their glow, / Each borrows from its sun" (1–4). Tennyson, the critic concludes, should outrank Keble "as 'our great Christian poet'" (636) by virtue of his greater breadth of feeling and his treatment of "[e]xternal nature" as "one great whole, the visible form and reflex of his own mind, with which it often becomes identified" (633). Clearly of "broad" sympathies, on this point the *Fraser's* critic coincides with more orthodox readers, such as an 1850 reviewer of *In Memoriam* in the moderate Nonconformist *Eclectic Review*: "A landscape [in this poem] is painted not only in itself, but in its relation to the human mind—. . . to be felt in and through it; its very spirit" ("Tennyson's In Memoriam" 338).

For both of these critics, *In Memoriam* replaces Keble's manufactured Chinese puzzle with a typological vision so internalized as to seem innate to emotion and perception rather than an imposed schema, an expression of "thoughts and desires" native to the "very spirit" of the human mind. In 1866, the year of Keble's death, a contributor to *The Quiver*, a cheap and widely circulating Evangelical weekly magazine, approves *In Memoriam* for this quality, singling out the description of a nightingale's song, "whose warble, liquid sweet, / Rings Eden thro' the budded quicks" (88.1–2). For this author, Tennyson shows that Eden can be treated "as a synonym for delight," and that traces of it are felt throughout the world, even in a poor man's garden (Bede 209–210). This is a very innocent reading of a lyric in which Tennyson indicates the impossibility of knowing or sharing the supposed "secret joy" of the bird (88.8). Yet in this section Tennyson does portray harmony in and with nature as a feeling, rather than a belief in stable typological correspondences between the natural world and spiritual realities: if now and then he does sense a "glory of the sum of things," it "will flash along the chords" of his poem "and go" (88.11–12).

Tennyson is practicing a more psychologized version of the perspective Colin Jager has detected in Wordsworth's *Prelude,* where Wordsworth replaces surety of a divine intention behind the designs and spiritual analogies he traces in nature with the *impression* of intention and significance created by his poetic response (*Book of God* 180–7). William Gladstone, in the 1859 *Quarterly Review*, caught well the quality so many of his contemporaries admired in Tennyson's renderings of natural scenes: "all [Nature's] images to him are clear and definite, and he translates them for us into the language of suggestion, emphasis, and refined analogy which links the manifold to the simple and the infinite to the finite" (480). Tennyson's internalized "suggestion" and "refined analogy," his version of the typology of everyday life, contributed to the ease with which his "New Christian Year" was claimed as part of a quasi-sacred national literature whose authority sat alongside, and sometimes merged with, the Bible's. For an increasing number of Victorians, *In Memoriam* could be diversely appropriated as a national scriptural text for an imagined British community, one that affirmed a spiritual significance in daily life and the natural world, and seemed to speak to one's inner life above the storm of controversy and without rigid and divisive imposition of theological schemes of interpretation.

Essential to Tennyson's typology of everyday life is the redefinition of "type" over the course of *In Memoriam*. In lyric 33, Tennyson concedes the legitimacy a traditional Christian "faith" sustained "thro' form" (33.9). It is centered in the Incarnation of Christ, the "flesh and blood" who forms a "type" of "a truth divine" (33.11, 16, 12), and so, implicitly, the whole sacramental system[11] and view of history typologically arranged to point toward Christ's earthly life and second coming. Indeed, the number of this stanza, 33, might itself be a type, recalling the traditional age of Christ at his death and resurrection. Yet lyrics 55 and 56 question the durability of this typological system, as the wish that "No life may fail beyond the grave" (55.2) is relegated to "the soul" (4), while "Nature" is left to cry "'A thousand types [species] are gone: / I care for nothing, all shall go'" (56.3–4). Tennyson famously reads nature's message from "scarped cliff and quarried stone" (56.2), drawing from Lyell's geological research to undermine the stability of traditional Christian typology, along with eighteenth-century natural theology and its arguments from design: "I found Him [God] not in world or sun, / Or eagle's wing, or insect's eye" (124.5–6). The application of "type" to the material world is drained of Christological and sacramental significance to become an abstract description of "a specific group or division of animals, plants, etc." (Shatto and Shaw 218).

---

11. See Blair's reading of this passage in *Form and Faith* (183–84).

Tennyson is left to preserve a typological vision of human history and destiny through "an odd formulation of human developmentalism," which moves "the future 'form' of humanity into another ambiguous, inchoate realm of spiritual, cultural un-animal" (Tomko 128). In lyric 118, Tennyson invokes a ghostly version of Christian typology validated by quasi-spiritual evolutionary development, so that "man" becomes the "herald of a higher race, / And of himself in higher place, / If so he type this work of time / Within himself" by "Mov[ing] upward, working out the beast" (118.12, 14–16, 27). The ambiguity of "working out"—expelling, developing latent potential or meaning—exemplifies Tennyson's strategy of relying on the "chang[ing] bearing of a word" (128.16) to break down rigid and vulnerable typological systems of the kind deployed by Keble while regaining some of their significance. Turning the material world and body into necessary stepping stones for the evolution of a higher race ("working out" as development), and, somehow, entry into a purer spiritual existence ("working out" as expulsion of "the beast"), Tennyson reclaims typological importance for the strivings of daily life and the intuitions received through nature of a higher existence.

The evolving significance of "type" contributes to the poem's emphasis, discussed in chapter 5, on secular time as "homogenous empty time," in which "the meaning of its important dates, like the anniversaries of Hallam's birth and death, are contingent rather than motivated by theology or cosmology" (Rowlinson 46). The poem's closing allusion to a divine design of historical time, the portrayal of Hallam as "a noble type" of a "crowning race" that will live in perfected knowledge of God and the universe (Epilogue.138, 128), is undercut by the sense that Hallam appeared "ere the times were ripe" (139): the promise of the final stanza rests on a foreshadowing type, Hallam, that has missed its proper time (Rowlinson 47), and so the great consummation of a future race unified with God might itself be uncertain. Rather than an exteriorly motivated and confirmed typology, the speaker's hope fitfully resides "in my spirit" (123.9). This empowers him to "mingle all the world with" memories of Hallam (129.12), and to feel that in continuing to love Hallam he participates in the progressive inclusion of all things in love, even "God and Nature," which previously seemed "at strife" (55.54): "Tho' mixed with God and Nature thou, / I seem to love thee more and more" (130.11–12).

Over the course of *In Memoriam,* the speaker drains time and space of inherited typological meaning, identifies his spirit as the sensitive refuge for faith in God's providential love, and then rereads the secular world through the divine love his spirit has learned to feel. Here typological interpretation is an intuitive art perhaps best developed through art. The speaker re-envisions the "Godless" secular "deep" (124.12), with its "vast eddies in the flood / Of onward time" (128.5–6), as an artwork, a poem, in process: "I see in part / That all, as in some piece of art, / Is toil cöoperant to an end" (128.22–24). This reworks St. Paul's contrast between present knowledge of God and intimacy with God in the new creation: "now I know in part; but then shall I know even as also I am known" (1 Cor. 13:12). Harboring unfulfilled eschatological hope is parallel to the act of reading an artwork for signs of its maker's synthesizing labor. This passage invites readers to imagine *In Memoriam* itself as a work in progress, and to regard their own movement through the multi-part poem as a typological act performed through printed type, an analogy for intuiting the apparently aimless events of secular time as components in God's redemptive composition. This is a "toil cöoperant," one in which author and reader continually negotiate the "chang[ing] bearing of a word" (128.16).

Nonetheless, public and inherited points of reference remain crucial to Tennyson's relocation of typological interpretation from ecclesiastical to psychological grounds. One such psychological relocation takes place in lyric 95, where the poet recounts experiencing a "trance" outdoors at night (95.43), in which he seemed to have a mystical experience of oneness with Hallam and the power behind all life. In the concluding lines, he says he awoke to the dawn as a breeze blew through trees and flowers "and said / 'The dawn, the dawn,' and died away; / And East and West, without a breath, / Mixt their dim lights, like life and death, / To broaden into boundless day" (95.60–64). The imagery remains so quietly suggestive that an 1850 *Eclectic Review* critic concludes Tennyson's "spiritual . . . art" has caught a deep meaning in the dawn somehow integral to common experience: "Have we not all heard such ineffable speech?" (338).

Yet perhaps this Nonconformist reviewer can feel Tennyson speaks for everyone because the "ineffable" quality of the voice heard through the morning breeze depends on the typological meanings that have colored dawn over the course of the poem. The dawn "broadens into [a] boundless day," and overwhelms the boundary of "life and death," because the rising sun has already been associated with collective longing for "the light that shone when Hope was born" (30.32) by Christmastides, village church bells, Prayer Book rubrics, biblical passages, and the hymnic and theological connotations of Tennyson's stanza and meter. The last of these associations is invoked just before the lines in question, as the poet describes his trance-like feeling of vaguely divine "pulsations" running through "the world" and "measuring out / The steps of Time" (40–42). The ensuing transformation of the "breeze" into a voice with "breath" silently revokes Nature's claim in lyric 56 that "The spirit does but mean the breath" (7), and faintly alludes to Jesus' words spoken to Nicodemus at night: "The wind bloweth where it listeth, and thou hearest the sound thereof, but canst not tell whence it cometh, and whither it goeth: so is every one that is born of the Spirit" (John 3:8). The turn from lyric 95 to the declaration in lyric 96—that faith will survive honest doubt because of an assisting "Power . . . in the night" (96.18)—gathers its force from this thick allusive and typological texture.

Similarly, as noted earlier, in the Epilogue Tennyson draws on the biblical view of marriage as a type of the approaching union of Christ and the Church, turning Cecilia's marriage (and ensuing impregnation) into a foreshadowing of humanity's progress toward a crowning race and the far-off divine event of creation's renewal. Elizabeth Chapman, in an 1888 commentary on *In Memoriam* highly recommended by Hallam Tennyson (*Memoir* I:298n), nicely articulates how "natural" Tennyson's internalized and domesticated typology of daily life could seem to Victorians. The "marriage" in the poem's Epilogue "is the very *type* of hope and of all things fair and bright and good, seeming to bring us nearer to the consummation for which we pray—that crowning race, that Christ that is to be" (E. Chapman 72; emphasis mine).

In an 1855 essay on "Tennyson," the Cambridge librarian and essayist George Brimley praises Tennyson in terms that resemble a declaration of faith: "we, who . . . admire him, have a reason for our faith" (226–27). Brimley portrays Tennyson's poems as a quasi-sacred national scripture, suggesting that they uniquely offer a typology of daily life for a modern British community.

> We find him possessing the clearest insight into our modern life, one who discerns its rich poetical resources, who tells us what we are and may be; how we can live free, joyous, and harmonious lives . . . He is showing to us an age in which an Englishman may live a man's life [and] find in his affections, studies, business, and relaxations scope for his spiritual faculties. (227)

Brimley was operating in a literary culture in which comparing faith in Tennyson's poetry to faith in the Bible was becoming more common. Just over ten years later, Alfred Austin, a poet jealous of Tennyson's success who would succeed him as laureate before fading from memory, could open an essay sneering at Tennyson's biblical status:

> If one were to enter a modern drawing-room filled with the average polite society of the day, and ... declare that Mr. Tennyson has no sound pretensions to be called a great poet, ... we suppose he would not create more astonishment, or be regarded more unanimously as a heretic, than would another ... who, before a committee of orthodox divines, exposed his utter disbelief in the inspiration of the Scriptures. (179)

As Brimley, Luther-like, takes his stand on Tennyson's poetry, he defends his faith by pointing to *In Memoriam* and Tennyson's 1842 poem "Morte d'Arthur" (with its framing introductory and concluding verses called "The Epic"), a foretaste of *Idylls of the King* (1859–85). In so doing, Brimley anticipates Charles LaPorte's recent argument that Tennyson's poetry, preeminently the *Idylls,* constitutes an effort to concede the implications of higher criticism, with its arguments for the Bible as a human and mythical literary text that nonetheless expresses spiritual truths, while creating a parallel instance of poetic inspiration that could be received as a part of a national mythology (LaPorte 68–69; 67–210). If Tennyson himself and sectors of his critical public came to place their faith in *Idylls* for achieving such a project (LaPorte 68, 93–94), most Victorian readers appeared to have agreed with the author of "'In Memoriam' and the Bible," published in 1874 in the evangelical *Leisure Hour,* who regarded *In Memoriam* as Tennyson's greatest expression of "Christian feeling" and, therefore, his "best known poem" (J. C. 71).

Brimley treats "Morte d'Arthur" as a mythical, national gospel whose full meaning is drawn out in coordination with the psalms and prophetic hymns of *In Memoriam.* He notices that Tennyson frames the poem as a reading given by a young poet, in a country house at Christmas, to a group of conservatives who are lamenting the apparent decline of faith. Within this context, the story of Arthur's glorious passing becomes "the answer of a Christian poet to" his day's "querulous lamentation ... over the decay of faith," and an affirmation that Arthurian Christian heroism endures: Victorian "men" who "fight the good fight" will be aided with the gift of "heavenly weapons," just as Arthur was given his Excalibur (241–42). After applying Tennyson's mythical national gospel to the typology of everyday life, Brimley connects it fluidly to the yearly reminder of the Christian Advent so important to *In Memoriam*:

> The Arthur of the round-table is gone to fairy-land; but the desire and hope that gave birth to the legends of chivalry yet live,—the dim prophecy that he will one day return and rule over Britain is ever accomplishing

itself. What mean those Christmas bells that tell us yearly Christ is born? Do they lie? No! they blend with all noble legends that speak of man's great deeds, of his vaster aspirations, of his yet unaccomplished hopes. They remind us of the prophecy to which fact is tending . . . To him whose heart is hopeful and brave, who will not be the slave of formulas [unlike, say, the Tractarians], 'Arthur is come again, and cannot die,' is the burden of the world's song; . . . 'Come with all good things, and war shall be no more,' [is] the strain that echoes in the clear distance, and most clear when the bells ring in the Christmas morn. (242)

Brimley quotes and paraphrases Tennyson's concluding lines to "Morte d'Arthur," where the narrator envisions Arthur's Second Coming in the form of a good Victorian gentleman, and then awakens to hear church bells ringing in the Christmas morn.

Brimley completes his canonization of Tennyson's national scripture by claiming *In Memoriam* as a national book of psalms and hymns. "We know," Brimley asserts, that "thousands of men and women" find "in *In Memoriam* the sort of consolation and strength they find in the Psalms of David" (276). *In Memoriam,* Brimley continues, contains "groans of despair" alongside "triumphant songs of faith," and in the background is "the scroll on which one reads from afar, '*I am the resurrection and the life.*' '*Blessed are the dead that die in the Lord*'" (277). The verses quoted by Brimley, John 11:25 and Revelation 14:13, are assigned in the Prayer Book's Order for the Burial of the Dead, which, as I noted earlier, subtly guides the family memorial service in lyric 30. Indeed, Tennyson's own allusions to these passages in that section might have prompted Brimley's. Brimley shows himself sensitive to the public forms of Tennyson's private faith discussed in this chapter—Christmas bells, Christmastide, the Prayer Brook, Scripture, the suggestion of hymnic form and hymn singing ("songs of faith"). The public coding of Tennyson's wandering cries and inward declarations of faith empowers Brimley's appropriation of *In Memoriam* as a more subjective, yet still nationally binding, version of David's Psalms and Victorian hymn books. He is also grateful for Tennyson's agreement with Lyell that essential human intuitions about God and immortality belong inside, leaving nature to roar undisturbed outside. Tennyson produces some of his "finest strains" in *In Memoriam* affirming intuitions of immortality in the face of "Comtian materialism" (279), even as he preserves this "passionate cleaving to a higher truth above nature" in an inner region, so that it requires no "falsification of science" (280). Unlike Keble, who, as discussed in chapter 4, would later be hymned as a British David in eulogies that poured forth at his death, Tennyson—for Brimley—practices a modern, internalized, and less sectarian typology of daily life, avoiding the "querulous lamentation of the Christian ritualist and dogmatist over the decay of faith" (241).

Brimley closes his defense of Tennyson's national scripture by quoting the well-known lyric 106 from *In Memoriam*. Both in Brimley's essay and in Tennyson's poem, the call to New-Year bells at the end of poem 106—"Ring in the Christ that is to be" (106.32)—absorbs reminders of Advent rung out by Christmas bells in earlier passages. Brimley introduces his closing quotation of lyric 106 as if he were simply repeating a text long recognized as sacred to the nation, and essential to readers' imagination of themselves within its spiritual community: "let us listen to the New-Year's hymn which . . . the people of England has taken for its national song of hope and prophecy of all good things to come" (281).

Readings of *In Memoriam* as a quasi-sacred national scripture were not isolated to theologically liberal Anglicans such as Brimley. A writer for the 1863 *Nonconformist* newspaper tells how, on "a lonely Sunday" evening "one of the passages from 'In Memoriam' sang itself through" his "wandering thoughts. Suddenly, and without any energy of will being brought to bear upon it, the dark mysterious words shot into light; the meaning, often sought for before, though never found, stood out clear and radiant." He turned back to the poem to find all the formerly perplexing passages "one after one, grow clear in their own brightness, and ring out their full diapason of thought" ("Moods and Tenses" 92). Perhaps alluding to the refrain "ring out" in lyric 106 of *In Memoriam,* the *Nonconformist* author also borrows language familiar among evangelicals for describing the Holy Spirit's elucidation of Scripture to explain his sudden awakening to the secrets of *In Memoriam*—and he is reading the poem on Sunday, when religious texts were regularly consulted for topics of "fruitful meditation" (92).

In 1860, a contributor to the Nonconformist *British Quarterly Review* connected such awakenings to the imagination of national spiritual community. The critic opens with a story meant to validate his faith in the native piety of English poetry. His neighbor in Sussex, Thompson, is secretary to a sewage company, a "practical, hard-working Englishman" no one would suspect of "keen sympathy with Mr. Tennyson" ("Les Contemplations" 71). The author recounts his surprise when, walking out into nature on a spring afternoon, he met "Thompson on the brow of a Sussex hill . . . in a reverie! His keen grey eyes were full of distant light" (71). The source of the sewage secretary's awakening was "Mr. Tennyson's poems": upon discovery of their mutual love for Tennyson, the two men felt an instant kinship, quoting "our favourite poet . . . to express how our senses grew alert to the throb of the glad earth whose accumulated life and motion made us half unconscious of our own" (71).

Separately led by the spirit to lose themselves in contemplation atop an English hill, these two Tennyson-loving Britons awaken to a psychological typology of everyday life. They descend in fellowship and shared reassurance of "the book-truth, that seeming discords have their due office in the symphony of creation," their "hearts . . . opened to the revelation around us of unfathomable wisdom and faultless law" (72). "Book-truth" seems an allusion to the Bible, but the immediate context points to "Mr. Tennyson's poems" (72). If these readers retain more natural theology than *In Memoriam*, they nonetheless experience the *sense* of Providence and spiritual harmony in nature that Tennyson's internalized typology sanctions. Their favorite canonical Tenysonian texts are Brimley's, "*In Memoriam*, and . . . the *Idylls of the King*" (73), and they share with Brimley a sense of the sacredness of Tennyson's national scripture to an imagined community of Britons: "the opening poem of *In Memoriam*," the critic concludes at his article's end, "is the heartbeat of England," and to be treasured above all the cynical criticism of human nature in "M. Hugo" (98). Here the critic arrives at a more jingoistic version of Patmore's claim that the measures of *In Memoriam* can rescue the British heart from a dangerous "syncope" to beat in time with the "A B C of Christian philosophy" ("In Memoriam" 553).

By the 1870s, there are more recognizably evangelical tributes to *In Memoriam*'s status as a semi-sacred national scripture. *The Leisure Hour*, a widely-circulating evangelical family magazine, criticized *In Memoriam*'s insufficient orthodoxy in 1863 ("Alfred Tennyson. Part II" 140), but by 1874 it ran an article on "'In Memoriam' and the Bible." For this critic, the national popularity of *In Memoriam* "lies in the fact that" Tennyson's use of "Scripture imagery" links the poem's "immortality . . . to the higher immortality of that Book of books—the Bible" (J. C. 73). To more firmly yoke the faith of (and in) Tennyson's poem to "the Book," the author identifies Scriptural allusions throughout *In Memoriam*, often tacitly rewriting departures from orthodoxy. He turns to lyric 55, where the poet despairs before Nature's "evil dreams" and "stretch[es] lame hands of faith, and grope[s], / . . . and call[s], / To what I feel is Lord of all" (55.6, 17–20). This, we are told, paraphrases Acts 17:27, where Paul tells the Athenians that God has arranged the circumstances of all societies "That they should seek the Lord, if haply they might feel after him, and find him." Paul goes on to declare the identity of the "UNKNOWN GOD" after whom he believes the Athenians have been groping (17:23). Stressing this connection, of course, accidentally turns Tennyson into a pagan, but the author wishes to imply that Tennyson, also, believes the "UNKNOWN GOD" has made himself known in Christ (17:31), and that each person typologically reenacts the passage of ancient cultures from darkness to revelation in their passage through doubt to reaffirmed faith. The critic reworks Tennyson's challenge to traditional typology in the following lyric, where he concludes all "hope of answer, or redress" is "Behind the veil, behind the veil" (56.58). Justified in detecting an "allusion to the veil of the tabernacle which concealed the presence of God," the *Leisure Hour* critic goes on to assert with the New Testament that "the Saviour has now passed" beyond that veil (72). In Tennyson's poetic cycle, however, removal of the veil is uncertain, since God largely remains an obscure intuition of the soul (124.3–24, 131.10, Epilogue.141–42). Yet the *Leisure Hour* author implies that Tennyson's biblical allusion can reinforce evangelical faith. No less than Brimley or the writer of *The British Quarterly Review,* the 1874 *Leisure Hour* critic partially rewrites *In Memoriam* for his purposes, in this case to bring its lines into dialogue with the Bible and Christian authority in ways that suit the needs of an imagined community of British evangelicals.

In keeping with this treatment of *In Memoriam,* the *Leisure Hour* critic describes the village near Tennyson's house in Surrey as "a place of pilgrimage" where visitors flock to catch "a glimpse of the poet" (71). On the next page, readers must negotiate a gigantic illustration of Tennyson's home while following the discussion of *In Memoriam*'s biblical allusions (72). Home and Bible, two major values of this magazine, sanctify Tennyson's *In Memoriam* as suitable family evangelical reading, perhaps even for sacrosanct Sunday afternoons. The initials of the contributor of this article, "J. C.," tempt a holy pun, as if Jesus Christ were extending biblical immortality to Tennyson's domesticated and national testimony of faith (73). Further encouraging Tennyson's incorporation into the home, *The Leisure Hour* ran an article in 1876 by the Rev. J. S. Stone on "The Home Aspect of Mr. Tennyson's Poems," in which the good reverend assured readers that the misty poet of *In Memoriam* could speak to "the ordinary public mind in relation to home scenes, and home affections, and home truths" (54). As the article's subtitle reminds readers, Stone is the author of the respectably evangelical "The Knight of Intercession," so that his opening commendation of Tennyson as a potential "prophet in his day" who deserves "devotion" can come across as a safely pious version of literary faith.

The suggestion of *The Leisure Hour* that Tennyson might offer good verses for Sunday reading was endorsed in a remarkable way in 1884 by *Sunday at Home,* an evangelical weekly magazine whose purpose was to convert the lower classes to spiritually nourishing Sunday afternoon reading. The magazine ran an article on "Gospel Notes in the Poetry of Alfred Tennyson" that claimed Tennyson as a reliable guide in "reverence before sacred truth" (180), and even portrayed his poetry as a "disinfectant" against the "Doubt" creeping into "our churches" and "literature" (181). To support this role for the poem, the "Gospel Notes" author applies a traditional technique of Christian—especially Protestant—biblical interpretation, compiling a catena of verses from *In Memoriam* to construct "the Creed, the Confession, the Litany, and Doxology of Tennyson." Selectively quoting from the introductory invocation of the "Strong Son of God" that Victorians so often used as a key for interpreting *In Memoriam* (see chapter 5), the critic, without noting the fact, combines these verses with the concluding stanza of lyric 56, which ends "What hope of answer, or redress? / Behind the veil, behind the veil" ("Gospel Notes" 181; *In Memoriam* 56.27–28).

This recalls the reconstructive appropriation of the same passage by the 1874 *Leisure Hour* critic. Here Tennyson is made to answer his own question in lyric 56 with his introductory stanzas, so that the public religious props—here the echoes of creeds and the Bible—on which the inward faith of *In Memoriam* depends become the summarizable content of the poetic cycle. Thus reconfigured, *In Memoriam* can serve a role recalling that praised by Brimley when he compared it to the Psalms of David, becoming a balm for "multitudes of living hearts, and millions of unborn suffering bereaved ones" ("Gospel Notes" 182). Indeed, the "Gospel Notes" author concludes by quoting, as reliable testimonies to a faith capable of enduring all modern doubt, most of the passages that earlier evangelical and High Church reviewers had condemned. Lyric 106 is rescued from potential charges of questioning or looking past the historical incarnation of Christ in its final line, "Ring in the Christ that is to be" (106.32). To the "Gospel Notes" writer, this means that Christ has yet to triumph in "the world" and "in the hearts of believers" in fulfillment of the messianic kingdom glimpsed by David in Psalm 72 (184). Lyric 106, in this view, extends the typological vision centered on Christ's first and Second Advents that had been long found by Christians in David's Psalms and other portions of the Old Testament. Applying familiar methods of biblical proof-texting and typological interpretation to Tennyson's *In Memoriam,* this evangelical critic treats it like a work of national scripture, one that testifies to the necessary bond between the British nation and Christianity: "we have . . . quoted enough to show that the faith of England's most popular poet . . . revolves round the great truths and revelations of Christ and Christianity as the loftiest inspirations of man and the most conservative influences of society" (185).

VI. TENNYSON'S MEASURED MINISTRY TO WORKERS

Tennyson's *In Memoriam,* then, made inward, private intuitions about immortality and God powerfully available for public consumption, appealing to many competing Victorian attempts to imagine national and denominational communities sustained by reading. It did so by seeming to dissolve public religious and cultural forms into the soul. Reviewers and commentators of every stripe joined in the open secret, even as they responded to the public textures of its inward confessions when using the poem to imagine their own religious communities and the spiritual character of their nation. Early on some of them, and by the 1870s many more of them, began to regard *In Memoriam* as a work of national scripture that provided an internalized typology of daily life for modern Britons. Yet by championing an inward faith in so publicly resonant a way, *In Memoriam* invited a diffusive sense of British piety that some called upon to validate control from above at home and military and imperial power abroad.

As Victorian reviewers often noted, the inward Christian experience of Tennyson's poem could be class coded: many anticipated, though not always with the same note of condescension, James Joyce's view of "Lawn Tennyson, gentleman poet" (qtd. Barton 183), observing that *In Memoriam's* appeal was strongest among English upper- and upper-middle-class readers, especially those with university educations.[12] The social and political undertones of *In Memoriam* seem intimately connected to its poetic tones—to the *In Memoriam* stanza that was immediately and widely praised by reviewers for its meditative and stately pace. That this measured progress is implicitly tied to visions of controlled social and political evolution Tennyson hints in lyric 113, where he expresses fear of revolution in lines borrowed from "Hail Briton!" He wrote this poem in the *In*

---

12. For example, "The Laureate and His School," *Dublin Review:* 363 and "Alfred Tennyson: Part II," *Leisure Hour:* 138.

Memoriam stanza in the early 1830s to express anxious disappointment over agitations leading to the 1832 Reform Act (Ricks I:527[13]).

In fact, Tennyson wrote a series of poems between 1831–34 using the ABBA stanza, all of them expressing fear of sudden political and social change and extolling the virtues of a land where "Freedom slowly broadens down / From precedent to precedent" ("You ask me, why, though ill at ease" [c. 1833] 11–12). After 1834, Tennyson dedicated the stanza he had used for containing fears of "banded unions" ("You ask me, why" 17) to channeling the struggle of doubt and faith in the wake of Hallam's death in poems that became *In Memoriam* (Ricks II:307, 311). Tennyson made these connections publicly available by publishing several of the political *In Memoriam* stanza poems in his 1842 volume,[14] and using the same stanza to hymn imperial Britain and the Queen in his first poem as Poet Laureate, "To the Queen" in 1851. Brimley appears to recognize the connection when he prefaces his comments on *In Memoriam* with a discussion of Tennyson's political poem in the same verse form, "Love Thou Thy Land" (274–75). By the 1860s, it would have been hard not to make this association, as newspapers reprinted debates over the 1866 Reform Bill showing Gladstone and his opponents both quoting "You ask me, why, though ill at ease," one of Tennyson's early political poems in the ABBA stanza, which he had just republished under the title "Britain" ("The Reform Bills" 284).

Whereas Dwight Culler limits the import of this stanza migration to Tennyson's Broad Church belief in intuitive process and gradual improvement rather than systematic solutions (159), I want to stress, as well, its relevance to fear of revolution and praise of measured direction from above. A dislike for firm religious systems, in other words, can sit well with discomfort over systematic political and economic change uncontrolled by wise elites. F. W. Robertson, the popular liberal Anglican minister based in Bristol, was one ardent admirer of *In Memoriam* who seized on the tacit analogy between the stately progress of Tennyson's Christian elegy and the firmly measured progress of Christian Britain. In his 1852 lectures on poetry to working men, Robertson reveals the social and class interests behind using *In Memoriam* to sanction Christian unity based on "fundamental" inward experiences. "The first maxim in religion and in art," Robertson tells his 1852 working-class audience, "is . . . cut your life adrift from all party," political, philosophical, or religious (182). Tennyson's poem can show work-

---

13. All quotations of poems by Tennyson other than *In Memoriam* come from Ricks' *The Poems of Tennyson*.

14. "You ask me, why, though ill at ease"; "Hail Briton!"; "Love thou thy land, with love far-brought"; "Of old sat Freedom on the heights."

ers the wisdom of ignoring Evangelical and High Church "religious periodicals" with their battles over "routine phrases" and watchwords (131), guiding them to locate a uniting faith not in "particular forms, either of words or ritual" (156), but in "intuitions of the Soul" (155).

Coming on the heels of Tennyson's promotion to Poet Laureate because of *In Memoriam,* the publication of Tennyson's "To the Queen" in the *In Memoriam* stanza, and the decisive suppression of the Chartist movement, Robertson's ban on public form and organization has a political charge. Not in the world of divisive forms and "party" organization, but in the non-demonstrative inward realm of intuitions, working Britons will discover their faith and their freedom. So long as working peoples' skepticism, anguish, and longing for a better world find expression through the ministrations of poets such as Tennyson, Robertson claims, these working-class readers will help preserve "England's freedom from revolution and conspiracies" (184). Revolution and conspiracies are the consequences of bottled-up frustration and doubt. Yet high poetry, such as *In Memoriam,* acts as a "safety-valve to the heart" (184), releasing negative emotions in noble expression. Two years before Robertson's lectures, Patmore had implied that the measured language of *In Memoriam* functioned like a stethoscope, through which the nation's heart could be heard quickening after a spiritual "syncope" to beat in time with basic Christian convictions. Robertson, by contrast, suggests *In Memoriam* might valuably slow pulses, rechanneling emotions "for which there is no available field of action" (184).

Robertson's view of poetry as a "safety-valve" for discharging otherwise dangerous emotional steam borrows from the poetics articulated by John Keble and the Tractarians,[15] and also despondently invoked in *In Memoriam:* "for the unquiet heart and brain, / A use in measured language lies; / The sad mechanic exercise, / Like dull narcotics, numbing pain" (5.5–8). Robertson supports his "safety-valve" theory by quoting Tennyson's poem "You ask me, why, though ill at ease," first published in 1842, and one of the early political poems that Tennyson wrote in the stanza of *In Memo-*

---

15. At Oxford in the heyday of Tractarianism, Robertson admired Newman and retained the Tractarians' emphasis on forms in religious devotion. Yet his "sympathy for the Tractarians" soon "hardened into opposition to their exclusiveness" (Blair, *Form and Faith* 172). Keble's 1838 review of Lockhart's life of Walter Scott for *The British Critic* is likely Robertson's source for the idea of poetry as a safety-valve: there Keble argues that poetic form "provides a 'safety-valve' for people who might otherwise develop actual 'mental disease' from the pressure of feeling" (Blair, *Form and Faith* 33). In his lectures to working-men, Robertson extends this principle from individual psychology to social stability: workers require poetry's controlled release of their discontent if they are to be restrained from marching in the streets and setting up barricades.

riam: "[Britain is] the land where, girt by friend or foe, / A man may speak the thing he will" (184). Poetry keeps free speech in good form, expressing emotions "which, unuttered, would make a man dangerous—or morbid—or mad," so that there "is no restless feeling left behind of something unsaid" (184–85). Modern poetry, especially poems such as *In Memoriam* suffused with basic Christian feelings, expresses unsatisfiable longing for a world unseen, and so should be recognized as the special inheritance of the working classes: "Does not such poetry therefore more peculiarly belong to the Working Men, whose life is desire, not enjoyment; aspiration, not contentment?" (185). Robertson is quick to ensure his statement is not misunderstood by his audience (which apparently contains employers as well as workers): "when we say Poetry elevates, let it not be understood of the improvement of physical comforts" (186).

This is, of course, simply realistic: reading *In Memoriam* is hardly going to resuscitate the Chartist movement or reform labor laws. But it is also proscriptive. The inward spiritual community and aspirations that *In Memoriam* could enable workers to imagine sharing with other Britons should not be confused with outward forms (or hasty reforms) and organized public demands. Yet workers should not resist calls to united action from the British state. Robertson notes that the 1848 revolution in France has brought an ambitious Napoleon III to power, and that working men might soon be called upon to serve as heroic Christian brothers of British soldiers (205). This will require their inward sense of Christian unity, and Tennyson can minister to the need. Robertson also champions this national faith as the source of Britain's imperial glory, citing British soldiers' heroic subjection of hill peoples in India as an example (204). If Robertson asks Bristol workers to embrace the inward force of modern Christian poems such as *In Memoriam,* he concludes praising the outward force of war and imperial conquest. For war, Robertson says, forces citizens to overcome sectarianism and self-interest and aspire to higher virtues (202). In battle Britons will discover brotherhood, even as Tennyson helps them believe their fellowship will survive death—at which point their aspirations for a better world could be realized.

Robertson uses Tennyson, then, to distinguish between the inner religious aspirations of poetry and the outward performances demanded of workers' bodies by the state. This move builds on the long process discussed in chapter 5, by which faith had come to seem the property of the individual mind. This opened the way for outward actions to become the property of the state as part of a process in post-Westphalian Europe, accelerated in England after the Toleration Act (1689) (McKeon 39–40), by which "the body was secularized in the sense that its needs, behaviors, and performances increasingly became the business of differentiated social spheres: the state, the economy, the medical professions, and so on" (Jager, *Unquiet Things* 114). Tennyson's *In Memoriam* and Christian poetry of its caliber can divert workers from making demands in the streets by uniting them around inward spiritual fundamentals, leaving their bodies to be secularized as the property of the state—and, Robertson suggests, the economy. He exclaims that "the Poetry of the coming age must come from the Working Classes" (168), for workers have learned the loyalty and devotion that exist in smoking factories, "the heroism of perseverance, and the poetry of invention, and the patience of *uncomplaining* resignation" (169; emphasis mine).

VII. AN INWARD AND IMPERIAL FAITH

As Robertson indicates, turning to inward experience as the basis for a vaguely Christianized British reading public was also easily tied—because divorced from creeds that could question, restrain, divide, or transcend national identity—to patriotic imperialism, a Christian civilizing ideal for a superior British nation. This version of British imagined community became increasingly available in print after the 1870s (McLeod, "Protestantism" 55–65), especially by "the heyday of imperialism" in the 1880s and 1890s (Carey 371), when imperialism was frequently "justified . . . as a spiritual enterprise through which the blessing of British rule would bring order and morality to the world" (33). For "Greater Britain" (7)—the "white, Christian, English-speaking" community that countless "publications" in these decades portrayed spanning Great Britain and its colonies in British North America, Australia, New Zealand, and southern Africa (8)—a "direct consequence" of spiritualized patriotic imperialism was "the creation of a loyal imperial fighting force that could be marshalled for the killing fields of the first imperial war, which was enthusiastically supported by the majority of the churches" (34–35).

In keeping with these developments, Tennyson's later poem "To the Queen" (1873) praises the British as the "mightiest of all peoples under heaven" (21), maintaining "Our ocean-empire" (29) only by virtue of "the faith / That made us rulers" (18–19). As LaPorte has observed, Tennyson wrote this poem as an epilogue to *The Idylls of the King* to fortify the point made throughout that national epic: "that the political strength that Christianity had given to the British nation was" as "imperiled in the nineteenth century" as it was in the legendary kingdom of Arthur (79). The "faith" of "To the Queen" is as much in Victoria's empire as in "Heaven" (46): Tennyson is discussing the "shame[ful]" lack of faith in imperial rule recently evidenced by proposals to cut off Canada from Greater Britain, since keeping it was "'too costly!'" (15–16). The "faith / That made us rulers" is a national conviction that British virtue, valor, and "common-sense" (61) will usher in "the goal of this great world / [which] Lies beyond sight" (59–60).

Such British Christian identity, while inheriting a Protestant emphasis on clear-sighted honesty (Carruthers 2), cuts loose from specific credenda to latch on to supposedly eternal human truths that each Briton will find confirmed by their inmost thoughts, and strengthened by familiar and nostalgic national religious associations. The nostalgic dimension of this vague Christian spirituality is evident in many of the comments on *In Memoriam* discussed in this chapter—Lushington's nostalgic praise for village church bells treasured by British sailors as the ringing echoes through their minds; Brimley's celebration of the way Tennyson's *In Memoriam* and *Idylls of the King* permit a fusion of national legend and Christian hope, together acting as a semi-sacred national scripture; the 1860 *British Quarterly Review* critic's praise of *In Memoriam* as the heartbeat of a basic English piety and reverence for the spiritual order in nature. This last critic builds on his faith in such English piety to justify Britain's role as a superior nation and the missionary of religion throughout the world ("Les Contemplations" 72). Ironically, Christian Britain becomes supposedly less sectarian—able, as Tennyson puts it in his poem "To the Queen," to include "The prayer of many a race and creed, and clime" (11)—as it becomes more explicitly *British* and imperial in its Christian virtue.

This is especially evident in "Akbar's Dream" (1892), which Tennyson completed and published in his last year of life, and which he said best expressed what he meant in poem 106 of *In Memoriam* when he called on New-Year bells to "Ring in the Christ that is to be" (32). By this phrase, Tennyson said, he meant the world in which "Christianity without bigotry will triumph, when the controversies of creeds shall have vanished" (*Memoir* I:326). The poem is a dramatic monologue framed by a narrator, in which the sixteenth-century Moghul emperor Akbar recounts to his chief minister, Abul Fazl, his struggle to create a religiously tolerant empire in northern and central India. As Blair has observed, in "Akbar's Dream" Tennyson reveals that he was not exclusively pledged to Christian forms and symbols as expressions of God and divine truth (*Form and Faith* 192). Blair rightly calls attention to Tennyson's consistent interest in comparative religion, and his late dedication to the idea that all religions are one, even as he continued to imply that Christianity provided the best model for the toleration he advocated (189–194).

Yet in focusing on Tennyson's permissive view of the relationship between form and faith in "Akbar's Dream," Blair risks underemphasizing Tennyson's endorsement of imperial arms and government as necessary ministers of toleration (194). Prioritizing the relative liberality of "Akbar's Dream" could also distract attention from the poem's contribution to a subject that I examined in chapter 3 in Matthew Arnold's later religious criticism: the strategic redefinition of "religion" to sanctify or enable state power. "Akbar's Dream" participates in the use of "religion" as a term in the comparative study of disparate cultures and social practices, and therefore the late nineteenth-century scholarly construction of "world religions" (Masuzawa 12–13, 18). This use of "religion" is an invention of political and scholarly discourses in Western modernity (Casanova, "The Secular" 62, 72–73). The concept is heavily tied to the needs of European colonial administrations faced with governing religiously diverse overseas populations often outnumbering the Christian populations of their metropoles: after 1882, when Britain added Egypt to an empire already containing India, it could be described by a Russian observer as "'in reality . . . a Mohamedan empire' ruled by a 'Christian minority'" (qtd. in S. Brown 302). In fact, the idea of "religions," or distinct thought systems and rituals binding people together, has long been deployed by states to categorize and regulate a plurality of practices and beliefs within their borders, whether in the case of imperial Rome, or in the case of the Mughal empire that forms the subject of Tennyson's "Akbar's Dream" (Calhoun, "Time, World, and Secularism" 349). As José Casanova observes, while this way of conceiving "religion" is Western in origin, it has now become a discursive reality on a global scale: used by individuals and societies around the world, it is—as an object of thought and discourse—"an undisputable global social fact" ("The Secular" 62). In this context, "religion" and "world religions" seem less neutral categories of analysis than instruments of political and cultural organization.

Tennyson's "Akbar's Dream" was produced by the turn-of-the-century study of comparative religion and philology that ultimately sponsored the concept of "world religions," and that contributed to "the colonial discourse of Orientalism," in which the West was positioned as the modern administrator and appreciator of the East and its—decidedly past—great cultures (Masuzawa 20–21).[16] Tennyson wrote "Akbar's Dream" in dialogue

---

16. McBratney recognizes the orientalism of "Akbar's Dream," even as he suggests the poem's "meditation on religion" is only awkwardly joined to its "apology for empire" and the idea that

with works by Orientalist philologist and comparative theologian Max Müller, and at the encouragement of Benjamin Jowett, the Oxford theologian and classicist, who supplied Tennyson with Orientalist books and urged him to write a poem on the theme "All religions are one" (*Memoir* II:372). One such book was Blochmann's translation (1872–77) of the *Ain-i-Akbari* by Akbar's advisor and chronicler Abu Fazl (Blair, *Form and Faith* 191–92). Given Tennyson's desire to promote interest in "the great religions of the world" (*Memoirs* II:401) and his engagement with late-century Orientalism, he appropriately prefaces "Akbar's Dream" with this inscription by Abul Fazl, quoted in Blochmann's preface to *Ain-i-Akbari*:

> AN INSCRIPTION BY ABUL FAZL FOR A TEMPLE IN KASHMIR
> (Blochmann xxxii)
> O God in every temple I see people that see thee, and in every language
> I hear spoken, people praise thee.
> Polytheism and Islám feel after thee.
> Each *religion* says, 'Thou art one, without equal.'
> If it be a mosque people murmur the holy prayer, and if it be a Christian
> Church, people ring the bell from love to Thee.
> [. . .] Thy elect have no dealings with either heresy or orthodoxy; for neither
> of them stands behind the screen of thy truth.
> Heresy to the heretic, and *religion* to the orthodox,
> But the dust of the rose-petal belongs to the heart of the perfume seller.
>
> (Ricks III:236; emphasis mine)

This epigraph enables Tennyson to position his poem as part of a prophetic interfaith dialogue initiated by enlightened officials in northern India's past imperial civilization. The British imperial laureate shares, and anticipates the realization of, hopes anciently cherished by the enlightened ancestors of Queen Victoria's Indian subjects. The word "religion" only appears in "Akbar's Dream" through this epigraph, as if Tennyson, assisted by Blochmann's translation, were simply unearthing the project this term contains to announce an opportunity for the modern West to complete

---

the "West" had "the power to resuscitate a dead or broken East for its own ends" (415). My point is that the poem's endorsement of British administration and curation of the East in fact requires the view of "religions" it promotes.

what the ancient East initiated.[17] Tennyson invokes the category "religion," in other words, to uphold the right of imperial states to oversee the "religions" of their subjects, as well as the capacity of imperial scholars and poets to discern, through the "screen[s]" of merely local temples and rituals, the cosmopolitan "truth" worth conserving. Indeed, the epigraph to "Akbar's Dream" might contain the only use of "religion" in Tennyson's *oeuvre* (A. Baker 573).

Tennyson devotes most of "Akbar's Dream" to Akbar's description of his efforts to establish open religious debate and an imperial religion that could embrace the best in all creeds. Akbar concludes his monologue by recounting a dream in which he foresees the failure of his ecumenical effort, but glimpses its completion by tolerant Christian Britain:

> From out the sunset [i.e., the West] there poured an alien race,
> Who fitted stone to stone [of my ideal ecumenical temple] again, and Truth,
> Peace, Love and Justice came and dwelt therein,
> Nor in the field were seen or heard
> Fires of Súttee, nor wail of baby-wife,
> Or Indian widow; and in sleep I said
> "All praise to Alla by whatever hands
> My mission be accomplished!" (182–89)

Citing the practice of Súttee, or Sati, a widow's throwing of herself on her husband's funeral pyre, which the British would follow Akbar in banning (1829), Akbar prophetically welcomes "whatever hands"—and, in the British context, guns—will be required to uphold the rule of "Love and Justice" over the "furious formalisms" of Hindu and Muslim dogmatists (55). Throughout the poem, Tennyson has Akbar portray as subhuman and irrational all those (other than himself) who make public and exclusive claims for their doctrines: Muslim "Ulama" are "like wild brutes

---

17. As Stevens and Sapra argue, though Tennyson's poem appears simply to confirm Western historicism—which places Western hegemony at the forefront of human progress—it also challenges the historical primacy of the West. In this view, Tennyson's epigraph signals not only a transfer of authority from ancient East to modern West but also recognition that "religious toleration, one of Western modernity's essential, self-defining concepts, is neither peculiarly Western nor modern" (411). Even so, this act of "provincializ[ing] Europe" (411) does not challenge British hegemony. Rather, Tennyson "unearths" further "evidence" that Victoria's empire rests on the supposedly universal compatibility of religious toleration with imperial governance. His poem insists that religious toleration is historically the creation of imperial state power, and that it requires that power to exist, at least at first.

new-caged—the narrower / The cage, the more their fury" (45–49), and "intolerant priests" are "cobras ever setting up their hoods" who must be "beat back" (156–58). This beating might require more than words. Akbar has won his ability to "do the right / Through all the vast dominion" by "a sword, / That only conquers men to conquer peace" (13–15). The implicit standards for religious participation in this imperial ecumenical community resemble those Talal Asad finds at work in many secularist understandings of the modern nation state—"religion has the option of either confining itself to private belief and worship or of engaging in public talk that makes no demands on life" (*Formations* 199).

If Akbar's regime—and Tennyson's ideal imperial Britain—promotes a "free Hall" of discussion, a public sphere "where each philosophy / And mood of faith may hold its own" (53–54), this requires, as Akbar explains, excluding or shaming all who believe their faith is more than a "mood," as they "clamour 'I am the Perfect Way, / All else is to perdition'" (33–34). In having Akbar allude to Christ's familiar claim of primary access to God (John 14:6), Tennyson singles out not only Muslims and Hindus who make doctrinal demands on public life but also contemporary British groups, such as evangelical proselytizers at home and abroad, who are vocal in their efforts to convert others to their path to God. At home, the poem suggests, shame is the best policy for enforcing a British public sphere that excludes strident religion. Tennyson's imagery of beasts and clamoring sects indicates that his poem on Akbar is one dose of the mocking medicine. In British India, as in Akbar's India, however, more forceful measures might occasionally be required from "the hand that rules, / With politic care, with utter gentleness" as it "Mould[s]" forms of faith "for all . . . people" (120–22).

This effort to imagine and enforce the limits of religion is deeply connected to Tennyson's presentation of his own verse as a universal language. Tennyson suggests that British poetry, especially his own, might enable the British imperial public to discern amidst the many chants and praises of diverse faiths "but one music, harmonizing 'Pray'" (144). Just after Akbar concludes his prophecy of Christian Britain arriving to fulfill his hope of a religiously tolerant empire, he overhears a morning "hymn" of interfaith worship that he—really, of course, Tennyson—composed, which declares that a "myriad" of "laureates" from every clime sing to "Him the Timeless" (199, 201). Akbar's state-sponsored hymn serves as a thinly veiled analogy to the way Victoria's laureate sees his widely circulating poetry furthering the unity of the British Empire.

Tennyson's poetry, then, recommended, and for some commentators enabled, the vaguely Christianized imperial British community that was invoked with increasing acceptance after the 1870s. Yet this vision of Christian Britain did not become the dominant or central point of allegiance for many Britons who continued to contribute to the public sphere; rather, it was just as often viewed in competition with more specific religious and irreligious imagined communities. In so far as reading publics and acts of reading were concerned, a vaguely Christian Britain became for many the explicit or assumed counterpoint against which to define a more compelling and specific form of imagined community. From this generalized sense of British Christendom both agnostic/atheistic and more orthodox poets in and after the 1870s sought relief, invoking reading communities that either defined themselves in opposition to the very idea of a Christian Britain or assumed a bond of unity that was both more exclusively and internationally Christian. The atheist James Thomson (B. V.), appealing to all skeptics in "this very Christian country" (*Speedy Extinction* 105), published *A City of Dreadful Night* (1874) as an inverted *Christian Year* whose inherited cycles and liturgical references are pointedly consumed or canceled in the vast entropic night of the modern world. Thomson opens by asking readers to receive his lines as the "voice" of "a brother / . . . out of sight" who is initiating them into a "sad Fraternity" (*The Complete Poems,* Proem.34–36), and includes a virtual image of this "congregation" in a church service stripped of (implicitly Anglican or Anglo-Catholic) "chant," "prayer," "priests," and "tinkling censers" (XIV.4–5), in which a preacher proclaims the death of God (23). As I discuss in the next chapter, with her final volume of poetry, *Verses* (1893), the Anglo-Catholic Christina Rossetti fashioned a late-century *Christian Year* that invited readers into a firmly international and ecumenical Christian communion.

This shows not the decline or privatization of Christianity in late nineteenth-century Britain, but its contested definition and its differentiation from other spheres of authority. Various British reading audiences were imagining themselves in terms of (even if against) a national imperial community that was still broadly Christian and Protestant, and vaguely sanctioned by Providence in its civilizing mission. Christianity, and attempts to distinguish public relations to and within it, remained central to imagining reading as participation in a community spanning the nation and empire; but an imagined spiritual identity *coextensive* with that imperial nation was difficult to sustain. Passing from the varying efforts to envision a spiritually united reading public by Coleridge, Maurice, and Arnold, and surveying the different permutations of the poetic paradigm Keble helped make widespread, a general and uneven trend emerges. The labor to imagine a *national* religious community through reading gives way to demarcations of religious and irreligious publics and counterpublics within a broadly "Christian" national public that itself floats loose from any single institution or religious group.

CHAPTER 7

CHRISTINA ROSSETTI'S *VERSES*

A Multi-Fashioned Community of Strangers

Just over a year before her death, Christina Rossetti published *Verses* (1893) with the Society for Promoting Christian Knowledge (SPCK), integrating into a united cycle 331 poems from three (largely prose) devotional books she had issued with the SPCK in the preceding decade.[1] Early into *Verses*, Rossetti's best-selling volume in the Victorian period, readers encounter a sonnet asking them to lend their voices to a communal prayer: "Lord, grant us . . . steadfast faces toward the Holy Land, / And confidence of hope, and filial fear, / And citizenship where Thy saints appear" ("Lord, grant us eyes to see and ears to hear" 1, 4–5).[2] Rossetti's language of "citizenship" appears several times in the New Testament to describe community between peoples from all nations within Christ's eschatological kingdom ("the Holy Land").[3] Yet given contrasting late-century attempts,

---

1. *Called to Be Saints* (1881), *Time Flies* (1885), and *The Face of the Deep* (1892).

2. Since *Verses* is made up of many individual poems and poetic sequences, I include the first line or, where provided, title of each poem, followed by line numbers. Unless otherwise noted, all quotations of Rossetti's poetry are from Crump and Flower's 2005 edition of *The Complete Poems*. When editors' comments are cited in the text, the volume is referred to as *CP*.

3. Eph. 2:18–20; Phil. 3:20–21. Unless noted otherwise, all citations of the Bible are from the Authorized Version. The term *citizenship* appears in modified form in the AV and English Revised Version renderings of Ephesians (2:19 "ye are . . . fellow citizens with the saints"). *Citizenship* is not used in the AV rendering of Philippians (3:20 "For our *conversation* is in heaven"), but it is in the English Revised Version (1881–85) (3:20 "For our *citizenship* is in heaven"). Ros-

examined in the previous chapter, to turn poetry into a quasi-national scripture for an imperial Christian Britain, Rossetti's call for transnational "citizenship" in a community whose hope will be fulfilled in an unseen "Holy Land" acquires contemporary and even countercultural importance. Only recently recovered by scholars for its artistry and complicated articulation of Rossetti's religious vision,[4] *Verses* deserves fuller recognition as Rossetti's late-century effort to involve readers in an imagined community of strangers—a widely scattered fellowship of saints whose binding hope in heavenly citizenship estranges them from exclusive identification with any national society, branch of the Church, or existing corner of the English-speaking literary market.

Such a construction of imagined community can seem naïve and abstract, an ideological fantasy of a united Christendom that never existed and that the increasing religious pluralism of nineteenth-century Britain would render impossible. As I discuss below, Rossetti's Anglo-Catholicism *would* encourage her to hope for a doctrinally and institutionally reconciled international Church. Yet such programmatic reconciliation is not the main practical or imaginative goal of *Verses*. Rather, Rossetti fashions a poetic cycle whose language, form, and structure can be appropriated to lesser or greater degrees by a wide range of English-speaking Christian and literary audiences, encouraging these strangers to imagine their membership in a community that hopes for an eternal society in which all will fully achieve their unique selfhood in unity with God and others.

This in many ways deeply traditional vision of a community of believers is therefore projected in a modern ideological form—a mass-mediated public—that is assumed in practice by all the writers discussed in this book. The "I" and "us" in the poems of *Verses* are intended to be received by strangers who are drawn by the volume into a public which is "in principle open-ended" (Warner, *Publics and Counterpublics* 73); and the "success" of this public address will be measured by "further attempts to cite, circulate, and realize the world understanding it articulates" (114). Firmly resisting the patriotic and imperial forms of spiritual community enabled by Tennyson's *In Memoriam* and promoted by many other figures later in the century (chapter 6), Rossetti's *Verses* redeploys the strategy of aligning the private reading of meditative poetic cycles with participation in a nation of Christian readers that John Keble's *Christian Year* and Tennyson's *In Memoriam*

---

setti seems to have been in the habit of comparing the Revised Version and Authorized Version. See her remarks in *Face of the Deep* (1892): 257, 549.

4. See especially David Kent ("W. M. Rossetti" and "Sequence and Meaning"), D'Amico (*Christina Rossetti*), Westerholm ("In Defense of *Verses*"), and Dieleman (*Religious Imaginaries*).

had so widely, if unintentionally, popularized (chapters 4–5). Like Keble and Tennyson, Rossetti created a poetic cycle that encouraged confusion of private reading with spiritual community by combining a series of separately written (and, in her case, published) poems. Rossetti's receptivity to Keble's precedent is hardly surprising, given her dedicated participation in the Anglo-Catholic movement he so deeply influenced, as well as her careful lifelong rereading of *The Christian Year*.[5]

In *Verses*, Rossetti adroitly reworks Keble's model to invoke an ecumenical and international Christian public at a time when new volumes of poetry were being forced into a relatively marginalized position within a market favoring cheap prose and anthologies of poetry (Erickson 345, 355–60), and when publishers and authors were competing to carve out a variegated array of readerships for distinct kinds and formats of literature (Weedon 100). *Verses* is comprised of eight sections[6] whose arrangement, as Karen Dieleman notes, quietly parallels the Anglican liturgy for Holy Communion (153–54). Yet only one section ("Some Feasts and Fasts") explicitly imitates *The Christian Year* in arranging poems according to the Anglican calendar. Rossetti adopts more ecumenical titles for the remaining seven sections (e.g., "Songs for Strangers and Pilgrims"), encouraging the volume's use by diverse Christian readers, and signaling her awareness of *Verses'* likely destiny as a sourcebook for more widely distributed anthologies aimed at specific religious groups and church parties.

In fact, when selecting poems from her previous SPCK volumes for inclusion in *Verses*, Rossetti appears to have been partly guided by her respect for the role anthologies played in distributing poems to readers who otherwise rarely purchased volumes of new poetry. Rossetti excluded from *Verses* fourteen of the poems that she had published in her SPCK prose books.[7] Most of these excluded poems could have easily fit the

---

5. D'Amico discusses CGR's illustrations of Keble's poems as well as the passages and lines she marked ("Christina Rossetti's *Christian Year*" 36–41).

6. "Out of the Deep Have I Called unto Thee, O Lord"; "Christ Our All in All"; "Some Feasts and Fasts"; "Gifts and Graces"; "The World. Self-Destruction"; "Divers Worlds. Time and Eternity"; "New Jerusalem and Its Citizens"; and "Songs for Strangers and Pilgrims."

7. Comparing lists of excluded poems by Rossetti's early biographer Henry Thomas Mackenzie Bell (287–88) and David Kent ("W. M. Rossetti" 26 n10) yields the following list of poems published in *Time Flies* (1885) and *The Face of the Deep* (1892) but excluded from *Verses*. I note page numbers in the earlier volumes on which the poems appear. *Time Flies:* "Pity the sorrow of a poor old dog" (p. 138), "Love is all happiness, love is all beauty" (p. 34), "A handy Mole who plied no shovel" (p. 40), "One swallow does not make a summer [A Rose which spied one swallow]" (p. 85), "Contemptuous of his home beyond" (p. 129); *Face of the Deep:* "What will it be, O my soul, what will it be?" (p. 35), "Lord, Thou art fullness; I am emptiness" (p. 36), "O Lord, I cannot plead my love of Thee" (p. 84), "Lord, comest Thou to me?" (p. 224), "Love us unto the end, and prepare

design of *Verses.* Yet Rossetti reprinted all but one[8] of the many SPCK poems that had been republished prior to her work on *Verses* in literary and religious anthologies in Britain and the United States. She must have known of at least four of these anthologies.[9] Apparently, Rossetti was careful to build on the relatively wide but disjointed anthologizing of her SPCK poems when compiling *Verses,* letting poems drop that had not been picked up elsewhere and artfully weaving into the structure of her collection those that had already attracted a variety of editors and readerships. Rossetti also compiled *Verses* with sensitivity to a literary market in which devotional poetry often failed to overleap the boundaries of a large and mainly middle-class religious reading public to attract the smaller but culturally central audiences of distinguished literary periodicals. *Verses* was able to reach across this devotional-literary divide, I argue later in this chapter, largely because of Rossetti's decision to capitalize on her pivotal role in the nineteenth-century sonnet revival by opening the volume with an accomplished sonnet sequence. Taken together, I argue, these strategies of arrangement eventually helped drive *Verses* itself—and Rossetti's agile

---

us" (p. 248: this is more of a prose prayer, a collect, than a poem proper), "I sit a queen, and am no widow, and shall see no sorrow" (p. 417), "Passing away the bliss" (p. 448), "Love builds a nest on earth and waits for rest" (p. 513), "Jesus alone:—if thus it were to me—" (p. 549).

8. The excluded poem is listed in the note above: "One swallow does not make a summer" (*TF* 85). This poem appeared with others from *Time Flies* in *From Queen's Gardens* (1889), an American anthology of verse by British women compiled by Rose Porter for Nims and Night (Ives 215–16). While Porter attributed the poems to Christina Rossetti, they were probably pirated without her or the SPCK's knowledge. Rossetti is unlikely to have known of the poem's prior inclusion in an anthology.

9. In 1882, one of Rossetti's poems from *Called to Be Saints* that was republished in *Verses* ("They scarcely waked before they slept [Holy Innocents]") appeared in a frequently reprinted anthology aimed at busy readers in pursuit of daily culture and devotion: *Five Minutes Daily Readings of Poetry* (London: Rivingtons, 1882). Rossetti corresponded with Rivingtons two years before this anthology's appearance (*Letters* II:252–53). It is unlikely that Rivingtons republished her SPCK poems without seeking permission. Henry Thomas Mackenzie Bell, Rossetti's biographer and friend, wrote the prefatory essay to an anthology edited by F. A. H. Eyles, *Popular Poets of the Period* (London: Griffith, Farran, Okeden, and Welsh, 1889), that included a biographical note on Rossetti as well as several poems from *Time Flies* later included in *Verses*: "Roses and Roses" and "If love is not worth loving, then life is not worth living" (Ives 216). Because of her connection with Bell, Rossetti almost certainly knew of the inclusion of the poems. William Garrett Horder included in his anthology *The Poet's Bible, Old Testament* (London: William Ibister, 1889 [1890]), with the permission of Rossetti and the SPCK, one poem from *Time Flies* that Rossetti reprinted in *Verses* ("'The half was not told me,' said Sheba's queen [She came from the uttermost part of the earth]") (Ives 217). Before she began work on *Verses,* Rossetti was aware that a large number of poems from *Time Flies* were to appear in Alfred H. Miles' famous *The Poets and the Poetry of the Century* (London: Hutchinson & Co., 1892) (Ives 221; see *Letters* for Rossetti's 1891 correspondence about the anthology and the poems from *Time Flies* [IV:250–51]). She included all of these poems in *Verses.*

effort to inspire a diverse readership with a vision of ecumenical Christian community—out of public consciousness, even as individual poems attracted critical attention and were reprinted in multiple forms.

My method of reading poems in this chapter could strike some as insufficiently attentive to literary aesthetics. Critics such as Joel Westerholm and Joshua Taft have rightly challenged the tendency "to read" Rossetti's late devotional poetry as a sign that the "poet . . . traded vigor for dogma" (Taft 311). Rather than perpetuating this impression through biographical or thematic criticism that leaves out traditional close reading practices, these critics have argued for the formal accomplishments of Rossetti's "repetitive but resourceful style" in her late devotional poetry (Taft 312). Such revisionary formalist criticism understandably prioritizes things such as Rossetti's use of genre conventions, rhyme, stanza structure, and paronomasia, as well as her evocation of multiple levels of meaning through grammatical ambiguity, sound pattern, and repetition and near repetition. Yet this approach risks assuming that carefully reading Rossetti's late verse simply means subjecting it to categories of formal analysis inherited from New Criticism. This can yield a richer understanding of Rossetti's artistry in terms still recognized within the literary academy (especially that portion of it devoted to poetry and poetics). Yet it can indirectly affirm the questionable belief that those elements of craft unique to Rossetti's devotional mode and aim are somehow unfit for serious consideration, the boring trappings of versified dogma that must be underplayed, apologized for, or peeled away to uncover "real" literary value. By contrast, although I frequently consider familiar elements of style in my reading of *Verses,* I highlight the ways in which Rossetti deftly constructs a poetic cycle whose method of arrangement, allusive language, and deployment of popular poetic forms (e.g., sonnets and roundels) would enable it—and its overarching image of transnational and ecumenical Christian community—to be engaged by a wide range of literary and Christian audiences in a diversified late-Victorian print market. When examining individual poems, I therefore foreground complex allusions to biblical phrases, liturgical structures, and hymns, as well as (in the chapter's conclusion) the multivalent nature of Rossetti's imagery and diction, which remains faithful to her Anglo-Catholic understanding of community while inviting appropriation by a range of denominations. I believe this way of reading *Verses* best accounts for its capacity to reach further into the Victorian reading public than any of Rossetti's other volumes.

Verses appeared when the British reading public had expanded beyond all previous boundaries, and not long before competing means of mass communication, such as the radio, signaled the beginning of the end of the age when print was Britain's dominant public medium. Published near the crescendo and twilight of one media age, *Verses* indicates another cultural turning point through its invitation to participate, by way of devoted reading, in an international Christian community that transcends any national or institutional body: the moment when efforts to imagine national spiritual communities had paradoxically encouraged some deeply Christian publics to be imagined in distinction from a nominally Christian British reading nation.

I. CITIZENS OF A BETTER COUNTRY: THE COMMUNION OF SAINTS AND INTERNATIONAL ECUMENISM

Over the last fifteen years, scholars have demonstrated the decisive influence on Rossetti's poetry and later prose exercised by Tractarian theology and Anglo-Catholic ecclesiology and ritualism.[10] After 1860, there was "a definite increase of interest in the doctrine of the Communion of Saints" within High Anglicanism, particularly among Anglo-Catholics, whose advocacy of ritualism[11] was at its zenith in this period (Lautz 81–82), and at whose major centers in London Rossetti consistently worshipped.[12] At its most basic, the doctrine describes the mystical union in Christ of members in the visible Church militant on earth with members in the invisible Church triumphant who have entered communion with God after death, "the great cloud of witnesses" (Heb. 12:1).

In her later life, Rossetti devoted increasing energy to cultivating in herself and her readers a sense of membership in the communion of saints and a longing for its final realization, beginning with *Called to Be Saints,*

---

10. In addition to studies by D'Amico and Dieleman mentioned above, see those by Mary Arseneau (*Recovering Christina Rossetti*), Dinah Roe (*Christina Rossetti's Faithful Imagination*), Emma Mason ("A Sort of Aesthetico-Catholic Revival"), and Kirstie Blair (the final chapter of *Form and Faith*).

11. Ritualism refers to "those ceremonial developments in the Church of England that were considered at the time to be making it approximate more closely to the services of the Roman Catholic Church," although its Anglo-Catholic apologists contended these adjustments were "entirely consistent with Anglican precedent and justified by the Anglican formularies" (Yates 1).

12. Henry William Burrows was incumbent of Christ Church, Albany Street, London, where Rossetti worshipped from 1843–76 before attending another leading Anglo-Catholic church by the same name in Woburn Square until her death in 1894. According to Burrows, Albany Street was the leading church of the Anglo-Catholic ritualist movement (Mason 117).

completed in 1876 as her sister Maria lay dying (Marsh 450), and published in 1881 with the SPCK. How the visible earthly Church communes with its invisible counterpart, the departed saints, and what those saints do prior to the resurrection, were points of debate among Victorian Christians.[13] Rossetti's position shapes the form of imagined community in *Verses*. Her poetry suggests an evolving perspective over the course of her career, but her "later devotional writings clearly present the . . . Anglo-Catholic tradition" defended by figures such as Newman before his conversion (Marshall, "What the Dead Are Doing" 58). In this view, while the "bodies" of the dead "decay, their souls enter Hades to await the Second Advent, Resurrection, and Judgment" (55). Drawing from Jesus' parable about Lazarus and the rich man (Luke 16:19–31), this tradition presents Hades as a divided region: one section is a place of unrelieved suffering (Hades proper), the other is Paradise, where souls of the faithful rest, experience loving communion with each other and God in Christ, possibly pray for the living, and await the day of their resurrection at Christ's return (56). In her 1892 devotional commentary on the Apocalypse, *Face of the Deep*, Rossetti has little interest in parsing the "historical drift of prophecy" (*Face of the Deep* 396), though the same study suggests a premillennial view (461–65).[14] *Face of the Deep* is the source for the majority of the poems in *Verses*, but in their new context, separated from surrounding prose commentary, these poems lose their distinctly premillennarian undertones.

The outline of redemptive history and Christian community assumed in *Verses* is pithily expressed in this short poem from the final section:

> Man's life is but a working day
>   Whose tasks are set aright:
> A time to work, a time to pray,
>   And then a quiet night.
> And then, please God, a quiet night

---

13. Within the Anglican Church, for example, parties argued for a number of positions, ranging from complete unconsciousness after death (soul sleep) to active existence in Paradise, an intermediate state between earth and heaven; few accepted the Roman Catholic doctrine of Purgatory. Most other Protestant denominations believed that the dead went straight to heaven or hell (Marshall, "What the Dead are Doing" 55–58).

14. At the time a "minority" position (Waller 477), this view held that the Second Coming would initiate a "Millennium" (*Face of the Deep* 461) beginning with the "First Resurrection" of the faithful dead (465; Rossetti implies she views this group as limited to faithful martyrs). It would be followed at the end of Christ's millennial reign by a general (second) resurrection of all the dead to stand before Christ at the final judgment, itself preceding the redemption of creation when the New Jerusalem descended to earth.

Where palms are green and robes are white;
A long-drawn breath, a balm for sorrow,
And all things lovely on the morrow.

This brief poem was first published as the entry for July 11 in *Time Flies* (1885), which Krista Lysack has described as "a project in timekeeping . . . that clocks eternity to 'man's daily time'" (465), seeking, through short daily readings that could occupy spare leisure moments, to coordinate "the impress of eternity" traditionally marked by "liturgical time" with the modern secular time measured not by feast days but by pocket watches, railway schedules, and work days (455). As I argued in chapter 4, Keble's *Christian Year* had well before this time become a popular means for adapting a vision of Christian history and community rooted in typology and liturgy to a sense of membership in a nation of individuals simultaneously progressing through the secular time charted by daily newspapers and clock hands. Recalling Keble's praise of those who ply "their daily task with busier feet" (31) because of shared Christian hope ("St. Matthew" 31), Rossetti encourages readers of this poem to regard even their most mundane "tasks" as "set aright" by God, recalling Ecclesiastes 3:1.[15] Yet the passive construction—"tasks are set aright"—permits multiple agencies to join providence in timing daily tasks, including the unyielding tick of the clock that governs "a working day," and the reader who rescues some of those moments for contemplating this poem, and, perhaps as a result, finding "a time to pray."

This complex intersection of temporal regimes is vital not only to the timekeeping of *Time Flies* but also to this poem's final home, *Verses,* and its project of aligning the activity of reading with imagined participation in a multidimensional communion of saints. If the poem's opening four lines outline the daily labor and nightly rest that structure every "Man's life," they also turn this small cycle in secular time into an analogy for the larger cycle of the "day" of "life" whose labor must end in the "night" of death. The last four lines rework the diurnal analogy yet again and blend it with eternal time, depicting rest for the saved in Paradise as a night's sleep almost casually broken when "sorrow" is entirely converted (by switching a single letter) into the loveliness of the "morrow," as the Second Coming, final resurrection, and Judgment usher in the community of the New Jerusalem and new creation. These two major sections of the poem are

---

15. "To every thing there is a season, and a time to every purpose under the heaven" (Ecc. 3:1).

bound together by the repetition of *are,* parallel syntax, and the anaphora of *And.* This establishes a shared grammar—a sense of simultaneity and even interchange—between the earthly, paradisiacal, and everlasting realms transected by the communion of saints. In this way, the present-tense of reading, of negotiating the printed page in secular time in spare moments between "a working day" and "a quiet night," becomes a point of contact with the eternity from which it is differentiated. The concentrated, reserved, repetitive construction of this poem also shapes private reading in ways that recall the ordering of time by communal liturgy, in that it resembles the collects and refrains of the Book of Common Prayer.

Semantic and sonic ambiguities maintain this delicate interplay between the eternal time signified by liturgy and the clocked, and often wearying, time that was increasingly turning Victorian "reading" of "devotional texts" into "a matter of sampling or grazing in one's available moments" (Lysack 458). The parenthetical "please God" at the poem's crucial turning point in the fifth line recognizes dependence on God's power and will ("if it please God") even as it implies a frustrated supplication ("please God!"). The "working day" of "life" is perhaps "but" short set next to eternity (1), yet still trying enough to compel "A long-drawn breath" in Paradise (7), which recalls the last breath on a death bed and seems to extend that breath into the repose of Paradise. Set so close to "morrow" (8), "drawn" nonetheless suggests the "dawn" into which weary readers (on earth) and resting saints (in Paradise) are together being "drawn." The "balm" offered for earthly "sorrow" in Paradise in line seven chimes with the "palms" in line six, so that the image of green fronds might momentarily blend with one of salved wounds on hands, a subtle reminder that the entire regenerative process depends on the sacrificial death of Christ after crowds laid palms before him upon his entry into Jerusalem. For the Anglo-Catholic Rossetti, these allusions would be connected to Holy Week and the Eucharist, overtly celebrated in the "Some Feasts and Fasts" section of *Verses* and central to her lived understanding of the communion of saints: in the Anglican rite of communion, the community is not only encouraged to remember and receive Christ's sacrifice but also to anticipate his Second Coming.

To encourage readers to imagine their passage through *Verses* as a form of participation in the communion of saints, Rossetti adapts Keble's strategy in *The Christian Year* of confusing private reception with shared activity in an unseen spiritual community. Rossetti most noticeably does so through the dizzying range of applications she gives to pronouns when arranging her poems in *Verses*. In "Lord, I believe, help Thou mine unbelief," originally from *Face of the Deep* (pp. 388–89) and integrated into a sonnet sequence in the opening section of *Verses,* the "I" of the poem could be spoken by both the poet and a receptive reader, but it is also the voice of the man in Mark 9:24, who brought his child to Jesus to be cured of seizures, and who upon being asked if he came in faith "cried out, and said with tears, Lord, I believe; help thou mine unbelief." This involves readers in a typological understanding of identity within a community extending across time, in which scriptural events and persons apply to their own experiences, a practice encouraged by *The Christian Year* and common to all nineteenth-century church parties (Landow 33, 48–50). By the next sonnet in the sequence, which was originally placed over three hundred pages earlier in *Face of the Deep* (p. 31), the voice of supplication has become communal, "Increase our faith" ("O Lord, on Whom we gaze and dare not gaze" 2). The implicit dialogue partner in these and many other poems, Christ, often directly converses with an "I" that remains open to imaginative alignment with the reader, the poet, and a wider community of individual believers across time and place: "Lord, what have I that I may offer Thee? / . . . Child, what is it thou hast not? / Thou hast all gifts that I have given to thee" ("Lord, what have I that I may offer Thee?" 1, 4–5). In other poems, the "I" speaks with enough specificity and retrospection to invite readers to imagine they are overhearing the author herself in meditation: "Thus I sat mourning like a mournful owl, / . . . When lo! The light cast off its nightly cowl" ("Heaviness may endure for the night," 9, 12). The poem "Passiontide" becomes a communal recollection of divine calls throughout history to "Come" that blend into an ever-present invitation, enacted in the time of reading, to receive grace in Christ,[16] and it ends as if placing the reader in a position to overhear the acceptance of unknown individuals merging with his or her own across time and space: "I come— and I—and I" (18). Even at the level of grammar, *Verses* encourages readers to imagine themselves in a community in which "I" is always voiced in the context of "a great cloud of witnesses" (Heb. 12:1).

Rossetti's vision of the communion of saints largely overlaps with views defended by highly-regarded Anglican biblical scholar and theologian N. T. Wright. Like Rossetti, Wright holds the option within Anglican theology of affirming Paradise as a resting place for the saints between death and

---

16. "Thou callest, . . . / 'Come, every one that thirsteth come'—'Come prove Me, knocking at my gate'— / (Some souls draw nigh!)—" (11–13). The first call quoted above alludes to God's invitation to his people in Isaiah 55:1 and Jesus' similar invitation in John 7:37; the second recalls Jesus' words in Matthew 7:7 (and Luke 11:9). The last parenthetical observation is, of course, at once present tense and applicable to any time.

before the final physical resurrection (171–74). Wright argues that this is an emphatically different picture of the afterlife than "going to heaven when you die," or the Platonic escape from materiality upon death often conflated with heaven in post-medieval Christian tradition and still dominant in popular Christian culture (18). For Wright, this later account of the afterlife turns upside down the perspective of canonical early Christian writings, which, as "in Revelation 21–22," portray "the new Jerusalem" not as rising from the earth, but as "coming down from heaven to earth, uniting the two in a lasting embrace" (19). Heaven and Earth are interlocking spheres of God's single created reality (251), destined to be joined at Christ's Second Coming, when he will judge injustice and oppression (138–45) and inaugurate a new creation free from corruption into which the dead receptive of God's reign will be raised to enjoy an exalted bodily life (104–5). For Wright, the New Testament writers see this new creation beginning with Jesus' physical resurrection (238). Although completed only at the final cosmic transformation, it is enacted in anticipation now through the life of Christ's followers in their worship, pursuit of justice, care of creation, and practice of love (208). When interpreting St. Paul's well-known reflection on love in 1 Corinthians 13 ("Though I speak with the tongues of men and angels, and have not charity . . ."), Wright produces what could almost be a summary of Rossetti's vision of the communion of saints in *Verses*:

> Love is not our duty; it is our *destiny*. It is the language Jesus spoke, and we are called to speak it so that we can converse with him. It is the food they eat in God's new world, and we must acquire the taste for it here and now . . . It is the resurrection life, and the resurrected Jesus calls us to begin living it with him and for him right now. (288)

In *Verses* Rossetti also portrays the life of the New Jerusalem as the land where "All love and only love can find a voice / Where God makes glad His Saints, for God is Love" ("All Saints" 13–14). In a poem placed shortly after this one, the "beginning" of this redeemed community is identified as "Love," as is its "course" and "goal" ("What is the beginning? Love" 1). Love stands not only for the actions of the Christian community but for the "God" who "is Love." This God is encountered in the incarnate, crucified, and resurrected Christ, who directly dialogues with the speakers of poems, whose positions the reader is invited to inhabit: "Feed My hungry brethren for My sake; / Give them drink, for love of them and Me: / Love them as I loved thee, when Bread I brake / In pure love of thee" ("Because He first loved us" 5–8). Referring to his crucifixion in colloquial terms that directly apply to the Eucharist ("when Bread I brake"), Christ makes the heart of High Church ritual the empowering motive for everyday care in fulfillment of his parable of the sheep and goats, according to which love shown "My hungry brethren" is love shown to him (Matt. 25:31–46). Christ roots the speaker's love in his own love and in the communion of the new creation, of which the communion meal is a foretaste.

The speaker responds accordingly, "Yet would I love Thyself, Lord, face to face, / Heart to heart, one day," and receives the reminder that by "today" filling "thy heart and hand to them and Me" (13–14), in the eschatological "Tomorrow thou shalt ask, and shalt not ask / Half I keep for thee" (11–12, 15–16). The speaker's love of others (and so of Christ) is to be returned in the future redeemed community with such unbelievable generosity that it will silence all requests for more, a silencing felt in the enjambment: "[thou] shalt ask, and shalt not ask / Half I keep for thee." That Christ "keep[s]" this gift suggests not only that he guards the reward but also—in agreement with N. T. Wright (208)—the counterintuitive idea that acts of love in this life are somehow stored up and multiplied in the new world of the New Jerusalem, rather like the fish and loaves in the feeding of the five thousand.

I engage in this comparison with Wright to demonstrate that in *Verses* Rossetti resists the radical separation of inward spiritual life from physical world that was broadly evident in Victorian print culture and affirmed so influentially by Tennyson's *In Memoriam* (1850) (see chapter 5). *Verses* is, admittedly, vulnerable to charges of otherworldliness. The literary couple Katherine Harris Bradley and Edith Emma Cooper, who wrote under the penname "Michael Field," published a sonnet "To Christina Rossetti" in *The Academy* shortly after Rossetti's death, in which they extended a Victorian fad—still popular today—of lamenting Rossetti's morbid desire to leave behind the world's "leafy light" (8): "thy moan was as a moan for ease / And passage through cool shadows to the night: / . . . [If only] Thou hadst breathed joy in earth and in thy kind" (3–4, 14). Their censure of Rossetti's disregard of "leafy light" suggests they had in mind one of the many poems she wrote (see her early "A Testimony") similar to the one that opens the section in *Verses* titled "The World. Self-Destruction": "The world,—what a world, ah me! / Mouldy, worm-eaten, grey: / Vain as a leaf from a tree" ("A vain Shadow" 1–3). Yet even in portraying earthly life "As veriest vanity" (5), this poem mixes admiration with frustration. "[W]hat a world, ah me!" could express lingering wonder as well as exasperation. A series of similes commands—rather than simply resigns—attention to multiple aspects of the world, recognizing "what is" to concede that it "passes away" (9): the world is "Vain as a leaf from a tree, / As a fading day, / . . . As the froth and the spray" (1–2, 6). The governing adjective "Vain," highlighted by grammar and by a trochee, at once evokes and sets aside the "vein" that is the life of the leaf, planting a subtle reminder of natural regeneration—fallen leaves form mold from which new life springs—that might faintly recall the hope, emphasized throughout *Verses,* of life in the new creation.

Nonetheless, those looking to charge Rossetti with dismal escapism could, on a flat reading, invoke this and related poems in her corpus that tempt equations between Rossetti's poetry and the "exercises in *contemptus mundi*" that Rodney Edgecombe detects in "the Tractarian lyric[s]" of Keble, Newman,[17] and Isaac Williams (33), which border on "a shared cult of mortification . . . tainted" by "masochism" (27). As Palazzo notes, beginning especially with Gilbert and Gubar in *The Madwoman in the Attic* (1979), critics interested in reclaiming Rossetti for feminism have tacitly or overtly accepted her apparent participation in Tractarian mortification in order to present Rossetti's poetics as a strategy of renunciation that defies patriarchy (7, 21). Yet Palazzo, who highlights the feminist potential of Rossetti's theology, turns to the later devotional writings that supplied poems for *Verses,* particularly *Called to Be Saints* (1881) and *Time Flies* (1885), to demonstrate how persistently Rossetti rooted her theology in the physical experiences and details of the natural world and domestic life (101).

Palazzo's feminist reading falls short when applied to *Verses,* in which "the lyrical 'I' is" generally "a universal Christian voice, unmarked by gender, rank, or office" and constituted by the "plural lyrical voice of . . . the communion of saints" (Dieleman 169–70). Yet *Verses* is perhaps the most triumphant affirmation of Palazzo's view that Rossetti's theology does not leave the world behind. *Verses* assumes that earth is not only preparatory to heaven but meant to be renewed in marriage to heaven. In the final stanza of "Sexagesima," from the section "Some Feasts and Fasts," Rossetti foreshadows this embrace by using chiastic syntax ("Earth . . . heaven . . . heaven . . . earth . . . Earth"); recycling "Earth" at the opening of the first and final line to stress its role as point of departure and renewal; and, through the strong enjambment between the second and third lines, making heaven's renewal hang upon the inclusion of earth:

---

17. In a recent dissertation, Mary Frank argues persuasively that Newman later renounced this otherworldliness. Beginning in the 1840s, she argues, Newman "goes from advocating a spirit of *contemptus mundi* and ascetical caution over the world's influence on the imagination to acknowledging the value of aesthetic experience for its tendency to connect the imaginer to the world, moving him to feel and surrender to his participation in it" (206).

> *Earth* may not *pass* till *heaven* shall *pass* away,
>   Nor *heaven* may be renewed
> Except with *earth:* and once more in that day
>   *Earth* shall be very good. (13–16; emphasis mine)

The original divine affirmation of creation's goodness (Gen. 1:31) will be reaffirmed in the re-creation already begun in Christ.

In fact, as Constance Hassett notes, in "Heaviness may endure for a night, but Joy cometh in the morning," a pair of sonnets from the last section of *Verses,* Rossetti performs a "mild satire on the speaker's whiningly intoned *contemptus mundi*" (215). The speaker begins the first sonnet complaining that "on this side of the grave" nothing is "of any stable worth" (1–2), but at the turn of the volta it becomes clear that the opening octave is a retrospective account delivered as if in the present. The speaker describes in the sestet how a sunrise exposed the self-absorbed folly of her lament: "Thus I sat mourning like a mournful owl, / And like a doleful dragon made ado, / Companion of all monsters of the dark: / When lo! The light cast off its nightly cowl, / . . . And all creation sang its hymn anew" (9–12, 14). The second sonnet continues with the speaker recalling how she was drawn out of solipsism by the sunrise into the song of a new creation, whose opening notes she caught in each detail of awakening nature, and in human actions that anticipate—and implicitly participate in—the resurrected community of love to come:

> While all creation sang its hymn anew
> What could I do but sing a stave in tune?
> Spectral on high hung pale the vanishing moon
> Where a last gleam of stars hung paling too.
> Lark's lay—a cockcrow—with a scattered few
> Soft early chirpings—with a tender croon
> Of doves—a hundred thousand calls, and soon
> A hundred thousand answers sweet and true.
> These set me singing too at unawares:
> One note for all delights and charities,
> One note for hope reviving with the light,
> One note for every lovely thing that is;
> Till while I sang my heart shook off its cares
> And revelled in the land of no more night.

Verses invites readers into a community whose "hope" is founded on faith that "all" authentic "delights and charities" in this life are rays preceding a sunrise, messengers from and participants "in the land of no more night." Hence in "To every seed his own body," Rossetti insists that resurrected saints will mysteriously correspond with what they were before their bodies decayed: "Bone to his bone, grain to his grain of dust: / A numberless reunion shall make whole / Each blessed body for its blessed soul, / Refashioning the aspects of the just" (1–4). Refashioned, restored yet transformed, each saint will emerge from the grave in the body and character sown by his earthly background and actions—so that the "grain of dust" in the first line is not only one of many scattered remains but also the grain, the seed of the sonnet's title, which is informed by verses in 1 Corinthians 15, the central New Testament passage about resurrection.[18] Before and after the resurrection each person's identity is also determined in terms of others:

> Each with his own not another's grace,
> Each with his own not another's heart,
> Each with his own not another's face,
> Each dove-like soul mounts to his proper place . . . (9–11)

Six of the sonnet's lines—the four above from the sestet and two in the octave—begin with "Each." This extended anaphora performs a sensuous, grammatical, and prosodic analogy to the diversity-in-unity, the continuity-in-difference, central to Rossetti's vision of the communion of saints. Visually the same, "Each" nonetheless acquires distinct accents—unstressed in "Each blessed body" (3) and stressed in the series of parallel phrases, "Each with his own" (9–11)—and meanings, first appearing as an adjective ("Each saint" [5]) and then a pronoun ("Each with his own"). Fittingly, this shift from specifying adjective to singular pronoun occurs at the turn of the octave, when the distinct parts of "Each saint" are reintegrated, and "Each" emerges as a reconsolidated and glorified individual. Then "Each" reappears as a distinguishing adjective as "Each dove-like soul" assumes its "proper"—fitting and unique—"place" within the eternal community. Throughout, the ground and goal of individuation is community within the "bless[ing]" and presence of the God who (as the title verse reminds) empowers reintegration at the individual and collective levels. The opening "numberless reunion" of "bone" and "grain of dust" in each

---

18. "But some man will say, How are the dead raised up? and with what body do they come? Thou fool, that which thou sowest is not quickened, except it die: And that which thou sowest, thou sowest not that body that shall be, but bare grain, it may chance of wheat, or of some other grain: But God giveth it a body as it hath pleased him, and *to every seed his own body*" (1 Cor. 15:35–38; emphasis mine).

believer's body is a microcosmic foreshadowing of the speaker's closing hope of reunion between members of Christ's body—despite the pain, evoked in the ending enjambment, of being wrung apart by death: "O faces unforgotten! if to part / Wrung sore, what will it be to re-embrace?" (13–14). Rossetti appropriately modulates the Petrarchan schema into a series of distinct yet overlapping embraces (*abbaabbacdccdc*). The final apostrophe to the departed ("O faces unforgotten") encourages readers to imagine, in advance of the exalted "re-embrace," a permeable boundary between themselves and the beloved dead, a momentary transcendence of time and distance subtly reinforced by the sonnet's shifting verb tenses— "A numberless reunion *shall make whole*" (2), "Each dove-like soul *mounts* to his proper place" (12), "what *will it be* to re-embrace?" (14).

In this understanding of the communion of saints, actions in this world may return as accusers in the Judgment inaugurating the new world, as Rossetti observed in *The Face of the Deep* shortly before compiling *Verses*: "complicated civilization produces or amasses riches: and the riches come to nothing except as accusers, and the lives cannot be silenced in the day of account. In that day many luxuries may turn out to have been unlawful, and the price of blood" (474). The depth of Rossetti's personal conviction on this matter is suggested by her sustained commitment—through personal involvement or through letter writing when illness confined her to home—to aiding victimized women, educating the poor, protesting vivisection, and defending minors sexually abused in London's human trafficking network (Arseneau 192 n.4). A few months before beginning work on *Verses* in 1892, Rossetti made her well-known statement to Edmund McClure, secretary for the SPCK and editor of her volumes for that society: "It is so easy from an armchair to exhort a man on a bench: I wish the scene could be varied occasionally, and that instead of a roomfull [*sic*] of 'Labour' to appease some heart and tongue of fire faced a roomful of 'Capital' to abate" (*Letters* IV 264). Reminders that actions toward the oppressed and vulnerable bear directly on one's participation in the new world punctuate *Verses,* as in one of the rare dramatic monologues, spoken by the Lazarus of Jesus' parable about the beggar and rich man (Luke 6:19–31), but also voiced by any of the impoverished who crowd Britain's towns. "I laid beside thy gate, am Lazarus: / See me or see me not I still am there, / Hungry and thirsty, sore and sick and bare" (1–3); one day "for me" there will be "plenitude an end of all desire: / But what for thee, alas! . . . / Fire and an unextinguishable thirst" ("Son, Remember" 9, 11–13). The reader is implicitly in danger of becoming the object—"thee"—of Lazarus' condemnation.

In *Verses,* then, Rossetti encourages her readers to see their individual and collective actions in the present as anticipating, even contributing to, the love that will rule creation at its redemption. This view of the community of saints underwrites an international ecumenism that contrasts with imperialist appeals to national imagined spiritual community published just before and after *Verses.* As demonstrated in chapter 6, a range of Victorians appropriated *In Memoriam* as a quasi-sacred national scripture whose authority sat alongside the Bible's. A central text was section 106, where the speaker calls upon ringing church bells to usher in a new millennium of enlightened Christianity, "Ring in the Christ that is to be" (106.32). Shortly before Rossetti began planning *Verses,*[19] Tennyson completed "Akbar's Dream" (1892), in which he indicated that the prayer of lyric 106 in *In Memoriam* could be answered by imperial Christian Britain as it molded forms of tolerant faith for all peoples under its dominion (see chapter 6). In "Akbar's Dream," Tennyson repeats the suggestion he had made in poetry since ascending to the laureateship that "political empire depends on the sovereign power of poetry" (Linley 421). The character speaking "Akbar's Dream," the sixteenth-century Moghul emperor Akbar, prophesies that Christian Britain will complete his project of establishing a religiously tolerant empire in India. Akbar then overhears a morning "hymn" of interfaith worship that he (or, really, Tennyson) composed, which declares that a "myriad" of "laureates" from every clime sing to "Him the Timeless" (199, 201). Similarly, Tennyson implies, his poetry will contribute to the ecumenical unity of the British Empire.

As discussed in the last chapter, such vaguely Christianized visions of Britain's imperial community became more common after the 1870s, especially in the 1890s. A few days after Rossetti published *Verses* in September 1893 (Ives 125), W. T. Stead, an eccentric Protestant and spiritualist, but an influential journalist and editor, issued his own call for a national literary scripture. In "Wanted, An English Bible!," Stead argues for "collecting our" own "Sacred Canon" (25) designed in analogy to the Bible and comprised of a condensed "history of our [Anglo-Saxon] race" alongside learned works, popular proverbs, sections of the Prayer Book, and passages from great poets, including "Tennyson" (26). Adopted as "a companion to the Bible in every English home" and introduced "for reading in our schools" (26), such a national scripture would instill "the religious side of imperial patriotism" (25) in "all English-speaking men," committing them to the "providential mission" of "their race" (26). Stead's vitriolic

---

19. On November 29, 1892, Christina told William Michael Rossetti that she was approaching Edmund McClure, secretary of the SPCK, with a plan she and William Michael had devised to collect the poems from her previous SPCK volumes into one volume (*Letters* IV:301).

activism and promotion of spiritualism were beginning to subtract from his tremendous influence in the 1880s, and the *Daily Paper* in which he published this call for an English Bible soon perished.[20] Yet he shores up the respectability of his plan for a national imperial scripture by including a response from Liberal politician, jurist, and academic, James Bryce. Bryce commends Stead's projected "English Bible," concluding that "the literature of a people is its lifeblood, and the key to both its national and religious development" (27).

Although Stead is more evangelistic and programmatic than Tennyson, the journalist and poet converge in thinking that the mission of the imperial state depends on literature's cultivation of the loyal imagination and supposedly British Christian values of its members. Hence Tennyson equates tolerant, ecumenical Christianity of the future with British liberalism's hatred of "the rancor of" exclusive "castes and creeds" ("Akbar's Dream" 62), and Stead praises the vaguely Protestant English resistance to "Sacerdotalism and tyranny" (26) and the English tradition of "liberty and self-government" going back to "the Magna Carta" (25). They also participate in widespread use of "racial terminology" to express British identity after the 1870s (McLeod, "Protestantism" 59), as when Tennyson's Akbar dreams of "an alien race" charged with fulfilling his ecumenical imperialism (182)—and, much more obviously, when Stead and Bryce portray the British as a homogeneous Anglo-Saxon race vivified by the lifeblood of its literature and driven by a providential mission to liberate the world (on its terms).

By contrast, "Now they desire a Better Country," a roundel from the final section of Rossetti's *Verses,* stages a short personified drama between "Love" and "Hope" that wittily revises Robert Herrick's "Corinna's going a-Maying" to suggest a profoundly eschatological and anti-nationalist perspective for the Christian community envisioned in *Verses.*

> Love said nay, while Hope kept saying
>   All his sweetest say,
> Hope so keen to start a-maying!—
>   Love said nay.
>
> Love was bent to watch and pray;
> Long the watching, long the praying;
>   Hope grew drowsy, pale and grey.

---

20. Nevertheless, Stead's journal the *Review of Reviews* had recently enjoyed enormous success, and continued to thrive until Stead's opposition to the Boer War of 1899–1902 severely curtailed its circulation. In 1890 its circulation was 300,000 (Altick 396).

>Hope in dreams set off a-straying,
> All his dream-world flushed by May;
>While unslumbering, praying, weighing,
> Love said nay.

Rossetti's "Hope," personified as male, plays the part of Herrick's persistent male speaker in "Corinna's going a-Maying" who "kept saying / All his sweetest say" to persuade his Corinna to join him in lovemaking and sensual delight before age and death removed the opportunity. Rossetti's "Love" rejects the proposition of Herrick's speaker to "Wash, dress, be brief in praying: / Few beads are best when once we go a-Maying!" (27–28). Indeed, to meet the roundel form's limitation to two rhymes, Rossetti might have begun by appropriating (and reversing the meaning of) the end rhymes of Herrick's famous couplet and then generated her rhyme scheme (and poem) in critical response. Love's "nay" determinedly denies or reworks Hope's "say," rebuffing Hope's "saying" and "a-maying" with "praying," and Hope's "a-straying" with meditative "weighing," even as rejected Hope suffers the fate feared by Herrick's speaker, missing his prime and declining into sleepy old age ("Hope grew drowsy, pale and grey").

Yet more is at stake than a playful defense of patient devotion against the *carpe diem* sensuality of a seventeenth-century poet-priest. Rossetti first published this roundel in *Time Flies: A Reading Diary* (1885), a popular meditation on the days of the year issued by the SPCK. There it appeared without a title under "May 5," a day popularly linked not only to youthful *eros* and hopes of spring but also to events central to English national mythology and modern European nationalism more broadly. On May 5, English barons renounced allegiance to King John, initiating the chain of events that would culminate in the Magna Carta a month later (1215); on the same day, the Estates-General convened, leading to the formation of the National Assembly (1789); and, as Rossetti would know as the daughter of an Italian nationalist exile and sister of the politically alert William Michael, on this day Giuseppe Garibaldi began the expedition of the Thousand (1860), giving birth to the unified Kingdom of Italy (1861).

Given these associations, Rossetti's roundel can be read as a rejection of the kind of hope promoted by works such as Tennyson's "Akbar's Dream" or Stead's "Wanted, an English Bible!" While Herrick's speaker calls Corinna to stray in sensual revelry in the fields, Rossetti's rejected Hope finally gives up his sweet "saying" to "set off a-straying" in "dreams," suggesting he does not physically depart but wanders in his head in ideological fields, lost in a "dream-world," which, as "flushed by May" suggests, is colored by mental intoxication and fever. Given the political associations of May 5, Hope represents not only heady young love retreating from disappointment into solipsistic and lurid fantasy but also the seductive ardor of imperialist nationalism. His might be the glowing eloquence that links "the Christ that is to be" (*In Memoriam* 106.32) with the "pour[ing]" of "an alien race" into benighted lands to enforce "Truth, / Peace, Love and Justice" ("Akbar's Dream" 182–84); it might be the enthusiasm that incorporates such poetic visions into a nationalistic "Sacred Canon" meant to spread "the religious side of imperial patriotism" to "every English home" ("English Bible" 25–26). When recalling and reworking the demand of Herrick's speaker to "Come . . . / And take the harmless folly of our time" (57–58), Rossetti might well have felt that the exhortation ironically glossed many appeals widely circulated in the final decades of the nineteenth century, the "heyday" of patriotic "imperialism" (Carey 371).

The manner in which Rossetti's Love says "nay" to Hope alerts readers to the roundel's eschatological undertones. "Love was bent to watch and pray" even as "Hope grew drowsy": this recalls Jesus' parable (Matt. 25:1–13) about five foolish virgins who fall asleep without putting oil in their lamps to meet the bridegroom, and who, after a rude awakening at midnight, are left outside the wedding feast into which five prepared and watchful virgins enter. Long interpreted as a parable about the Church's need to live in faith and love in expectation of the Second Coming, the parable's closing line has resounded ominously through Christian tradition, including Rossetti's own poetry: "Watch therefore, for ye know neither the day nor the hour wherein the Son of man cometh" (25:13). In Rossetti's roundel, Love plays the part of the wise virgins, remaining "unslumbering" by not falling into Hope's easy dreams of (among other things) nationalist fulfillment. Love is sustained by another, unspoken hope: the Bridegroom coming to his eschatological wedding feast with the resurrected communion of saints.

When Rossetti removed this poem from *Time Flies* and inserted it into *Verses*, she deprived it of the "May 5" heading with its associations of erotic and nationalistic longing, but she strengthened its resistance to nationalism. The new heading for the poem, "Now they desire a Better Country," is one of many biblical phrases that Rossetti devised to head previously untitled poems when extracting them from earlier SPCK books for inclusion in *Verses*. It comes from an extended celebration in Hebrews 11 of the faithful who prior to Christ's first advent endured disappointment, oppression, and exile while awaiting "the [Messianic] promise" witnessed by the readers of Hebrews (11:39). The patient pre-messianic faithful now serve as a "great . . . cloud of" exemplary "witnesses" (12:1) for the readers of Hebrews, who with them will "be made perfect" (11:40) by "Jesus the author and finisher of our faith" (12:2). Rossetti's selected phrase invokes the community of saints emphasized throughout *Verses,* and the full verse of which it is part includes this community in a period of exile as they, like the pre-Christian exiled saints and previous generations of Christian saints, await a better country: "But now they desire a better country, that is, a heavenly: wherefore God is not ashamed of them, to be called their God: for he hath prepared for them a city" (11:16). Here again Hope's desire "to start a-maying!" is implicitly the longing to slumber in nationalistic dreams rather than live in anticipation of union with the Bridegroom in the eschatological nation of the faithful.

Opposition to nationalism is consistent throughout *Verses,* as in another previously untitled poem that Rossetti titled with a passage from the same section of Hebrews, "The General Assembly and Church of the Firstborn." First published in *Face of the Deep* (1892), this poem reappears in *Verses* in a section dedicated to "New Jerusalem and Its Citizens," and its title affirms the connection between this eternal community of saints and its earthly members, including Rossetti's Christian readers.[21] The rhyme-scheme of this eighteen-line poem is an extended, more interwoven, variation on the Shakespearean sonnet (*ababcbcdcdedefefgfg*), mirroring the poem's focus on a diversity of "nations" (2) and individuals brought into concord through the "Lord Jesus Christ" (18), whose name rhymes with the act—"sufficed" (17)—of eschatological fulfillment he effects: "Raptures and voices one while manifold, / . . . Home-comers out of every change and chance, / . . . Aspects which reproduce One Countenance" (5, 13, 15). International and celebratory of the "manifold" ways in which nations and individuals can be themselves while also images of Christ's "One Countenance," Rossetti's vision of the communion of saints always locates "Home" in a region in which no earthly state or patriot can claim priority. Perhaps this strand of *Verses,* its continual portrayal of nationalist and imperialist versions of community as illusory even as it recommends the internationalism of the New Jerusalem, prompted one of its first reviewers to remark that several poems seemed "the national songs of Heaven" (L. Johnson 59).

While the communion of saints is fundamental to *Verses,* other strands of Anglo-Catholicism in the 1890s also contributed to Rossetti's portrayal

---

21. "But ye are come unto mount Zion, and unto the living God, the heavenly Jerusalem, and to innumerable hosts of angels, *to the general assembly and church of the firstborn* who are enrolled in heaven, and to God the Judge of all, and to spirits of just men made perfect, and to Jesus the mediator of a new covenant" (Heb. 12:22–24; emphasis mine).

of this community as "manifold" and estranged from nationalistic belonging. Several of the poems discussed thus far are from "Songs for Strangers and Pilgrims," the last section in *Verses*. Since this section follows "New Jerusalem and Its Citizens," it recalls, as Dieleman notes, the movement of the Anglican service, which "ends with a parting blessing" in acknowledgment that the "eschatological promise of communion" is not yet fulfilled: "the participants still depart into a world in which they consider themselves but pilgrims" (153). This subtle liturgical movement also stresses the paradoxical status of the community imagined in *Verses:* they are alienated from full identification with current homelands by their uniting hope in a future one. Crucially, the heading of the final section, "Strangers and Pilgrims," comes from the passage in Hebrews about patient exile and communal perfection in Christ from which, as mentioned above, Rossetti drew titles for several poems in the final sections of *Verses:* "These all died in faith, not having received the promises, but having seen them afar off, . . . and confessed that they were *strangers and pilgrims on the earth*. For they that say such things declare plainly that they seek a country . . . But now they desire a better country, that is, a heavenly" (Heb. 11:13–16; emphasis mine).

This suggests that as Rossetti revised and retitled poems from her earlier SPCK publications for inclusion in *Verses,* she was contemplating the degree to which membership in the community of saints meant exclusion or self-distancing from other communities, particularly those that prioritized national identity. Many Anglo-Catholics shared this perspective in the 1890s. The rise of Anglo-Catholic ritualism in the 1850s and 1860s provoked widespread fear of a Romanizing mutiny against British Protestant virtues, generating decades of savage journalism, damning *Punch* cartoons, riots, and massive petitions targeting Anglican ritualists. This pushed the government to criminalize ritualism with the Pubic Worship Regulation Act (1874). The act, and the imprisonment of Anglo-Catholic priests in which it resulted, motivated "many" prominent "Anglo Catholics," including "even Gladstone," to sympathize with the idea that the Anglican Church should be disestablished to protect it from the state's authoritarian control—an option which early Tractarians, such as John Keble, had themselves considered (Reed 136).

With one in eight churches in London adopting ritualist practices by 1895 (Reed 257), Anglo-Catholics were no longer a persecuted minority, but it was hard for Anglo-Catholics to shake their sense of alienation from Protestant Britain and vulnerability to attack in mass culture. Ritualism in London seems to have reached new heights in the 1880s (Mason

117), and damning portrayals of Anglo-Catholics such as Edward Pusey as sadomasochistic secret agents of Rome in Walter Walsh's *Secret History of the Oxford Movement* (1897) could still stir up Protestant outrage and horror (Reed 255). Yet by 1899 Charles Wood, Lord Halifax, the longtime president of the English Church Union, which promoted Anglo-Catholic principles and practices in the Church of England, admitted the bored "indifference" of "the great mass of the country" to the ritualist controversy ("Crisis" 178). Halifax could, however, still point to controversy over ritualism in Parliament, the dailies (particularly the *Times*), and statements by the Archbishop of Canterbury (175). When Rossetti began arranging *Verses*, Anglo-Catholicism had largely faded from a national scandal to a tolerated eccentricity (Janes 182) that had become increasingly middle class and almost respectable (Reed 262–64). Yet Anglo-Catholics retained the feeling of being strangers in the dominantly Protestant imagined community of Britain.

Verses, with its emphasis on exile and anti-nationalism, indicates Rossetti's sympathy for Anglo-Catholic suspicions about close alliances between church and state, as well as her own residual sense of outsider status. Rossetti and the many Anglo-Catholics with whom she worshipped and cooperated on literary projects would not have taken kindly to Tennyson's suggestion to "let the hand that rules, / With politic care, with utter gentleness, / Mould" forms of faith "for all his people" ("Akbar's Dream" 120–22). Yet *Verses* also shares the ecumenical and international view of Christian communion embraced by many late-century Anglo-Catholics. Inheriting the Tractarian sense of the Anglican Church as not Protestant, but a branch of the true Catholic Church, the majority of Anglo-Catholics had throughout the nineteenth century longed for the reconciliation of Christendom, even as they sought to uphold their freedom from both the state and the Papacy (Bentley 95). Early dreaming of restoring a "'Catholic' Church of England," by the 1890s most Anglo-Catholics "had become content to see" their beliefs "tolerated as the mark of a party" (Reed 258). Lord Halifax, quoted above, had led an effort "between 1890 and 1896" to "initiate such a renewal of relations between the Holy See and the authorities of the English Church as might eventually pave the way for the reunion of Western Christendom" only to have the proposal shot down by a Papal Bull ("Crisis" 174). By 1899, Halifax published an essay in *The Nineteenth Century*, calling for the more moderate goal of "reconciliation" between parties of the "Anglican Communion" as a first step toward the greater unity of "the Church of Christ" (186–87). He turned to Christina Rossetti for a model of how such a tolerant and ecumenical—yet Christ-focused—

Christendom might be imagined, concluding with a quote from her SPCK book *Face of the Deep*:

> Strength attaches to union, resource to multiplicity . . . Alas for the offences of former days, and of these days, . . . which have torn to shreds Christ's seamless vesture! Nevertheless, inasmuch as multiplicity is allied to resource, let us . . . make capital of our guilty disadvantage. Let us be provoked to good works by those with whom we cannot altogether agree, yet who in many ways set us a pattern . . . Cannot we—I at least can learn much from the devotion of Catholic Rome, the immutability of Catholic Greece, the philanthropic piety of Quakerism, the zeal of many a "protestant." And when the Anglican Church has acquired and reduced to practice each virtue from every such source, holding fast meanwhile her own goodly heritage of *gifts and graces,* then may those others likewise learn from her, until to every Church, congregation, soul, *God be All in all*. (*Face of the Deep* 301–2[22]; emphasis mine)

Rossetti wrote this passage in response to her reading of Revelation in years immediately preceding *Verses* (Marsh 549). In the phrases I have italicized above, she anticipates the titles of two sections in *Verses*: "Christ Our All in All" and "Gifts and Graces." In ways that have never been adequately appreciated, this meditation on unity-in-diversity forecasts what I regard as a central, ecumenical ambition of Rossetti's last collection of poems. *Verses* aims to bring the "gifts and graces" of various Christian audiences into play by a language and structure that are nonetheless attuned to Rossetti's own Anglican "goodly heritage" in order that Christ might "be all in all" within a diversified community of saints united by their commitment to live now as citizens of the New Jerusalem.

This might explain the fact that when compiling *Verses* Rossetti drew so heavily from *Face of the Deep*, the work in which she most carefully contemplated how the earthly life of the communion of saints related to life in the New Jerusalem. She pursues the theme of "multiplicity" in the above quote from *Face of the Deep* throughout *Verses*. For example, the sixth portion of *Verses*, "Diverse Worlds. Time and Eternity," includes a roundel, "Behold, it was very good," whose final two stanzas follow saints entering Paradise from Earth, preserving in the transfer the multiplicity

---

22. Apparently Halifax was not able to extend his ecumenism quite so far as Rossetti's. As shown above, Rossetti included "the philanthropic piety of Quakerism" in her list of scattered virtues; in his quotation, Halifax omitted the phrase, writing instead: "the immutability of Catholic Greece, the zeal of many Protestants?" (187).

that a more conventional imagination might erase. "The multi-fashioned saints bring praise to Thee, / As doves fly home" (6–7), and yet in Paradise perch "on divers branches of their tree [Christ]," so that "in each degree / All things are fair"—that is, pleasing but also equitable and just (8, 10–11). Apparently, for Rossetti, the sectarian divisions she lamented in *Face of the Deep* are capable of transformation into concordant diversity in the Church triumphant. The "multi-fashion[ing]" of saints on earth, a word that suggests divine creative resourcefulness exercised through a multitude of mediums, will somehow be preserved and yet harmonized out of discord. "Songs for Strangers and Pilgrims," the last section of *Verses*, contains a roundel, "The end is not yet," which both alludes to Christ's words about "the end" coming after "this gospel of the kingdom" is preached to "all nations" (Matt. 26:14) and fashions into a reiterated, almost liturgical, phrase—"Home by different ways" (repeated lines 1, 4, 11)—the ecumenical theme introduced in a poem from the volume's first section: "Come home by different roads from near or far" ("Lord, make us all love all . . ." 6). The international Christian community envisioned in *Verses* is rooted neither in quasi-religious racial qualities that equip an English nation to deliver freedom to its empire (Stead) nor in a vague divine mission for the British state to promote tolerance by restraining the public demands and even altering the forms of competing faiths (Tennyson). Rossetti's international ecumenism celebrates "multi-fashioned" and "diverse branches," acknowledging diverse communal and individual practice of faith rooted in one "tree."

II. A *CHRISTIAN YEAR* BETWEEN AND BEYOND EXISTING PUBLICS

In *Verses*, Rossetti frequently decides to promote the communion of saints through poetic forms that she or other poets had introduced with relative popular success. Algernon Charles Swinburne was largely responsible for "populariz[ing] the" roundel "form" with his *Century of Roundels* (1883), dedicated with permission to Christina Rossetti (*CP* 1169). Two years later, in a manuscript of *Time Flies*, Rossetti singles out "Now they desire a Better Country," which I analyzed in the previous section, as "My first roundel" (*CP* 1056), indicating that Swinburne inspired her experiments with the form. She included a large number of roundels in *Time Flies* and *Face of the Deep*, of which fifty-six made it into *Verses*. As Dieleman notes, the roundel form approximates "the concision, pattern, yet variety of the Anglican collects" that had so deeply shaped Rossetti's religious imagination (147). The form's structure, eleven lines joined by two rhyming sounds and an opening phrase recycled in the fourth and final lines, "fits well with a religious tradition that believes so strongly in remembering its past through frequent repetition of a centuries-old liturgy" that nevertheless gains fresh application with each recitation (151).

In "Now They Desire a Better Country," the refrain of "Love said nay" remains constant amidst Hope's increasingly delusional descent into an autoerotic and nationalistic "dream-world," acting as a resistant liturgical refrain repeated over time that expands in significance as allusions to Matthew 25 and Hebrews 11 align Love's words and posture with that of the Church enduring through the ages in anticipation of the New Jerusalem. Rather than contributing to a quasi-national scripture of the kind Stead and Tennyson differently imagined, Rossetti drew poetic forms from surrounding literary culture, blending them with—and thereby potentially extending to a wider audience—habits of mind that were trained by her own Anglican liturgical worship and that were fundamental to her vision of the communion of saints. *Verses* is Rossetti's effort to create a *Christian Year* capable of motivating a variety of audiences attuned to distinct aspects of poetry and Christianity to imagine themselves in an international and ecumenical Christian community.

When Rossetti began to conceive *Verses* as a project for the SPCK in November 1892 (*Letters* IV:301), experience would have taught her to expect the poems in her volume to gain their widest and most diverse circulation when extracted from its covers in periodical reviews and anthologies. Even as Tennyson, Stead, and others made grandiose claims for poetry's spiritual and imperial influence in the 1890s (neither they nor most of their contemporaries considered novels part of the nation's scripture), most new poetry was actually selling to a smaller proportion of the reading public than it had over sixty years earlier (Erickson 255)—and that proportion had always been a minority (346). Of the roughly 30 million people able to read in Great Britain in the 1890s (Weedon 51),[23] at the most one million could be expected to purchase new books of poetry (Erickson 350). As a result, publishers kept average prices (five shillings) and print runs (500) of new poetry volumes at relatively the same levels that were common in the 1830s (255), even as the best-selling newspapers went for

---

23. Weedon estimates the size of the potential reading public for 1891 at 88 percent of the total population, which was 38,000,000 by the 1900 census.

pennies and reached circulations nearing or topping 1,000,000 (Altick 395–6). Novels normally started near five shillings but customers could expect them to drop to 6d after a few years (Weedon 144); cheap fiction, priced below a shilling, often enjoyed first editions of 100,000 (71), and by the time the SPCK published *Verses* at the reasonable price—for a new poetry volume—of 3s6d, this was in fact the price of 63 to 75 percent of all books sold that year (Weedon 106–7).

Stead's proposal "to pillage" the "poets" for passages to use in his "English Bible" was only a brutal statement of a widespread practice (26). The real money and high sales for poetry were in anthologies that could deliver a range of poems to readers for a relatively low price and for a variety of special purposes, whether polemical compilations such as Revd. Orby Shipley's Anglo-Catholic and ritualist collections of the 1860s (to which Rossetti contributed [Blair, *Form and Faith* 214]); religious compilations designed for devotional reading or congregational singing; increasingly specialized and academic collections of the best of national culture for aspiring readers (Guillory 43); material for students in the textbook market fanned by the expansion of education discussed in chapter 3 (Weedon 103); or specialty collections of popular forms, such as the sonnet (Houston, "Valuable by Design" 266). Sales for *Sonnets of this Century* (1886)—30,000 in ten years—were impressive but not atypical (Erickson 355). Religious poetry collections usually did even better. *The Cloud of Witnesses* (1891) gathered selected poems and passages under a title whose allusion to the communion of saints would have pleased Rossetti when she included her poem in the collection. Within eight years, it sold over 80,000 copies (Ives 219).[24]

These figures put into perspective the sales and reach of Rossetti's *Verses*. As scholars have recently become fond of noting, it was Rossetti's best-selling volume, with 21,000 copies printed by 1912 and perhaps several thousand more by 1925.[25] Yet Tennyson, the century's great violator of poetry's market limitations, witnessed *Enoch Arden* (1864) quickly sell three times as many copies—60,0000—in its first edition (Erickson 349); *In Memoriam* sold 25,000 copies in just over a year (350). Rossetti, as when she contributed to Shipley's Anglo-Catholic collections and *The Cloud of Witnesses*, often found her poetry in demand for anthologies whose contemporary circulations far surpassed anything she published in volume

---

24. The signed poem by Rossetti included in the volume was "Watch with me, Jesus, in my loneliness" from "Old and New Year Ditties," a sequence first published in *Goblin Market and Other Poems* (1862) (Ives 219).

25. Noted on back of the title page of the 1925 edition, the last issued by the SPCK.

form. Rossetti would have known that her poems in *Verses* were in all probability going to owe their greatest distribution to pillagers serving a multitude of purposes and audiences.

New volumes of devotional poetry did, however, achieve higher sales throughout the century than their secular counterparts (Erickson 346–47). As noted in chapter 4, Keble's *Christian Year* was the century's single-volume poetic blockbuster. Rossetti would have had reason to be more sanguine about a good distribution for *Verses* than she would for her earlier volumes with Macmillan, but experience would have taught her that *Verses* had to overcome the partition between "devotional" and "general" literature in Victorian publishing and evaluation. As publishers' lists for secular imaginative literature continued expanding in the nineteenth century, they began to exclude religious or devotional literature.[26] This occurred despite the fact that the crowded field of religious publishing remained healthy and, in the aggregate, larger. Partly a result of different trade practices, the division was also due to high-end publishers' growing sense that they had to appeal to an expanding and ideologically dispersed middle-class audience interested in intellectual and creative literature. For this reason, an increasing number of major book publishers and leading literary reviews provided relatively neutral venues for contesting viewpoints on religion and politics, promoted imaginative literature that avoided didacticism and controversial doctrines, and kept denominational labels in the background, lest they be pushed into one of the sectarian fields (Altholz 92).

Rossetti had negotiated the distinction between "general" and "devotional" literature throughout her career. At the suggestion of her brother Dante Gabriel (hereafter Gabriel), Christina divided *Goblin Market and Other Poems* (1862), her first public volume, between unmarked, general poems placed in the front and explicitly "Devotional Pieces" removed to the end.[27] She and her secular publisher, Macmillan, followed this format until *A Pageant and Other Poems* (1881), in which pieces were not labeled

---

26. "The proportion of religious works in the list of a general publisher rapidly decline[d]" in the last part of the century: "religion formed a third of Macmillan's [Rossetti's publisher] list in 1849, a fifth in 1869, and only a seventeenth in 1889" (P. Scott, "The Business of Belief" 214).

27. Gabriel helped Christina secure Alexander Macmillan's interest in *Goblin Market*. When Gabriel first mentioned the prospect to Christina, he advised her to divide her volume between general and devotional poetry: "It seems to me that the only plan—so large a section of your poems being devotional—would be to divide the volume into two distinct sections" (*The Correspondence of Dante Gabriel Rossetti* II:349 Letter 61.11). Jan Marsh speculates that Gabriel recommended this arrangement to Christina because he had heard something from Macmillan "about the vast amount of pious poetry offered for publication nowadays" (Marsh 269).

"devotional." Even in this volume, however, Rossetti arranged[28] her poems in the same way: general poems came first, followed by devotional poems. Arseneau argues that Rossetti's division of poems "re-enact[s]" her sense of "the Bible's economy of gradual revelation" across Old and New Testaments, so that general poems in the opening of a volume disclose their hidden levels of spiritual meaning in light of devotional ones later in the volume (130). This strategy of arrangement also indicates Rossetti's anticipation of a dual-stream reception, whereby readers, reviewers, and anthologizers most interested in poetry of either a general or devotional nature could direct their attention to the section of immediate interest. Rossetti seems to have operated on this principle when sending poems to anthologizers. Soon after *Goblin Market* appeared, the Anglo-Catholic Rev. Orby Shipley asked Rossetti to send him pieces from the devotional section of that volume for his popular *Lyra Eucharistica* (1863); Rossetti sent them with two unpublished devotional works she knew would suit his purposes (Marsh 299).[29] Later she sent Samuel Waddington a number of her most reprinted general sonnets and a few of her devotional ones for the diverse audience he was likely to seek with his *English Sonnets By Living Writers* (1881) (*Letters* II:226).[30]

When she was conceptualizing *Verses*, Rossetti would have had good reasons for supposing that the division between general and "devotional" literature could result in the exclusion of her devotional poems from the educated, relatively elite literary market catered to by reviewers of *The Athenaeum* and *The Academy*. In 1881, Christina responded to a letter from her brother Gabriel in which he had expressed concern that she would harm her poetic standing by continuing to publish with the SPCK (*Letters* II:256–57). By writing strictly devotional poetry and prose for the SPCK, Gabriel seems to have assumed, his sister would undermine her claim to be a poet who was admired for her artistic accomplishment. This was likely also Gabriel's concern when he wrote his sister twenty years earlier asking her to divide her poetry in *Goblin Market* into devotional and general sections. Gabriel would, in fact, be justified in fearing disregard for Christina's SPCK publications by the *Athenaeum* crowd. Writing for a transatlantic intellectual and literary audience in *The Atlantic Monthly* a few months

---

28. Rossetti insisted on controlling the arrangement and correction of poems in her volumes. See her 1875 letter to Macmillan on this subject (*Letters* II:42).

29. Sabine Haass reports that Shipley's first edition of *Lyra Eucharistica* (1,250 copies) quickly sold out (55).

30. Ives notes the sonnets included: "If Only," "Rest," "The World," "Autumn Violets," "After Communion," "On the Wing," "After Death" (204).

after Rossetti's death, William Sharp recalled Rossetti telling him that "the literary world that praised her so much studiously ignored" her "little known prose books" for the SPCK ("Some Reminiscences" 745). Yet these "little known prose books" actually markedly increased Rossetti's distribution.[31] Sharp assumes that "the literary world" would normally overlook SPCK devotional prose publications when in search of literary value, no matter how wide a circulation those works achieved in other sectors of the market.

Soon after its appearance in 1893, a reviewer of *Verses* for *The Athenaeum* confirms Sharp's assumptions, observing that if the poems in *Verses* had been left dispersed in Rossetti's works of devotional prose, they would have likely remained the special interest of "the religious public" ("Verses" 842). Yet now, "collected" under the general title *Verses* and unhindered by the "interruption of the edifying prose," the poems comprise a book that might still "be largely . . . read for its devotional tendency by people who will not see the difference between such verse and the verse of the late Frances Ridley Havergal.[32] But it will [also] be appreciated for its actual poetic value by all who care for Miss Rossetti's work, that is to say, by all who care for poetry" ("Verses" 842). Rossetti, who kept up with journals such as *The Athenaeum* and whose associates included leading *Athenaeum* reviewers such as Theodore Watts-Dunton, would have been aware of this tendency to distinguish between the devout but poetically insensitive multitude and the aesthetically attuned elect. When, in the 1881 letter mentioned above, she responded to Gabriel's fears about the damage her SPCK publications would do to her poetic fame, Rossetti seems to have counted the costs of directing her efforts fully to the "devotional" side of the market, even as she remained optimistic about her ability to appeal beyond its margins: "I dontt [*sic*] think harm will accrue from my S. P. C. K. books even to my standing: if it did, I should still be glad to throw my grains of dust into the religious scale. I am seriously hoping, however, to get up a vol. of poems before so very very long. There are a few poems in my Saint's Day book" (*Letters* II:257).

Rossetti did not approach her SPCK editor, Edmund McClure, with the idea of collecting the poems from her devotional prose until 1892, and her brother William claimed that he proposed the idea to her (*Letters*

---

31. W. K. Lowther Clarke notes that "7,000 of *Time Flies* were sold, and *The Face of the Deep* went into six editions" ("Introduction").

32. The Anglican poet and hymn writer perhaps best known for her hymn "Take my life, and let it be / Consecrated, Lord, to Thee."

IV:301). When, however, Christina assures Gabriel in the 1881 letter above that she plans to issue another volume of poetry and then immediately mentions the poems in her most recent SPCK book, *Called to Be Saints*, she indicates that she has been considering such a move long before William encouraged her to make it. In any case, she quickly saw the wisdom of the maneuver and followed through with it. No longer subordinated to meditations on the saints' lives (*Called to Be Saints* 1881), daily devotionals (*Time Flies* 1885), or biblical commentary (*Face of the Deep* 1892), the poems in *Verses* had the chance, confirmed by the 1893 *Athenaeum* reviewer above, of reaching beyond the devotional market.

Rossetti, who had long kept abreast of the SPCK's publishing agenda through its annual and monthly reports (*Letters* IV:352), would have been aware that *Verses* coincided with the society's missionary and market aims. The SPCK's reports would have kept Christina informed of the society's efforts to sell books to members at reduced prices for free distribution to the poor (Clarke, *A History* 148, 192), and they would also have reminded her of the SPCK's worldwide book grant program, which could feasibly get *Verses* into the hands of a wide range of laborers, soldiers, recovering addicts and prostitutes, hospital patients, emigrants, school children, and transatlantic and international audiences in and far beyond the empire (Allen and McClure 459–60). When dialoguing with Gabriel about the dangers of publishing with the SPCK in 1881, Christina could have read the society's Annual Report for that year, which reemphasized its commitment to meeting "the Christian needs of the age" with low-priced literature whose "large and catholic spirit" avoided points of denominational controversy and penetrated beyond the society's distribution network to reach markets supplied by "general booksellers" (Allen and McClure 196–97). Working on *Verses* in London in 1892, Rossetti would have been aware that the SPCK held a major public meeting there in which its mission of reaching across classes and literary markets was reemphasized (Clarke, *A History* 152). In collecting *Verses* for the SPCK, then, Rossetti secured a publisher committed to a broad distribution that at least partly complemented the ecumenical, international vision she held of the communion of saints, as well as her desire to attract literary audiences alongside devotional ones.

Shortly after *Verses* appeared, *The Speaker,* a weekly addressing a relatively small intellectual liberal audience, indicated that the SPCK had followed its aim of penetrating diverse markets in the material presentation of Rossetti's volume. The reviewer singles out *Verses* as both a "spiritual" and "poetical" achievement, notifying readers that "its production is very dainty and beautiful" ("Miss Rossetti's 'Verses'" 588).[33] A month earlier, the *Times* highlighted the book's distinctive appearance, noting that it was "printed in red and black on hand-made paper" (Ives 125). Until at least 1904 (Ives 128), *Verses* kept its 1893 form, with a gilt title and top edge, and ample margins around the poems inside, which were bordered by red lines whose endings formed crosses as they met, or Oxford corners (Glaister 354–55). The "hand-made paper" noticed by the *Times* is laid paper, or paper made in a mold,[34] and the distinctive horizontal lines in the paper of *Verses* would indicate to a connoisseur of books a deliberately classic or artisanal appearance, as would the uneven deckle edges.[35]

Such techniques were characteristic of Anglo-Catholic and High Church publications in the nineteenth century. Dressing *Verses* so finely for the market would have been expensive, and the fact that the price for the volume remained reasonable indicates the SPCK followed religious rather than profit motives (as did Rossetti, who willingly surrendered all profits to the society [Kooistra 146]). Yet Dieleman goes too far when she concludes that the material presentation of *Verses* is the "response" of the SPCK to "High Church aesthetics *rather than* middle-class social aspirations" (156; emphasis mine). The aesthetic packaging that appealed to High Church readers was also commonly used to single out poetry as a specialty commodity for gift giving and appreciation by upwardly mobile middle-class readers.[36] Attention to middle-class readers' aspirations would be entirely in keeping with a society that had in 1881 announced its commitment to "ceaseless adaptations to its changing environment" as

---

33. Other 1893 reviewers noticed the cultural flag the SPCK raised with the packaging of *Verses,* associating the volume with the "golden realm of poetry" ("Recent Verse," *Saturday Review* 476).

34. Technically this paper could be made by machines in the nineteenth century (Carter 130). Even so, the practice of imitating laid paper was, as the *Times* indicates, a deliberate effort by publishers and paper-makers to give the impression of rarity and cultural quality (Carter 130).

35. The "chain lines" of laid paper (Glaister 91), or the heavier lines produced by wire mesh with which it is made, are normally vertical (272). Horizontal, or "turned chain lines," are less common and are particular to paper made in the late seventeenth and eighteenth centuries (487).

36. Anthologies and reprints of both general literary poetry and religious poetry frequently capitalized upon the association of fine material presentation with cultural prestige. The SPCK issued gift books in gilt titles and top edges, as in the case of a 1900 printing I have seen of *The Oxford Complete Edition of the Poetical Works of the Elizabeth Barrett Browning* (London, SPCK 1900). In possession of the Armstrong Browning Library (Baylor University), this volume was presented as a gift book by the United Methodist Church Juvenile Missionary Society in Sheffield (as the inscription indicates). One year after the 1898 reprinting of *Verses,* Thomas B. Mosher published what might have been a pirated edition of Rossetti's sonnet sequence *Monna Innominata* in a form resembling *Verses,* including laid paper, untrimmed edges, and deep brown reddish ink on the title page (Ives 155).

it sought to promote "true religion" through "almost the entire field of literature" (Allen and McClure 196–97). A steady and self-sacrificial supporter of this endeavor like Rossetti would have been able to appreciate the multi-directional appeal of the red-crossed Oxford corners that she discovered the SPCK had chosen for the border of *Verses* in June 1893. Expressing her admiration of "the pretty red lined page" to McClure, Rossetti was in all probability approving the crossover those "pretty" crossing lines performed between appeals to devotional and aspiring literary audiences (*Letters* IV:328).

With this diverse reception in mind, Rossetti designed *Verses* as a late-century *Christian Year* poised to draw from, and (through future anthologizing and reviewing) circulate back out into, diversified markets for poetry. The most obvious structural debt of *Verses* to *The Christian Year* is the third section, "Some Feasts and Fasts," in which Rossetti retitled and regrouped poems to follow the feasts of the church calendar, though she did so more selectively and flexibly than had Keble (Dieleman 161–62). Immediately noticed by reviewers as a renovation of Keble's design,[37] this section also suggests Rossetti's greater sensitivity than her Tractarian predecessor to the diversity of ways in which readers would encounter her poems. In keeping with the goal of the SPCK to reach a broader literary audience, Rossetti allots only one of *Verses*' eight sections to an explicitly liturgical scheme, and the arrangement of her poems suggests her anticipation of *Verses*' likely future as a sourcebook for anthologies. Section headings of *Verses*—such as "Christ our All in All," "Some Feasts and Fasts," and "Gifts and Graces"—help the reader to perceive the thematic relationships of poems but also enable the editor to select pieces according to category and purpose. Rossetti's own long experience with anthologies would have taught her that "Some Feasts and Fasts" might catch the eye of an anthologist such as the ritualist Orby Shipley, or indeed—as it did[38]— serve the SPCK's own effort in the later nineteenth century to promote the Church's seasons through tracts and relevant collections of reprints (Allen and McClure 459). The less explicitly Anglican section, "Songs for Strangers and Pilgrims," might attract the Congregational minister William Garrett Horder, who had recently included a poem republished by Rossetti in this section of *Verses* in his popular collection *The Poet's Bible, Old Testament* (1890).

---

37. The critic for the 1893 *The Saturday Review* observed that the section was "a kind of calendar like the *Christian Year*" ("Recent Verse" 476).

38. As Kooistra notes, Rossetti's devotional poetry and prose was mined for such a tract ten years after *Verses* was published: *Redeeming the Time: Daily Musings for Lent from the works of Christina Georgina Rossetti* (London: SPCK, 1903) (182).

Horder had also enjoyed success with *Congregational Hymns: A Hymnal for Free Churches* (1884), in which Rossetti had willingly included a devotional poem,[39] and he and others seeking to meet the large Victorian demand for hymnals would have looked carefully at *Verses*. This much is assumed by the rising man of letters, Edmund K. Chambers, in his review of *Verses* for *The Academy,* when he encouraged "the hymnbook compilers" to "take the opportunity to diversify their doggerel with a little literature," singling out "We know not a voice of that River" in *Verses* (164).[40] When Chambers' review appeared, this poem had, in fact, already been included in a High Church hymnal published by the SPCK, *Church Hymns with Tunes* (1893) (Ives 253), and five other poems published in *Verses* were recollected in the *Wintersdorf Hymnal* the same year (252).

Rossetti's longstanding comfort with anthologizers recycling her devotional poems indicates that she constructed her late-century *Christian Year* with an eye to the variety of paths readers would take into *Verses,* as well as the ways poems within could be expected to fan out from the collection, itself a kind of anthology, to reach an extensive and variegated field of readers (and congregations) in fresh anthologies and hymnals. *Verses* seems built less to be a final "home" than a junction for readers—and editors and reviewers—travelling "by different roads from near or far" ("Lord, make us all love all" 6). It aims for a place between many sectors of the late nineteenth-century reading public in the hope of pointing diverse audiences, through a multitude of venues, toward "reunion" in the eschatological community beyond (4).

III. THROWING SONNETS INTO—AND OUT OF—THE RELIGIOUS SCALE

One dimension of the arrangement of *Verses* seems particularly conducive to the SPCK's effort to breach the wall between "devotional" and "general" literature and win a wide audience by attracting general booksellers and positive reviews in journals such as *The Athenaeum* and *The Academy.*

---

39. "Weary in Well-Doing," first published in *The Prince's Progress* (1866). See *Letters* for Rossetti's endorsement of this volume and poem's inclusion (III:264).

40. This is a roundel, whose refrain structure, as earlier discussed, resembles the liturgical patterns of Rossetti's own worship as an Anglo-Catholic. Noticing that such a "refrain" might also be "effective in congregational singing," Chambers wisely omits the poem's title, "Whitsun Monday" (it is in the "Feasts and Fasts" section of *Verses*), thereby encouraging its appropriation by a more interdenominational range of editors (164).

Rossetti introduces *Verses* with a sonnet sequence, "Out of the Deep Have I Called unto thee, O Lord," which at once capitalizes upon her prominent standing as a sonneteer and reworks the religious and literary associations of the form to bring her vision of the community of saints to a range of readers. Opening with this sonnet sequence was a closely considered move on Rossetti's part. She took sonnets scattered through books published nearly a decade apart and arranged them into a thematically interrelated sequence, deliberately departing from chronological order by taking most of the sonnets from her final devotional book, *The Face of the Deep* (Taft 317).

The material presentation of the sonnet sequence advertises *Verses* both to those attuned to the aesthetics of devotional publications and to those seeking opportunities for refined cultural consumption—and, of course, to those who found themselves in both camps. Set apart by their title page and the one introducing the following section of *Verses,* the seventeen sonnets serve as a highly wrought entryway, with the Oxford-cornered red borders enclosing no more than two sonnets per page. This display mirrors that of Victorian sonnet anthologies, in which sonnets frequently appear in red borders with generous margins, a material and economic signifier of their aesthetic and cultural value (A. Chapman, "Sonnet and Sonnet Sequence" 105). Poised to draw in readers of *The Athenaeum,* this format also frames the sonnets within beautiful, ordered spaces marked at each corner by the cross-forming Oxford corners, associating the printed page with sacred church spaces. Many Anglican, especially Anglo-Catholic, readers had become accustomed to this analogy between page and church space through Isaac Williams' sonnet sequences, *The Cathedral* (1838) and *The Altar* (1847)—the last of which Rossetti owned, annotated, and illustrated (D'Amico and Kent 93). Keble had influentially argued that the sonnet was suited to the reserved expression that he and other Tractarians recommended in poetry and devotion (Phelan 89). As Wordsworth's *Ecclesiastical Sonnets* (first published as *Ecclesiastical Sketches* in 1822) reminds, the sonnet's use as a devotional and religious form extended beyond Anglo-Catholic circles, and because of its brevity and concentration, it was often likened by critics to a "Collect" (Russell Part I:402). Rossetti had herself increasingly identified the sonnet form with devotion over the course of her career (Phelan 96). She published nearly eight times as many sonnets—fifty-six—in *A Pageant and Other Poems* (1881) as in *Goblin Market* (1862) or in *The Prince's Progress* (1866). In *Verses,* the number climbed to sixty-four, roughly one-fifth of the poems in the volume, meaning that in her last and most explicitly devotional collection of verse, Rossetti included more sonnets than any other form of poetry.

Rossetti not only shared in the association of the sonnet with devotion, she was also at the center of enthusiasm for sonnets that swept much of the late-Victorian literary world. Seventeen anthologies of sonnets were published in Britain between 1800 and 1900, the majority of which (eleven) appeared after 1867, six of them in the time in which Rossetti was working on poetry eventually gathered in *Verses* (Houston, "Valuable by Design" 266). Living poets were as active in producing new sonnets as were anthologists in collecting samples from mainly dead poets. John Holmes has compiled a (far-from-comprehensive) list of sixty-six sonnet sequences published in the century, fifty-nine of which appeared after 1850 (168–69). Added to these sequences, were an untold number of sonnets that crowded sections of anthologies, newspapers, periodicals, and volumes of verse (Houston, "Towards a New History" 148). The output was so great and enthusiasm so high that Samuel Waddington felt he could justify dealing with copyright law and financial risk to anthologize only breathing writers in his *English Sonnets by Living Writers* (1881), claiming that the "work of one generation" of sonneteers, "both as regards number and execution," might have "rival[ed] that of all its predecessors" ("Preface" vi). Esteemed literary critics, many of whom wrote sonnets themselves, were no less assiduous in generating historical-critical studies of the sonnet aimed at serious poetry readers.[41] By 1882, Edward Dowden, one of the first professors of English literature, could humorously suggest in *The Academy* that "A perplexed Chancellor of the Exchequer might do worse nowadays than introduce a tax on sonnets; the consumption of them is large, and shows no tendency to decline . . . ; a staff of Inspectors of Sonnets, with ample salaries, would be . . . selected from the critics of our leading literary journals" (129). A sonneteer and sonnet critic himself, Dowden would have profited from the legislation. By 1901, William Archer could ask with some disgust, "Who is there in these days, that has not written one or two passable sonnets?" (qtd. Golden 134).

Rossetti moved in the circles most responsible for inspiring this interest in sonnets. After 1870, her brother Gabriel was widely hailed as "the greatest of all living sonneteers" (Noble 469), a title secured with his *House of Life* sequence (1881), and he inspired a second generation of sonneteers who were active during the 1870s and 1880s, several of whom Christina personally knew.[42] Christina attended lectures by, and assisted the work of,

---

41. Jennifer Wagner has located sixteen historical-critical studies of the sonnet published between 1814 and 1888, half of them appearing after 1863, mainly in distinguished literary periodicals and sonnet anthologies (192–93).

42. See John Holmes' discussion of the "Sons of Gabriel," his term for the male sonneteers inspired by *The House of Life,* many of whom Christina knew (36–43); Houston discusses the

scholars interested in recovering and translating Renaissance Italian sonnets. One of them, Charles Tomlinson, was a close associate. She owned his study of Dante's and Petrarch's sonnets, *The Sonnet: Its Origin, Structure, and Place in Poetry* (1874), which was frequently cited by anthologists and periodical critics.[43] She and Gabriel would have kept up with reviews of this and related sonnet literature as well as the historical-critical essays on the sonnet that appeared in periodicals to which they contributed work, such as *The Athenaeum, The Academy, The Cornhill Magazine*, and *The Fortnightly Review*;[44] and their friend, Theodore Watts-Dunton, was noted for his criticism of sonnets in *The Athenaeum*. In 1880, when Rossetti and Gabriel were at work on their sonnet sequences *Later Life* and *The House of Life*, they presented David Main's popular *A Treasury of English Sonnets* (1880) to their mother for her birthday, and each wrote a "sonnet on the sonnet" to accompany it. Main's anthology included a second volume aimed at students of the sonnet, with numerous samples from living sonneteers, including Christina and Gabriel.[45] That same year, she and Gabriel were sending off sonnets to Waddington for his *English Sonnets by Living Writers* (1881) (*Letters* II:226).

When, therefore, Rossetti selected the sonnet she first wrote to go with her mother's copy of Main's anthology as the dedication of *Pageant* (1881), she must have hoped that its first lines would catch sonnet-hunting eyes: "Sonnets are full of love, and this my tome / Has many sonnets" (1–2). The maneuver was successful. Rossetti soon gained a substantial critical reputation with the two sonnet sequences in *Pageant, Monna Innominata: A Sonnet of Sonnets* and *Later Life: A Double Sonnet of Sonnets*; and her standing as a leading sonneteer was increased by the wider circulation of these and other sonnets in sonnet anthologies published in Britain and the United States between 1882–90.[46] Amplifying her earlier strategy of using

---

influence of Gabriel on women sonneteers ("Towards a New History" 162–64).

43. Rossetti also received Tomlinson's book of sonnets, *Sonnets* (1881), which he dedicated to her (Marsh 471–72).

44. Between them, Gabriel and Christina contributed to all these periodicals (A. Chapman and Meacock 466, 475), in which important essays on sonnet literature appeared. Their letters show that they were in the habit of sending each other numbers in which one of them would have special interest. One such article might have been William Davies' "The Sonnet," published in the January 1873 *The Quarterly Review*. Davies had been in correspondence with Gabriel since 1862 (Chapman and Meacock 142), and Christina knew of him through Gabriel (*Letters* II 221–22). Davies' article was often cited by sonnet anthologists and reviewers in periodicals.

45. Main included Christina's sonnet "Remember" (292–93).

46. Shortly after Rossetti's death, Alice Law could claim in *The Westminster Review* that Rossetti's "monument of" highly "finished work" almost "dwarfs" that of "Mrs. Browning," especially her "numerous exquisite sonnets—among which the *Monna Innominata* threaten to rival Mrs.

a prefacing sonnet to advertise the many sonnets in *Pageant,* in *Verses* Rossetti opened with a sonnet sequence that was almost certain to catch the attention of anthologizers and sonnet critics.

Christina is likely to have read James Ashcroft-Noble's important essay on "The Sonnet in England" for the 1880 *Contemporary Review.*[47] Like many other literary critics and reviewers, Noble praises the sonnet form for its tight constraints, since they exert pressure on a writer's artistry and call forth the skilled and devoted interpretation of readers: "[the sonnet] must have an artistic perfection which shall stand the test of that frequent and loving examination to which, in virtue of its very brevity, it makes a claim" (Noble 452). For Noble and other sonnet critics and anthologists, sonnet reading is a sign of sensitive perception and literary refinement. Good sonnet-reading eludes the undisciplined, who "expect . . . to find the meaning upon the surface, in vivid and graceful lines which they may read as they run" (Russell Part I:403). According to Thomas H. Caine, a protégé of Gabriel and editor of *Sonnets of Three Centuries* (1882), those who make their way through historical-critical studies of the sonnet will belong to a "limited company" ("Preface" viii). Critics and anthologists offered the sonnet, and critical essays on it, to readers from all levels of the middle class as a means for rising above the low-grade distractions of the mass market to cultivate the authentic enjoyment of poetry practiced by a self-selecting literary community.[48] Positioned as the portico to *Verses,* then,

---

Browning on her own ground" (453). As noted earlier, Thomas Mosher produced an exquisitely packaged edition of *Monna Innominata* for a U.S. audience in 1899 (Ives 155–57). Ives describes numerous anthologies, religious and secular, in which Rossetti's sonnets, especially those from *Monna Innominata* and *Later Life,* were republished between 1882 and 1890 (Ives 206–17). We can be certain that Rossetti knew about the appearance of her sonnets in many of these anthologies (e.g., Rossetti wrote the editor of the 1883 *English Poetesses* [Ives 206–7] about her inclusion [*Letters* III:156–57]).

47. Given her habit of keeping up with the top literary periodicals, such as *The Contemporary Review,* she was likely to seek out the essay, since it began as a review of Main's anthology, which, as mentioned above, she purchased for her mother, and in which a sonnet of her own had appeared.

48. William Sharp, like Caine a protégé of Gabriel, edited *Sonnets of This Century* (1886), stating in his sixty-page introduction that the collection, priced at 1s, was meant to initiate "the reader unacquainted with the true scope of our sonnet-literature and of the technique of the sonnet itself, and to illustrate its development and capacities" (xxi). Even as Sharp acknowledges his lower-middle-class readers' constraints, recommending the sonnet's brevity to those who seek cultivation with scant time for leisure, he resorts to the familiar opposition between the discriminating reading he is recommending and the distractions of the swarming literary market: "[The sonnet's] conciseness is an immense boon in these days when books multiply like gossamer-flies in a sultry June; it is realised that if good a sonnet can be speedily read and enjoyed, that if exceptionally fine it can with ease be committed to memory, and that if bad it can be recognized as such at a glance, and can be relegated to oblivion by the turning of a single page" (xxv).

the introductory sonnet sequence could potentially reach a variety of audiences: those of many classes seeking religious devotion; educated readers of *The Academy* intent on honing their cultural and literary perceptiveness on the sonnet form; the wider body of middle-class readers who might not have warmed to close discussions of the sonnet but who nevertheless helped sonnet anthologies sell; and, of course, those readers who would fall into several of these groupings at once.

Readers familiar with *In Memoriam* might have detected an echo upon turning with the *volta* of Rossetti's first sonnet into its ninth line. "Alone Lord God, we see not yet we know" (9) recalls Tennyson's well-known line in the introductory stanzas to *In Memoriam*: "We have but faith: we cannot know; / For knowledge is of things we see" (Intro. 21–22). Whereas Tennyson encourages relegation of faith to the inward realm of feeling in distinction from the empirical domain of scientific knowledge, Rossetti returns to the traditional identification of faith *as* evidence of a reality now hidden.[49] The double reading permitted by Rossetti's syntax—"we see not yet, we know" rather than simply "we see not *but* we know"—indicates, together with anxiety over not seeing, certainty in one day seeing what is now unseen. The allusion quietly introduces, for the biblically sensitive reader, the echoes of Hebrews 11–12 which, as I have shown, amplify and resound as the volume proceeds, and which undergird the overriding invitation to readers to imagine themselves in a diverse community whose nation is ultimately found in the new creation. The revisionary dialogue between the openings of *Verses* and of *In Memoriam* would have been helped, at least for readers of contemporary sonnet criticism, by critics' sometimes loose application of "sonnet sequence" to any series of relatively homogeneous short lyrics, such as Tennyson's "Short swallow-flights of song" in *In Memoriam* (48.15; Phelan 107–11).

The sonnet is placed directly beneath the sequence's title, "Out of the Deep, Have I Called unto Thee, O Lord," which comes from *De Profundis* (Psalm 130) and would be repeated by faithful uses of the Prayer Book each month. The Psalm, like the sonnet, is a cry of individual and communal anguish, fear of God's distance, and, ultimately, patient hope. The sonnet's governing images of night and dawn carry forward the Psalmist's turn from fear of abandonment and divine judgment to determination to wait "for the Lord more than they that watch for the morning" (130:6). Rossetti's sonnet thereby again resembles the introduction of *In Memoriam*, which combines a communal confession of hope in the "Strong Son of

---

49. "Now faith is the substance of things hoped for, the evidence of things not seen" (Heb.11:1).

God, immortal Love" (Intro. 1) with ensuing "wild and wandering cries" of confusion and doubt (39). Yet Rossetti's sonnet is loyal to Keble's emphasis on a community formed by shared religious knowledge and an analogical and typological vision of the world.[50] Rossetti conveys this vision in a more subtly articulate manner than *The Christian Year,* rewarding the patient attention of readers accustomed to the "frequent and loving examination" of fine details recommended by late Victorian sonnet critics and anthologists (Noble 452):

> Alone Lord God, in Whom our trust and peace,
> Our love and our desire, glow bright with hope;
> Lift us above this transitory scope
> Of earth, these pleasures that begin and cease,
> This moon which wanes, these seasons which decrease:
> We turn to Thee; as on an eastern slope
> Wheat feels the dawn beneath night's lingering cope,
> Bending and stretching sunward ere it sees.
> Alone Lord God, we see not yet we know;
> By love we dwell with patience and desire,
> And loving so and so desiring pray;
> Thy will be done in earth as heaven today;
> As yesterday it was, tomorrow so;
> Love offering love on love's self-feeding fire.

Rossetti evokes the struggle between patient waiting and anxious longing through a series of subtle formal and semantic turns. For Dieleman, "alone," the leading word of the first line and *volta,* refers "not to a lonely speaker or a lonely God but to God as the one-and-only to whom the believing community turns" (169). Yet "alone" surely gains its suggestiveness by shifting between this meaning ("only") and "solitary," acknowledging the loneliness that the faithful "we" in the sonnet are often in this life made to feel, individually and corporately. The sonnet silently performs the traditional Christian pun underlying Tennyson's address to the "Strong Son of God" in *In Memoriam* and Keble's equally famous "Sun of my soul! Thou Saviour dear" from the opening of *The Christian Year* ("Evening" 12): the Son is the sun toward which the community of *Verses* leans "sunward" (8), turning in faith—but also need and exhaustion—with the "turn" of

---

50. In this case, that knowledge is comprised by familiarity with scripture, and perhaps Prayer Book devotions, by which the sequence's title gains its depth, as well as the typological suggestion that the Psalmist's cry is that of every believer who now anticipates Christ's second coming.

the fifth line into the sixth (6). Strengthened by assonance, the sixth line introduces an analogy between the "we" of the community and "Wheat" that "feels the dawn beneath night's lingering cope, / Bending and stretching sunward ere it sees" the Son's rise (7–8). This leaning silently carries the community across the *volta* into the renewed address to God ("Alone Lord God"), even as this turn—of the sonnet and the supplication—occurs across a full stop that recalls the cloak of mortal "night's lingering cope," which still screens believers from "see[ing]" the incomparable God toward whom they now, often in isolation, must grope. Rossetti delicately emphasizes this impression of blind grasping just before the *volta*, following the mildly personified "bending" of wheat with more human and willfully anxious "stretching." This suggestion of stretching hands itself combines with the aural texture of the immediately preceding "l*inge*ring co*pe*" to evoke the *grope* of human *fingers*.

If, in opening her multifaceted late spin on *The Christian Year*, Rossetti recalls the introductions to Keble's *Christian Year* and Tennyson's *In Memoriam*, she does so in a manner that redirects the wandering of the later poetic cycle toward the surer communal faith of the former, but without sacrificing the fineness of craft that would appeal to those schooled in the late-Victorian culture of sonnet reading. Despite its assured tone and reliance on biblical knowledge, the Prayer Book's emphasis on Psalm 130, and Tractarian practices of analogy, this sonnet nonetheless involves those entering *Verses* in imagining faith less as a set of prescribed affirmations than a drama of exasperation, longing, and (re)turning, which is enacted alone and communally over time—and in the subtle turning of a phrase and line. The last seven lines, in fact, contain participles and gerunds ("lingering," "bending," "stretching," "loving," "desiring," "offering," "self-feeding") that suggest the time of waiting and longing described in the poem includes the present time and act of reading.

Westerholm hears in the "pleasures that begin and cease" of this sonnet an intertextual revision to "the 'grating roar' of pebbles on Matthew Arnold's 'Dover Beach' (1867), which 'Begin, and cease, and then again begin'" (192). Unlike Arnold's poem, here there is no unending cycle: the earthly pleasures are of transitory scope, and "the moon wanes without waxing; the seasons decrease without growing full" (Westerholm 192). In pairing references to Christ as the sun with the "moon which wanes" (5), Rossetti might also be reworking Keble's well-known schematic analogy in "Septuagesima Sunday": "The Moon above, the Church below, / . . . all their radiance, all their glow, / Each borrows of its Sun" (13, 15–16). "This moon which wanes" might allude to the earthly Church, an imperfect visible manifestation of the community of saints. Reflecting the Son in its passage on "earth" (4), the Church appears to wane with corruption and weariness without bearing a harvest amidst "these seasons which decrease" (4). Yet while the Church seems dead and cold, it is also a field of "Wheat," collectively and—with every stalk—individually stretching toward the Son whose love sustains it now and will, according to the parable (Matt. 13:24–30), purify it of tares in the harvest of the kingdom. The heat of Christ's divine light is "love" (2), which each member of the Church "feels" even as the night lingers (6–7). "By love we dwell with patience and desire" (10), and "we know" even when "Alone" we are in an unseen community with God and others that will one day be available for all to "see." That community becomes partially visible through individual and corporate acts of mercy and sacrifice, as each member repeats what he or she has been taught to pray by the Son while awaiting his dawn: "Thy will be done in earth as heaven today; / As yesterday it was, tomorrow so" (12–13).

The sun-lit fire quietly implied in the second line—"Our love and our desire, glow bright with hope"—openly ignites on the altar of the final line, as if the wheat mentioned in lines 6–8 had been quietly offered to the flames: "Love offering love on love's self-feeding fire" (14). This final conflagration dizzyingly reveals that offering "Our love" to God and others is also God ("Love") offering through us, so that even amidst the night "By love we" already "dwell" with Love (10), and his "self-feeding fire" fuels and is mirrored in our mortal acts of love and the new ones they feed. Likely to intrigue a reader of *The Athenaeum,* this intricate pattern of imagery also lends support to a network of biblical images that a much wider and diverse audience could be expected to appreciate. It recalls Paul's command to offer one's body as a living sacrifice to God in acts of obedient charity (Rom. 12:1); the fulfillment of Old Testament ritual in Christ's loving sacrifice upon which Paul's command depends (Eph. 5:1–2); and the claim that God is love so that those who love dwell in God (1 John 4:16).

Rossetti in this opening sonnet gently recalls the parable of the wheat and tares. In the next sonnet of the sequence, she draws out the implications of this allusion, referring in the first line to the "Seven vials" of God's "wrath" in Revelation (15:7), to be poured out against humanity in the final judgment. Yet Rossetti glances at judgment only to amplify the last line of the first sonnet, with its portrayal of Christian love enkindled by and dimly replicating the "self-feeding fire" of divine love:

> Seven vials hold Thy wrath: but what can hold
> Thy mercy save Thine own Infinitude

> Boundlessly overflowing all good,
> All lovingkindness, all delights untold?
> Thy Love, of created love the mould . . . . (1–5)

In this sonnet sequence and in sonnets distributed across *Verses,* Rossetti builds upon her reputation among late Victorian sonnet enthusiasts as a master of the Petrarchan sonnet. With *Sonnets from the Portuguese* (1850) Elizabeth Barrett Browning most influentially revived, for Victorians, the Petrarchan amatory sonnet sequence, rekindling interest in the Petrarchan form. By the time Gabriel and Christina established themselves as preeminent Petrarchan sonneteers with *House of Life* (1881) and *Monna Innominata* (1881), many sonnet critics agreed that the ideal form of the sonnet was Petrarchan.[51] Christina, who had showcased her knowledge of Italian models in *Monna Innominata* with a series of epigraphs in Italian from Dante and Petrarch, and who had boldly opened the sequence with a preface inviting comparison with Browning's *Sonnets from the Portuguese,* was generally acknowledged as the greatest English practitioner of the Petrarchan sonnet after her brother's death in 1882.[52] The general rules of the Petrarchan form—its division into an octave and sestet, and the "most approved mode of rhyming" the octave in the ABBAABBA pattern (Davies 188)—were constantly rehearsed for readers.[53] Whenever critics detailed the ideal sonnet's parts, especially its octave-sestet division, they stressed that the "one thing most needful in the sonnet is what may be called impressive unity" (Noble 449); each part must be "a member of one body" (Davies 190), giving the strong impression of "unity in multiplicity."[54] In her two most widely discussed and anthologized sonnet sequences, Rossetti had heavily relied upon readers' sensitivity to Petrarchan unity in multiplicity. *Monna Innominata: A Sonnet of Sonnets* requires readers to recognize that its fourteen sonnets form a larger whole, a giant "octave" of eight sonnets followed by a "sestet" of

---

51. In 1880, Noble asserts that "[we must] allow the name of sonnet without qualification to be given only to those specimens on the Italian model; other fourteen-line poems being set apart by a distinguishing prefix, such as illegitimate, irregular, or Shakespearian" (449).

52. Writing in *The National Review* a few months after Rossetti's death, Arthur Benson favorably contrasted Christina's sonnets with her brother's more "exotic" work (760).

53. To list just a few instances—John Dennis "The English Sonnet" (1872) 581; Davies "The Sonnet" (1873) 188; Tomlinson, *The Sonnet* (1874) 2.

54. I quote from "Oneness of All" in William Bell Scott's *Outside the Temple* (1875) sonnet sequence, written in the Petrarchan form under the influence of Gabriel (10). Scott's sonnet is one of many examples of the way in which the unity-in-multiplicity of the Petrarchan sonnet was thematized by Victorian sonneteers.

six. *Later Life: A Double of Sonnet of Sonnets* goes even further, asking to be read as a doubled macro-sonnet with an "octave" of sixteen sonnets, and a "sestet" of twelve.

The very terms used by late nineteenth-century sonneteers and reviewers when reflecting on the Petrarchan form—"member of one body," "unity in multiplicity"—tempt comparisons with Rossetti's view of the communion of saints. In *Later Life,* Rossetti makes this suggestive analogy central to the structure of her sequence, inviting the acute "few" (5) to notice that the *volta* between the octave and sestet of the sixteenth sonnet precedes the *volta-of-voltas* in the overarching *Double Sonnet of Sonnets,* the turn from the doubled "octave" of sonnets 1–16 into the doubled "sestet" of sonnets 17–28. In the octave of the sixteenth sonnet, on the brink of this coincidence of divisions, Rossetti teases careful sonnet readers with a message of deepest importance to her: "Our teachers teach that one and one make two: / Later, Love[55] rules that one and one make one: / Abstruse the problems! neither should we shun, / . . . Both [totals are] provable by me, and both by you" (16.1–3, 8). In terms that highlight the irony of a devout woman poet "teach[ing]" in violation of St. Paul's prohibition (Marshall, "'Abstruse the Problems!'" 302–3), Rossetti insinuates that the very structure of her doubled sonnet of sonnets defies the inherited wisdom of "the common run" (6) that "one and one" must always "make two"—that men and women are forever divided into roles of authority and submission, that such hierarchies pertain permanently to the church, that the grave irrevocably divides those on either side of it. "Yield[ing]" this traditional perspective its temporary "due" (4),[56] Rossetti counsels readers to receive her sonnet sequence's multiply split-yet-united structure as a witness to the "rule" of "Love," Christ, who declares that in the final sum "one and one make one" within his communion of saints, which is the focus of sonnets 23–28 in *Later Life*—and in which, to return the phrases of the sonnet critics to their roots in 1 Corinthians 12, each is "a member of one body" (1 Cor. 12:12).

---

55. As Rossetti has clarified earlier in the first line of sonnet 5 in *Later Life,* "Love" (as in *Verses*) stands not only for the theological virtue but also for its source, Christ: "Lord, Thou Thyself art Love" (1).

56. The immediately preceding sonnet opens "Let woman fear to teach and bear to learn" (15.1). As many have noted, Rossetti accepted her Church's (and Victorian society's) traditional distinctions between men's and women's roles (as in her famous letter to August Webster, *Letters* II:158–59), even as she imagined that in the New Jerusalem "woman . . . will be made equal with men and angels; arrayed in all human virtues, and decked with all communicable Divine graces" (*Face of the Deep* 310).

The analogy between the Petrarchan form and the multidimensional communion of saints so cleverly staged in *Later Life* also informs *Verses*. Yet Rossetti maintains the connection in a less heady and ornate fashion, rewarding the trained eye of sonnet aficionados while meeting the desire for devotion among a wider body of readers who might be put off by experiments such as "A Double Sonnet of Sonnets." In *Verses*, Rossetti frequently aligns her handling of the *volta* with the divided-yet-united nature of the community she projects, and with acts of participation in this communion.

With its *volta*, the seventh sonnet in the opening sequence recalls and then faithfully looks past the dividing wall of "Death" through which the speaker must pass before fully communing with "Christ" (1) and his "saints" (7): "[They are] Loving and loved thro' all eternity. / [*volta*] Death is not death, and therefore do I hope" (8–9). In the penultimate sonnet of the introductory sequence, the speaker prays to be unified both with "him who yearns for union yet to be" and with those already assembled in Paradise (6). The *volta* marks the distance of separation—a distance traversed by the speaker's supplicating sigh, which imaginatively fulfills its own request, reaching, by way of shared participation in Christ, the transformed ears of those who have gone ahead. "[Lord, make me] At one with all who throng the crystal sea / And wait the setting of our moons and suns. / [*volta*] *Ah, my beloved ones gone on before*" (16.7–9; emphasis mine), how "beautiful must be your aspects now; / Your unknown, well-known aspects in that light" (12–13).

This theme of Christ as the present link to the future is taken up in the following and final sonnet of the sequence, "Light of Light." Placed just before the division between two sections of *Verses* in the original 1893 printing, this sonnet nonetheless points to the unity "of all lights that be" (4) in "Christ our Light" (1), a thought that looks ahead to the title page of the next section: "Christ Our All in All." By virtue of the sonnet's placement, its second line becomes a prompt to reading as well as an address to Christ: "O Christ our Light, Whom even in darkness we / (*So we look up*) discern and gaze upon" (1–2; emphasis mine). In anticipation of the turn to the title at the top of the next page, this tacit command to a reader's eyes becomes insistent at the turn of the *volta*: ". . . [other lights than Christ are hid in] places higher than man's degree. / [*volta*] Who *looks* on Thee *looks* full on his desire, / Who *looks* on Thee *looks* full on Very Love: / *Looking*, he answers well, 'What lack I yet?'" (8–11; emphasis mine). Negotiating *voltas* and divisions between poems becomes a means of imaginative participation in the communion of saints.

In *Verses,* Rossetti resists the nationalizing tendencies of late-century sonnet critics and anthologists, who often argued that in the Elizabethan period "the sonnet" had been successfully "transplanted" from Italy to Britons' "native land" (Dennis 581), and that there was "no more remarkable sign of" the nation's high cultural "times than the steadily growing public appreciation of the sonnet" (Sharp, *Sonnets of this Century* xxv). In sustaining the Petrarchan sonnet's revival, these critics claimed, sonnet readers were contributing to "the growth of a higher and healthier poetical taste" during a new Elizabethan period of literary glory under Victoria (Russell Part I:406–7). Critics therefore felt compelled to demonstrate that "the form" had "become thoroughly naturalized, and acclimated to our insular severity" (Waddington 182).

By the 1870s, the *English* Petrarchan sonnet was being treated as a crowning jewel in the national cultural treasury[57] and a focal point for anxiety over the prestige and boundaries of the national community entered through study of its form. Commentators frequently used the language of miscegenation and transplantation: if the Petrarchan form was the most "legitimate" (Dennis 581), then Shakespearean and other local island variants had to be defended as nonetheless natural to "English soil" (Noble 471). Crossbreeds, Sharp observed, could "be regarded as English bastards of Italian parentage or as Italian refugees disguised in a semi-insular costume" (*Sonnets of this Century,* lviii). By 1881, Rossetti's friend Theodore Watts-Dunton hit on a novel solution: Victorian adaptations of the Petrarchan sonnet, such as Christina's, could be called the "contemporary English sonnet" ("A Pageant" 328), a national achievement based on wave-like patterns in human emotions and nature whose laws were now being grasped by scientific Englishmen, but which had been intuitively captured by Renaissance Italians in the Petrarchan form.[58] The effort to justify national sonnetry was dogged by the feeling that the Petrarchan form was an "Italian exotic" (Noble 471) whose rhymes and restraints were not fully "consonant with the genius of the English language" (Davies 194).

Rossetti's Italian heritage was well-known to reviewers, and they frequently traced the qualities of her poetry and sonnets to her Italian blood.[59]

---

57. Hence Main's title: *A Treasury of English Sonnets;* note the pointed claim for England made in that title.

58. Watts-Dunton exemplified his views in "The Sonnet's Voice: A Metrical Lesson by the Sea-Shore," published in 1881 in *The Athenaeum.* This sonnet was much-discussed and frequently reprinted, and Sharp and Caine embraced its principles in introductions to their anthologies.

59. This tendency remained strong when critics focused on Rossetti's religious poetry: see Lily Watson for *The Leisure Hour* ("Christina G. Rossetti" 245) and Rossetti's friend Katharine Tynan

She was therefore aware of the national, and nationalist, lens through which her poetry—especially her sonnets—would be read. Prior to *Verses,* she occasionally counted on her public association with Italian exoticness to redirect attention from exclusive nationality to citizenship in the New Jerusalem. In *Pageant,* for example, she included "Italia, Io Ti Saluto! [Italy, I salute you!]," which drew on memories of her 1865 visit to Italy. Returning from Italy, the speaker accepts her loss of the southern "country half my own" (6) to resume duty in her "bleak" northern home (8). Nonetheless, she is vulnerable to recurrent yearning for "the sweet South" (1). The speaker regards her northern abode as the temporary setting in which to fulfill her earthly tasks before the event foretold at every corner by internal and end rhymes: "[I come back to] Where *I* was born, bred, look to *die*; / Come back to do my day's work in its day, / Play out my play— / Amen, amen, say *I*" (2–5; emphasis mine). Rather than exclusively identifying herself with a nation, the speaker locates herself in the tension between the allure of Italy and her obligation to England. Through her chiastic refrain ("Amen, amen, say I. / . . . Amen, I say" [5, 8]), she practices acceptance of daily obedience in response to an implicit divine providence, suggesting her ultimate destination is an unseen and sweeter country for which "out of reach" Italy is only an analogy (10). This suggestion is bolstered by Rossetti's placement of the poem between one obliquely about the Last Judgment ("Pastime") and another about "The mystery of Life, the mystery / Of Death" ("Mirrors of Life and Death" 1–2).

In the sequence of Petrarchan sonnets opening *Verses,* Rossetti develops the analogy implicit in earlier poems between her "southern" heritage and membership in the eternal country of the communion of saints. The seventh sonnet opens with a series of paradoxes: "It is not death, O Christ, to die for Thee: / Nor is that silence of a silent land / Which speaks Thy praise so all may understand" (1–3). As in Psalm 19,[60] the "silence" of the "land," of nature, is portrayed as a universal messenger proclaiming God's glory. Silence is therefore not a sign of absent life, or, ultimately, a "silent land" of the dead, but an echo from a country where "band[s] / Of saints" from every nation gather round Christ and carry "worship" to its highest pitch (6–7). Inspired to "sing / . . . humbl[y]" in concert with this cosmic song (10–11), the speaker culls "offering[s]" from her "heart-field" that recall the

---

for *Bookman* ("The Poetry of Christina Rossetti" 79).

60. "The heavens declare the glory of God; and the firmament sheweth his handiwork. Day unto day uttereth speech, and night unto night sheweth knowledge. There is no speech nor language, where their voice is not heard. Their line is gone out through all the earth, and their words to the end of the world" (19:1–4).

association of Rossetti's sonnets with southern lands (12), even as they turn attention upward, much as the heliotrope follows the sun: "A handful of sun-courting heliotrope, / Of myrrh a bundle, and a little balm" (13–14). The next sonnet, "Lord, grant us eyes to see and ears to hear," reaffirms in a communal voice that true "citizenship" is "where Thy saints appear" (5).

Chambers, in his review of *Verses* for *The Academy* discussed earlier, suggests that Rossetti's special aptitude for "the sonnet" derives from "her Italian blood," as do her "tones of speech . . . which do not belong to our country" and her "intimate sense of spiritual beauty" (163). Even as he returns to conflicted racial vocabulary[61] to describe the sonnet's place in the nation's cultural treasury, Chambers' appreciation for Rossetti's skill as a sonneteer leads him to concentrate his review on her promotion of a supranational community of Christian love. The first poem Chambers discusses—and quotes in full—is the fifth sonnet of the opening sequence, with its international focus on "myriads of earth's myriads" gathered in "reunion" before Christ ("Lord, make us all love all" 2, 4). Catching this sonnet's call to love all in this life in preparation for ultimate "reunion," Chambers declares such "Love is the keynote of Miss Rossetti's book" (163). Indeed, Chambers begins, centers, and concludes his review by fully or partially quoting sonnets from the opening sequence of *Verses*, most of which I have analyzed as central contributions to Rossetti's negotiation between her vision of the community of saints and her sensitivity to late-century sonnet discourses.[62]

Chambers demonstrates Rossetti's wisdom in opening her late-century *Christian Year* with a Petrarchan sonnet sequence. Readers of Chambers' review who were at all interested in the steady wave of sonnets, sonnet sequences, and anthologies still entering the market might well conclude that Rossetti's capacity to construct "a sonnet . . . with infinite art" (163) was reason to follow Chamber's implicit recommendation: "It is with a pride of possession that one puts her new volume upon the shelf, to return to again and again for refreshment" (162). Significantly, Chambers makes this commendation shortly before his first quotation from the introductory sonnet sequence. In the process of approving the volume's passage between the fields of strictly "devotional" and aesthetically treasurable poetry, how-

---

61. Whereas Chambers felt the Italian quality of Rossetti's tones of speech and habits of mind could be described as "a physiological expression of the unique character of her work," he still claims her as an "exotic" part of "English literature" (163).

62. The sonnets quoted, in order, are: "Lord, make us all love all: that when we meet" (pp. 162–63), "Nerve us with patience, Lord, to toil or rest" (163), and "It is not death, O Christ, to die for Thee" (164).

ever, he pauses to reaffirm how unusual the transition is, indicating how much it might have been helped along by Rossetti's decision to advertise that her book had many sonnets. Although "in a sense published before," he remarks, "practically [these verses] are new to lovers of literature, whose attention is not always called to the publications of the S. P. C. K." (162).

If Chambers felt compelled to apologize for "traces of" *The Christian Year* in *Verses*,[63] Lily Watson did not when writing a few months later for the *Sunday at Home*, an evangelical magazine aimed at encouraging Sunday reading among readers of all classes, and reaching an audience perhaps eight times as large as *The Academy*.[64] Yet reflecting, perhaps, the journal's struggle to sustain itself in the challenging market of the 1890s (Lloyd "Sunday at Home"), and to fulfill its mission of reaching readers turned off by dry religious literature (Altholz 55), Watson is careful to present *Verses* as both "highly devout" and aesthetically "choice" enough to have been already "enthusiastically received" (425). She is quick to point out that *Verses* opens with "seventeen exquisite sonnets" and selects as her first—and full—quotation the initial sonnet, "Alone Lord God, in Whom our trust and peace" (426). Indeed, Watson's attention to the enthusiastic reception of *Verses* suggests she has already perused the top opinion-setting literary journals, and she shows clear signs of having read Chambers' earlier review.[65] For a moment, at least, in the words of a sonnet that Chambers and Watson both quoted to capture "the keynote" to the "book" (Chambers 163; L. Watson 426), Rossetti's multidimensional appeal in *Verses* seemed poised to draw, "by different roads from near or far," a wide range of readers into contact with her vision of the community of saints ("Lord, make us all love all" 6).

---

63. "In various ways they are not without traces of their origin [in devotional musings published by the SPCK]. A cycle of verses written, as some of Miss Rossetti's are, to fit the feasts and fasts of the Prayer Book, must needs, one think, want something at times of spontaneity" (162). On the next page, Chambers does his best to brush away those traces, remarking that while Rossetti's religious poetry is of a rare and authentic stamp, "viewed merely as poetry, the *Christian Year* is inconsiderable" (163).

64. *The Academy* started with a circulation of 16,000 in 1869 (Altick 395), and in the economically competitive market of the 1890s, that number is more likely to have sunk than climbed, despite the reduction of the journal's price to a few pennies by 1874 (C. Kent "Academy"). *Sunday at Home*, by contrast, soared to 130,000 by 1865, and even though its sales and circulation declined by 1895, it must have still reached a considerably larger readership than *The Academy* (Lloyd "Sunday at Home").

65. Like Chambers, Watson structures her review around sonnets; quotes and discusses "Lord, make us all love all" (426) and "Whitsun Monday" (427); emphasizes that the "sonnet form" is "adapted to Christina Rossetti's genius" (426); and identifies the "keynote of the whole book" as "Love to God, and love to man" (426).

IV. CONCLUSION: THE "MULTICHORD" HARMONY AND DISSOLUTION OF *VERSES*

Given Rossetti's design of *Verses* for appropriation by multiple audiences (and editors), Watson's concluding remark in *Sunday at Home* is perceptive, and might be addressed to editors as well as readers: "Christians of all shades of faith will find here something that they can appropriate as the utterance of their own heart" (428). Watson demonstrates her own advice, highlighting passages that permit an evangelical emphasis upon individual salvation and personal devotion: "the poems are utterances of intense devotion; the devotion of a ransomed soul clearly apprehending its own guilt and nothingness, clinging to the Saviour" (426). Injecting the poem under discussion[66] with her own sense of evangelical melodrama, Watson nonetheless showcases the multivalent nature of Rossetti's language in *Verses*: faithful to Rossetti's Anglo-Catholicism, it is appropriable by a range of denominations. This quality accords with Rossetti's assumption that even in "heaven" (9) the song of the saints is "multichord" in tone ("Tremble, thou earth, at the Presence of the Lord" 8).

In "Christ Our All in All," a section whose heading identifies Christ as the source of plenitude for the cosmos, the Church, and the future world,[67] and under a subheading emphasizing unexpected conversion to Christ,[68] Rossetti places a poem ecumenical in tone. "Lord, grant us grace to mount by steps of grace" is a communal supplication to Christ to "Call us . . . home" through life's difficult pilgrimage (21). The second line contains a telling, and unrepeated, shift from the plural to the singular first person:

> Lord, grant us grace to mount by steps of grace
>   From grace to grace nearer, my God, to Thee;
>   Not tarrying for tomorrow,

---

66. "O Lord, when Thou didst call me, didst Thou know" from the "Christ Our All in All" section.

67. Consider the title's scriptural resonances: "[Having raised Christ from the dead, God exalted him] above all principality, and power, and might, and dominion, and every name that is named, not only in this world but also in that which is to come: and hath put all things under his feet, and gave him to be the head over all things to the church, which is his body, the fullness of him that filleth all in all" (Eph. 1:22–23). "[By Christ] were all things created," and "by him all things consist. And he is the head of the church" (Col. 1:15, 17, 18).

68. The subheading is "And now why tarriest thou?"—from Paul's account of his conversion from persecuting to joining Christians, a transformation he completed by responding to Ananais' call to be baptized: "And now why tarriest thou? arise and be baptised, and wash away thy sins, calling on the name of the Lord" (Acts 22:16).

> Lest we lie down in sorrow,
>   And never see
> Unveiled Thy Face. (1–6)

"Nearer, my God, to Thee" is the refrain of Sarah Flower Adams' hymn by that title, first published in the Unitarian *Hymns and Anthems* (1841). Also portraying life as a hard journey to nearness with God, Adams' hymn had been altered into more orthodox shape by later editors and achieved enough popularity to be selected by the band as the *Titanic* sank in 1912 (Blain "Sarah Flower Adams"). Nonetheless, Adams' Unitarianism might have been a deciding factor in the exclusion of her work from a representative anthology of nineteenth-century women's hymns, *Lady Hymn-Writers* (1892) (J. R. Watson 423, 429), published the same year that Rossetti published the poem above in *Face of the Deep*. There Rossetti placed the poem only a few pages (298–99) before she made the ecumenical appeal I discussed earlier in this chapter, where she encouraged Anglicans to absorb "every virtue from every" body of the universal Church while "holding fast" to their "own goodly heritage of gifts and graces," until "to every Church, congregation, soul, God be All in all" (302).

"Lord, grant us grace" appears to be Rossetti's effort to model such ecumenical receptivity through the diction and texture of her poetry. By incorporating Adams' line into her own poetic supplication, Rossetti engages a tradition of Dissenting hymn singing at odds with, and arguably more democratic than, Anglo-Catholic choral services that she attended in London, in which priests and all-male choirs, surpliced and set apart in a chancel, led congregants through hymns and the sung liturgy. In absorbing this Nonconformist influence, Rossetti is also extending the implicit critique noticed by Dieleman throughout *Verses* of the gap between Anglo-Catholic celebration of the communion of saints and the stratification that ritualism introduced into Anglican worship (134). Perhaps because of its hybrid nature, Rossetti's poem was not only set to music by the choir director at her ritualist church and sung at her funeral (Ives 280–81) but also later adopted in interdenominational hymnals (252).

Rossetti includes Adams' Unitarian hymn in her multichord harmony, allowing it to bear critically on the stratification within her Anglo-Catholic worshipping community. Yet she thereby turns the focus of Adams' lines in an Anglican and Trinitarian direction. This becomes clearer by turning to a stanza in Adams' poem from which Rossetti borrows her opening imagery ("grant us grace to mount by steps of grace"). Here Adams alludes to the ladder seen by Jacob in his dream (Gen. 28:11–17):

There let the way appear,
>   Steps unto heaven;
All that thou send'st to me,
>   In mercy given:
Angels to beckon me
Nearer, my God, to thee—
>   Nearer to thee! (Adams 15–21; *Hymns and Anthems*)

As here, Adams pares down each of her stanzas to a half-line that accentuates her request for proximity to God ("Nearer my God, to thee— / *Nearer to thee!*"; emphasis mine), even as that half-line's concentrated and intimate form, always prefaced by a separating dash, anticipates the desired passage from longing imperative ("[Let me be] Nearer to thee!") to fulfilled indicative ("[I am] Nearer to thee!"). In the opening stanza, Rossetti catches up Adams' individually voiced hymn ("nearer, my God, to Thee") in an otherwise communal supplication reminiscent of collects in Anglican worship ("Lord, grant us grace"), and points the narrowing lines of her stanzas not only to God in general, but to Christ in particular, in anticipation of the day when he will be beheld with "Unveiled . . . Face" (6). Given the section's heading ("Christ our All in All"), Rossetti's final lines make this shift in focus unavoidable and locate it within her vision of the communion of saints: "Call us too [as you have the saints gone on ahead] home from sorrow / To rest in Thee tomorrow; / In Thee our Best, / In Thee our All" (21–24). The third stanza recalls Jesus' words at the feeding of the four thousand,[69] quietly affirming Rossetti's conviction that Christ is encountered in the communion meal, and yet implying hope for inclusion of all who, such as Adams, might in Rossetti's view come to Christ "from far": "Lord, strengthen us; lest fainting by the way / We come not to Thee, we who come from far" (13–14).

Except for scanty allusions to Anglo-Catholic church architecture and devotion,[70] in *Verses* Rossetti uses language that can resonate with a variety of Christian perspectives even as it retains her own and prioritizes her

---

69. "[Jesus told his disciples] I have compassion on the multitude, because they have now been with me three days, and having nothing to eat: and if I send them away fasting to their own houses, they will faint by the way: for divers of them came from far" (Mark 8:2–3).

70. "Earth has clear call of daily bells" compares the sky to "A chancel-vault of gloom and star" (2), and "Love understands the mystery, whereof" refers to the act of "Silently telling" a "bead-history" (9), a reference to praying with a rosary. Yet the first poem was composed in 1858 (*CP* 1026), when Rossetti was much more actively involved in ritualist publications (see chapter 6 of Blair's *Form and Faith*); and the second appears under the ecumenical subheading "Judge nothing before the time."

focus on the communion of saints. This is true even of a poem Mason has cited to support her interpretation of the collection as a "handbook of ritualist ceremony" (123), "All Saints," where Rossetti describes the ascent of saints from earth to Paradise: "Lo! Like a stream of incense launched on flame / Fresh Saints stream up from death to life above" (9–10). A fellow parishioner of Rossetti at Christ Church Woburn would readily conclude with Mason that the "saints spread their incense-filled haze around so that heaven begins to resemble the intense interiors of Christ Church" (126). Yet evangelical readers could just as easily connect the imagery to passages in the New Testament that endorse offering up oneself as a living sacrifice to God (Rom. 12:1), compare Christ's crucifixion to "sweetsmelling" incense (Eph. 5:2), and liken "the prayers of God's people" to "smoke of the incense" streaming up to God in heaven from "a golden censer" (Rev. 8:3–4).

For this reason, the *Wesleyan Methodist Magazine,* noted for its conservative evangelicalism and reaching a wide denominational audience, could shortly after Rossetti's death focus with approval on "Christina Rossetti and Her Message," observing that "'Verses'" had "largely" increased an "audience" for her poetry that was "not yet nearly so wide as it ought to be" (Smellie 203). Focusing almost exclusively on *Verses,* the reviewer catches Rossetti's "constant picture of the Christian on earth" as a "pilgrim" (205), as well as the communal and ecumenical emphasis of this estranging hope, giving it a slightly evangelical twist: "across all boundaries of time and creed," she belongs "to the Church, catholic and eternal, which glories in the cross, and in Him who hastened to it for the joy of redeeming us" (204).

Yet Rossetti's appropriable language in *Verses* probably contributed to the process by which her editors helped ensure the volume's retreat from the public eye and its total disappearance after the last SPCK edition in 1925. This 1925 edition notes that "21,000 *copies*" were "*[p]rinted to 1912.*" The title page of the 1898 *Verses* advertises itself as the "Twentieth Thousand" printing, which suggests that only 1,000 copies had been printed between 1898 and 1912, even though 20,000 were issued between 1893 and 1898. Reviewing Rossetti's life and poetry shortly after her death in December 1894, the High Church *Guardian* newspaper indicates the likely reason for this decline. While, as expected, the *Guardian* reviewer praises the devotional poetry of *Verses,* he nonetheless says "the more studied [collected] *Poems* [of 1890] reduces" the SPCK's volume "to comparative unimportance" ("Christina Rossetti" 51). The critic demonstrates the tendency of many late-Victorian readers to prefer collected anthologies of a poet's work over individual volumes (Erickson 354). According to the *Guardian* critic, the Macmillan edition had already been reprinted "five times" when his review appeared (51), meaning that it had kept pace with *Verses*. The next year, Christina's brother William Michael Rossetti helped ensure the decline in demand for *Verses* with his competing edition of *New Poems by Christina Rossetti, Hitherto Unpublished or Collected* (Macmillan 1896).

After 1898, interest in *Verses* as a single volume seems to have subsided, since no further printings were made until 1904. At that point, after granting permission to William to include the poems from *Verses* in his edition of *The Poetical Works of Christina Georgina Rossetti* (Macmillan 1904), the SPCK reprinted *Verses* itself, apparently hoping to ride the renewed attention its poems might gain through *Poetical Works* (Ives 128). Yet in his preface to *Poetical Works,* William asserted that *Verses* lacked "any very definite plan" (vi), and he reinforced the misimpression through his own severely scrambled and tenuous rearrangement of *Verses* in *Poetical Works* (D. Kent, "W. M. Rossetti" 19–21). This, combined with William's claim that *Verses* contained "many of" Rossetti's "finest devotional poems" (v), no doubt encouraged readers to feel that poems originally combined in *Verses* could be best appreciated in *Poetical Works* without wasting money on the supposedly shoddily arranged SPCK volume. The SPCK did not bring *Verses* out again until 1912. The competing efforts of Rossetti's publishers helped drive *Verses* out of public notice even as they ensured its poems were reprinted in new venues.

Indeed, Rossetti probably aided this disappearing act by so successfully making the poems in *Verses* appeal to multiple markets through her opening sonnet sequence, grouping of poems in categories that could attract editors, and use of ecumenical, appropriable language.[71] This multipronged strategy might have also played into widespread turn-of-the-century portrayals of Rossetti's devotional poetry as the mystical outpourings of a cloistered spirit. In the 1890s, reviewers and commentators for the general market tended to regard *Verses* as a loose anthology, treating poems as isolated, artful revelations of Rossetti's innermost soul.[72] For a number of review-

---

71. Kegan Paul might have been encouraged to include poems from *Time Flies* (also in *Verses*) in the 1893 edition of *Living English Poets* because of the initial success of *Verses* (Ives 221); several poems from *Verses* also appeared in hymnals, one—*Church Hymns with Tunes* (1893)—produced by the SPCK (Ives 253), and another for a general press, the University of Glasgow (*Hymns of Faith and Life* [1896]) (Ives 252). During the same period, as noted above, Rossetti's sonnets from *Verses* were circulating through the general and religious press.

72. The 1893 *Athenaeum* reviewer of *Verses* characterized the poems as short, artfully finished "noting[s] of the sensations of the soul" (842), disregarding the international and ecumenical vision of Rossetti's collection: "It is herself, really, that she puts into these poems, her deepest self;

ers, Rossetti's exquisite expression of her deep religious feelings confirmed, in ways consonant with the persistent view of women as uncritically and essentially religious, an inherent spiritual dimension of humanity of the kind promoted by the Victorian cult of poetry.[73]

As Lootens has argued, by the turn of the century Rossetti's poetry was being diluted of its "religious struggles" and "ambitions" to become the watery, quasi-sacred confessions of a resigned virgin saint (182). Even critics for religious periodicals tended to portray her devotional poetry as the work of "a chaste and nun-like spirit," losing sight of Rossetti's vision of the community of saints (Kenyon 750). It quickly became an established *topos* among reviewers and editors of all stripes to liken the saintly Rossetti to images of the young Virgin modeled upon her in Gabriel's paintings of *The Girlhood of Mary Virgin* (1849) and *Ecce Ancilla Domini!* (1853).[74] In

---

and they give adequate expression to that, to the real self" (843). Arthur Symons, in his essay on Christina Rossetti for Alfred H. Miles' landmark *The Poets and Poetry of This Century* (1892), later reprinted as *The Poets and the Poetry of the Nineteenth-Century* (1907; edition cited here), came to a similar conclusion: "In all these poems we are led through phase after phase of a devout soul; we find a sequence of keen and brooding moods of religious feeling and meditation, every word burningly real and from the heart, yet in every word subjected to the keenest artistic scrutiny" (8–9).

73. Theodore Watts-Dunton opens his "Reminiscences of Christina Rossetti" for *The Nineteenth Century* by positioning himself as an authoritative hagiographer and apostle of a poetic gospel: "the time will come—it *must* come—when every authoritative word about one so beloved, every scrap of testimony from every witness, howsoever unworthy, will be accounted sacred by those to whom poetry is almost a religion" (355). Yet he contains and feminizes the devotional quality of her poetry by emphasizing her "sweet" womanly "sainthood" (355), describing the effects of her poetry on him as a kind of return to the spiritual womb: "It seemed to me to come from a power which my soul remembered in some ante-natal existence" (357).

74. Katharine Tynan, a late friend of Rossetti, in a review for *The Bookman* shortly after *Verses* appeared, says that the young Rossetti "lives for us in 'The Girlhood of Mary,'" and she turns the painting into a prophecy of the poet's life: "her mournful face, as of one pre-sanctified, pre-destined to great honour and a sorrow greater than all sorrows. The face of the 'blessed Mary, pre-elect'" whose later poems "are the poetry of a saint, with the yearnings of an exile" (78). Later comparisons with the picture include Sharp's in 1895 reminiscences for *The Atlantic Monthly* (749) and Watson's in the 1895 evangelical *The Leisure Hour* (245). William Michael Rossetti probably cemented the connection with his preface to *New Poems* (1896), where he includes as a frontispiece a pencil drawing by Gabriel of Christina when she was around 18, suggesting that it was "a slight study preliminary to the picture *Ecce Ancilla Domini* (National Gallery)" (xiii). The pencil drawing reappeared as the frontispiece of *Poetical Works*. Canonization of Rossetti as a domesticated virgin saint seems to be complete in the 1896 *London Quarterly Review*, a Wesleyan Methodist periodical. The article, reviewing *New Poems* and *Verses*, recalls William's note about the pencil sketch of Christina, and then describes this drawing itself, not the paintings, in saintly terms: "The lovely head, inclined a little forward, has such a mild inquiring eagerness in its full earnest eye and delicately parted lips as might beseem a fair young seraph, 'desiring to look into' the great mystery of God manifested in the flesh. Nothing could better symbolize the life-long attitude of Christina Rossetti, as revealed in the poems with which she continued to enrich English literature during more than forty years" (9–10).

an effort to reach different strands of the market with fresh arrangements of the same stock of poetry, between 1895 and 1932 the SPCK published specialty collections drawn from different sections of *Verses* (e.g., *Gifts and Graces* in 1911), along with appreciations of Rossetti's devotional poetry (D. Kent "W. M. Rossetti" 19; Kooistra 172–85). Many of these publications reprinted Gabriel's paintings and repeated the association of Rossetti with domesticated sainthood (Kooistra 173–76). One of the more egregious examples occurs in the final 1925 SPCK reprinting of *Verses*, where Gabriel's painting is included as the frontispiece but mistitled "The Girlhood of the Virgin," as if the picture were transparently about Christina's by-now-familiar status as a sweet "saintly soul" (Clarke "Introduction"). Even as W. K. Lowther Clarke, secretary of the SPCK, continues this marketing tradition in his introduction to the volume, he concedes its limited appeal.[75] He portrays the collection as a "cheap" specialty product for "the religious public," and gives only vague and token attention to its "unity of purpose" before seeking to renew its lease on life by inviting pillaging: "Many of the poems alluded to above are sought after by makers of anthologies" ("Introduction").

Many of its reviewers and editors, whether aiming at religious or general audiences, converged in underplaying Rossetti's attempt in *Verses* to bring readers into an imagined Christian community that transcended ecclesiastical and national boundaries. They overplayed the degree to which the volume could be treated as a collection of isolated spiritual expressions. Taken together, these forms of evaluation and repackaging unraveled the communal organization of Rossetti's *Verses* in ways that affirmed existing partitions between "devotional" and "general" reading publics; contributed to a hazy survival of the national cult of poetry; and facilitated fresh efforts to tap specialized audiences.

Rossetti's ecumenical and international project in *Verses* was from this angle a partial defeat. Its structure and reception bear exceptionally sensitive witness to the sheer multiplicity of attempts to conceive and address readerships by the century's end, as well as the growing estrangement between deeply Christian and vaguely spiritual and nationalistic visions of communities entered while reading. Yet, as I have argued, Rossetti would not have

---

75. Clarke had reason to think so. Already by 1898, a critic for *The Athenaeum* indicated that the minor cult of santa Christina had alienated a rising literary generation from *Verses* and her other devotional works: "to the younger generation, at least, her early work is her best, and we would gladly exchange the whole of her 'sacred prose' and nine-tenths of her religious verse for one more poem like 'Venus' Looking Glass'" ("Christina Rossetti: a Biographical and Critical Study" 109).

been surprised that her last and most popular volume of poetry experienced this degree of reorganization, reinterpretation, and redistribution. Had she lived to witness the fate of *Verses,* she might have appreciated the fact that so many reviewers, editors, and anthologizers outside Anglicanism could, at least for a time, and however partially, respond to her "multichord" song of "a better country."

CONCLUSION

THE END OF PRINT-MEDIATED CHRISTIAN BRITAIN AND THE RISE OF DIGITAL SPIRITUAL COMMUNITIES

Between the 1820s and 1890s, I have argued, several forces interacted in British national life with an intensity unparalleled before or after: a voluntary religious market emerged even as print became a dominant medium by which an increasing number of people charted their daily lives in secular time and imagined themselves in a national community that provided the context for their actions. Rather than an inherently secularizing phenomenon, this print-mediated form of national imagination was powerfully shaped by competing efforts to imagine the nation as a Christian community and the place of one's own religious group within that collective. As Christian agencies and authors fought for audiences and swelled the daily tide of print, readers became adept at imagining themselves in or between far-flung spiritual communities shared with strangers who were simultaneously navigating life in a British nation and empire densely interconnected by the circulating printed page. Generated by, and generating, this uniquely modern form of religious and national imagination were new rhetorical strategies, theories and theologies of reading, journalistic tropes, poetic genres, and vast schemes for educational and ecclesiastical reform. The activity was prodigious and far-reaching, from Samuel Taylor Coleridge's print-mediated seminars with future members of the clerisy; to Frederick Denison Maurice's social theology of media and schemes for converting newspapers and periodicals into platforms for imagining British Christian unity; to Matthew Arnold's faith in a poetic National Church to give ethical cohesion to an emerging mass-mediated democracy; to John Keble's transformation of a poetic cycle into a means of participating in a virtual congregation, and the many reinterpretations and reformations of his model within journalistic commentary and later poetic cycles by poets such as Alfred Tennyson and Christina Rossetti.

Rossetti's *Verses* (1893), the most innovative late adaptation of Keble's poetic paradigm, anticipates in its design and fate the late-century dilution and twentieth-century dissolution of these forms of imagined British Christian community. As discussed in chapter 7, Rossetti adroitly deployed the arrangement, poetic forms, and multivalent language of *Verses* to appeal to diverse reading audiences and methods of periodical reviewing, advertising, and publishing that mediated poetry to an increasingly differentiated late-Victorian print and religious market. Rossetti's attempt to draw the divergent paths of publishers, editors, critics, and readers into contact with her ecumenical and international vision of the communion of saints ultimately made it all the easier for poems in *Verses,* soon after its successful publication, to be extracted, reinterpreted, and repackaged in ways that reaffirmed existing divisions between "devotional" and "general" reading audiences, and between distinct religious readerships. The fate of *Verses* is more than an intriguing irony. It indicates the late nineteenth-century diversity of Christian identity and the rising interest in other religious expressions, such as spiritualism, forms of Eastern religion, and theosophy (S. Brown 381); the manifestations of this diversifying religiosity in print (McKelvy, *The English Cult of Literature* 256–64);[1] and the need of publishers of "general" literature, such as Macmillan's, to distinguish themselves from any single religious audience in order to reach an ideologically-dispersed middle-class readership (Altholz 92; P. Scott, "The business of belief" 214).

---

1. Several figures important to my narrative in this book directly contributed to late-century alternative religious expressions and their bibliographic manifestations. The eccentric Protestant journalist W. T. Stead, discussed in chapter 7, began in the 1890s to mix his evangelicalism with spiritualism, automatic writing, and collaboration with mediums. In 1895, he founded a journal, *Borderland,* to spread awareness of spiritualism (S. Brown 384). William Sharp, a friend of the Rossettis mentioned in chapter 7, participated in revived interest in Britain's pre-Christian myths and legends, founding the *Pagan Review* in 1892 (S. Brown 389). Henry Sidgwick, the theistic but skeptical Cambridge philosopher discussed in chapter 5, hoped that systematic analysis of spiritualism would provide incontrovertible evidence for belief in an intelligent higher power and personal immortality—the "minimum of faith" he praised Tennyson for defending in *In Memoriam.* In 1882, he joined other intellectuals in founding the Society for Psychical Research (still active), which sponsored studies and conducted a scholarly journal on telepathy, hypnotism, spiritualism, and automatic writing (S. Brown 390).

While the large majority of late-century Britons remained within the Christian tradition (S. Brown 381), tensions were also developing between Christian and imperial nationalist forms of imagined community. Most British Christians continued to view the empire as God's means to "diffuse Christianity, commerce and civilisation" to supposedly less advanced and unenlightened races (323): in the 1890s, enthusiasm surged for both missions (432) and empire, especially during celebrations of Queen Victoria's Diamond Jubilee in 1897 (434). Yet missionaries and their supporters at home had consistently been among the most articulate critics of aggressive imperialism (Carey 14), and after the late 1870s there were, especially among Nonconformists, occasional public demonstrations and printed protests against the sacrifice of Christian morality to militaristic and economic expansionism (S. Brown 298). By 1904, reports on use of concentration camps in the Second Boer War (1899–1902), murder and mutilation in the Congo rubber trade, and virtual slave labor in South African mines were compelling Christians across denominations to question the sanctity of British imperialism (436–37). Rossetti's rejection of giddy imperialism and invocation of an international and ecumenical Christian community in *Verses,* then, was not wholly against the grain, and it was in sympathy with ecumenical world missionary conferences and international denominational alliances that were proliferating among British and North American Protestants by the late 1880s. These partnerships, and their networks of publication and communication, marked the "emergence" of "world churches [that] had grown beyond their British and colonial roots" (Carey 372).

This international networking facilitated imagination of global Christian communities at a critical distance from nationalist or imperialist ones, as demonstrated by the 1910 World Missionary conference in Edinburgh, at which an ecumenical and international body of Protestant delegates condemned the economic exploitation and human oppression of Western imperialism; began to confess racial discrimination within their own missionary societies; and demonstrated new respect for other religions. The interdenominational cooperation and desire for Christian unity emerging from this and related conferences sowed the seeds that would produce the World Council of Churches in 1948 (S. Brown 439–40). As the new century progressed, "all the British churches would become detached from both their national origins, and their transitory connection with the British World, and become part of world Christianities, putting aside their imperial past as rapidly as possible" (Carey 374).

Taken together, diversification of Britain's religious and print market, and the growing willingness of British churches and missionary societies to look to the world rather than Britain for Christian union, diluted the bond between active Christian allegiance and British national imagination. This dilution of Christian Britain is connected to its rapid dissolution after the 1960s. As I have argued throughout this book, a century unmatched in churchgoing and growth of voluntary religious organizations (C. Brown 9, 45–57) was also the century in which it became easier to conceive of participation in Christian community as a virtual act that did not require being at church. Especially after the 1820s, discourses of Christian identity and membership circulated and competed in print on a scale never before or after matched (C. Brown 39), and the paradoxical long-term result was that many Britons became accustomed to imagining and symbolically asserting their Christian allegiance in place of regularly practicing it in worship. Church attendance probably reached an historic peak by mid-century, at around 50 percent, with noticeable decline after 1880[2] and a steeper fall after 1940, even as basic affiliation with a church body grew continuously from 1800 and peaked at 19.3 percent in 1910 (C. Brown 162–63). By the 1950s, respectable connection with a church had reached a new high even as few adults frequented one: in Scotland, whose situation Callum Brown suggests is representative of Britain at this time, at least "44 per cent of" people "had a church affiliation (including Sunday school enrolments), but only about 12 per cent of the people attended church on a given Sunday" (166).

In other words, after the 1880s maintaining a symbolic yet passive bond to a church remained important for many Britons, and rites of passage such as baptism experienced growth during the first four decades of the twentieth century (C. Brown 166)—yet the pews continued to empty. Christianity exercised wide, if diluted, discursive power through the 1950s, as evidenced by massive participation in Bill Graham's evangelistic crusades (173). Families' links to churches, however, depended in large part on women, who were still expected to uphold ideals of female piety and domesticity inherited from the nineteenth century. As church attendance by adult males declined at the turn of the century, women made up around two-thirds of those who attended services (S. Brown 400). When, with the revolution in youth culture beginning around 1958, this domestic ideology began to crumble, so did the public force and practice of Christianity (C. Brown 179), with most "indices of religiosity in Britain" entering a "free fall" after 1963 (188) and generations growing up after the 1960s

---

2. The crucial decade for decline in church attendance seems to have been the 1890s. Available evidence shows decline for several areas of Britain from around 45 percent in 1851 to around 25 percent by 1913 (S. Brown 399).

increasingly perceiving Christianity as out of touch with their ethical concerns and daily lives (190).

If, then, Christian Britain was vanishing by the 1960s, *print*-mediated Christian Britain had already begun to unravel seriously by the 1920s—a development foreshadowed by the aims and diversified reception of Rossetti's *Verses* in the 1890s. In the 1920s, print was being displaced as a primary medium of national imagination and virtual religious community, even though there was (and still is) a rise in the quantity of printed material produced and consumed (Weedon 54). The telecommunications revolution that has since reshaped the modern world had already been faintly predicted by use of telegraphy in message sending and printed news since the 1850s (Roberts). The telephone was also beginning to become a familiar (if still rare) oddity by the 1890s; by 1912 a unified telephone system would be available throughout most of Britain, increasingly replacing the simultaneity imagined and approximated through print and telegraphy with an audible exchange in present time (Freshwater). A communications revolution Walter Ong has called the "second orality" was well underway (11).

The explosion in broadcasting after the First World War soon spurred formation of the BBC, which became a public corporation in 1926 and helped transform radio waves into a dominant medium of national imagination. That same year the BBC formed the Central Religious Advisory Committee (CRAC), which ruled out competition between religious groups invited to broadcast (Briggs 270) and through the 1950s limited expression to a supposedly nonsectarian and "mainstream" Christianity (273). BBC officials often imagined diffusion of this national Christianity in deliberately non-ecclesiastical terms, with the founding General-Director John Reith remarking that attendance at Church was desirable but dispensable (275), and R. J. E. Silver, the Head of Audience Research, proudly declaring in 1956 that the BBC's religious programming brought Christian teaching and worship to one-half of the people who declared themselves non-church-goers (269). Attuned to the changes in Britain's religious environment described above, in 1965 Director-General Hugh Greene departed from earlier BBC directors by declining to portray the BBC as an agency that catered to a Christian country and Christian values; in 1977 the CRAC recognized that Britain was a country of multiple religious traditions and described its mission as the broad presentation of "beliefs, ideas, issues, and experiences in the contemporary world . . . related to a religious interpretation or dimension of life" (280). By the 1960s, the combined influence of television and radio-broadcast pop music were enabling a youth counterculture in Britain that was beginning to reject many of the values sustained in the print-mediated Christian Britain of days past (C. Brown 178–79).

Rossetti's attempt to network the divergent paths of late-Victorian readers into an imagined international and ecumenical community distantly prefigures a phenomenon new to this millennium, the "virtual ekklesia," or "online congregation," that has "no geographic existence" and is constituted by the aggregate activity of Internet users (Howard 13). Religious community is moving online (Howard 21), with, for example, 64 percent of Americans using the Web for religious or spiritual matters in 2004 (Hoover, Clark, and Rainie i), and "one-in-five Americans" shared "their religious faith online" in "an average week" in 2014 ("Religion and Electronic Media" 1). In concluding, I want to suggest how the story told by *Imagined Spiritual Communities in Britain's Age of Print* remains relevant to our Internet age long after the nineteenth-century world concerned has faded into the texts by which it was mediated—many of which have been remediated to me through digital databases. While, in keeping with the focus of my study, I highlight Christian "virtual ekklesia" emanating from the English-speaking North-Atlantic world, I do not believe these developments are more deserving of attention than the myriad forms of online spiritual community emerging around the world. My observations, for example, could be differently applied to, and are in fact partly drawn from, scholarship on the way the Internet is transforming Islamic imagined communities (Turner 150–51).

Both online imagined spiritual communities and the print-mediated ones I discuss are constituted by replacing locations with distributed media. Coleridge performs this substitution when addressing the reader of *Aids to Reflection* (1825) as if they are in a seminar on spiritual reflection: "we are in the silent school of Reflection" (*AR [CC]* 84). Though Coleridge invites his reader to imagine the "remediation" (Bolter and Grusin 273), or representation and refashioning, of voice and place in the printed word, his paradox of "silent" communication pushes this illusion of immediacy into "hypermediacy" (19), awareness of the medium—print—that takes the place of place in order for the imagined encounter to occur.

Similarly, to take place online spiritual communities need their media to take place away. *Reddit* is a massive social-networking website to which registered community members, or "redditers," post comments, links, images, and other content and then vote entries "up" or "down" to determine their position on the site's pages. The site's lexicon foregrounds its user-generated nature—readers are editors—and its "redditers" can create "subreddits," or smaller interest-based subscriber communities. The nearly

100,000 subscribers to the "Christianity" subreddit submit prayer requests, seek spiritual and life counsel, share their faith, post and discuss innumerable items related to Christianity from around the Web, and, if they wish, supplement such asynchronous posting with synchronous communication in linked chat forums. With user icons and comments indicating they represent places from around the world and perspectives within and without Christianity, these redditers imagine themselves in a diversely shared community by remediating acts formerly confined to churches, homes, and other shared locations in a virtual forum whose evolving content—itself remediated from every corner of the virtual globe—*is* the place they gather. At any moment, a redditer can glance at a sidebar to see how many virtual "neighbors are here now" ("Christianity"); beneath this post is a list of related, often more specific, subreddits (e.g., "RadicalChristianity") into which one might move. The virtual community of the "Christianity" subreddit, whose only location is a global medium, recalls Christina Rossetti's late-Victorian vision of a host of "multi-fashioned saints" participating in an international community that transcends any single national or institutional space ("Behold, it was very good" 6).

Keble inspired many competing dreams of communal (if not always international) worship in a virtual church when he invited readers of *The Christian Year* (1827) to confuse private acts of reading with shared liturgical acts in a service—"And now before the choir we pause" ("Trinity Sunday" 21). Virtual churches abound on the Internet, with the website for Andy Stanley's nondenominational evangelical North Point Community Church in Atlanta offering not only popular podcasts of his sermons but also live streaming of services through *NorthPointOnline.TV* so that "you can connect with a local church—no matter where you are" (*NorthPointOnline.TV*). North Point is part of a global network of churches, and its ministry model is paralleled by another nondenominational church-based virtual community and global network, *LifeChurch.TV,* which also broadcasts "live" worship services and other "online experience[s]" (*LifeChurch.TV*). These institutionally backed virtual ecclesiae exemplify "religion online," an extension of offline religious activity into digital networks (Fitzgerald 122). Their synchronous global services are meant not only to reach those unable or unwilling to enter physical churches but also to draw the unaffiliated to locations in their church networks.

As their explicit analogies to TV and broadcasting indicate, these nondenominational evangelical initiatives largely remediate the strategies of radio and televangelists into the world of digital social networking, and they maintain at least notional connections between their virtual global communities and ones bound by brick-and-mortar churches. In this second quality, they distantly resemble attempts by nineteenth-century Anglicans such as Keble to extend site-based worship into a world of circulating texts that was quickly eluding any form of comprehensive religious institutional control, in the hope that virtual approximations of liturgical practices in volumes such as *The Christian Year* might not only reshape private reading but also guide Britons back to the buildings of their national church. Yet, as shown by the reception history of Keble and his poetic model that I provide in chapters 4 through 7, the nineteenth-century print-mediated virtual church could quickly circulate, and be reimagined, without any necessary link to location. In this way it anticipates not only "religion online" but also "online religion," the use of online networking to create new and wholly digital spiritual interactions (Fitzgerald 122). A new phenomenon in religious history—congregations whose members use digital bodies to engage in "real-time" worship in digital spaces—is multiplying on Second Life, a massively multiplayer online (MMO) environment in which members assume digital avatars who communicate by text and voice in an enormous virtual world where they build homes, do business, have sex, and attend all sorts of user-generated venues, including churches. Although Facebook has displaced Second Life as a global networking tool, as of 2013 the virtual world had 36 million registered citizens (Reahard).

Among Second Life's many virtual churches, mosques, temples, and spiritual centers, *The Anglican Cathedral of Second Life* holds "live" Sunday worship, daily prayer, social events, and bible studies. Already, in ways that recall Maurice's development of a theology of media in which even newspaper advertisements acquired a nearly sacramental quality, *The Anglican Cathedral of Second Life* is being pushed by its medium into new theological territory. Its presiding bishop recently issued a paper on virtual sacraments, in which he argued that Baptism and Holy Communion cannot be practiced online, but they can be commemorated and spiritually received there ("Sacraments on Epiphany Island").

These developments of religion online and online religion recall and remediate strategies pursued in print by authors in this book, and the imagined communities sustained in Britain's printed age and our Internet age both take away place to take place. Not surprisingly, tensions marking Britain's print-mediated spiritual communities also define today's global and digitally mediated ones. The first of these is a conflicted relationship between institutional religious authority and what Robert Glenn Howard calls "vernacular authority" in his study of online Christian fundamentalist community—authority generated within an imagined social entity not by an institution or centralized leadership, but by the repeated choices of lay believers to connect through media and the "larger shared volition" that this connection creates (7, 18–21).

All of the authors and their respondents studied in this book acted within the ambiguous space created between institutional and vernacular authority by Britain's print networks. If Keble, as Anglican priest and poet, sought to reclaim the authority of his Church over British readers' imaginations, he did so through a poetic medium and system of distribution and evaluation that exceeded his Church's control. As the century progressed, Anglicans opposed to Keble's Tractarian principles, Nonconformists, and Roman Catholics used journalistic commentary on *The Christian Year*, adoption of it in worship services or routines of reading, and appropriations of its poetic paradigm to further their competing visions of spiritual and national community in a cluttered religious marketplace. In revising and redistributing Keble's model, Tennyson and Rossetti similarly offered an authority and medium for imagining spiritual community over which no single church could claim supervision. Coleridge, Maurice, and Arnold publicized visions of institutional reform and strategies of interpretation meant to defend a leading role for the Church of England in the reading nation. Yet they each did so by invoking and partially creating, through their activity and influence, versions of an intellectual clerisy that was within and beyond that Church. When Arnold, in his 1876 address on "The Church of England" to Anglican clergy at Sion College in London, exhorted his audience to transform themselves into "a great national society for the promotion of . . . *goodness*" (CPW VIII:65), his endorsement of their authority rested on his own vernacular authority as a widely publicized and controversial commentator on the Church and society.

If *LifeChurch.TV* seeks to extend institutional church authority into the virtual world, it simultaneously assumes and empowers the vernacular authority of Internet users who may or may not find its solicitation effective. *The Anglican Cathedral of Second Life* now "works under the authority of Bishop Christopher Hill of Guildford, England," yet it is shepherded by a part-time teacher and Anglican lay pastor along with an interdenominational and international body of lay volunteers ("The Leadership Team"). Furthermore, it owes its foundation not to a bishop or Church outreach, but to the self-motivated cooperation of lay Anglicans in Kansas and New Zealand ("History"). Both *LifeChurch.TV* and *The Anglican Cathedral of Second Life*, of course, cannot supervise how their worship services will be remediated as users incorporate them into their own evolving networks of association—possibly by posting their reactions to Facebook or the "Christianity" forum on *reddit*.

Bloggers provide perhaps the closest online analogy to the extra-institutional, print-mediated authority variously exercised by nineteenth-century figures such as Matthew Arnold, Christina Rossetti, and the evangelical-spiritualist and maverick journalist discussed in chapter 7, W. T. Stead. Some popular religious bloggers occupy a dual role as minister and media guru (e.g., Nadia Bolz-Weber, a Lutheran minister who runs the blog *Sarcastic Lutheran*); others advertise their participation in a church community or tradition (e.g., Sarah Bessey on the blog under her name, or Eve Tushnet on hers); and still others make their difficulty in committing to any local Christian community a subject of reflection (e.g., Rachel Held Evans on the site under her name). As even this brief review indicates, many popular Christian bloggers today are women, a trend in harmony with the fact that in 2004 "55% of the online faithful" in America were "women" (Hoover, Clark, and Raine i), and predictions by sociologists that "women will be and to some extent already are the important 'taste leaders' in the emergent global spiritual marketplace" (Turner 154).

Even the short survey above of the varied institutional affiliations of Christian women bloggers indicates that sociologists such as Bryan S. Turner might be too quick to assume that online religion primarily contributes to individualistic spiritual expression and consumption (153–55).[3] Participants in a lay Catholic catechism reading group recently pointed to bloggers such as Eve Tushnet as lay voices who help them reconcile official teachings of their Church with the demands of wider discourse communities in the contemporary world (Milburn).[4] A forum on "The Virgin Birth: Fact, Fiction, or Truth?" recently hosted by Lutheran blogger Nadia Bolz-Weber (mentioned above) generated over nine hundred comments within a few days, with respondents of differing Christian denominations from

---

3. A recent Pew Research survey, for example, "suggests that" for Americans "religious engagement through TV, radio, and the internet generally complements—rather than replaces—traditional kinds of religious participation, such as going to church" ("Religion and Electronic Media" 1).

4. Humorously titled the Super Official Catechism Reading Group (SOCRG), this group meets at St. Peter's Catholic Student Center next to Baylor University (Waco, TX). Primarily composed of Baylor graduate students, the group holds informal discussions of the Catholic catechism and Catholic life. At my request, on December 3, 2014, the group discussed the topic "Imagined spiritual communities in the digital age." My knowledge of their comments is based on a *Microsoft Word* report (December 4) from a regular participant, Michael Milburn, my research assistant.

around the world declaring and discovering camaraderie, even as some distanced themselves from their church institutions. One self-identified "cradle Roman Catholic" sympathized with Nadia (Joseph (the original), "Re: The Virgin Birth"), sharing his belief in the Virgin Birth but disbelief in the Immaculate Conception, and citing the latter as one reason for his "exit from RC teaching and worship practice" ("Re: Felicity"). In response, "an employee of the Catholic Church" in "Zimbabwe" who is "struggling with" aspects of her "faith," expressed her alienation from the dogmatism of her local church hierarchy along with her newfound sense of solidarity: "It feels good to know there are others [like me] out there in the world" (Felicity Sibindi).

Imagined Spiritual Communities helps to illuminate a second tension within online religion—between its balkanizing and consensus-building power. A parallel conflict characterizes all the cases of authorship and reception discussed in this book, particularly in my accounts of Maurice and Arnold in chapters 2 and 3. A "newspaper," Maurice remarks in 1852, "which speaks to us the notions and phrases of one school or party is a Respirator. We get our own breath returned to us again" (*Friendship of Books* 89). An age historically unmatched for circulation of news and new views, Maurice suggests, could paradoxically increase the possibility of sealing off ideological enclaves from fresh air, as party and sectarian newspapers remove the work of imagining community to the partisan page, instead of a locale shared with potentially diverse neighbors. Howard offers a similar warning in his study of online Christian fundamentalism: "with participatory [online] media, a feedback loop has emerged between individual expression and individual consumption of media content" (156), as some people have used social media's relative freedom from geographic proximity and financial and technological barriers to mass communication to "create self-filtering enclaves" (158).

When Maurice protested the divisive effects of church-party periodicals, and Arnold warned about anarchy fueled by the vast media industry of "Puritan" Nonconformists, they were reacting to a much less participatory media world in which the means of mass communication were still largely limited to persons and groups with access to financial and organizational power. Yet their anxieties about media-enforced enclaves, and Arnold's readiness to uphold what he imagined to be "the main current of [the nation's] thoughts" (CPW VIII:334), resemble Howard's fear that those caught in online feedback loops will lose their capacity to participate in "the" supposed "mainstream" of public life and opinion (Howard 17). Without contesting the valid concerns over bigotry and marginalization expressed by these nineteenth- and twentieth-century analysts of media-driven imagined communities, one might notice how closely these concerns can be tied to anxiety over challenges to the liberal state's supervisory power. Arnold's fear over supernatural claims that could challenge the state's authority, and his willingness to condone state violence to maintain that order, are congruent with Tennyson's late nod of approval, in "Akbar's Dream" (1892), to the imperial military force that might be required to quiet the "furious formalisms" of Hindu and Muslim fundamentalists in India (55). These attitudes are in turn uncomfortably similar to those that sometimes surface in debates now being waged in the government and media in the United States and elsewhere about the need of a secular democratic state to drop bombs abroad to quell the fury of religious extremists,[5] or to monitor the spread of "terrorism" and—note the wide applicability of the term—"radicalization" in personal digital communications and internet use by private citizens.[6]

A question asked by Maurice in an 1858 sermon on "The Sleep of the Church" has been continually in mind as I have finished this book and contemplated its bearing on our virtual age: "Are we to live in an age in which every mechanical facility for communication between man and man is multiplied ten-thousandfold, only that the inward isolation, the separation of those who meet continually, may be increased in a far greater measure?" (*Sermons in Lincoln's Inn* V:24). While Maurice is commenting on the sectarianism of the press, his ensuing defense of the "Sacraments" and their empowerment of an ethic of love and social engagement (24) reveals he is most concerned with a third tension, between virtual and real-world community: people might become so immersed in media-saturated worlds as to become incapable of the lived spiritual communion that can empower "acts of blessing to those who are near and to those who are afar off" (25). Much of Maurice's career can be understood as an attempt to avert mass-mediated isolation by converting virtual worlds entered through print into portals to actual spiritual communion and mutual service at the local and national levels. Sociologists have recently used different terms to predict the near fulfillment of Maurice's misgivings: "Religion as an agent of social change has been . . . compromised

---

5. For a recent consideration of these and related issues see Jerry Mark Long and Alex S. Wilner, "Delegitimizing al-Qaida: Defeating an 'Army Whose Men Love Death.'"

6. Controversy has recently been sparked by the Cybersecurity Information Sharing Act (CISA), a bill introduced to the U.S. Senate (July 10, 2014), which is directly related to the defeated Cybersecurity Intelligence Sharing and Protection Act (CISPA) (Craig; "S.2588-Cybersecurity Information Sharing Act of 2014").

by the loss of any significant contrast between the sacred and the world," as digital communications networks expand a global spiritual marketplace based on the low-commitment consumerism that fuels global capitalism (Turner 155).

Yet some virtual spiritual communities are motivating social change. Rachel Held Evans, the nondenominational Christian blogger cited above, recently held a "Rally to Restore Unity" in the face of theological and political polarization in the United States, generating online round-table discussions and hundreds of images and blog posts that promoted interdenominational unity, and raising money to provide clean water for communities in Ethiopia and Sierra Leone (Evans). This is one of many small-scale, real-world manifestations of vernacular virtual spiritual community that complement online global collaboration between individuals, local congregations, and non-profits and parachurch organizations to improve human well-being, such as projects facilitated by UrbanPromise Honduras, World Vision, Compassion International, and, with a mission to rectify economic inequality and labor abuse in the United States, Interfaith Worker Justice. The dreams of spiritual communion rehearsed in this book failed during or died with print-mediated Christian Britain. Even so, many of the tensions and aspirations that defined those imaginative responses to the printed age are being uploaded in new form to the virtual age.

BIBLIOGRAPHY

"Alfred Tennyson. Part II." *The Leisure Hour* 28 Feb. 1863: 136–40. *ProQuest: British Periodicals.* Web.

Allen, Peter. *The Cambridge Apostles: The Early Years.* London: Cambridge UP, 1978.

Allen, W. O. B. and Edmund McClure. *Two Hundred Years: The History of the Society for Promoting Christian Knowledge, 1698–1898.* London: SPCK, 1898.

Anderson, Benedict. *Imagined Communities: Reflections on the Origins and Spread of Nationalism.* Rev. ed. London: Verso, 1991.

The Anglican Cathedral of Second Life. The Anglican Cathedral of Second Life, 2007. Web. 22 Dec. 2014.

———. "History." n.d. Web. 22 Dec. 2014.

———. "The Leadership Team." n.d. Web. 22 Dec. 2014.

———. "The Sacraments on Epiphany Island." n.d. Web. 22 Dec. 2014.

apRoberts, Ruth. *Arnold and God.* Berkeley: University of California Press, 1983.

"Archer Gurney's Poems." *The English Review* Apr. 1852: 104–41. *ProQuest: British Periodicals.* Web.

Arnold, Matthew. *The Complete Prose Works of Matthew Arnold.* Ed. R. H. Super. 11 vols. Ann Arbor: University of Michigan Press, 1960–77.

———. *The Letters of Matthew Arnold.* Ed. Cecil Y. Lang. Charlottesville: University of Virginia Press, 1996-2001.

———. *Reports on Elementary Schools, 1852–1882.* Introd. F. S. Marvin. New ed. London: Wyman and Sons Ltd., 1908.

Arseneau, Mary. *Recovering Christina Rossetti: Female Community and Incarnational Poetics.* Houndmills, UK: Palgrave Macmillan, 2004.

Altholz, Josef. *The Religious Press in Britain, 1760–1900*. New York: Green Wood Press, 1989.

Altick, Richard D. *The English Common Reader: A Social History of the Mass Reading Public, 1800–1900*. Chicago: The University of Chicago Press, 1957.

Asad, Talal. *Formations of the Secular: Christianity, Islam, Modernity*. Stanford: Stanford University Press, 2003.

———. *Genealogies of Religion: Discipline and Reasons of Power in Christianity and Islam*. Baltimore: The Johns Hopkins University Press, 1993.

[Austin, Alfred.] "The Poetry of the Period: Mr. Tennyson." *Temple Bar* May 1869: 179–94. *ProQuest: British Periodicals*. Web.

Baker, Arthur E. *A Concordance to the Poetical and Dramatic Works of Alfred, Lord Tennyson*. 1914. London: Routledge and Kegan Paul Ltd., 1965.

Baker, Luke. "Iraqi Conflict Has Killed a Million Iraqis: Survey," *Reuters* (Jan. 30, 2008). Web. 29 Oct. 2012.

Barbeau, Jeffrey W. *Coleridge, The Bible, and Religion*. New York: Palgrave Macmillan, 2008.

Barton, Anna. *Alfred Tennyson's In Memoriam: A Reading Guide*. Edinburgh: Edinburgh University Press, 2012.

Bede, Cuthbert. "Modern Edens." *The Quiver* Dec. 1866: 209–12. *ProQuest: British Periodicals*. Web.

Beer, John. *Romantic Influences*. New York: St. Martin's Press, 1993.

Bell, [Henry Thomas] Mackenzie. *Christina Rossetti: A Biographical and Critical Study*. Boston: Roberts Brothers, 1898.

Benson, Arthur Christopher. "Christina Rossetti." *The National Review* 26 Feb. 1895: 753–63. *ProQuest: British Periodicals*. Web.

Bentley, James. *Ritualism and Politics in Victorian Britain: The Attempt to Legislate for Belief*. Oxford: Oxford University Press, 1978.

Bessey, Sarah. *Sarah Bessey*. 2005–2014. Web. 17 Dec. 2014.

The Bible. King James Version. Zondervan Corp., L. L. C. *BibleGateway.com*. Web.

———. English Revised Version. *The Bible Hub*. By Biblios. Web.

"Birmingham Scepticism." *London Quarterly Review* Apr. 1871: 310–31. *ProQuest: British Periodicals*. Web.

Blain, Virginia H. "Sarah Flower Adams." *Oxford Dictionary of National Biography*. Oxford University Press, 2004–2013. Web.

Blair, Kirstie. "Church Going." *The Oxford Handbook of Victorian Poetry*. Ed. Matthew Bevis. Oxford: Oxford University Press, 2013: 762–82.

———. *Form and Faith in Victorian Poetry and Religion*. Oxford: Oxford University Press, 2012.

———. "Introduction." *Keble in Context*. Ed. Kirstie Blair. London: Anthem Press, 2004. 1–16.

———. "Keble and *The Christian Year*." *The Oxford Handbook of English Literature and Theology*. Ed. Andrew Hass, David Jasper, and Elizabeth Jay. Oxford: Oxford University Press, 2007. 607–23.

———. "Keble and the Rhythm of Faith." *Essays in Criticism* 53.2 (2003): 129–50.

———. "Transatlantic Tractarians: Victorian Poetry and the Church of England in America." *Victorian Studies* 55.2 (Winter 2013): 286–98.

———. *Victorian Poetry and the Culture of the Heart*. Oxford: Clarendon Press, 2006.

Blake, William. *Blake's Poetry and Designs*. Ed. John E. Grant and Mary Lynn Johnson. New York: W. W. Norton and Co., 2007.

The Book of Common Prayer. Oxford: Clarendon Press, 1815.

Bolter, Jay and Richard Grusin. *Remediation: Understanding the New Media*. Cambridge: Massachusetts Institute of Technology Press, 2000.

Bolz-Weber, Nadia. "The Virgin Birth: Fact, Fiction, or Truth?" *Sarcastic Lutheran*. Patheos, 17 Dec. 2014. Web. 17 Dec. 2014.

[Bradley, Katherine Harris and Edith Emma Cooper] Michael Field. "To Christina Rossetti." *The Academy* 4 April 1896: 284.

Briggs, Asa. "Christ and the Media: Secularization, Rationalism, and Sectarianism in the History of British Broadcasting, 1922–1976." *Secularization, Rationalism, and Sectarianism: Essays in Honour of Bryan R. Wilson*. Ed. Eileen Barker, James A. Beckford, and Karel Dobbelare. Oxford: Clarendon Press, 1993: 267–86.

Bright, Rev. J. S. "Autumn Leaves." *Evangelical Magazine and Missionary Chronicle* Oct. 1866: 629–35.

Brimley, George. "Alfred Tennyson's Poems." *Cambridge Essays, Contributed by Members of the University*. London: J. W. Parker and Son, 1855.

Brooke, Stopford A. *Life and Letters of Frederick W. Robertson, MA*. Boston: Ticknor and Fields, 1865.

Brose, Olive J. *Frederick Denison Maurice: Rebellious Conformist*. Athens: Ohio University Press, 1971.

Brown, Callum. *The Death of Christian Britain: Understanding Secularisation, 1800–2000*. 2nd ed. London: Routledge, 2009.

Brown, Stewart J. *Providence and Empire: Religion, Politics and Society in the United Kingdom, 1815–1914*. Harlow, UK: Pearson Longman, 2008.

Bruce, Steve. *Secularization: In Defence of an Unfashionable Theory*. Oxford: Oxford University Press, 2011.

Byron, Lord Gordon. "Dedication" to *Don Juan*. *Romanticism: An Anthology*. Ed. Duncan Wu. 4th ed. Malden, MA: Blackwell, 2012. 959.

Caine, Thomas Hall, ed. *Sonnets of Three Centuries: A Selection*. London: Elliot Stock, 1882. *Google Books*. Web.

"Calendar for 1895." *All the Year Round* 29 Sept. 1894: 58. *ProQuest: British Periodicals*. Web.

"Calendar for the Week." *Reynolds's Weekly Newspaper* 27 Mar. 1887: 4. *ProQuest: British Periodicals*. Web.

Calhoun, Craig. "Time, World, and Secularism." *The Post-Secular in Question: Religion in Contemporary Society*. Ed. Philip S. Gorski et al. New York: New York University Press, 2012. 335–64.

Calleo, David P. *Coleridge and the Idea of the Modern State*. Yale University Press, 1966.

Canuel, Mark. *Religion, Toleration, and British Writing, 1790–1830*. Cambridge: Cambridge University Press, 2002.

Carey, Hilary M. *God's Empire: Religion and Cosmopolitanism in the British World, c. 1801–1908.* Cambridge: Cambridge University Press, 2011.

Carlyle, Thomas. *Past and Present.* Introd. and notes by Chris R. Vanden Bossche. Ed. Chris R. Vanden Bossche, Joel J. Brattin, and D. J. Trela. Berkeley: University of California Press, 2005.

Carruthers, Jo. *England's Secular Scripture: Islamophobia and the Protestant Aesthetic.* London: Continuum, 2011.

Carter, John. *ABC for Book Collectors.* 6th ed. Correction and Additions by Nicolas Barker. New Castle, Delaware: Oak Knoll Books, 1992.

Casanova, José. *Public Religions in the Modern World.* Chicago: University of Chicago Press, 1994.

———. "The Secular, Secularizations, Secularisms." *Rethinking Secularism.* Ed. Craig Calhoun et al. New York: Oxford University Press, 2011. 54–74.

Chadwick, Owen. *The Victorian Church.* 2 vols. 1966, 1970. London: SCM Press, Ltd., 1987.

Chambers, Edmund K. "*Verses.* By Christina G. Rossetti. (SPCK)." *The Academy* 24 Feb. 1894: 162–64. *HathiTrust Digital Library.* Web.

Chapman, Alison. "Sonnet and Sonnet Sequence." *A Companion to Victorian Poetry.* Ed. Richard Cronin, Alison Chapman, and Antony H. Harrison. Oxford: Blackwell, 2002: 99–114.

——— and Joanna Meacock. *A Rossetti Family Chronology.* Houndmills, UK: Palgrave Macmillan, 2007.

Chapman, Elizabeth Rachel. *A Companion to In Memoriam.* 2nd ed. 1901. Folcroft Library Editions, 1973.

Chapman, Raymond. *Faith and Revolt: Studies in the Literary Influence of the Oxford Movement.* London: Weidenfeld and Nicholson, 1970.

Christensen, Torben. *Origin and History of Christian Socialism, 1848–1854.* Aarhus: Universitetsforlaget, 1962.

"Christianity." *Reddit.* Reddit Inc., 2014. Web. 17 Dec. 2014.

"Christina Rossetti: a Biographical and Critical Study." *The Athenaeum.* 22 Jan. 1898: 109. *ProQuest: British Periodicals.* Web.

"Christina Rossetti." *The Guardian* 9 Jan. 1895: 51. *Access Newspaper Archive.* Web.

Claeys, Gregory. "Robert Owen." *The Oxford Dictionary of National Biography (DNB).* Online ed. Oxford University Press, 2004–2012. 29 March 2012. Web.

Clarke, W. K. Lowther. *A History of the S. P. C. K.* London: SPCK, 1959.

———. "Introduction." *Verses.* London: SPCK, 1925.

Coleridge, John Taylor. *A Memoir of the Rev. John Keble, M. A., Late Vicar of Hursley.* 2nd ed. 2 vols. Oxford: James Parker and Co., 1869.

———. "The Rev. John Keble." *The Guardian* 11 April 1866: 372. *Access Newspaper Archive.* Web.

Coleridge, Samuel Taylor. *Aids to Reflection in the Formation of a Manly Character.* Ed. John Beer. Princeton: Princeton University Press and Routledge, 1993.

———. *Biographia Literaria; or Biographical Sketches of my Literary Life and Opinions.* Ed. James Engell and W. Jackson Bate. Princeton: Princeton University Press and Routledge, 1983.

———. *Confessions of an Inquiring Spirit.* Ed. Henry Nelson Coleridge. London: William Pickering, 1840. Armstrong Browning Library. 19th Century Collection.

———. *On the Constitution of the Church and State According to the Idea of Each.* Ed. John Colmer. Princeton: Princeton University Press and Routledge, 1976.

———. *Essays on His Times.* Ed. David Erdman. 3 vols. Princeton: Princeton University Press and Routledge, 1978.

———. *The Friend.* Ed. Barbara E. Rooke. 2 vols. Princeton: Princeton University Press and Routledge, 1969.

———. *Lay Sermons.* Ed. R. J. White. Princeton: Princeton University Press and Routledge, 1972.

———. *Lectures on Literature, 1808–1819.* Ed. R. A. Foakes. 2 vols. Princeton: Princeton University Press and Routledge, 1987.

———. *Marginalia.* Ed. H. J. Jackson and George Whalley. Vol. 3. Princeton: Princeton University Press and Routledge, 1992.

———. *The Notebooks of Samuel Taylor Coleridge.* Ed. Kathleen Coburn and Anthony John Harding. 5 vols. Princeton: Princeton University Press, 1957–2002.

———. *Opus Maximum.* Ed. Thomas McFarland and Nicholas Halmi. Princeton: Princeton University Press and Routledge, 2002.

———. *Shorter Works and Fragments.* Ed. H. J. Jackson and J. R. de J. Jackson. 2 vols. Princeton: Princeton University Press and Routledge, 1995.

———. *Table Talk,* Ed. Carl Woodring, 2 vols. Princeton: Princeton University Press and Routledge, 1990.

Colley, Linda. *Britons: Forging the Nation 1707–1837.* New Haven: Yale University Press, 1992.

Connell, Phillip. *Romanticism, Economics and the Question of 'Culture.'* Oxford: Oxford University Press, 2001.

Cook, Chris. *The Routledge Companion to Britain in the Nineteenth Century, 1815–1914.* London: Routledge, 2005.

Cox, Jeffrey L. "Master Narratives of Religious Change." *The Decline of Christendom in Western Europe, 1750–2000.* Ed. Hugh McLeod and Werner Ustorf. Cambridge: Cambridge University Press, 2003. 201–17.

Craig, Caroline. "CISPA returns as CISA—and it's just as terrible for privacy." *Infoworld.* InfoWorld, Inc., 20 June 2014. Web. 27 Dec. 2014.

Crimmins, James E. "William Paley." *The Oxford Dictionary of National Biography (DNB).* Online ed. Oxford University Press, 2008. Web. 23 July 2010.

Culler, Dwight. *The Poetry of Tennyson.* New Haven: Yale University Press, 1977.

Currie, Robert, Alan Gilbert, and Lee Horsley. *Churches and Churchgoers: Patterns of Church Growth in the British Isles Since 1700.* Oxford: Clarendon Press, 1977.

D'Amico, Dianne. *Christina Rossetti: Faith, Time, and Gender.* Baton Rouge: Louisiana State University Press, 1999.

———. "Christina Rossetti's *Christian Year:* Comfort for 'the weary heart.'" *The Victorian Newsletter* 72 (Fall 1987): 36–42.

——— and David A. Kent. "Rossetti and the Tractarians." *Victorian Poetry* 44.1 (Spring 2006): 93–103.

Davies, William. "The Sonnet." *The Quarterly Review* 134 (January 1873): 186–204.

Dennis, John. "The English Sonnet." *Cornhill Magazine* 25 (May 1872): 581–82. *ProQuest: British Periodicals.* Web.

Dickens, Charles. *Bleak House.* Ed. and introd. Nicola Bradbury. London: Penguin Books, 1996.

———. *Hard Times.* Ed. and introd. Kate Flint. London: Penguin Classics, 2003.

Dicks, Bella and Joost Van Loon. "Territoriality and Heritage in South Wales: Space, Time and Imagined Communities." *Nation, Identity, and Social Theory: Perspectives from Wales.* Ed. Ralph Fevre and Andrew Thompson. Cardiff: University of Wales Press, 1999. 207–32.

Dieleman, Karen. *Religious Imaginaries: The Liturgical and Poetic Practices of Elizabeth Barrett Browning, Christina Rossetti, and Adelaide Procter.* Athens: Ohio University Press, 2012.

Dowden, Edward. "*Sonnets of Three Centuries*, ed. By T. Hall Caine." *The Academy* 25 Feb. 1882: 129–30. *ProQuest: British Periodicals.* Web.

Eagleton, Terry. *Literary Theory: An Introduction,* 2nd ed. Minneapolis: University of Minnesota Press, 1996.

"Ecclesiastical Notes." *Nonconformist* 4 April 1866: 261–62. *Access Newspaper Archive.* Web.

Edgecombe, Rodney Stenning. *Two Poets of the Oxford Movement: John Keble and John Henry Newman.* Madison: Farleigh Dickinson University Press, 1996.

Eliot, T. S. "In Memoriam." In John Dixon Hunt, 1970. 129–37.

Erickson, Lee. "The Market." *A Companion to Victorian Poetry.* Ed. Richard Cronin, Alison Chapman and Antony H. Harrison. Malden, MA: Blackwell, 2002. 345–60.

Evans, Rachel Held. "10 Cool Things We've Done in 1,000 Posts." *Rachel Held Evans.* Evans Freelance, 24 Sept. 2012. Web. 17 Dec. 2014.

Everett, Glenn. "The Reform Acts." *The Victorian Web.* Web. Nov. 1, 2012.

Felicity Sibindi. "Re: Joseph (the original)." *Sarcastic Lutheran.* Nadia Bolz-Weber, 17 Dec. 2014. Web. 17 Dec. 2014.

Fitzgerald, William. *Spiritual Modalities: Prayer as Rhetoric and Performance.* University Park: The Pennsylvania State University Press, 2012.

Frank, Mary C. "*Ex Umbris et Imaginibus in Veritatem:* Wilfrid Ward and the Art of Newman." Diss. Baylor University, 2013.

Freshwater, R. "UK Telephone History." *The Telephone File: A Historical Web Site about* UK *Customer Telephone Apparatus & Systems.* 20 Dec. 2010. Web. 19 Dec. 2014.

Frey, Anne. *British State Romanticism: Authorship, Agency, and Bureaucratic Nationalism.* Stanford: Stanford University Press, 2009.

Froude, James Anthony. *Thomas Carlyle: A History of His Life in London, 1834–1881.* New impression. 2 vols. London: Longmans, Green and Co., 1919.

Froude, Richard Hurrell. *Remains of the Late Reverend Richard Hurrell Froude.* 2 vols. London: Printed for J. G. and F. Rivington, 1838–39.

Genung, John Franklin. *Tennyson's In Memoriam: Its Purpose and Its Structure, a Study.* 2nd ed. Boston: Houghton, Mifflin and Co., 1884.

Gigante, Denise. *Life: Organic Form and Romanticism.* New Haven: Yale University Press, 2009.

Gilbert, Sandra M. and Susan Gubar. *The Madwoman in the Attic: The Woman Writer and the Nineteenth-Century Literary Imagination.* New Haven: Yale University Press, 1979.

Gilmartin, Kevin. *Print Politics: The Press and Radical Opposition in Early Nineteenth-Century England.* Cambridge: Cambridge University Press, 1996.

[Gladstone, W. E.] "Tennyson's Poems." *The Quarterly Review* Oct. 1859: 454–85. *ProQuest: British Periodicals.* Web.

Glaister, Geoffrey Ashall. *Encyclopedia of the Book.* 2nd ed. New Castle, Delaware: Oak Knoll Press & The British Library, 1996.

Golden, Arline. "Victorian Renascence: The Revival of the Amatory Sonnet Sequence, 1850–1800." *Genre* VII (June 1974): 133–47.

"Gospel Notes in the Poetry of Alfred Tennyson." *Sunday at Home* 22 Mar. 1884: 180–85.

Greenfeld, Liah. *Nationalism: Five Roads to Modernity.* Cambridge: Harvard University Press, 1992.

Greenfeld, Liah and Jonathan Eastwood. "The Class Nature of Nationalism." In Guntram H. Herb and David H. Kaplan, 2008. 1–13.

Groth Lyon, Eileen. *Politicians in the Pulpit: Christian Radicalism in Britain from the Fall of the Bastille to the Disintegration of Chartism.* Aldershot: Ashgate, 1999.

Guillory, John. *Cultural Capital: The Problem of Literary Canon Formation.* Chicago: Chicago University Press, 1993.

Haass, Sabine. "Victorian Poetry Anthologies: Their Role and Success in the Nineteenth-Century Book Market." *Publishing History* XVII (1985): 51–64.

Habermas, Jürgen. *The Structural Transformation of the Public Sphere: An Inquiry into a Category of Bourgeois Society,* trans. Thomas Burger. Cambridge, MA: MIT Press, 1989.

Hair, Donald. "Tennyson's Faith: A Re-examination." *University of Toronto Quarterly* 55.2 (Winter 1985/6): 185–203.

Halifax, Charles Wood, Lord. "The Present Crisis in the Church of England." *The Nineteenth Century* Feb. 1899: 173-187. *ProQuest: British Periodicals.* Web.

Harrison, Antony H. "Victorian Culture Wars: Alexander Smith, Arthur Hugh Clough, and Matthew Arnold in 1853," *Victorian Poetry* 42.4 (Winter 2004): 509–20.

Harrison, J. F. C. *A History of the Working Men's College.* London: Routledge & Kegan Paul, 1954.

Harrison, Peter. *'Religion' and the Religions in the English Enlightenment.* Cambridge: Cambridge University Press, 1990.

Hassett, Constance W. *Christina Rossetti: The Patience of Style.* Charlottesville: The University Press of Virginia, 2005.

Haweis, Rev. Hugh Reginald. *Poets in the Pulpit.* 1880. London: S. Low, Marston, Searle, and Rivington, 1889. Armstrong Browning Library.

[Hazlitt, William.] "Mr. Coleridge's Lay-Sermon." *Examiner* 12 Jan. 1817: 28–29. *ProQuest: British Periodicals.* Web.

Hedley, Douglas. *Coleridge, Philosophy, and Religion.* Cambridge: Cambridge University Press, 2000.

Hempton, David. "Established churches and the growth of religious pluralism: a case study of christianisation and secularisation in England since 1700." In McLeod and Werner Ustorf, 2003. 81–98

Herb, Guntram H. and Gruia Badescu. "Introduction." *Nations and Nationalism: A Global Historical Overview.* Vol. 1. Ed. Guntram H. Herb and David H. Kaplan. Santa Barbara: ABC-CLIO, 2008. xvii–xx.

Herrick, Robert. "Corinna's going a-Maying." *The Oxford Book of English Verse: 1200–1900.* Ed. Arthur Quiller-Couch. Oxford: Clarendon, 1919. *Bartleby.com.* Web.

Hill, Alan. *Tennyson, Wordsworth and the 'Forms' of Religion.* Lincoln: Tennyson Society, 1997.

Holmes, John. *Dante Gabriel Rossetti and the Late Victorian Sonnet Sequence: Sexuality, Belief and the Self.* Hampshire, UK: Ashgate, 2005.

Holmes, Richard. *Age of Wonder: How the Romantic Generation Discovered the Beauty and Terror of Science.* New York: Pantheon Books, 2008.

———. *Coleridge: Darker Reflections, 1804–1834.* New York: Pantheon Books, 1988.

Honan, Park. *Matthew Arnold: A Life.* New York: McGraw-Hill Book Co., 1981.

Hood, Edwin Paxton. "John Keble," *Eclectic Review* 10 May 1866: 428–41. *ProQuest: British Periodicals.* Web.

Hoover, Steward M., Lynn Schofield Clark, and Lee Raine. "64% of wired Americans have used the Internet for spiritual or religious purposes." *Pew Internet and American Life Project.* The Pew Charitable Trusts, 7 April 2004. Web. 18 Dec. 2014.

[Hopkins, Manley.] "The Poetry of Sorrow." *The Times* 28 Nov. 1851: 8. *Times Digital Archive, 1785–1985.* Web.

Hostettler, John. *Voting in Britain: A History of the Parliamentary Franchise.* Chichester, England: Barry Rose, 2001.

Houston, Natalie. "Towards a New History: Fin-de-Siècle Women Poets and the Sonnet." *Victorian Women Poets (Essays and Studies 2003).* Ed. Alison Chapman for the English Association. Cambridge: D. S. Brewer, 2003. 145–64.

———. "Valuable by Design: Material Features and Cultural Value in Nineteenth-Century Sonnet Anthologies." *Victorian Poetry* 37.2 (Summer 1999): 243–72.

Howard, Robert Glenn. *Digital Jesus: The Making of New Christian Fundamentalist Community on the Internet.* New York: New York University Press, 2011.

Hunt, John Dixon, ed. *Tennyson's In Memoran: A Casebook.* London: Macmillan, 1970.

Hymns and Anthems. London: Charles Fox, 1845. *Google Books.* Web.

"In Memoriam." *The Atlas* 15 Jun. 1850: 379. *Access Newspaper Archive.* Web.

Ives, Maura. *Christina Rossetti: A Descriptive Bibliography.* New Castle, DE: Oak Knoll Press, 2011.

Jackson, J. R. de J., ed. *Samuel Taylor Coleridge: The Critical Heritage.* New York: Barnes & Noble, Inc., 1970.

———, ed. *Samuel Taylor Coleridge: The Critical Heritage, 1834–1900.* Vol. 2. London: Routledge, 1995.

Jager, Colin. *The Book of God: Secularization and Design in the Romantic Era.* Philadelphia: University of Pennsylvania Press, 2007.

———. *Unquiet Things: Secularism in the Romantic Age.* Philadelphia: University of Pennsylvania Press, 2014.

Janes, Dominic. *Victorian Reformation: The Fight over Idolatry in the Church of England, 1840-1860.* Oxford: Oxford University Press, 2009.

J. C. "'In Memoriam' and the Bible." *The Leisure Hour* 31 Jan. 1874: 71–73. *ProQuest: British Periodicals*. Web.

J. H. F. "The Tennysonian Stanza: and a Passage from 'In Memoriam.'" *The Illustrated Times* 10 Jan. 1863: 27. *Access Newspaper Archives*. Web.

"John Keble." *The Guardian* 11 April 1866: 371. *Access Newspaper Archive*. Web.

"John Keble." *Month* Jan.–June 1866: 441–58.

"John Keble." *Morning Post* 2 April 1866: 5. *19th Century British Newspapers: Part II*. The British Library. Web.

Johnson, Lionel. "Literature: Miss Rossetti and Mrs. [Cecil Frances] Alexander." *The Academy* (25 July 1896): 59–60. *ProQuest: British Periodicals*. Web.

Johnson, Maria Poggi. "The Christian Year and the Typological Imagination in John Keble's Parochial Sermons." *Pro Ecclesia* 9.4 (Fall 2000): 414–28.

Jones, Mark. "Alarmism, Public-Sphere Performatives, and the Lyric Turn: Or, What is 'Fears in Solitude' Afraid of?" *Boundary 2* 30.3 (2003): 67–105.

Jones, Tod E. *The Broad Church: A Biography of the Movement*. Lanham, Maryland: Lexington Books, 2003.

Joseph (the original). "Re: The Virgin Birth: Fact, Fiction, or Truth?" *Sarcastic Lutheran*. Nadia Bolz-Weber, 17 Dec. 2014. Web. 17 Dec. 2014.

———. "Re: Felicity Sibindi." 17 Dec. 2014. Web. 17 Dec. 2014.

Kaiser, David Aram. *Romanticism, Aesthetics, and Nationalism*. Cambridge: Cambridge University Press, 1999.

Kaufmann, Michael W. "The Religious, The Secular, and Literary Studies: Rethinking the Secularization Narratives in Histories of the Profession." *New Literary History* 38.4 (Autumn 2007): 607–28.

Keble, John. *The Christian Year: Thoughts in Verse for Sundays and Holydays throughout the Year*. New York: D. Appleton and Co., 1896; Rep. Detroit: Gale Research Company, 1975.

———. *Occasional Papers and Reviews*. Ed. E. B. Pusey. Oxford: James Parker and Co., 1877.

———. "On the Mysticism Attributed to the Early Fathers of the Church" [1841]. *Tracts for the Times*. Vol. 5 (1838–1840). London: J. G. F. & J. Rivington, 1840–.

———. *Sermons Academical and Occasional*. Oxford: John Henry Parker, 1847.

———. "Sunday Lessons: The Principle of Selection." *Tracts for the Times*. Vol. 1 (1833–1834). London: J. G. & F. Rivington, 1839.

Keen, Paul. *The Crisis of Literature in the 1790s*. Cambridge: Cambridge University Press, 1999.

———. "'With an Industry Incredible'; Politics, Writing, and the Public Sphere." *A Concise Companion to the Romantic Age*. Ed. John Klancher. Wiley-Blackwell, 2009: 99–118.

———, ed. *The Popular Radical Press in Britain, 1817–1821*. Vol. 2. London: Pickering & Chatto, 2003.

Kent, Christopher. "The Academy (1869–1916)." *Dictionary of Nineteenth-Century Journalism*. Ed. Laurel Brake and Marysa Demoor. *ProQuest: C19: The Nineteenth Century Index*. Web.

———. "Higher Journalism and the Mid-Victorian Clerisy," *Victorian Studies* 13.2 (Dec. 1969): 181–98.

Kent, David. "Sequence and Meaning in Christina Rossetti's Verses." *Victorian Poetry* 17.3 (Autumn 1979): 259–64.

———. "W. M. Rossetti and the Editing of Christina Rossetti's Religious Poetry." *The Pre-Raphaelite Review* 1 (May 1978): 18–27.

Kenyon, James B. "Dante Gabriel Rossetti and His Sister Christina." *Methodist Review.* New York. Sept. 1896: 743–53. *Google Books.* Web.

King, Joshua. "Patmore, Hopkins, and the Problem of the English Metrical Law." *The Hopkins Quarterly* 38.1–2 (print) and *Victorian Poetry* 49.2 (electronic: Project Muse) (June 2011): 31–49.

———. "A Post-Secular Victorian Study: Religion, Reading, and Imagining Britain." *Nineteenth-Century Prose* 39.1–2 (Spring/Fall 2012): 58–70.

Kingsley, Charles. "Tennyson." *Fraser's Magazine* Sept. 1850: 245–55. *ProQuest: British Periodicals.* Web.

Kitson, Peter J. "Political Thinker." *The Cambridge Companion to Coleridge.* Ed. Lucy Newlyn. Cambridge: Cambridge University Press, 2002: 156–69.

Klancher, Jon. *The Making of English Reading Audiences.* Madison: U of Wisconsin P, 1987.

Kline, Daniel. "'For rigorous teachers seized my youth': Thomas Arnold, John Keble and the Juvenilia of Arthur Hugh Clough and Matthew Arnold." *John Keble in Context,* ed. Kirstie Blair. London: Anthem Press, 2004. 143–58.

Knight, Frances. *The Nineteenth-Century Church and English Society.* Cambridge: Cambridge University Press, 1995.

Knight, Mark and Emma Mason. *Nineteenth-Century Religion and Literature: An Introduction.* Oxford: Oxford University Press, 2006.

Knights, Ben. *The Idea of the Clerisy in the Nineteenth Century.* Cambridge: Cambridge University Press, 1978.

Kooistra, Lorraine Janzen. *Christina Rossetti and Illustration: A Publishing History.* Athens: Ohio University Press, 2002.

Korshin, Paul J. *Typologies in England: 1650–1820.* Princeton: Princeton University Press, 1982.

Kriegel, Lara. "The Pudding and the Palace: Labor, Print Culture, and Imperial Britain in 1851." *After the Imperial Turn: Thinking with and through the Nation.* Ed. Antoinette Burton. Durham: Duke University Press, 2003. 230–45.

Kumar, Krishan. *The Making of English National Identity.* Cambridge: Cambridge University Press, 2003.

Lake, William C. "Mr. Keble and 'The Christian Year.'" *Contemporary Review* May/August 1866: 314–37. *ProQuest: British Periodicals.* Web.

Landow, George P. *Victorian Types, Victorian Shadows: Biblical Typology in Victorian Literature, Art, and Thought.* Boston: Routledge & Kegan Paul, 1980.

LaPorte, Charles. *Victorian Poets and the Changing Bible.* Charlottesville: University of Virginia Press, 2011.

"The Late John Keble." *The Times* 6 April 1866: 5. *Times Digital Archive, 1785–1985.* Web.

"The Late Rev. John Keble." *Daily News* 2 April 1866: 2. *Access Newspaper Archive.* Web.

"The Laureate and His School." *The Dublin Review* Apr. 1864: 363–85. *ProQuest: British Periodicals.* Web.

Lautz, Boniface, O. S. B. *The Doctrine of the Communion of Saints in Anglican Theology, 1833–1963.* Ottawa: University of Ottawa Press, 1967.

Law, Alice. "The Poetry of Christina G. Rossetti." *The Westminster Review* 143 January 1895: 444–53. *ProQuest: British Periodicals.* Web.

Lawson, John and Harold Silver. *A Social History of Education in England.* London: Methuen and Co Ltd., 1973.

Leadbetter, Gregory. "Coleridge and the 'More Permanent Revolution.'" *The Coleridge Bulletin* 30 (Winter 2007): 1–16.

Lecourt, Sebastian. "Matthew Arnold and Religion's Cosmopolitan Histories." *Victorian Literature and Culture* 38 (2010): 467–87.

"Les Contemplations." *The British Quarterly Review* Jul. 1860: 71–98. *ProQuest: British Periodicals.* Web.

"Letters on Clerical Subscription." *The Patriot* 4 Feb. 1864: 75. *Access Newspaper Archive.* Web.

Lewes, George Henry. "Tennyson's New Poem." *The Leader* 22 June 1850. In John Dixon Hunt, 1970. 64–69.

Lewis, C. S. *The Abolition of Man, or Reflections on Education with Special Reference to the Teaching of English in the Upper Forms of Schools.* Oxford: Oxford University Press, 1943.

LifeChurch.TV. LifeChurch.tv, 2014. Web. 18 Dec. 2014.

Linley, Margaret. "Nationhood and Empire." Cronin, Chapman and Harrison. 421–37.

Livingston, James C. *Matthew Arnold and Christianity: His Religious Prose.* Columbia: University of South Carolina, 1986.

Lloyd, Amy. "Sunday at Home (1854–1940)." *Dictionary of Nineteenth-Century Journalism.* Ed. Laurel Brake and Marysa Demoor. *ProQuest: C19: The Nineteenth Century Index.* Web.

"London, Saturday." *Morning Post* 7 April 1866: 4. *19th Century British Newspapers: Part II.* The British Library. Web.

Long, Jerry Mark and Alex S. Wilner. "Delegitimizing al-Qaida: Defeating an 'Army Whose Men Love Death.'" *International Security* 39.1 (Summer 2014): 126–64.

Lootens, Tricia. *Lost Saints: Silence, Gender, and Victorian Literary Canonization.* Charlottesville: University Press of Virginia, 1996.

Lushington, Franklin. "In Memoriam." *Tait's Edinburgh Magazine* Aug. 1850. In John Dixon Hunt, 1970. 71–84.

Lysack, Krista. "The Productions of Time: Keble, Rossetti, and Victorian Devotional Reading." *Victorian Studies* 55.3 (Spring 2013): 451–70.

Main, David A. *A Treasury of English Sonnets.* Manchester: Alexander Ireland and Co., 1880. *Google Books.* Web.

Marchand, Leslie. *The Athenaeum: A Mirror of Victorian Culture.* Chapel Hill: University of North Carolina Press, 1941.

Marsh, Jan. *Christina Rossetti: A Writer's Life.* New York: Viking, 1995.

Marshall, Linda E. "'Abstruse the Problems!': Unity and Divisions in Christina Rossetti's *Later Life: A Double Sonnet of Sonnets.*" *Victorian Poetry* 32.3–4 (Autumn–Winter 1994): 299–314.

———. "What the Dead Are Doing Underground: Hades and Heaven in the Writings of Christina Rossetti." *The Victorian Newsletter* 72 (Fall 1987): 55–60.

Martin, Meredith. *The Rise and Fall of Meter: Poetry and English National Culture, 1860–1930.* Princeton: Princeton University Press, 2012.

Mason, Emma. "'A Sort of Aesthetico-Catholic Revival': Christina Rossetti and the London Ritualist Scene." *Outsiders Looking In: The Rossettis Then and Now.* Ed. David Clifford and Laurence Roussillon. London: Anthem Press, 2004.

Masuzawa, Tomoko. *The Invention of World Religions: Or, How European Universalism Was Preserved in the Language of Pluralism.* Chicago: The University of Chicago Press, 2005.

Mathieson, Margaret. *The Preachers of Culture: A Study of English and Its Teachers.* London: George Allen & Unwin Ltd., 1975.

Maurice, Frederick Denison. *The Friendship of Books and other Lectures.* Ed. T. Hughes. 4th ed. London: Macmillan and Co., 1889.

———. *The Kingdom of Christ.* 2 vols. London: J. M. Dent & Co., 1938.

———. *Learning and Working. Lectures Concerning this Time and the Times of Old.* Cambridge: MacMillan and Co., 1855.

———. *The Life of Frederick Denison Maurice, Chiefly Told in His Own Letters.* Ed. (John) Frederick Maurice. 2 vols. London: Macmillan and Co., 1884.

———. "National Tales of Ireland." *Westminster Review* Apr. 1828: 422–40. *ProQuest: British Periodicals.* Web.

———. "On Right and Wrong Methods of Supporting Protestantism. A Letter to Lord Ashley." London: J. W. Parker, 1843.

———, John Ludlow, et al., eds. *Politics for the People.* London: John W. Parker, 1848. Armstrong Browning Library. 19th Century Collection.

———. "Reasons for Not Joining a Party in the Church, A Letter to the Ven. Samuel Wilberforce, Archdeacon of Surrey: Suggested by the Rev. Dr. Hook's Letter to the Bishop of Ripon, on the State of Parties in the Church of England." London: J. G. F. & J. Rivington, 1841. *Project Canterbury.* Transcribed Charles Wohlers, 2006. Web.

———. *Sermons on the Prayer-Book and the Lord's Prayer.* London: Macmillan and Co., 1880.

———. *Sermons Preached in Lincoln's Inn Chapel.* New ed. Vol. 5. London: Macmillan and Co., 1892.

———. *Social Morality: Twenty-One Lectures Delivered in the University of Cambridge.* London: Macmillan and Co., 1869.

———. *Sermons on the Sabbath-Day, on the Character of the Warrior, and on the Interpretation of History.* London: J. W. Parker, 1853.

———. "Sketches of Contemporary Authors: No. II—Mr. Jeffrey and the Edinburgh Review." *The Athenaeum* 23 Jan. 1828: 49–50. *ProQuest: British Periodicals.* Web.

———. "Sketches of Contemporary Authors: No. III—Mr. Southey." *The Athenaeum* 29 Jan. 1828: 65–66. *ProQuest: British Periodicals.* Web.

———. "Sketches of Contemporary Authors: No. V—Mr. Wordsworth." *The Athenaeum* 19 Feb. 1828: 113–15. *ProQuest: British Periodicals.* Web.

———. "Sketches of Contemporary Authors: No. IX—Sir Walter Scott." *The Athenaeum* 11 Mar. 1828: 217–19. *ProQuest: British Periodicals.* Web.

Mayhew, Henry. *London Labour and the London Poor.* Introd. John D. Rosenberg. Vol. 3. New York: Dover Publications Inc., 1968.

McBratney, John. "Akbar's 'Fane': Tennyson's Reclamation of the East." *Victorian Poetry* 31.4 (Winter 1993): 411–17.

McCullagh, Thomas. "A Collection of Hymns for the Use of the People called Methodists." *The London Quarterly Review* Jan. 1876: 356–80. *ProQuest: British Periodicals.* Web.

McKelvy, William R. "Children of the Sixties: Post-Secular Victorian Studies and Victorian Secularization." *Nineteenth-Century Prose* 39.1–2 (Spring/Fall 2012): 17–32.

———. *The English Cult of Literature: Devote Readers, 1774–1880.* Charlottesville: University of Virginia Press, 2007.

McKeon, Michael, *The Secret History of Domesticity: Public, Private, and the Division of Knowledge.* Baltimore: Johns Hopkins University Press, 2005.

McLeod, Hugh. "Protestantism and British National Identity, 1815–1945." *Nation and Religion: Perspectives on Europe and Asia.* Ed. Peter van der Veer and Hartmut Lehmann. Princeton University Press, 1999. 44–70.

———. *Religion and Irreligion in Victorian England: How Secular was the Working Class?* Bangor: Headstart History, 1993.

———. *Religion and Society in England, 1850–1914.* New York: St. Martin's Press, 1996.

McLeod, Hugh and Werner Ustorf, eds. *The Decline of Christendom in Western Europe, 1750–2000.* Cambridge: Cambridge University Press, 2003.

Milburn, Michael. "Imagined spiritual communities in the digital age." Report on a discussion of the Super Official Catholic Reading Group (SOCRG). St. Peter's Catholic Student Center (Waco, TX). 4 Dec. 2014. *Microsoft Word* file.

Miles, Robert. *Romantic Misfits.* Basingstoke: Palgrave Macmillan, 2008.

———. "Trouble in the Republic of Letters: The Reception of the Shakespeare Forgeries." *Studies in Romanticism* 44.3 (2005): 317–40.

"Miss Rossetti's 'Verses.'" *The Speaker* 25 November 1893: 588. *ProQuest: British Periodicals.* Web.

"Moods and Tenses: II. Exaltations." *The Nonconformist* 4 Feb. 1863: 92–93. *Access Newspaper Archive.* Web.

Morris, Jeremy. *F. D. Maurice and the Crisis of Christian Authority.* Oxford: Oxford University Press, 2005.

Murray, Nicholas. *A Life of Matthew Arnold.* New York: St. Martin's Press, 1996.

"Musical, Dramatic, Literary, and Artistic News and Gossip." *Evening Herald* 28 Dec. 1861: 5. *Access Newspaper Archive.* Web.

Neville, Graham. *Coleridge and Liberal Religious Thought.* London: I. B. Taurus, 2010.

"New Poetry—Tennyson, Browning, and Taylor." *The English Review* Sept. 1850: 65–92. *ProQuest: British Periodicals.* Web.

Newlyn, Lucy. *Reading, Writing, and Romanticism: The Anxiety of Reception.* Oxford: Oxford University Press, 2000.

Noble, James Ashcroft. "The Sonnet in England." *The Contemporary Review* XXXVIII July–Dec. 1880: 446–71. *ProQuest: British Periodicals.* Web.

NorthPointOnline.TV. North Point Ministries Inc., 2014. Web. 17 Dec. 2014.

"Note on Sales: Keble's 'The Christian Year.'" *Times Literary Supplement* 14 July 1927: 492. *TLS Historical Archive: 1902–2005.* Gale-Cengage Learning. Web.

"Notices of New Books. The Inner Life. A Poem." *The Christian Witness* May 1867: 236.

Nunokawa, Jeffrey. "In Memoriam and the Extinction of the Homosexual." *ELH* 58.2 (1991): 427–38.

Nussbaum, Martha. *Not for Profit: Why Democracy Needs the Humanities.* Princeton: Princeton University Press, 2010.

Nye, Eric W. "John Sterling." *The Oxford Dictionary of National Biography (DNB).* Online ed. Oxford University Press, 2004. Web. 23 July 2010.

Ong, Walter J., S. J. *Orality and Literacy: The Technologizing of the Word.* London: Routledge, 2004.

Palazzo, Lynda. *Christina Rossetti's Feminist Theology.* Houndmills, Basingstoke, UK: Palgrave, 2002.

Patmore, Coventry. "Maud and other Poems." *The Edinburgh Review* Oct. 1855: 498–519. *ProQuest: British Periodicals.* Web.

———. "In Memoriam." *North British Review* Aug. 1850: 532–55. *ProQuest: British Periodicals.* Web.

Pearse, Meic. *Why the Rest Hates the West: Understanding the Roots of Global Rage.* Downers Grove: Intervarsity Press, 2004.

Perkins, Mary Anne. *Coleridge's Philosophy: The Logos as Unifying Principle.* Oxford: Clarendon Press, 1994.

Phelan, Joseph. *The Nineteenth-Century Sonnet.* Houndmills, UK: Palgrave, 2005.

"Poetical Theology and Theological Poetry." *Fraser's Magazine* Nov. 1868: 623–41.

Pope, Alexander. *The Poems of Alexander Pope.* Ed. John Butt. New Haven: Yale University Press, 1963.

Potkay, Adam. "Wordsworth, Henry Reed and Bishop Doane: High-Church Romanticism on the Delaware." *Wordsworth in American Literary Culture.* Ed. Joel Pace and Matthew Scott. Houndmills, UK: Palgrave Macmillan, 2005. 101–20.

Prickett, Stephen. "Coleridge and the Idea of the Clerisy," *Reading Coleridge: Approaches and Applications,* Ed. Walter B. Crawford. Ithaca: Cornell University Press, 1979. 252–73.

Reahard, Jeff. "Second Life readies for 10th anniversary, celebrates a million active users per month." *Massively.* Joystiq: AOL Inc., 20 June 2013. Web. 21 Dec. 2014.

Reardon, Bernard M. G. "Frederick Denison Maurice." *The Oxford Dictionary of National Biography (DNB).* Online ed. Oxford University Press, 2006. Web. 23 July 2010.

———. *From Coleridge to Gore: A Century of Religious Thought in Britain.* Worcester: Longman, 1971.

"Recent Verse." *The Saturday Review* 76 (Oct. 21, 1893): 476–77. *ProQuest: British Periodicals.* Web.

Reed, John Shelton. *Glorious Battle: The Cultural Politics of Victorian Anglo-Catholicism.* Nashville: Vanderbilt University Press, 1996.

Rees, Henry D. "Free Church Hymn-Writers. II.-The Rev. William Tid Matson." *The Puritan: An Illustrated Magazine for Free Churchmen* July 1899: 485–87.

"The Reform Bills." *The Patriot* 7 June 1866: 384. *Access Newspaper Archive.* Web.

"Religion and Electronic Media: One-in-Five Americans Share Their Faith Online." Pew Research Center, 6 Nov. 2014. Web. 18 Dec. 2014.

Rigg, James Harrison. "The Guardian Newspaper." *London Quarterly Review* July 1866: 403–27. *ProQuest: British Periodicals.* Web.

Roberts, Steven. "The Companies and the News." *Distant Writing: A History of the Telegraph Companies in Britain between 1838 and 1868.* The British Library: The UK Web Archive. 4 Dec. 2012. Web. 18 Dec. 2014.

Robertson, Frederick W. *Lectures and Addresses on Literary and Social Topics.* 1858. 2nd ed. Boston: Ticknor and Fields, 1869.

Roe, Dinah. *Christina Rossetti's Faithful Imagination: The Devotional Poetry and Prose.* Houndmills, Basingstoke, UK: Palgrave Macmillan, 2006.

Rossetti, Christina. *The Complete Poems.* Ed. R. W. Crump, with notes and introduction by Betty S. Flowers. London: Penguin, 2005.

———. *The Face of the Deep: A Devotional Commentary on the Apocalypse* (1892). Sixth ed. London: Society for Promoting Christian Knowledge, 1911.

———. *The Letters of Christina Rossetti.* 4 vols. Ed. Antony H. Harrison. Charlottesville: University Press of Virginia: 1997–2004.

———. *Time Flies: A Reading Diary.* London: SPCK, 1897.

———. *Verses.* London: SPCK, 1893.

———. *Verses.* London: SPCK, 1898.

———. *Verses.* London: SPCK, 1925.

Rossetti, Dante Gabriel. *The Correspondence of Dante Gabriel Rossetti.* 9 vols. Ed. William E. Fredeman. Cambridge: D. S. Brewer, 2002–2010.

Rossetti, William Michael, ed. *The Germ: Thoughts towards Nature in Poetry, Literature and Art.* London: Elliot Stock, 1901.

———, ed. *New Poems by Christina Rossetti, Hitherto Unpublished or Collected.* London: Macmillan and Co., 1896.

———, ed. *The Poetical Works of Christina Georgina Rossetti, with Memoir and Notes, etc.* London: Macmillan, 1904.

"The Rossettis." *The London Quarterly Review* Oct. 1896: 1–16. *ProQuest: British Periodicals.* Web.

Rowlands, John Henry Lewis. *Church, State, and Society: The Attitudes of John Keble, Richard Hurrell Froude, and John Henry Newman, 1827–1845.* Worthing, West Sussex: Churchman Publishing, 1989.

Rowlinson, Matthew. "History, Materiality and Type in Tennyson's *In Memoriam.*" *Darwin, Tennyson and their Readers.* Ed. Valerie Purton. London: Anthem Press, 2013. 35–48.

Ruskin, John. *Modern Painters.* 5 vols. New York: John Wiley & Sons, 1882.

———. *The Stones of Venice.* 3 vols. New York: John Wiley & Sons, 1890.

Russell, C. W. "Critical History of the Sonnet" (2 Parts). *The Dublin Review* 27 (1876): 400–30; 28 (1877): 141–80.

Ryan, Robert. "The Genealogy of Honest Doubt: F. D. Maurice." *The Critical Spirit and the Will to Believe.* Ed. David Jasper and T. R. Wright. New York: St. Martin's Press, 1989. 120–30.

"S.2588-Cybersecurity Information Sharing Act of 2014." *Congress.Gov.* The Library of Congress. 10 July 2014. Web. 27 Dec. 2014.

Sanders, Charles Richard. *Coleridge and the Broad Church Movement.* Durham: Duke University Press, 1942.

Sanders, Mike. *The Poetry of Chartism: Aesthetics, Politics, History.* Cambridge: Cambridge University Press, 2009.

Scherer, Matthew. "Landmarks in the Critical Study of Secularism." *Cultural Anthropology* 26.4 (2011): 621–32.

Schlossberg, Herbert. *Conflict and Crisis in the Religious Life of Late Victorian England.* New Brunswick: Transaction Publishers, 2009.

Scott, Patrick. "The Business of Belief: The Emergence of 'Religious' Publishing." *Sanctity and Secularity: The Church and the World (Studies in Church History, X).* Ed. Derek Baker. Oxford: Basil Blackwell, 1973. 213–24.

———. "Rewriting the Book of Nature: Tennyson, Keble, and *The Christian Year.*" *Victorians Institute Journal* 17 (1989): 141–55.

Scott, William Bell. *Poems.* London: Longmans, Green, and Co., 1875. *Google Books.* Web.

Shairp, William. "John Keble." *Studies in Poetry and Philosophy.* 1868. Port Washington, N. Y.: Kennikat Press, 1970.

Sharp, William. "Some Reminiscences of Christina Rossetti." *The Atlantic Monthly* 70 (June 1895): 736–49.

———, ed. *Sonnets of this Century.* London: Walter Scott, 1886.

Shaw, Marion. "*In Memoriam* and *The Christian Year.*" *John Keble in Context.* Ed. Kirstie Blair. London: Anthem Press, 2004. 159–74.

Sheehan, Jonathan. "When Was Disenchantment? History and the Secular Age." In Warner, Vantwerpen, and Calhoun, 2010. 217–42.

Shelley, Mary. *Frankenstein, or the Modern Prometheus: The 1818 Text.* Ed. Marilyn Butler. Oxford: Oxford University Press, 1993.

Sherman, Kevin Miguel. "An Imagined Community of Avatars? A Theoretical Interrogation of *Second Life* as Nation through the Lens of Benedict Anderson's Imagined Communities." *Creating Second Lives: Community, Identity and Spatiality as Constructions of the Virtual.* Ed. Astrid Ensslin and Eben Muse. New York: Routledge, 2011. 32–54.

Smellie, A. "Christina Rossetti and Her Message." *Wesleyan Methodist Magazine* (March 1895): 203–6. *ProQuest: British Periodicals.* Web.

St. Clair, William. *The Reading Nation in the Romantic Period.* Cambridge: Cambridge University Press, 2004.

Stead, William Thomas. "Wanted, An English Bible! Suggestion for Its Compilation.—With Criticisms by Mr. Bryce." *The Daily Paper* (Oct. 4, 1893): 25–27.

[Sterling, John.] "The English Periodical Press." *The Athenaeum and Literary Chronicle* 7 Aug. 1828: 695–96. *ProQuest: British Periodicals.* Web.

Stevens, Paul and Rahul Sapra, "Akbar's Dream: Moghul Toleration and English/British Orientalism." *Modern Philology* 104(3) (2007): 379–411.

Stewart, Garrett. *Dear Reader: The Conscripted Audience in Nineteenth-Century British Fiction.* Baltimore: The Johns Hopkins University Press, 1996.

Stone, J. S. "The Home Aspect of Mr. Tennyson's Poems." *The Leisure Hour* 22 Jan. 1876: 54–56. *ProQuest: British Periodicals*. Web.

"Stratagem." *The Christian Witness.* 1 May 1871: 261.

Sussman, Herbert L. *Fact into Figure: Typology in Carlyle, Ruskin, and the Pre-Raphaelite Brotherhood.* Columbus: Ohio State University Press, 1979.

Symons, Arthur. "Christina G. Rossetti. 1830–1894." *The Poets and the Poetry of the Nineteenth Century: Christina G. Rossetti to Katharine Tynan.* Ed. Alfred H. Miles. London: George Routledge and Sons, Ltd., 1907. 1–16.

Taft, Joshua. "The Forms of Discipline: Christina Rossetti's Religious Verse." *Victorian Poetry* 51.3 (Fall 2013): 311–30.

Taylor, Charles. "Apologia pro Libro suo." In Warner, VanAntwerpen, Calhoun, 2010. 300–21.

———. *A Secular Age.* Cambridge: Harvard University Press, 2007.

———. "Western Secularity." *Rethinking Secularism.* Ed. Craig Calhoun et al. New York: Oxford University Press, 2011. 31–53.

Tennyson, Alfred. *In Memoriam.* Eds. Susan Shatto and Marion Shaw. Oxford: Clarendon Press, 1982.

———. *The Poems of Tennyson.* Ed. Christopher Ricks. 2nd ed. 3 vols. Berkeley: University of California Press, 1987.

Tennyson, G. B. *Victorian Devotional Poetry: The Tractarian Mode.* Cambridge: Harvard University Press, 1981.

Tennyson, Hallam. *Alfred Lord Tennyson: A Memoir by His Son.* 2 vols. New York: The Macmillan Co., 1897.

"Tennyson's In Memoriam." *The Eclectic Review* (Sept. 1850): 330–41. *ProQuest: British Periodicals.* Web.

Thompson, John B. *The Media and Modernity: A Social Theory of the Media.* Stanford: Stanford University Press, 1995.

Thomson, James. *The Complete Poetical Works of James Thomson.* Ed. J. Logie Robertson. London: Oxford University Press, 1951.

Thomson, James (B. V.). *The Complete Poems.* Arlington, VA: Charles & Wonder Purveyors of Fine Literature, 2012.

———. *The Speedy Extinction of Evil and Misery: Selected Prose of James Thomson (B. V.).* Ed. William David Shaefer. Berkeley: University of California Press, 1967.

Thwaite, Ann. *Emily Tennyson: The Poet's Wife.* London: Faber and Faber, 1996.

Tomko, Michael. "Varieties of Geological Experience: Religion, Body, and Spirit in Tennyson's *In Memoriam* and Lyell's *Principles of Geology.*" *Victorian Poetry* 42.2 (Summer 2004): 113–33.

Tomlinson, Charles. *The Sonnet: Its Origin, Structure, and Place in Poetry.* London: John Murray, 1874.

Tucker, Herbert. "The Fix of Form: An Open Letter." *Victorian Literature and Culture* 27 (1999): 531–35.

Turner, Bryan S. "Post-Secular Society: Consumerism and the Democratization of Religion." *The Post-Secular in Question: Religion in Contemporary Society.* Ed. Philip S. Gorski et al. New York: University Press, 2012. 135–58.

Tushnet, Eve. *Eve Tushnet*. Patheos, n.d. Web. 17 Dec. 2014.

Tynan, Katharine. "The Poetry of Christina Rossetti." *The Bookman* Dec. 1893: 78–79. *ProQuest: British Periodicals*. Web.

Van Young, Eric. "The Limits of Atlantic-World Nationalism in a Revolutionary Age: Imagined Communities and Lived Communities in Mexico, 1810–1921." *Empire to Nation: Historical Perspectives on the Making of the Modern World*. Ed. Joseph W Esherick, Hasan Kayali, and Eric Van Young. Lanham: Rowman & Littlefield Pub., Inc., 2006. 35–67.

[Vernon, John Richard.] "Quiet Thoughts." *Sunday at Home* 30 Mar. 1868: 340–43. *ProQuest: British Periodicals*. Web.

"Verses." *The Athenaeum* 16 Dec. 1893: 842–43. *ProQuest: British Periodicals*. Web.

Vidler, Alex R. *F. D. Maurice and Company*. London: SCM Press Ltd., 1966.

Waddington, Samuel. *English Sonnets by Living Writers*. London: George Bell and Sons, 1881.

Wagner, Jennifer. *A Moment's Monument: Revisionary Poetics and the Nineteenth-Century English Sonnet*. Madison: Farleigh Dickinson University Press, 1996.

Waller, John O. "Christ's Second Coming: Christina Rossetti and the Premillennialist William Dodsworth." *Bulletin of the New York Public Library* 73.7 (Sept. 1969): 465–82.

Warner, Michael. *Publics and Counterpublics*. New York: Zone Books, 2002.

Warner, Michael, Jonathan VanAntwerpen, and Craig Calhoun, eds. "Introduction." *Varieties of Secularism in a Secular Age*. Cambridge: Harvard University Press, 2010.

Watson, J. R. *The English Hymn: A Critical and Historical Study*. Oxford: Clarendon Press, 1999.

Watson, Lily. "Christina G. Rossetti." *The Leisure Hour* Feb. 1895: 245–48. *ProQuest: British Periodicals*. Web.

———. "Christina Rossetti." *Sunday at Home* 5 May 1894: 425–28. *ProQuest: British Periodicals*. Web.

Watts[-Dunton], Theodore. "A Pageant and other Poems." *The Athenaeum* 10 September 1881: 327–28. *ProQuest: British Periodicals*. Web.

———. "Reminiscences of Christina Rossetti." *The Nineteenth Century* 37 (Feb. 1895): 355–66. *ProQuest: British Periodicals*. Web.

Weedon, Alexis. *Victorian Publishing: The Economics of Book Production for a Mass Market, 1836–1916*. Aldershot: Ashgate, 2003.

Wellings, Ben. "England." In Guntram H. Herb and David H. Kaplan, 2008. 158–68.

Westerholm, Joel. "In Defense of *Verses:* The Aesthetic and Reputation of Christina Rossetti's Late Poetry." *Renascence* 51.3 (Spring 1999): 191–203.

William, Braden. "The Works of George Herbert," *The British Quarterly Review* (July 1867): 97–125. *ProQuest: British Periodicals*. Web.

Williams, Isaac. "On Reserve in Communicating Religious Knowledge." *Tracts for the Times*. Vol. 4 (1836–1837). London: Printed for J. G. & F. Rivington, 1839.

———. "On Reserve in Communicating Religious Knowledge" [Part 2]. *Tracts for the Times*. Vol. 5 (1838–1840). London: J. G. F. & J. Rivington, 1840.

Williams, Raymond. "Advertising: the Magic System." *Culture and Materialism: Selected Essays*. 1980. London: Verso, 2005. 170–95.

———. "Communications and Community." *Resources of Hope: Culture, Democracy, and Socialism*. London: Verso, 1989. 19–31.

———. "Means of Communication as Means of Production." *Problems in Materialism and Culture: Selected Essays*. London: Verso, 1980. 50–66.

Wordsworth, William. *The Excursion*. Ed. Sally Bushell, James A. Butler, Michael C. Jaye, and David García. Ithaca: Cornell University Press, 2007.

———. *The Prose Works of William Wordsworth*. Vol. 1. Oxford: Clarendon Press, 1974.

Wright, Luke Savin Herrick. "*On the Divine Ideas:* The Systematic Theology of Samuel Taylor Coleridge." *Coleridge's Assertion of Religion: Essays on the Opus Maximum*. Ed. Jeffrey Barbeau. Leuven, Belgium: Peeters, 2006. 53–72.

———. *Samuel Taylor Coleridge and the Anglican Church*. Notre Dame: University of Notre Dame, 2010.

Wright, N. T. *Surprised by Hope: Rethinking Heaven, the Resurrection, and the Mission of the Church*. New York: HarperOne, 2008.

Yates, Nigel. *Anglican Ritualism in Victorian Britain, 1830–1910*. Oxford: Oxford University Press, 1999.

Yonge, Charlotte. *Musings over "The Christian Year" and "Lyra Innocentium."* 2nd ed. Oxford: James Parker and Co., 1872.

INDEX

Allen, Peter, 60, 174, 303

Altholz, Josef, 63–64, 67, 68, 70, 117, 146, 159, 165, 181, 184, 186, 259, 280, 290n1, 304

Altick, Richard D., 9, 75, 89, 100, 117, 148, 249n20, 258, 280n64, 304

Anderson, Benedict, 3–4, 6, 8, 46, 47–48, 58–59, 59n1, 63, 84–85, 86, 91, 92, 130, 147–50, 303. *See also* imagined community, national

Anglo-Catholicism, 66n2, 157, 160, 161, 180, 183, 184, 186, 230; Arnold on, 122; Christina Rossetti and, 16, 233, 234, 236, 237, 237n10–12, 238, 240, 252–56, 257, 258, 260, 263, 266, 281, 282, 283–84, 283n70; Maurice on, 69, 71; and Public Worship Regulation Act (1874), 253; *Verses* and, 236, 240, 252–54, 255, 263, 265n40, 266, 281, 282, 283–84, 283n70. See also *Christian Year, The*; Christianity; Church of England; Evangelicalism; High Church; Nonconformity and Dissent; Roman Catholicism; Tractarianism; *Verses*

apRoberts, Ruth, 106, 108n7, 110, 303

Arnold, Matthew, 7, 10, 11, 13, 16, 18, 51, 96–126, 156, 226, 230, 272, 290, 297, 298, 299, 300, 303; on anarchy, 100, 101, 109, 112, 116, 117, 119, 299; appropriation of theological authority, 98, 124–125; on the "best self," 98, 101, 102, 110, 115–17, 119; on Bible, Anglican liturgy, and Prayer Book as "charming" and "poetic" ethical language for binding together the reading nation, 13, 98, 99, 102, 104, 105–22; and "buffered self" and "immanent frame," 103–4, 114–15; comparison with Coleridge and Maurice, 11, 13, 96–97, 230, 297; "critical tact" and unacknowledged claim to inspiration, 124–25; on culture, 13–14, 98, 101–2, 119, 120, 123–25; on humanizing power of secular poetry, 102, 108, 111, 111n8, 112; influenced by *The Christian Year*, 106; on middle-class leadership of reading nation, 100, 101, 110, 114; mischaracterized as advocating "replacement" of institutional Christianity with poetry and culture, 13–14, 97, 98–99, 125; on regulative force and violence of the state, 109, 115, 116, 118, 119, 123, 124, 125, 300. *See also* Anglo-Catholicism; British Christian community, imagined; Broad

Church; Chartism; *Christian Year, The;* Church of England; clerisy; education; Evangelicalism; High Church; imagined community, national; nation-state; Nonconformity and Dissent; public sphere; publics; religion; Roman Catholicism; secular; secularization; Tractarianism; working classes

Arnold, Mathew, works of: *A Bible-Reading for Schools: The Great Prophecy of Israel's Restoration (Isaiah, Chapters 40–66),* 110–12, 115; "The Church of England,"116, 297; "A Comment on Christmas," 117n10; *Culture and Anarchy,* 98, 100, 101, 107, 109, 117, 119, 120, 156; "Dover Beach," 272; "Emerson," 107; "Irish Catholicism and British Liberalism," 117n10, 121; *Isaiah of Jerusalem,* 110–112, 114, 116–17; *Isaiah XL–LXVI,* 111–12, 113–14, 115, 116; "A Last Word on the Burials Bill," 117–22, 117n10, 119n11; *Literature and Dogma,* 99, 101, 102, 104, 109, 110, 114, 115, 119, 122, 123, 125; *St. Paul and Protestantism,* 104, 109–10; "A Psychological Parallel," 106, 117n10; *Reports on Elementary Schools,* 102, 110, 111, 111n8, 112, 116, 303; "The Study of Poetry," 98–99, 102

Arseneau, Mary, 237n10, 247, 260, 303

Asad, Talal, 6–7, 56n16, 119, 135, 229, 304

Austin, Alfred, 213–14, 304

Badescu, Gruia, 5, 310

Baker, Arthur E., 117, 228, 304

Baker, Luke, 56n15, 304

Barbeau, Jeffrey W., 50, 304, 321

Barton, Anna, 202, 220, 304

Beer, John, 52n12, 304, 306

Bentley, James, 254, 304

Blain, Virginia H., 282, 304

Blair, Kirstie, x, 129n2, 130, 131n5, 135, 196, 304–5; *Form and Faith in Victorian Poetry and Religion,* 11, 66n2, 105–6, 107n6, 108, 118, 160, 160n2, 163n5, 164, 165, 168n8, 174, 190, 199, 204, 210n11, 222n15, 225–26, 227, 237n10, 258, 283n70; *Victorian Poetry and the Culture of the Heart,* 106, 203n8

Blake, William, 55, 305

Bolter, Jay, 139n12, 294, 305

Bradley, Katherine Harris ("Michael Field"), 243, 305. See also Cooper, Edith Emma

Briggs, Asa, 293, 305

Brimley, George, 218, 219, 221, 305; on Tennyson's poetry as semi-sacred national scripture, 213–16, 217, 225

British Christian community, imagined: competing visions of print-mediated unity, 2, 3, 4, 14–15, 125–26, 131, 166–67, 155–58, 220, 289, 297; demarcation of divergent publics and counterpublics within broadly or vaguely Christian reading nation, 12, 15–16, 186–88, 229–31, 237, 290, 290n1; dilution and dissolution of print-mediated Christian Britain, 16–17, 290–94, 301; imagined in tension with international Christian community, 16–17, 237, 248, 291–92; imagined through printed page more than any single religious group's sites or institutions, 8–10, 10n5, 12–13, 16–17, 48, 74, 76, 92, 96–97, 99–100, 123, 131–35, 147, 155–58, 182–83, 292, 297; and Protestantism, 3, 4, 6, 8, 11, 13, 14, 15–16, 61–62, 69, 70–71, 72–73, 102, 104–5, 109–10, 118, 121–22, 126, 133–34, 149, 155, 156, 157, 158, 180, 181, 182, 183, 187, 199, 225, 226, 230, 249, 253–54, 291; and questioning/sanctifying imperialism, 16–17, 62, 224, 225, 230, 248–49, 291–92. See also *Christian Year, The;* Christianity; Church of England; education; imagined community, national; *In Memoriam, A. H. H.;* media; nation-state; newspapers and periodicals; public sphere; publics; religion; secular; secularization; *Verses;* voluntary religious association; working classes

Broad Church, 155–56; and Arnold, 13, 97, 106; and Coleridge, 13, 22, 97; and High Church and Tractarian poetics, 106; and *In Memoriam, A. H. H.,* 160, 184; limits of category, 13, 97; and

Maurice, 13, 97, 106; and Tennyson, 160, 163n5, 163–64, 184, 221. *See also* Cambridge "Apostles"; Christianity; Church of England; Evangelicalism; High Church; Tractarianism

Brose, Olive J., 60, 68, 70, 73, 305

Brown, Callum, 9, 10, 11, 76, 100, 292, 293–94, 305

Brown, Stewart J., 5, 226, 290, 290n1, 291, 292, 292n2, 305

Bruce, Steve, 5, 305

Butler, Marilyn, 40n8, 318

Byron, Lord Gordon, 44, 305

Caine, Thomas Hall, 269, 269n48, 277n58, 305

Calhoun, Craig, 179, 180, 226, 305, 306, 318, 319, 320

Calleo, David P., 46, 48, 306

Cambridge "Apostles": and Coleridge, 22, 53, 60, 174; and Maurice, 22, 53, 60, 65, 174; and Tennyson, 174. *See also* Broad Church; clerisy

Canuel, Mark, 23, 35–36, 35n6, 306

Carey, Hilary M., 6, 224, 251, 291, 306

Carlyle, Thomas, 140, 141, 306

Carruthers, Jo, 5, 122, 225, 306

Carter, John, 263n34, 306

Casanova, José, 5, 8, 44, 190, 226, 306

Chadwick, Owen, 133, 157n15, 306

Chambers, Edmund K., 265, 265n40, 279, 279n61, 280, 280n63, 280n65, 306

Chapman, Alison, 266, 268n44, 306, 308, 310, 313

Chapman, Elizabeth Rachel, 213, 306

Chapman, Raymond, 66n2, 306

Chartism, 57–58, 74–75, 76, 77, 82, 89, 187, 222, 223; and Arnold, 109, 115; and *In Memoriam, A. H. H.*, 222; and Maurice, 74–77, 78, 89. *See also* Reform Acts; voting; working classes

Christensen, Torben, 76, 77, 81, 82, 89, 306

Christian Socialism: Maurice and, 74, 74n4, 82. *See also* socialism; working classes

Christian Year, The (Keble), 106, 129–58, 131n5, 173, 181, 230, 234n5; and "analogy" and typological interpretation, 130–31, 130n4, 137–46, 139n13, 147–48, 150–55, 158, 208–9, 239, 241, 271; and Church Calendar, 129, 137, 144, 147, 150, 152–53, 158, 165, 174, 192–93, 195, 195n3, 234, 264, 264n37; and doctrine of reserve, 130n4, 134–35, 134n7, 136–37, 144, 146, 152; and interdenominational reception and competing uses of, 1, 3, 126, 131, 139–40, 139n13, 144, 146, 147, 150, 155–58, 166, 167, 196–97, 208, 290, 295, 297; as poetic cycle that turns private reading into participation in national Christian community, 1, 3, 14–15, 16, 97, 125, 130–31, 144, 146, 147–158, 166–67, 169, 171, 208, 230–31, 233–34, 290, 295, 297; popularity and influence, 2, 129–30, 129n1, 129n2, 130n3, 146, 154, 167, 259; and reassertion of Book of Common Prayer and Church of England's discipline over private reading, 14, 131–37, 141, 143, 147, 150, 155, 183, 296; and secular time of print-mediated national imagination, 147–55, 158, 239; and "typology of everyday life," 208. *See also* Anglo-Catholicism; British Christian community, imagined; Church of England; High Church; hymn; *In Memoriam, A. H. H.*; poetic form and genre; religion; secular; secularization; Tractarianism; *Verses*

Christian Year, The (Keble), discussion of poems in: "Christmas Day," 192–93, 200; "Eighteenth Sunday after Trinity," 142; "Evening," 166, 169–70, 171, 172, 271; "Monday in Easter Week," 150–54; "Morning," 144, 169, 171, 172, 195, 201; "Septuagesima Sunday," 138, 151, 209, 272; "St. Bartholomew," 165; "St. Mark's Day," 156; "St. Matthew's Day," 145–46, 181–82, 181n13, 239; "St. Thomas' Day," 144–45, 208; "Sunday next before Advent," 150; "Third Sunday in Lent," 170; "Thursday before Easter,"

141–44; "Trinity Sunday," 152, 295; Twentieth Sunday After Trinity," 165; "Wednesday before Easter," 140, 144

Christianity: active versus passive identification with, 10, 16–17, 292; bibliographic manifestations of late-century alternatives to, 290, 290n1; church affiliation, 9, 292, 298; church attendance, 9, 55, 76, 107, 237n12, 282, 292–93, 292n2, 296, 298n3; public vitality of in nineteenth-century Britain, 10, 230, 292. *See also* Anglo-Catholicism; British Christian community, imagined; Broad Church; Christian Socialism; Church of England; Evangelicalism; High Church; imagined community, national; Methodism; nation-state; Nonconformity and Dissent; religion; Roman Catholicism; secular; secularization; voluntary religious association

Church of England: and 1851 census, 9, 11; loss of exclusive privileges, 6, 8–9, 10n4, 11, 99, 99n3, 157–58, 157n15; Arnold on role in creating national imagined spiritual community, 13, 97, 98, 99, 102–5, 107, 113–14, 116, 117, 118, 120–21, 125, 297; Maurice on role in creating national imagined spiritual community, 4, 12, 61, 71, 74, 74n4, 76, 82, 83, 86, 87, 90, 92, 95, 96–97, 163n1, 297; position as cultural center of gravity, 11; Tennyson on Church and state, 163, 163n5. *See also* Anglo-Catholicism; British Christian community, imagined; Broad Church; *Christian Year, The*; Christianity; clerisy; Evangelicalism; High Church; *In Memoriam, A. H. H.*; Methodism; nation-state; Nonconformity and Dissent; online and digital spiritual community; religion; secularization; Tractarianism; *Verses*; voluntary religious association

Claeys, Gregory, 82, 306

Clark, Lynn Schofield, 294, 298, 310

Clarke, W. K. Lowther, 261n31, 262, 287, 287n75, 306

clerisy, 2, 12–13, 22, 23, 43n10, 47n11, 53n13; and Arnold, 51, 103, 297; class and gender limits of Coleridge's clerisy, 23–25; Coleridge on clerisy and Church of England, 22, 43–44, 45, 50, 51, 289, 297; Coleridge on clerisy as agents of national spiritual imagination through education, Anglican devotion, and mass media, 22, 23, 38, 43n10, 43–52, 53, 297; influence of Coleridge's mass-media mission for, 52–54, 59; Maurice on, 25, 52–54, 59, 60, 73, 79–80, 297; and vocation of the humanities, 25, 55–56. *See also* British Christian community, imagined; Cambridge "Apostles"; Church of England; education; newspapers and periodicals; public sphere

Coleridge, Henry Nelson, 47, 60, 307

Coleridge, John Taylor, 132, 150, 154, 171n9, 306

Coleridge, Samuel Taylor, 1, 2, 11–13, 16, 21–56, 96–97, 132, 174, 230, 294, 297; elitism and views of reform, 23–25, 51–52, 54, 79–80, 90; and fiction of direct address to reader in virtual classroom of reflection, 2, 23, 25, 33, 37- 42, 43, 52, 59, 290, 294; on Logos as source of right Reason and principles governing reality, 23, 26–29, 32, 33, 35, 36–38, 39, 41, 42, 46, 54, 55, 59, 174–75; on manipulative appeals to "reason" and "the reading public," 34–35; on mass media as primary influence on national imagination because of differentiation of modern society, 44–45, 47–49, 51–52; on mass media fueling self-interest and commercial power, 47n11, 48–49, 51–52; on print culture and utilitarian empiricist materialism (the epoch of the Understanding), 22–23, 29–33, 35, 39, 41, 42, 49; on vitalism and resistance to fully disenchanted world, 39–42, 41n9. *See also* British Christian community, imagined; Broad Church; Cambridge "Apostles"; Church of England; clerisy; education; newspapers and periodicals; public sphere; publics; secularization; working classes

Coleridge, Samuel Taylor, works of: *Aids to Reflection*, 1, 1n1, 2, 21–56, 35n6, 59–60, 174, 175, 294, 306; *Biographia Literaria*, 32, 34, 35, 35n5, 39, 40, 42, 44, 53,

53n13, 54, 90, 307; *Confessions of an Inquiring Spirit*, 49, 50, 307; *Essays on His Times*, 48, 49, 307; *The Friend*, 25, 29, 35n6, 41, 43, 43n10, 45, 46, 47, 48, 49, 51, 307; *Lay Sermons*, 24–25, 30, 51, 307; *Lectures on Literature*, 21, 26, 29, 43n10, 47n11, 307; *Marginalia*, 26, 307; *Notebooks*, 47n11, 307; *On the Constitution of the Church and State, According to the Idea of Each*, 2, 22, 23, 24, 35n6, 38, 43, 44, 45–46, 48, 49, 50, 307; *Opus Maximum*, 26, 41, 307; *The Statesman's Manual*, 23, 24, 31, 34, 43n10, 51, 307; *Table Talk*, 47, 51, 307

Colley, Linda, 8, 61–62, 63, 134n6, 148, 149, 307

Connell, Phillip, 51–52, 307

Cook, Chris, 100n4, 307

Cooper, Edith Emma, 243, 305. See also Bradley, Katherine Harris

Cox, Jeffrey L., 10, 307

Craig, Caroline, 300n6, 307

Crimmins, James E., 30, 307

Culler, Dwight, 221, 307

Currie, Robert, 149, 307

D'Amico, Dianne, 233n4, 234n5, 237n10, 266, 307

Davies, William, 268n44, 274, 274n53, 277, 307

Dennis, John, 274n53, 277, 308

Dickens, Charles, 85–86, 149, 158, 308

Dicks, Bella, 3, 4, 308

Dieleman, Karen, x, 233n4, 234, 237n10, 244, 253, 256–57, 263, 265, 271, 282, 308

Eagleton, Terry, 98, 116, 308

Eastwood, Jonathan, 5, 309

Edgecombe, Rodney Stenning, 130n4, 244, 308

education, 2, 8–9, 11, 17, 23, 24, 43–52, 58, 70, 99, 100n5, 116, 133, 220, 258, 289; Arnold on humanistic state education awakening citizens to their "best selves" in a spiritually united reading nation, 13, 100, 101–3, 110–111, 123, 125; Elementary Education Act of 1870, 9n4, 100, 110; Elementary Education Act of 1880, 9n4, 100, 100n5; and humanizing members of the reading nation through poetry study, 98, 102, 110–13, 111n8, 122, 221–24; Maurice on education as key to awakening mass-mediated Christian Britain from sectarianism and class conflict, 54, 72–73, 74n4, 79–81, 82, 86, 94; Maurice's Working Men's College, 54, 82, 93–94. *See also* British Christian community, imagined; Church of England; clerisy; public sphere; secularization; working classes

Eliot, T. S., 176–77, 308

Erickson, Lee, 234, 257, 258, 259, 284–85, 308

Evangelicalism, 9, 59, 100–101, 120, 121, 139, 140, 160, 161, 166, 168, 178, 179, 185, 186, 187, 199, 201, 202, 216, 222, 229, 284, 290n1, 295–96, 298; and Evangelical distinguished from evangelical, 66n2; and *Evangelical Magazine and Missionary Chronicle*, 139n13, 305; *The Leisure Hour*, 162, 214, 217–20, 220n12, 277n59, 286n74, 303, 311, 319, 320; Maurice on print-mediated warfare with Tractarianism and High Church party, 66–73; *The Quiver*, 209, 304; *The Record*, 68, 69, 70, 72; *Sunday at Home*, 165, 168–69, 172–73, 185–86, 219, 280, 280n64–65, 281, 309, 313, 320. *See also* Anglo-Catholicism; Church of England; High Church; Methodism; Nonconformity and Dissent; Tractarianism

Everett, Glenn, 100n4, 308

Fitzgerald, William, 295, 296, 308

Frank, Mary C., 244n17, 308

Freshwater, R., 293, 308

Frey, Anne, x, 45, 308

Froude, James Anthony, 165, 308
Froude, Richard Hurrell, 67, 108, 109, 120, 165, 308

Genung, John Franklin, 191–92, 309
Gigante, Denise, 40, 41, 41n9, 309
Gilbert, Alan, 149, 307
Gilbert, Sandra M., 244, 309
Gilmartin, Kevin, 33, 309
Gladstone, W. E., 210, 221, 253, 309
Glaister, Geoffrey Ashall, 263, 263n35, 309
Golden, Arline, 267, 309
Greenfeld, Liah, 5, 309
Groth Lyon, Eileen, 76, 124, 309
Grusin, Richard, 139n12, 294, 305
Gubar, Susan, 244, 309
Guillory, John, 258, 309

Haass, Sabine, 260n29, 309
Habermas, Jürgen, 12, 96, 96n1, 124, 125, 309
Hair, Donald, 174, 174n10, 309
Halifax, Charles Wood, Lord, 254–55, 255n22, 309
Harrison, Antony, 109, 306, 308, 309, 313, 317
Harrison, J. F. C., 93, 94, 309
Harrison, Peter, 180, 309
Hassett, Constance W., 245, 309
Haweis, Rev. Hugh Reginald, 190, 196, 309
Hazlitt, William, 23–24, 31, 310
Hedley, Douglas, 27, 30, 35, 36, 310
Hempton, David, 9, 10, 310
Herb, Guntram H., 5, 309, 310, 320
Herrick, Robert, 249–51, 310
High Church, 66n2, 81, 107n6, 131n5, 190, 206–7, 219, 222, 243, 263, 265; Arnold as heterodox inheritor of High Church and Tractarian stress on regulated poetic, religious, and social form, 105–9, 113–14, 118, 120–21, 122; *The Christian Remembrancer*, 68, 70; and *English Review*, 159–60, 161, 175, 178, 182, 184–85, 186, 187–88, 204, 206, 207, 303, 315; and *The Guardian*, 154–55, 156, 284–85, 306, 311; Maurice on High Church and Tractarian print-mediated warfare with Evangelicalism, 66–73. *See also* Anglo-Catholicism; Broad Church; *Christian Year, The*; Church of England; Evangelicalism; poetic form and genre; Tractarianism; *Verses*
Hill, Alan, 163, 310
Holmes, John, 267, 267n42, 310
Holmes, Richard, 37, 40, 310
Honan, Park, 109, 116, 310
Hood, Edwin Paxton, 145, 146, 310
Hoover, Steward M., 294, 298, 310
Hopkins, Manley, 206–7, 310
Horsley, Lee, 149, 307
Hostettler, John, 100n4, 310
Houston, Natalie, 258, 267, 267n42, 310
Howard, Robert Glenn, 294, 296–97, 299, 309
hymn, 107n6, 109, 119n11, 121, 125, 139, 221, 229, 248, 261n32; and *Christian Year, The*, 144, 150, 152, 166, 171, 171n9, 172, 201; and *In Memoriam, A. H. H.*, 15, 162, 190, 199, 200–203, 212, 214, 215–16; and *Verses*, 236, 265, 265n40, 282–83, 285n71. *See also* poetic form and genre

imagined community, national: enablement by mass print media, 3–4, 47–48, 58–59, 63, 84–85, 86, 91, 92, 130, 147, 148, 149–50; and religion, 4, 6, 7, 8, 7n3, 15–16, 58–59, 86, 92, 130, 147, 148, 149; "spiritual" communities, 7. *See also* British Christian community, imagined; *Christian Year, The*; Christianity; *In Memoriam, A. H. H.*; media; nation-state; newspapers and periodicals; public sphere; religion; secular; secularization; *Verses*

INDEX   329

In Memoriam, A. H. H. (Tennyson), 14–16, 125, 159–231, 233–34, 243, 248, 251, 258, 270–72, 290n1, 319; and Book of Common Prayer, 172–73, 190, 199, 200, 200n5–6, 202, 212, 215; and "buffered self" and "immanent frame," 176, 179–80; and church bells, 15, 190, 191, 195–99, 200, 212, 215, 216, 225; and Church calendar (especially Christmas Eve and Christmas), 172, 190, 191–98, 199–201, 212, 214–15, 216; comparison with *The Christian Year* by Victorians, 162, 163, 164–67, 169–71, 182, 188, 189, 199, 200, 208–10; complication of idea that faith is privatized in modern nations, 15, 163, 189–90; "differentiation" of scientific and poetic authority, 177–78, 190; diverse uses of to imagine spiritual community and place in nation's spiritual landscape, 160–66, 168–69, 171–73, 178–79, 183–88, 189, 190–91, 195, 197, 203–4, 207, 212, 216–20, 221–24, 225, 229–30; division of inward faith from outer secular world, 173–82, 190, 210–12, 215–16; and domestic devotion as national community, 196, 197, 199–201, 202–3, 218; and formal creeds, 161, 162, 168, 169, 171, 173, 174, 175, 182, 186, 190, 191, 194, 219; homoeroticism of, 178, 178n11, 206–7; and inalienable minimum of faith, 160–61, 174–75, 183–85, 186, 189, 191, 192, 203–4, 215, 221–23, 225; and internal, epistemological and private construction of "religion" in Western societies, 179–82, 187, 188, 191–92, 199, 223–24; and internalized "typology of everyday life," 15, 208–20; introductory stanzas interpreted by Victorians, 167–73, 182, 186, 190, 191, 217; as national scripture, 208–20, 225; private testimony of faith enabled by public religious and cultural forms, 15, 161–63, 171, 172, 173, 182, 190–220; and secular cycles and liturgies, 193–95; use for repressive and imperialist versions of sacred British community, 191, 220–31. *See also* British Christian community, imagined; Broad Church; Chartism; Church of England; *Christian Year, The*; hymn; poetic form and genre; religion; secular; secularization; *Verses*; working classes

Iraq War, 56, 56n15, 304

Islam, 4–5, 227–29, 294, 300

Ives, Maura, 235n8–9, 248, 258, 258n24, 260n30, 263, 263n36, 265, 268–69n46, 282, 285, 285n71, 310

Jager, Colin, x, 7, 7n3, 136, 209–10, 223–24, 310–11

Janes, Dominic, 254, 311

Johnson, Maria Poggi, 136n9, 311

Jones, Mark, 37n7, 311

Jones, Tod E., 52n12, 97, 311

Kaiser, David Aram, 44, 311

Kaufmann, Michael W., 98, 311

Keble, John, 2–3, 7, 9, 14, 16, 18, 67, 97, 105–6, 108, 125–26, 129–58, 162–67, 169, 170–72, 171n9, 181, 188–89, 192–95, 195n3, 200–201, 204, 208–9, 211, 215–16, 222, 222n15, 230, 233–34, 234n5, 239, 240, 244, 253, 259, 264, 266, 271–73, 290, 295–97, 311; on "analogy" and disciplines of typological interpretation, 135, 136, 136n9, 137–46, 139n12–13, 147–48; anxiety over "feverish thirst after knowledge" and confidence in private judgment stimulated by print culture, 131–37, 141–43, 147, 158, 183; conservatism of, 133–34, 134n6, 183; and "reserve" as strategy for resisting excesses of print culture, 134–35, 134n7, 137, 147; on sacred poetry and print culture, 136–37. *See also* Anglo-Catholicism; British Christian community, imagined; *Christian Year, The*; Church of England; High Church; *In Memoriam, A. H. H.*; religion; Roman Catholicism; Tractarianism; *Verses*; working classes

Keble, John, works of: "National Apostasy" sermon (*Sermons*), 9, 57, 158; *Occasional Papers and Reviews*, 136–37, 311; "On the Mysticism Attributed to the Early Fathers of the Church" (*Tracts for the Times*), 135–37, 137n10, 138, 151, 311; "Sacred Poetry" (*Occasional Papers*), 136–37; *Sermons Academical and Occasional*, 9, 67, 132, 134, 134n6, 158, 311; "Sunday Lessons: The Principle of Selection" (*Tracts for the Times*), 137, 143, 311. See also *Christian Year, The*

Keen, Paul, 31, 33, 34, 36, 64, 311

Kent, Christopher, 53, 53n13, 280n64, 311–12

Kent, David, 233n4, 234n7, 266, 285, 287, 308, 312

Kingsley, Charles, 74, 169, 173, 177, 178, 185, 186, 197, 202n7, 312

Kitson, Peter J., 24, 25, 35, 312

Klancher, Jon, 33, 35, 43n10, 63, 311, 312

Kline, Daniel, 106, 108, 312

Knight, Frances, 70, 312

Knight, Mark, x, xi, 11, 312

Knights, Ben, 22, 312

Kooistra, Lorraine Janzen, 263, 264n38, 287, 312

Korshin, Paul J., 149n14, 208, 312

Kriegel, Lara, 3, 312

Kumar, Krishan, 5, 8, 312

Lake, William C., 155–56, 312

Landow, George P., 139, 140, 143, 147, 149n14, 199, 208, 241, 312

LaPorte, Charles, x, 214, 224–25, 312

Lawson, John, 100, 100n5, 313

Lautz, Boniface, O. S. B., 237, 313

Leadbetter, Gregory, 24, 25, 313

Lecourt, Sebastian, 120, 313

Lewis, C. S., 46, 313

Linley, Margaret, 248, 313

Livingston, James C., 99, 102, 104, 313

Lloyd, Amy, 280, 280n64, 313

Long, Jerry Mark, 300n5, 313

Lootens, Tricia, 286, 313

Ludlow, John, 74, 76, 77, 80, 83, 84, 314

Lushington, Franklin, 197, 225, 313

Lysack, Krista, 239, 240, 313

Main, David A., 268, 268n45, 269n47, 277n57, 313

Marchand, Leslie, 21n1, 313

Marsh, Jan, 238, 255, 259n27, 260, 268n43, 313

Marshall, Linda E., 238, 238n13, 275, 313–14

Martin, Meredith, x, 112–13, 314

Mason, Emma, x, xi, 11, 237n10, 237n12, 253–54, 284, 312, 314

Masuzawa, Tomoko, 226, 314

Mathieson, Margaret, 98, 314

Maurice, Frederick Denison, 1, 16, 57–95, 106, 160, 163n1, 230, 297, 314; debts to and differences from Coleridge's approach to print media and national spiritual community, 2, 4, 11–13, 22, 25, 53–55, 59–63, 73, 79–80, 86, 90, 93, 96–97, 297; early journalistic work, 62, 63–66; on imperialism, 62; on mass print media as primary means of awakening to national Christian community, 4, 13, 58, 59, 74, 76, 82, 83–92, 93, 95, 96–97, 290, 300; sacramental understanding of media and print culture, 92, 296; on sectarianism, social fragmentation, and exclusive imagined communities fueled by print culture (especially periodicals), 2, 4, 58, 63–73, 78–79, 81, 88, 93, 299, 300; on Universal Society or Kingdom of Christ, 54, 60–61, 62, 66, 69, 79, 86–87, 90, 94, 174–75. See also Anglo-Catholicism; British Christian community, imagined; Broad Church; Cambridge "Apostles"; Chartism; Church of England; Christian Socialism; clerisy; High Church; education; Evangelicalism; media; nation-state; newspapers and periodicals; public sphere; publics; Roman Catholicism; working classes

Maurice, Frederick Denison, works of: "On Books," 87 (*The Friendship of Books*); "The Divine Interpretation of History" (*Sermons on the Sabbath-Day*), 86–87, 314; *The Friendship of Books,* 1n1, 63, 87, 88, 89, 93, 299, 314; *The Kingdom of Christ,* 22, 54, 60–61, 62, 68, 69, 79, 86, 90, 314; *Learning and Working,* 94, 314; "The National Tales of Ireland," 66, 314; "On Right and Wrong Methods of Supporting Protestantism," 70–73, 314; "On the Use and Abuse of Newspapers" (*The Friendship of Books*), 1, 88–92; *Politics for the People,* 66, 74n4, 74–86, 88, 90, 91, 314; "Reasons for Not Joining a Party in the Church," 68–70, 314; *Sermons on the Prayer-Book and the Lord's Prayer,* 57–58, 314; *Sermons Preached in Lincoln's Inn Chapel,* 88, 93, 300, 314; "Sketches of Contemporary Authors: No. II—Mr. Jeffrey and the Edinburgh Review," 64, 314; "Sketches of Contemporary Authors: No. III—Mr. Southey," 64–65, 314; "Sketches of Contemporary Authors: No. V—Mr. Wordsworth," 65–66, 314; "Sketches of Contemporary Authors: No. IX—Sir Walter Scott," 63, 314; *Social Morality,* 62, 314

Mayhew, Henry, 78, 315

McBratney, John, 226–27n16, 315

McClure, Edmund, 247, 248n19, 261, 262, 264, 303

McCullagh, Thomas, 171n9, 315

McKelvy, William R., x, 5–6, 6n2, 99, 130, 133, 134n7, 290, 315

McKeon, Michael, 8, 180, 199, 223, 315

McLeod, Hugh, 8, 9, 61, 76, 78, 100, 101, 122, 224, 249, 315

Meacock, Joanna, 268n44, 306

media: constitution of communities, 18, 294; hypermediacy, 294; Maurice on social theology of media and reading, 86–88, 90, 92, 93, 289, 296; radio, 237, 293–94, 295, 298n3; remediation, 81, 139, 139n12, 151, 294, 295, 298; sacramental quality attributed to print, 92, 296; telecommunications revolution, 17, 293; telegraphy, 9, 88, 293; telephone, 293; television, 293–94, 295–96,

298n3. *See also* British Christian community, imagined; newspapers and periodicals; online and digital spiritual community; print market; public sphere; publics; religion

Methodism, 26, 263n36; and *The London Quarterly Review,* 156, 171n9, 173, 178–79, 187, 286n74, 304, 315, 317; and *The Methodist Review,* 286, 312; and *Wesleyan Methodist Magazine,* 284, 318. *See also* Church of England; Evangelicalism; Nonconformity and Dissent

Miles, Robert, 33, 34, 315

Morris, Jeremy, 61, 62, 67, 74n4, 75, 86, 315

Murray, Nicholas, 105, 108–9, 115, 315

nation-state: liberal secularist views of religion's place in national society, 8, 104, 124, 229; Maurice on nation-state as providential form of society and theology of nationhood, 58, 61–62, 66, 86–87, 92, 94; regulative force and violence of, 8, 109, 115, 116, 118, 119, 123, 123–24, 125, 256, 300, 300n5–6. *See also* British Christian community, imagined; Christianity; Church of England; clerisy; imagined community, national; public sphere; religion; secular; secularization

Neville, Graham, 61, 315

Newlyn, Lucy, 31, 312, 315

Newman, John Henry, 66n2, 67, 68, 107, 107n6, 108, 222n15, 238, 244, 244n17

newspapers and periodicals: *The Academy,* 243, 252, 260, 265, 265n40, 267, 268, 270, 279, 279n61, 280, 280n63–65, 305, 306, 308, 311; *The Athenaeum,* 21, 21n1, 55, 60, 64–66, 260, 261, 262, 265, 266, 268, 273, 277n58, 285n72, 287n75, 306, 314, 318, 320; *The Atlas,* 167–68, 310; avoidance of divisive rhetoric, 117, 259; Coleridge on the press as medium of divine guidance of nation, 49–51; *The Contemporary Review,* 117, 117n10, 155–56, 267, 269, 269n47, 274, 274n51, 277, 312, 315; *The Edinburgh Review,* 34, 40, 64, 65, 183–84, 185, 316;

The Evening Herald, 160n4, 315; *The Fortnightly Review*, 117, 117n10, 268; *Fraser's Magazine*, 52–53, 166, 167, 169, 208–9, 312, 316; growth of religious press, 67; *Illustrated Times*, 201, 311; *The Leader*, 161, 313; *Macmillan's Magazine*, 117; Maurice on sectarian periodical audiences, 4, 58, 63–73, 78–79, 81, 88, 299; Maurice on newspaper ads and notices as medium of national Christian community, 83–86, 89–92, 290, 296; *The Morning Post*, 139–40, 146, 311, 313; *The Quarterly Review*, 34, 40, 64, 136–37, 210, 268n44, 274, 274n53, 277, 307, 309; *Tait's Edinburgh Magazine*, 197, 313; *Times, The*, 89, 117, 118, 146, 206–7, 254, 263, 263n34, 310, 312; *The Westminster Review*, 64, 66, 72, 82, 268–69n46, 313, 314. See also British Christian community, imagined; clerisy; Evangelicalism; High Church; Methodism; media; Nonconformity and Dissent; print market; public sphere; publics; Roman Catholicism; Tractarianism; working classes

Noble, James Ashcroft, 267, 269, 274, 274n51, 277, 315

Nonconformity and Dissent, 8, 9, 9n4, 34, 35, 70, 71, 81, 119n11, 133, 156, 157n15, 160, 161, 171, 282, 291, 297; Arnold on as agent of anarchy in print culture and politics, 100–101, 102, 105, 109–10, 112, 117–18, 120–21, 122, 124, 125, 299; and *British Quarterly Review*, 1, 2, 166, 181n13, 186, 195n3, 216–17, 218, 225, 313, 320; and *The Christian Witness*, 185, 201, 202, 316, 319; and *Eclectic Review*, 145, 146, 191, 195, 209, 212, 310, 319; and *Nonconformist*, 72, 100–101, 110, 118, 156–57, 166, 216, 308, 315; and *North British Review*, 146, 184, 203–4, 316; and *The Patriot*, 166, 200, 221, 313, 317; *The Puritan*, 201, 317. See also Anglo-Catholicism; Church of England; Evangelicalism; High Church; Methodism; Tractarianism

Nunokawa, Jeffrey, 207, 316

Nussbaum, Martha, 55, 55n14, 316

Nye, Eric W., 21, 316

Ong, Walter J., S. J., 293, 316

online and digital spiritual community, x, 18; *Anglican Cathedral of Second Life*, 55, 296, 297–98, 303; compared with print-mediated spiritual communities, 294–301; *LifeChurch.TV*, 295–96, 297–98, 313; *NorthPointOnline.TV*, 295–96, 316; online religion and religion online, 295, 296, 298, 299; *Reddit*, 294–95, 298, 306; Second Life, 55, 296; vernacular authority, 296–99; virtual ekklesia, 294; virtual sacraments, 296. See also British Christian community, imagined; media; publics; religion

Palazzo, Lynda, 244, 216

Paley, William, 29–31, 32, 33, 173, 174

Patmore, Coventry, 160, 160n3, 183–85, 184n14–15, 186, 203–5, 204n9, 207, 217, 222, 316

Pearse, Meic, 3, 316

Perkins, Mary Anne, 27, 316

Phelan, Joseph, 266, 270, 316

poetic form and genre: New-Critical bias about poetic form and devotional poetry, 236; *In Memoriam, A. H. H.* and persuasions of poetic form, 177–78, 182, 204–7; religious and political associations of meter and stanza form of *In Memoriam, A. H. H.*, 201–7, 212–13, 220–21, 221n14; *Verses* and the roundel, 236, 249, 250, 251, 255, 256–57, 265n40; *Verses* and sonnet form and revival, 235, 326, 252, 265–280, 267n41–42, 268n44–269n48, 274n51–54, 277n57–59, 279, 279n61, 285. See also *Christian Year, The*; High Church; hymn; *In Memoriam, A. H. H.*; *Verses*

Pope, Alexander, 151, 316

Potkay, Adam, x, 131n5, 316

Prickett, Stephen, 44, 316

print market: circulation of poetry in anthologies and periodicals, 234, 258–59, 264, 266, 267, 268, 269, 269n48, 284–88; competitiveness and diversification of in late-Victorian period, 234,

236, 258, 259, 262–64, 280n64, 287, 290; division between "devotional" and "general" publishing, 16, 235, 259, 259n26–27, 260–64, 263n33–36, 265, 266, 270, 276, 279–280, 280n63–64, 287, 287n75, 290; factors behind nineteenth-century growth of, 9; practices of religious publishers, 235, 258, 259, 259n26–27, 261–62, 261n31, 263–64, 263n33–36, 264n38, 265, 266, 280, 280n64, 290; price and circulation of newspapers and periodicals, 9, 75, 89, 100, 148, 234, 257–58, 280n64; price of new books, 258; price and sales of new poetry volumes, 234, 257–58; price and sales of novels and fiction, 234, 258. *See also* newspapers and periodicals; religion

public sphere (republic of letters), 124; history and fate of, 12, 96, 96n1, 33–4; Coleridge's spiritual republic of letters, 12, 22, 23, 25, 26, 33–38, 43–52, 53–55, 59, 93; Maurice's modeling of through fictional dialogues on London penny steamers, 77–82; privatization of religion in public spheres of nations, 4–5, 15, 44, 119, 163, 180, 183, 189–90, 191, 199, 223–24, 230–31; revisions to ideal by Coleridge and Maurice, 11–13, 96–97; Tennyson on religion in public sphere of imperial Britain, 229–30. *See also* British Christian community, imagined; nation-state; publics; religion; secular; secularization

publics, 12, 34, 63–64, 66, 123, 186–87, 223, 231, 237, 287; counterpublics, 12, 33, 34, 122, 187–88, 231; *the* public, 34–35, 96n1, 122–23, 187. *See also* British Christian community, imagined; newspapers and periodicals; print market; public sphere; voluntary religious association

Raine, Lee, 298, 310

Reahard, Jeff, 296, 316

Reardon, Bernard M. G., 52, 316

Reed, John Shelton, 253, 254, 316

Reform Acts, voting: Chester Square suffrage protests, 109; Hyde Park suffrage protests, 109, 116, 119; Redistribution Act (1885), 100n4; Reform Act (1832), 61–62, 221; Reform Act (1867), 99–100, 100n4; Reform Act (1884), 99–100, 100n4. *See also* Chartism; working classes

religion: Arnold's strategic redefinition of religion and Christianity for British public sphere under regulatory state, 7, 13–14, 99, 102–5, 119, 120, 123–25, 226; conditions of public presence of in mid-Victorian print culture, 182–88, 189, 199; divergent constructions of, 6–7, 7n3, 8, 13; internal, epistemological, and private construction of in Western societies, 7, 7n3, 179–182, 187, 188, 191–92, 199, 223–24; Keble's resistance to beliefs-based view of, 135–36, 136n9; Tennyson's participation in construction of "religions" and "world religions" to support imperial state, 226–29, 228n17. *See also* British Christian community, imagined; Christianity; imagined community, national; *In Memoriam, A. H. H.*; nation-state; print market; public sphere; secular; secularization; voluntary religious association; working classes

Ricks, Christopher, 221, 221n13, 227, 319

Roberts, Steven, 293, 317

Robertson, Frederick W., 160, 165, 221–24, 222n15, 317

Roe, Dinah, 237n10, 317

Roman Catholicism, 4, 8, 15, 67, 158, 160n3, 179–80, 237n11, 238n13, 253, 297, 298, 298n4, 299; Arnold on, 104–5, 117n10, 118, 120–21, 122, 124–25; and Catholic Relief Act (1829), 9n4, 61, 157n15; Christina Rossetti on, 254, 255; *The Dublin Review*, 181, 187, 201, 220n12, 266, 269, 277, 313, 317; Keble on, 14, 135, 155, 183; Maurice on, 61–62, 65; *The Month*, 152, 157, 311

Rossetti, Christina, 7, 14, 125, 230, 232–288, 290n1, 293, 297, 298, 317; on communion of saints and its ecumenical and international character, 16, 232, 233,

234, 236, 237–48, 238n13–14, 251–53, 252n22, 254–57, 262, 265, 266, 270, 274, 275–76, 278–80, 281–84, 285n72, 286, 287, 288, 294, 295; composition, arrangement, and selection of poems for *Verses*, 232, 232n1, 234–35, 234n7–235n9, 248, 248n19, 250–51, 252, 253, 255–56, 257–58, 261–62, 264–65, 266, 268–69, 270, 276, 279, 281, 281n67–68, 285; opposition to nationalism and imperialism, 233, 248–54, 257, 277–79, 291; portrayed as sweet cloistered saint, 285–87, 285n72–287n75; reading of *The Christian Year* by, 234, 234n5; role in Victorian sonnet revival and appeal to reputation as sonneteer, 235, 265–80, 267n42, 268n43–269n47, 274n52, 277n59, 285; sensitivity to divisions and trends in late-Victorian print market, 16, 234–36, 257–59, 259n27, 260, 260n28, 260n30, 261–62, 264–70, 269n48, 278–280, 287, 290; strategy of engaging wide range of audiences in *Verses*, 16, 233, 235, 236, 255, 257, 260, 261–64, 263n36, 265–66, 268–70, 271, 272, 273, 274, 276, 279–280, 281–86, 290, 294; on women's and men's roles in the communion of saints, 275, 275n56. *See also* Anglo-Catholicism; British Christian community, imagined; *Christian Year, The*; Church of England; High Church; *In Memoriam, A. H. H.*; poetic form and genre; print market; Roman Catholicism; Tractarianism; *Verses*; working classes

Rossetti, Christina, works of: "After Communion," 260n30; "After Death," 260n30; "Autumn Violets," 260n30; *Called to Be Saints*, 232n1, 235n9, 237–38, 244, 262; *The Face of the Deep: A Devotional Commentary on the Apocalypse*, 232n1, 233n3, 234–35n7, 238, 238n14, 241, 247, 252, 255–56, 261n31, 262, 266, 275n56, 282, 317; *Goblin Market and Other Poems*, 258n24, 259, 259n27, 260, 266; "If Only," 260n30; "Italia, Io Ti Saluto!" 278; "*Later Life: A Double Sonnet of Sonnets*, 268, 269n46, 275, 275n55–56, 276; "Mirrors of Life and Death," 278; *Monna Innominata: A Sonnet of Sonnets*, 263n36, 268, 268–69n46, 274–75; *New Poems by Christina Rossetti, Hitherto Unpublished or Collected* (ed. Rossetti, William Michael), 285, 286n74; "Old and New Year Ditties," 258n24; "On the Wing," 260n30; *A Pageant and Other Poems*, 259–60, 266, 268, 278; "Passtime," 278; *Poems* (1890), 284; *The Poetical Works of Christina Georgina Rossetti, with Memoir and Notes, etc.* (ed. Rossetti, William Michael), 285, 286n74; *The Prince's Progress*, 265n39, 266; "Remember," 268n45; "Rest," 260n30; "Sonnets are full of love, and this my tome," 268; "A Testimony," 243; *Time Flies: A Reading Diary*, 232n1, 234–35n7, 235n8–9, 239, 244, 250, 251, 256, 261n31, 262, 285n71, 317; "Watch with me, Jesus, in my loneliness," 258n24; "Weary in Well-Doing," 265n39; "The World," 260n30. *See also Verses*

Rossetti, Dante Gabriel, 140, 259, 259n27, 260, 261–62, 267, 267n42, 268, 268n44, 269, 269n48, 274, 274n54, 286, 286n74, 287, 317

Rossetti, William Michael, 248n19, 250, 261–62, 285, 286n74, 317

Rowlands, John Henry Lewis, 133, 317

Rowlinson, Matthew, 211, 317

Ruskin, John, 140, 141, 317

Russell, C. W., 266, 269, 277, 317

Ryan, Robert, 160, 174, 174n10, 195n2, 205, 206, 318

Sanders, Charles Richard, 21, 22, 52n12, 54, 318

Sanders, Mike, 115, 124, 318

Sapra, Rahul, 228n17, 318

Scherer, Matthew, 124, 318

Schlossberg, Herbert, 67, 68, 318

Scott, Patrick, 164, 170, 192, 260n26, 290, 318

Scott, William Bell, 274n54, 318

secular: divergent constructions of, 6–7, 8; secular time of print-mediated national imagination, 8, 84–85, 147–155, 158, 239–40, 289; Western distinction between "religious" and "secular" realms and categories and their development in dialogue, 6–8, 103–4, 124, 158, 176–80, 193–95, 211–12, 226–29. See also *Christian Year, The*; imagined community, national; *In Memoriam, A. H. H.*; nation-state; religion; secularization; *Verses*

secularization: of body as property of the state and economy, 8, 223–24; of Britain, 292–94, 292n2; debated or discredited narratives of 3, 6, 6n2; and differentiation, 47–49, 51–2, 103, 177–78, 190, 224, 230–31, 290; literary studies and misrepresentations of Arnold to support "replacement" of religion with secular culture and literature, 13–14, 97, 98–99, 125; and multiple modernities, 8; national imagination and, 4, 5, 6, 8, 86, 149–50, 230–31, 289; of state 9n4, 163n5. See also British Christian community, imagined; *Christian Year, The*; Christianity; Church of England; imagined community, national; *In Memoriam, A. H. H.*; nation-state; public sphere; religion; secular; *Verses*; voluntary religious association; working classes

Sharp, William, 261, 269n48, 277, 277n58, 286n74, 290n1, 318

Shatto, Susan, 159n1, 167, 169n6, 210, 319

Shaw, Marion, 159n1, 164, 167, 169n6, 170, 210, 318, 319

Sheehan, Jonathan, 180, 318

Sherman, Kevin Miguel, 3, 318

Silver, Harold, 100, 100n5, 313

socialism, 72, 82–84. See also Christian Socialism; working classes

Society for Promoting Christian Knowledge (SPCK), 102, 134, 232, 234–35, 235n8, 235n9, 238, 247, 248n19, 250, 251, 253, 255, 257, 258, 258n25, 260–64, 263n31, 263n36, 264n38, 265, 280n63, 284–85, 285n71, 287, 287n75, 303. See also Church of England; print market; *Verses*

St. Clair, William, 9, 318

Stead, William Thomas, 248–49, 249n20, 250, 256, 257, 258, 290n1, 298, 318

Sterling, John, 21–22, 21n1, 54, 318

Stevens, Paul, 228n17, 318

Stewart, Garrett, 37n7, 319

Sussman, Herbert L., 140, 141, 319

Taft, Joshua, 236, 266, 319

Taylor, Charles, 319; on "buffered self," 40–41, 103, 176, 179–80; on disenchantment of the world, 40–41, 176, 179–80; on distinction between "religious" and "secular" realms, 6, 7, 103, 176, 179; on "excarnation" of Christianity and Christian practice, 180; on "immanent frame" of modern secular life, 7–8, 103–4, 176, 179. See also religion; secular; secularization

Tennyson, Alfred, 7, 125, 156, 159–231, 233, 234, 256, 258, 271, 272, 290, 290n1, 297, 319; as author of quasi-sacred national scripture, 209, 213–20, 248, 257; awareness of connections between *In Memoriam* and *The Christian Year*, 164, 167, 188; and division of inward faith from secular natural world, 173–75, 190, 243, 270; fear of revolution and praise of rule from above, 220–21, 228–29; and forms in worship, 163n5; and homoeroticism, 206–7; influence of by Samuel Coleridge and F. D. Maurice, 174–75; introductory stanzas to *In Memoriam* regarded as creed of, 168, 219; journey through doubt to spiritual hope in *In Memoriam* seen as representing British nation and human condition, 14–15, 161, 163–4, 184–85, 190, 191, 195, 196–97, 203–4, 212, 217–18, 220, 221–22; and justification of British Christian imperialism, 15–16, 224–231, 248, 249, 250, 251, 254, 300; as laureate, 183, 195, 207, 221, 222, 229, 248; portrayal of class limitations of, 220, 220n12; praised as nineteenth-century Britain's great Christian poet, 167, 185, 195n2, 209, 214, 219, 220; on tolerant control of religion by imperial state, 225–29, 228n17, 248, 249, 254; as witness to innate foundations of faith, 14–15, 183–85, 220. *See also* British Christian community, imagined; Broad Church; Cambridge "Apostles"; *Christian Year, The;* Church of England; *In Memoriam, A. H. H.;* nation-state; public sphere; religion; secular; secularization; *Verses;* working classes

Tennyson, Alfred, works of: "Akbar's Dream," 163n5, 225–29, 226n16, 228n17, 248, 249, 250, 251, 254, 300; "Hail Briton!," 220, 221n14; *Idylls of the King*, 214, 217, 224–25; "Love thou thy land, with love far-brought," 221, 221n14; "Morte d'Arthur" and "The Epic," 214–15; "Of old sat Freedom on the heights," 221n14; "To the Queen," 221, 222, 224–25; "You ask me, why though ill at ease" (later retitled "Britain"), 221, 221n14, 222–23. See also *In Memoriam, A. H.H*

Tennyson, Emily (née Sellwood), 168–171, 205; devotional use of *In Memoriam*, 168n6–8, 168–171

Tennyson, G. B., 129, 129n2, 130n4, 319

Test Acts, repeal of (1828), 9n4, 67, 157n15

Thompson, John B., 3, 48, 319

Thomson, James, 151–52, 319

Thomson, James (B. V.), 230, 319

Thwaite, Ann, 168, 168n7, 319

Tomko, Michael, 173–74, 176, 182, 211, 319

Tractarianism (Oxford Movement): Keble and, 67, 130, 130n4, 131, 131n5, 132, 134–37, 144, 222, 222n15, 253, 264, 266, 297; and *The Tracts for the Times*, 66n2, 67, 68, 69, 72, 132, 135–37, 157; *See also* Anglo-Catholicism; *Christian Year, The*; Church of England; Evangelicalism; High Church; *Verses*

Tucker, Herbert, 160n2, 184, 319

Turner, Bryan S., 294, 298, 300–301, 319

Tynan, Katharine, 277–78n59, 286n74, 320

Van Loon, Joost, 3, 4, 308

Van Young, Eric, 3, 48, 320

VanAntwerpen, Jonathan, 179, 180, 319, 320

Vernon, John Richard, 165, 185–86, 320

Verses (Rossetti, Christina), 232n2, 232–288; allusions to Anglican liturgy and ritual (especially Communion), 234, 234n6, 236, 240, 243, 253, 256, 257, 264, 265n40, 283, 283n70; "analogy" and typological interpretation, 271, 271n50, 272; appropriable language of, 236, 281–84, 285, 288, 290; appropriation in anthologies and periodical reviews, 16, 234, 235, 235n8–9, 257–59, 264, 264n38, 265, 281, 284, 285–86, 285n71, 286–88, 290; and Book of Common Prayer, 240, 270, 271n50, 272 ; and Church calendar, 240, 264, 281n64; compared with Keble's *Christian Year,* 14, 16, 125, 230, 233–34, 239, 240–41, 264, 265, 271, 271n50, 272, 2879–80, 280n63, 290; compared with Tennyson's *In Memoriam*, 14, 16, 125, 233–34, 243, 248, 251, 270–72; decline and dissolution of, 16, 236, 284–88, 290; and ecumenical, international, and transhistorical communion of saints, 16, 230, 232–33, 236, 237, 238–48, 251–52, 255–56, 257, 265, 266, 270, 276, 278–84, 283n70, 286, 287–88, 290, 291; estrangement and exile of Christian community, 16, 251–54, 284; and intersection of secular time of reading with eternity, 239–40, 272, 276; material presentation of, 262–64, 263n33–36, 266, 276; opposition to nationalism and imperialism, 16, 230, 233, 248–52, 253, 254, 257, 277–80, 291; price and sales of, 14, 16, 258, 258n25, 284–85; reception of by wide range of Christian and literary commentators and audiences, 16, 236, 261–63, 264, 264n37–38, 265, 265n40, 279–280, 279n61–280n65, 281, 284, 285–88, 290, 293; resistance to division between spirituality and the physical body and world, 243–48, 270. *See also* Anglo-Catholicism; British Christian community, imagined; *Christian Year, The*; Church of England; High Church; hymn; *In Memoriam, A. H. H.*; print market; poetic form and genre; secular; secularization; Tractarianism

Verses (Rossetti, Christina), discussion of poems in: "All Saints," 242, 284; "Alone Lord God, we see not yet we know," 270–73, 280; "Because He first loved us," 242; "Behold, it was very good," 255–56; "Earth has clear call of daily bells," 283n70; "The end is not yet," 256; "The General Assembly and Church of the Firstborn," 252; "Heaviness may endure for the night," 241, 245–46; "Holy Innocents," 235n9; "If love is not worth loving, then life is not worth living," 235n9; "Light of Light," 276; "Lord, grant us eyes to see and ears to hear," 232, 279; "Lord, grant us grace to mount by steps of grace," 281–83, 281n68; "Lord, I believe, help Thou mine unbelief," 240–41; "Lord, make us all love all," 256; "Lord, what have I that I may offer Thee?" 241; "Love understands the mystery, whereof," 283n70; "Man's life is but a working day," 238–40; "Now they desire a Better Country," 249–52, 256, 257; "O Lord, on Whom we gaze and dare not gaze," 241; "O Lord, when Thou didst call me, didst Thou know," 281n66; "Out of the Deep Have I Called Unto Thee, O Lord," 234n6, 266, 268–69, 270–80; "Passiontide," 241, 241n16; "Roses and Roses," 235n9; "Sexagesima," 244–45; "She came from the uttermost part of the earth," 235n9; "Son, Remember," 247; To every seed his own body," 246, 246n18, 247; "Tremble, thou earth, at the presence of the Presence of the Lord," 281; " "A vain Shadow," 243; "What is the beginning? Love," 242; "Whitsun Monday" ("We know not a voice of that River"), 265, 265n40.

Vidler, Alex R., 59, 61, 320

voluntary religious association: print-mediated competition for religious allegiance, 9–11, 100, 183, 199, 289, 292; rise of voluntary establishment and religious market, 8–9, 183, 199, 289, 292; Toleration Act (1689), 8, 199, 223–24. *See also* British Christian community, imagined; Christianity; Church of England; publics; religion; secularization

Wagner, Jennifer, 267n41, 320

Waller, John O, 238n14, 320

Warner, Michael, 12, 96n1, 122–23, 179, 180, 186–87, 233, 320

Watson, J. R., 144, 282, 320

Watson, Lily, 277n59, 280, 280n65, 281, 286n74, 320

Watts[-Dunton], Theodore, 261, 268, 277, 277n58, 286n73, 320

Weedon, Alexis, 234, 257, 257n23, 258, 293, 320

Wellings, Ben, 62, 320

Westerholm, Joel, 233n4, 236, 272, 320

William, Braden, 1, 1n1, 2–3, 166, 181n13, 195n3, 320

Williams, Isaac, 67, 135, 135n8, 136, 137, 147, 244, 266, 320

Williams, Raymond, 73, 89, 90, 320–21

Wilner, Alex S., 300n5, 313

Wordsworth, William, 65–66, 102, 131–32, 131n5, 146, 184n14, 209–10, 266, 321

working classes: Arnold on, 100, 101, 102, 105, 109, 110, 111, 112–13, 114, 115–17, 119, 120, 121, 122; Christina Rossetti's concern for, 247, 262; Coleridge's elitism regarding and concern for, 23–25; Keble's fear of "feverish thirst after knowledge" and reliance on private judgment among, 133–35, 134n6; Maurice's efforts to reach as readers in print-mediated national spiritual community, 74–86, 93–95; Maurice's paternalistic vision of means of communication and working classes, 54, 73, 80–81, 89, 92, 93, 94; and newspapers and periodicals, 74–86, 75, 89, 100, 148, 165, 280; Robertson's "safety-valve" theory of working-class poetry reading, 221–24, 222n15; stereotyped as indifferent to religion, 76, 101; "taxes on knowledge," 89, 100; Tennyson's anxiety over, 220–21. *See also* British Christian community, imagined; Chartism; Christian Socialism; clerisy; education; *In Memoriam, A. H. H.*; newspapers and periodicals; Reform Acts, voting; socialism

Wright, Luke Savin Herrick, 41, 43, 50, 321

Wright, N. T., 241–42, 243, 321

Yates, Nigel, 237n11, 321

Yonge, Charlotte, 143, 144, 150, 152, 154. See also *Christian Year, The*

LITERATURE, RELIGION, AND POSTSECULAR STUDIES
LORI BRANCH, SERIES EDITOR

Literature, Religion, and Postsecular Studies publishes scholarship on the influence of religion on literature and of literature on religion from the sixteenth century onward. Books in the series include studies of religious rhetoric or allegory; of the secularization of religion, ritual, and religious life; and of the emerging identity of postsecular studies and literary criticism.

Imagined Spiritual Communities in Britain's Age of Print
    Joshua King

Puritanism and Modernist Novels: From Moral Character to the Ethical Self
    Lynne W. Hinojosa

Conspicuous Bodies: Provincial Belief and the Making of Joyce and Rushdie
    Jean Kane

Victorian Sacrifice: Ethics and Economics in Mid-Century Novels
    Ilana M. Blumberg

Lake Methodism: Polite Literature and Popular Religion in England, 1780–1830
    Jasper Cragwall

Hard Sayings: The Rhetoric of Christian Orthodoxy in Late Modern Fiction
    Thomas F. Haddox

Preaching and the Rise of the American Novel
    Dawn Coleman

Victorian Women Writers, Radical Grandmothers, and the Gendering of God
    Gail Turley Houston

Apocalypse South: Judgment, Cataclysm, and Resistance in the Regional Imaginary
    Anthony Dyer Hoefer

www.ingramcontent.com/pod-product-compliance
Lightning Source LLC
Chambersburg PA
CBHW030127240426
43672CB00005B/52